ACPL IT
DISCARDED

SO-ATF-954

Developmentally based
psychotherapy

DEVELOPMENTALLY BASED PSYCHOTHERAPY

DEVELOPMENTALLY BASED PSYCHOTHERAPY

Stanley I. Greenspan, M.D.

INTERNATIONAL UNIVERSITIES PRESS, INC.
Madison   Connecticut

Allen County Public Library
900 Webster Street
PO Box 2270
Fort Wayne, IN 46801-2270

Copyright © 1997, Stanley I. Greenspan, M.D.

All rights reserved. No part of this book may be reproduced by any means, nor translated into a machine language, without the written permission of the publisher.

International Universities Press and IUP (& design) ® are registered trademarks of International Universities Press, Inc.

Library of Congress Cataloging-in-Publication Data

Greenspan, Stanley I.
    Developmentally based psychotherapy / Stanley I. Greenspan.
        p.   cm.
    Includes bibliographical references and index.
    ISBN 0-8236-1199-X
    1. Developmental therapy. 2. Personality development. 3. Ego (Psychology)   I. Title.
    RC489.D46G74   1995
    616.89′14—dc20   95-17189
                                                                CIP

Manufactured in the United States of America

Contents

Chapter 1   Introduction to Developmentally
Based Psychotherapy   1

Chapter 2   Principles of Developmentally Based
Therapy   7

Chapter 3   Regulatory Processes   71

Chapter 4   Engaging and Relating   135

Chapter 5   Boundary-Defining Gestures,
Behaviors, and Affects   161

Chapter 6   Self- and "Other"-Defining Complex
Gestural, Behavioral, and Affective
Patterns   189

Chapter 7   Representational Elaboration   225

Chapter 8   Clinical Techniques to Facilitate
Representational Capacities   253

Chapter 9   Representational Differentiation
(Emotional Thinking)   313

Chapter 10   Tactics to Foster Representational
Differentiation   361

Conclusion   381
Appendix   The Clinical Assessment of
                    Developmental Levels   385

References   427
Name Index   447
Subject Index   451

Chapter 1

Introduction to Developmentally Based Psychotherapy

Most psychotherapists use a developmental framework in their clinical work. Many recent developmental discoveries, however, have not yet found their way into this evolving frame of reference.

Developmentally Based Psychotherapy presents a new developmental theory that unifies and extends the practice of psychotherapy. It formulates therapeutic strategies based on recent discoveries of early presymbolic levels of adaptive and disturbed personality functioning, emerging understanding of the phases of development throughout the course of life, and observations of the biological aspects of symptom and character formation.

Over the past forty to fifty years, there has been an increase in both the types of problems presenting for psychotherapy and the available therapeutic approaches. Typical problems include circumscribed difficulties, such as anxiety states and phobias, and a growing range of character pathologies and borderline conditions dealing with self-esteem, narcissism, depression, relationships, and psychological boundaries. The growing array of

1

psychotherapeutic techniques to meet these diverse problems includes psychodynamic, object relations, and supportive approaches, as well as behavioral strategies and short-term therapies which use relationships, transference phenomenon, or guidance.

Many experienced therapists, however, rather than following a specific approach, have evolved their own unique eclectic approaches, which often contain a number of dynamic, relationship, and behavioral principles, coupled with what has been described as "nonspecific" factors, all seasoned with an emerging developmental framework that organizes and directs the therapeutic effort. The following list describes some of these tried and true tactics: (1) Forming a relationship that conveys a sense of warmth and acceptance and yet has boundaries that must be respected; (2) empathizing with the patient's difficulties as well as joys and satisfactions; (3) helping the patient fully describe problems, strengths, the subtleties in their relationships, and the full range of their feelings; (4) expanding the patient's ability to elaborate intentions, wishes, feelings, and fears; (5) assisting the patient in recognizing patterns in relationships, feelings, and difficulties; (6) increasing self-awareness of feelings, intentions, and interactive patterns that are not obvious to the patient; (7) helping the patient identify opposing tendencies or conflicts; (8) using imagery to understand inner life and, when appropriate (as in cognitive behavioral therapy), explore or construct new images to guide behavior; (9) breaking down complex behavioral patterns into smaller, learnable steps; (10) creating conditions for behavioral change (as in the differential reinforcement, i.e., encouragement or reward, of selected "appropriate" behaviors); (11) increasing tolerance for anxiety through systematic exposure to images or situations that are difficult (as in a desensitization procedure); and (12) helping with regulating and organizing attention and mood through support and guidance.

Many strategies on this list make "developmental sense." They contain the elements that promote emotional growth. In employing a variety of useful approaches, however, therapeutic efforts can sometimes work at cross purposes. Consider, for example, a person who never had successful relationships and avoids them. He is inadvertently pushed out of therapy by a therapist who begins interpreting his "passive-aggressiveness" and his unwillingness to be committed and motivated when he keeps trying to change appointments. A different therapist empathizes with the patient's need to control the relationship, and at the same time tries to build a relationship by becoming as flexible as possible, offering telephone consultations and changes within a reasonable range. He does much better with this patient who was just learning to form relationships and was not yet able to reflect on the feelings associated with relating to others.

Alternatively, consider a person who was on the verge of talking about longing or needy feelings that he had avoided for a long time. He was introducing these feelings by talking about how the therapist was not active enough and did not at that very moment meet his needs. The therapist offers advice to show he is a giving, caring person, but in so doing, misses an opportunity to help the patient become more aware of and learn to elaborate feared-and-avoided longing feelings.

In these two examples, an understanding of exactly where the patient is in his emotional development and therapy would enable the therapist to pick the right technique; in the first instance, providing more support for developing relationships and in the second instance providing more opportunity to explore feelings rather than to meet expressed needs directly.

In addition, with the greater diversity of approaches currently available, individuals often select the type of therapy that they feel would be helpful to them. This "choice," however, can be a two-edged sword. On the one hand, it gives the patient a chance to choose. On the other hand, it provides an opportunity for the patient to select an approach that may fit with and actually support his characterological difficulties rather than help him get over them. For example, a patient who has a fundamental problem with experiencing and finding symbols or words for a range of feelings may understandably select an approach that emphasizes only changing behavior or using medication, even though his most significant problem has to do with learning to experience and elaborate feelings. Alternatively, a person who is comfortable talking and is already a poet of his or her feelings, but avoids certain types of life endeavors, may elect a type of "talking" therapy or a therapist that enables him to "continue to hide out" from avoided challenges. Similarly, an individual who tends to control his feelings may elect a cognitive-behavior therapy because he is attracted to its precise, planned nature. Images can be anticipated. Such an approach, however, may support an unrealistic desire to control his inner world.

We need to move to a position where the patient does not simply knock on the door to obtain what he wants (because what he wants may not always be what is needed), but where the therapist helps educate the patient about what approach would provide emotional growth.

Seasoned therapists tend to construct their own developmental road map to deal with these challenges and guide their efforts. They also use theoretical concepts related to developmental understanding of the personality, such as concepts of separation and individuation developed by Margaret Mahler and those on the formation of the self described by Heinz Kohut.

Most clinicians of all persuasions, however, believe there is a need for a more systematic understanding of human development, for example, in psychodynamic approaches to fill in the missing pieces of emotional development and in behavioral approaches to identify better the most relevant patterns of behaviors, thoughts, and reinforcers.

Clinical observations and studies during the last twenty years have made it possible to construct a more comprehensive developmental framework. The pioneering developmental discoveries of Freud and Anna Freud, as well as Piaget, Erikson, Mahler, and Kohut, have been added on to by a variety of studies (see Appendix for review). For example, we have been able to conduct clinical studies of development in the face of family and psychosocial challenges, biological and maturational challenges, and in normative contexts. From these observations, we have constructed a systematic, biopsychosocial developmental model (Greenspan, 1989, 1992).

In the following chapters of *Developmentally Based Psychotherapy*, we will examine the implications of these insights about human development and emotional learning for the practice of psychotherapy. We will build a model of psychotherapy that is grounded in the processes of emotional and cognitive growth. This model, which incorporates therapeutic principles that many clinicians have found helpful, will facilitate clinical observation, judgment, planning, and research. Most importantly, this developmental road map will make it possible to construct new strategies, particularly for the most difficult clinical conditions.

For example, it has constructed new tactics to work with a wide range of clinical problems, including the following types of challenges:

1. Physical and temperamental differences in patients including five characteristic constitutional types that predispose to anxiety disorders, disturbances in affect, aggressive or antisocial behavior, tendencies toward self-absorption and reality testing problems, oppositional defiant and compulsive patterns, and problems with regulating attention, impulses, and behavior.
2. Problems in forming, maintaining, and deepening relationships, including dealing with relationship capacities that are superficial, unstable, rejection-sensitive, and/or avoidant.
3. Difficulties at the deepest levels of character structure, including distorted affective expectations and responses, such as suspiciousness, and depressive, impulsive, and passive avoidant patterns.
4. Deficits in the ability to form inner images (mental representations) and construct feeling states, wishes, and fantasies from preverbal intentions and dispositions.
5. Problems in building logical, reality-based bridges between different intentions, wishes, and feelings, self and other images, and engaging adaptively in relationships and feelings characterizing such advanced levels of development as forming an integrated capacity for morality,

carrying out the responsibilities of adulthood and parenthood, and negotiating the aging process.

A new developmental paradigm for psychotherapy is especially important at this time. Numerous approaches are being
used, but in an unintegrated manner. Classical psychoanalytic
and derivative approaches are being used less and less, both because of the number of individuals with severe psychopathologies
that lie outside the range of classical analytic techniques and the
economics of mental health services, demanding shorter, less in-
depth approaches. Short-term eclectic, supportive, behavioral, somatic, and guidance-oriented approaches are on the increase.

With these current trends, there is some danger that we will
lose in-depth understanding of the mind. Developmentally based
approaches, however, have the potential for investigating the
depth of the mind in a way that stays close to clinical observations.
Building on the insights of reconstructive work, a comprehensive
developmental model preserves the dynamic, in-depth focus so
necessary for a functional understanding of human beings. At the
same time, it provides the basis for developing techniques that
can meaningfully extend the practice of psychotherapy.

Chapter 2

Principles of Developmentally Based Therapy

The overarching principle of a developmentally based approach to psychotherapy is mobilization of the developmental processes associated with an adaptive progression of the personality throughout childhood and adulthood. The therapeutic relationship is the vehicle for mobilizing developmental processes in the therapy sessions and for helping the patient create developmentally facilitating experiences outside the therapy situation.

Patients present to therapy with a variety of challenges, some of the most familiar of which have to do with anxieties and conflicts that interfere with healthy adaptation. More commonly, however, patients present with ongoing characterologic difficulties where patterns of experiencing emotions, thoughts, and behaviors are either unmodulated, constricted, or reflect developmentally early interactions, rather than age-appropriate ones. Still other patients present with deficits in core capacities, such as emotional or behavioral regulation, or the organization of affect and thought. This latter group also often demonstrates patterns of interaction related to very early levels of character formation.

7

Helping patients verbalize feelings, alter their behaviors, and alter patterns of thinking are all potentially helpful for aspects of a problem or certain narrowly defined problems. Rarely, however, do they provide the basis for facilitating the overall growth of the personality, and often may not suffice to reverse the more challenging types of symptoms or behaviors. A series of principles will now be described that form the basis for a developmentally based approach to psychotherapy. These principles outline processes that attempt to mobilize the individual's capacity for an overall developmental progression, as well as overcoming severe emotional and characterological challenges.

The first and foremost principle in the developmental model is that we try to build on the patient's natural inclinations and interests to try to harness a number of core developmental processes at the same time. These core processes have to do with self-regulation, forming intimate relationships, engaging in simple boundary-defining gestures, and complex preverbal, self-defining communication. They also have to do with representing internal experience, including representing and abstracting wishes, intentions, and affects, and finally to become able to differentiate these internal representations and build bridges between them. Where the patient has not reached a certain level, the therapist engages him or her at the levels that have been mastered, and begins the process of working toward experiences that will facilitate the new levels.

In traditional psychoanalytic and psychodynamic therapies, it is mistakenly assumed that many patients can use a highly differentiated representational system to perceive, interpret, and work through earlier experiences and conflicts. Patients are thought to regress from higher to lower levels of thoughts, affect, wish and behavior while retaining the necessary ego functions for representation and self reflection. For example, as noted in the previous chapter, we sometimes assume that almost all patients can picture and verbalize their wishes and feelings, and step away from the urgency of their feelings long enough to explore where they came from and what they mean. Most patients, however, do not have a highly differentiated representational system. Many cannot represent wishes and affects or can barely represent only certain wishes or affect states, let alone explore their meanings. Others cannot sustain relationships or regulate mood impulses or sensations. More often than not, these limitations are *not* regressions from advanced states of ego organization, but limitations or constrictions stemming from the types of interactions that were experienced during development. Therefore, one must work clinically at a number of developmental levels at once. We cannot maintain an illusion that patients function at a higher developmental level than they do.

The core developmental processes that we see in normal development can go awry in one form or another, resulting in various kinds of psychopathology. For each of the stages and processes, which will be described in detail in the following chapters, a patient may have a deficit or a constriction. A deficit means the processes that ordinarily are mastered at that stage were not mastered. A constriction means the processes for a particular stage were partially mastered. The patient may have a constriction in terms of the range of emotions mastered or the stability of the processes under challenges. For example some patients may have a deficit in representing any affect and instead act out their feelings. Other patients may only have a constriction in representing selected feelings such as anger or may loose their capacity when anxious. Through the psychotherapeutic process, these developmental stages and processes are reworked. For example, the withdrawn patient needs to be engaged; the patient who escapes into fantasy needs to learn to build on the communications of others; and the concrete, acting out patient needs to learn to symbolize or represent intentions, wishes, and affects. Developmentally based psychotherapy creates a therapeutic relationship where all the core levels are supported at the same time. The therapist attempts to mobilize attention, engagement, prerepresentational and representational communication patterns, and when they are not present helps the patient construct them.

Mobilizing developmental process does not mean structuring experience. The therapist must follow the patient's internal inclinations through his spontaneous communications. The patient's affects, behaviors, and words tell the therapist where the patient is in his development. They also create an emotional–personal basis for growth.

Some of the traditional perspectives in therapy only support one or two of these core developmental processes and not others. Approaches which tend to integrate more of these developmental processes are going to be more potent in helping individuals overcome difficulties. The developmental model also offers a framework for comparing different therapeutic approaches and seeing which ones are likely to be helpful, under which circumstances, and for which kinds of psychopathologic conditions.

The second principle involves the therapist always meeting the individual that he or she is working with at the patient's specific developmental level. It is essential not to make the mistake of communicating with the patient in a manner that is inappropriately abstract or primitive. For example, some individuals do not have the capacity for verbal expression of emotions. They may operate on a more primitive level where affect spills over immediately into behavior. They stomp and yell and scream when they are angry; they cling when they are needy. They don't commonly (unless you put the words in their mouths) say, "I feel angry" or "I miss you so much that I think about you all the time." We often put those words in a patient's mouth, yet they really may not be able to abstract affect in that way. If such patients should begin to act out aggressively or withdraw after the therapist's vacation, for example, offering them an interpretation like, "Gee, you must have missed me and are showing me your anger by stubbing out your cigarettes on my couch," will go right over their heads. The patient may nod, but if he is operating at a more primitive level, he simply won't get it. It won't be a meaningful intervention because the patient would have to be at a very highly differentiated level to process that kind of interpretation. Not only would such a patient need to be able to represent affect, he would have to be able to see connections between different affects ("I missed you, and therefore I'm mad"), and he would have to be able to self-observe while he was seeing this connection.

We find ourselves inadvertently pitching a high-level interpretation when the patient is still at an earlier level, and often the exchange has little value to it. It makes us feel we are earning our fee, and not just sitting there wasting our time, but it is not very meaningful to the patient beyond conveying our interest or concern. The challenges of regulating and attending, relating with depth and intimacy, and sending and responding to nonverbal gestural cues without distortion can occupy the therapeutic stage for a considerable period of time. Ignoring these issues or seeing them as secondary to problems at a higher level can create rather than help overcome therapeutic obstacles.

We often make the parallel error of underestimating the patient's developmental level. Take, for example, a person who is capable of representing affects and understanding connections. We may try to overnurture them by being extra supportive and empathetic, not realizing that we are infantilizing them. They may actually operate at a level where they can see connections between different wishes and affect states and figure out things on their own. Thus, we may inadvertently lull them into a state of greater dependency than they need to be.

It is evident, then, that we have to make an initial developmental diagnosis of the patient's character structure (see Appendix). In focusing on the developmental level a patient has more or less attained in his communicative capacities, one also looks at the different themes of emotional life, including dependency and closeness; pleasure, excitement, and sexuality; assertiveness, curiosity, competition, anger, and aggression; self-limit-setting; and empathy and more mature forms of love. These themes encompass much of the emotional human drama.

When considering the above themes, remember that dependency includes separation anxiety, and that the flip side of aggression includes fears and worries about aggression. We look at the degree to which a developmental level can organize certain themes and not organize others. For example, how does a person deal with dependency and closeness? Does he use highly differentiated, extended representational capacities, or just gestures? Does he become aloof and distant when he is dealing with themes of dependency, avoiding engagement almost entirely? It should be pointed out, however, that the person invariably communicates about all these emotional themes in one way or another. Even disengagement and aloofness are ways of communicating.

As indicated earlier the clinician needs a sense of the developmental levels mastered by a given patient in terms of the relative degree of deficit in any level versus mastery at that level. He or she also needs to have a sense of the range and specific types of emotions or experiences that can be organized at each particular level, in terms of the different thematic, affective domains. With this knowledge to hand the clinician is in a good position to anticipate some of the issues that will be coming up in his or her therapeutic interventions. The clinician can anticipate whether the main issue will be fostering engagement and relatedness, or whether it will be even more basic, such as helping the person organize behaviors, affects, and thoughts; or whether the main issue will be in helping the person broaden his or her ability to elaborate certain feelings and themes.

As the therapist gets a sense of where his patient is developmentally, and anticipates where some of the initial therapeutic goals and objectives will lie, he or she is also anticipating some of the issues that may get played out between clinician and patient. Consider a concrete example. The patient misses sessions and is aloof as the therapy sessions come to an end. The therapist may be tempted to say, "I can see that you've become a little bit aloof and preoccupied every time you seem to be angry with me. This seems to occur just before the end of the session as you're anticipating my ushering you out of the door. Frequently, you miss the next session."

If, however, the therapist sees the patient is not able to represent affects and see connections between them, the only way he might have of dealing with that coolness is through the quality of his or her own engagement and relatedness. In fact, drawing a patient's attention to the possible sequence of his thoughts may have no impact. Such an intervention may be contraindicated because it may drive the patient away from therapy, overloading him with representational information which he cannot comprehend and which he may experience as hostile and threatening.

When patients have been driven from therapy by having been asked prematurely to look at connections between feelings that they cannot yet represent, therapists often mistakenly think it is because they are pushing the patients to look at "repressed feelings" too quickly (i.e., by interpreting their anger or sexual wishes). In many instances, however, the problem is not so much the premature discussion of a repressed or unconscious impulse, but is instead the inability to relate to patients at their own developmental levels. It is this inability that such patients experience as sadistic and rejecting. It tends to overload patients who already may be feeling overloaded by their own affects, which they can barely organize or represent.

The clinician might well wonder how he would use developmental understanding to deal with a person who was becoming more aloof before the end of the session, but who had not achieved a mastery of representational capacities to handle such feelings. He might, for example, as the patient was beginning to withdraw, metaphorically reach out by using an especially soothing tone of voice and assuming a gentle facial expression and nonthreatening motor gestures. He might also empathize aloud with the fact that sometimes beginnings and endings are best approached gradually. The therapist may focus on behavioral and some general affective components of the transition, and not on feelings. He might try to see the adaptive side of the patient's becoming aloof, which is to prepare for what may be a very difficult transition (e.g., "sometimes it's easier to say goodbye slowly"). A developmentally derived, seemingly supportive comment is not of less value than a representational one. It greets the patient where he is developmentally, much as later on in the therapeutic relationship, an insight about the sequence of the patient's thoughts and feelings may greet the patient where he or she is at that particular point.

In addition to commenting on how hard it is to make the transition, and doing extra wooing and reaching out with voice and gesture (of course being respectful of the person's need to also keep his distance), the therapist might also pay attention to the apprehension around leaving. He might talk in a very concrete sense (using behavioral imagery) about what will happen the next day or during the next session. What will it be like when the person returns? What might the person want to look at or talk about? Also, he might ask in a rather concrete, behavioral sense about what experiences the person might anticipate between the two sessions—things that will be going on at home, school, or work. In this way, there are concrete behavioral details of a person's life that are helping to make a transition from the images at the end of the session to the images between the sessions or of the next session. This sort of bridge will help the patient make the transition, yet it does not push him to abstract feeling states, such as how he feels about leaving or how he will feel while away. It creates a sense of security for the next steps in the therapeutic process.

An early step in the therapeutic relationship, therefore, is to gain a sense of where the person is developmentally so that the clinician can select an approach that is therapeutically appropriate. It is worth emphasizing that the diagnostic process used to determine the developmental level of the patient and its relationship to more traditional diagnostic categories, need not be confined to the initial set of interviews. In a developmental psychotherapeutic approach, the therapist is continually monitoring and revising his or her impressions of the person's developmental level. As therapy proceeds and development moves ahead, the developmental level may well be moving to higher and more progressive levels. In fact, the most appropriate way of assessing the progress in therapy is through assessing the shifts in the patient's developmental level and the broadening of experiential realms that can be organized at each level (see Appendix). This, along with changes in symptoms, is the appropriate way to look at the efficacy of psychotherapy (Greenspan and Scharfstein, 1981).

The third principle is that a therapist should aim to effect change by helping the patient negotiate the developmental level or levels he has not mastered, or only partially mastered. They may have been bypassed earlier in life, which at present is in evidence as a deficit or constriction. In facilitating the negotiation of a developmental level, the therapist is not simply a commentator or insight giver, but a *collaborator in the construction of experience.* The therapist does this within the traditional boundaries of the therapeutic relationship, and not by role-playing or reenacting "real" relationships. Collaborating in the construction of experience should not be confused with historical tactics, such as a "corrective emotional experience" where the therapist may, for example, deliberately take an extra vacation to stimulate certain feelings in the patient. Such contrived strategies can undermine the naturally occurring affects that will characterize the therapeutic relationship.

Rather, the therapist uses the tools of communication available to him or her within the confines of the therapeutic role of following and dealing with the patient's spontaneous communications, verbal and nonverbal. As a collaborative constructor of experience, the therapist is aware of the different developmental levels of the therapeutic relationship. He does not limit himself to exploring only the more representational levels. He is also aware of the importance of the interactive experience, guided by the patient's natural inclinations. He responds to the patient's inclinations and communications, rather than initiating the themes, but does so at multiple developmental levels. As a collaborator of experience, the therapist has to be especially aware of his or her own countertransference tendencies so that the therapeutic explorations reflect the patient's natural, spontaneous inclinations and communications at multiple developmental levels. The therapist listens, empathizes, and offers developmentally useful communications, while the patient explores his experiences as best he can. In maintaining the integrity of the therapeutic relationship, he allows for future transference configurations.

While the subsequent chapters will provide the principles and clinical illustrations to amplify how the roles of constructor and collaborator work, a brief illustration may be helpful at this point. Consider a patient who tends to withdraw during the sessions and become aloof and mechanical in his affect. Traditionally, the therapist might be very patient and comment once or twice about the patient's aloofness or tendency to withdraw, but not do anything to alter that state of withdrawal directly, other than comment on it intellectually. Months, or even years, may go by with a relatively mechanical therapist and an equally mechanical patient, with little or no affect exchange taking place. If the patient were at an advanced representationally differentiated level and could abstract affect and see connections, the therapist might be able to effect change by this approach. For example, the therapist might muse along the lines of, "Every time you seem mad at me, you tend to withdraw." Such a comment may help open up the patient's associations.

But with the patient who is not representationally differentiated, and who is, instead, primitively organized and tends to withdraw anytime he feels intensity of affect of any kind, the therapist must pay attention to and focus on subtleties in the patient's nonverbal behavior and affective tone. Let us postulate, for example, that this person's mother was intrusive and his father was very emotionally removed. Neither parent successfully found a way to woo this very sensitive person into a more intimate pattern of relating. The therapist pays careful attention to his mood and physical sensations while the patient is in various states of attention and relatedness. The therapist, rather than using the tone he uses with most other patients, needs to find a particular tone and rhythm (e.g., using voice tone and rhythm and facial gestures, to maintain a sense of relatedness) that will work with this particular patient. The establishment of this pattern may be a critical first therapeutic step. Rather than comment on how the patient is afraid of his direct gaze, the therapist maintains the rhythms that increases relatedness and wonders about what type of voice tone or looks the patient finds most comforting. For example, the therapist notes that when he talks assertively and looks directly at the patient the patient becomes more aloof. When he talks softly and looks slightly to the side of the patient, only periodically looking directly at him or her, the patient is more engaged.

The therapist and patient then observe and experience different states of relatedness together; they explore at the same time. Initially, they do not explore historical or even current complex patterns of wishes and feelings. They explore, in a supportive manner, aspects of their interaction (e.g., the patient may be helped to see if he finds the therapist's voice soothing or irritating). The therapist uses the boundaries of the therapeutic relationship in a new way, but still maintains those boundaries.

In general, the therapist is attempting to first broaden the range of experiences dealt with at the developmental level where the patient is. For example, if the patient avoids assertion or aggression or intimacy, the therapist's initial goal is to facilitate a full range of feelings at his current level. The next goal is to help the patient move up to the next level. For each developmental level, each chapter will discuss in some detail how to meet these two goals.

The fourth principle, while generally accepted in most dynamic therapies, is often ignored. The therapist should always promote the patient's self-sufficiency and assertiveness. The way learning occurs in life, and particularly in the psychotherapeutic process, is through the person's own active discovery in the context of the relationship he develops with the therapist. For example, it is often not helpful to make comments on the person's behavior or affects, while the person nods acceptingly, and then goes on free associating. On the other hand, it is the active learning done by the patient himself, as opposed to the passive nodding acceptance of what the therapist says and does, that proves to be more helpful. Always promote the person's own assertiveness, self-sufficiency, and active construction of their experiences, as opposed to the more passive, compliant acceptance of what we may have to offer them. Not infrequently, in the enthusiasm of the moment, we assume that the patient's nod or compliant free associations along the lines we suggest is proof of the value of our insight.

Part of the individual's self-sufficiency is rooted in his or her ability to create growth producing experiences in other relationships in addition to the therapeutic one. As a particular issue is being mastered, the therapist needs to actively explore factors that might be interfering with the patient taking this step.

The therapeutic goal, then, is to build on the patient's natural inclinations and interests (i.e., follow his lead) and look for opportunities to collaborate in recreating developmental experiences that are going to help the individual negotiate for the first time, or renegotiate, aspects of development that he was never able to resolve for himself. The preceding four generic principles of (1) harnessing core processes; (2) meeting patients at their developmental levels; (3) renegotiating bypassed levels; and (4) promoting the patient's self-sufficiency, form the framework of this developmental approach to therapy.

These four principles, however, rest on an understanding of the six core developmental processes that are part of all therapeutic relationships (Greenspan, 1989, 1992). Of special importance to better understanding the developmental basis of psychotherapy is the fact that the representational system, so central to most dynamic therapies, only deals with the most surface aspects of ego functioning. The ability to represent experience and elaborate representations, and the ability to differentiate between representations, are the two levels of ego functioning acquired in later stages of ego development (i.e., when children are already verbal and symbolic). There are four earlier levels that must also be dealt with, which deal with the way experience is organized pre-representationally. They include how regulation (sensory reactivity and processing) occurs; the way early engagements and relationships are formed and elaborated; and how early simple and complex, intentional, gestural communication becomes a part of a prerepresentational pattern of mental organization.

By being aware of early stages of ego development, the therapist has greater empathetic range. He can go beyond empathy to be an actual facilitator of new ego development. While intuitive therapists have always been able to empathize with early affective states, most therapists will be aided by a theoretical road map indicating what sensory, regulatory, gestural, behavioral, and affective signposts to look out for. Blind spots due to countertransference phenomena and the therapist's own experiences naturally limit one's empathetic range to some degree.

The patient who does not come into therapy at a level of representational differentiation requires assistance in moving up the developmental ladder. Remember, only the rare representationally differentiated patient is capable of abstracting affect states, making connections between them in the present and the past, and observing their relevance for his or her behavior, moods, and wishes. For most patients, the therapist must negotiate two roles: empathizer-clarifier (and eventually interpreter), regulator-engager-interacter, and collaborative constructor of experience. The therapist's dual role will be highlighted in later chapters describing clinical work on early and later states of ego organization.

AFFECT AND INTERACTION: THE BASIS FOR EGO DEVELOPMENT AND INTELLIGENCE

The therapist's role is based on the critical notion that development occurs from interaction. This notion emerged from our observation that both emotional and intellectual growth depend on affective interactions and these interactions can be harnessed in various contexts. Putting affect and interaction in the central role in mobilizing development as well as change and growth in the therapeutic situation is supported by our observations of infants and children. In this model, interactions are, in a sense, the fuel that mobilizes the mind's various functions. These interactions create opportunities for affective interchange and these affects are then vital to the way in which the mind organizes itself and functions. Each interaction gives rise to affects such as pleasure, annoyance, surprise, sadness, anger, curiosity, and so forth. Variations in the quality and intensity of these and other affects make for almost infinite variety of affect patterns. As will become clear shortly, the affects, in many respects, operate as the orchestra leader, organizing and differentiating the mind's many functions. Affects stemming from interactions become the foundation for both ego growth and differentiation and, more broadly, for intelligence (Greenspan, 1979). Developmentally based therapy promotes intelligence as well as emotional growth and serves as a general and basic mobilizer of developmental processes. While ego growth is not a surprising concomitant of affective interchanges, cognitive or intellectual abilities are not usually thought of as stemming from interactive and affective patterns. To see why they do, consider the following.

A child is learning to say "hello." Is this seemingly simple cognitive task learned by the child being taught to say hello only to close friends, relatives, and those who live within a quarter mile of his house? Does he think to himself with every new person, "Where does this person live in relationship to me?" Or, is the decision when to say hello mediated by an affective cue, such as a warm feeling in one's own body as one sees a familiar, friendly face, which, without even thinking, leads to the smile, the hello, and an extended hand. If it's the latter, we would promote it by creating opportunities for interactions where the child could link his affects, thoughts, and behaviors.

In an even more elaborate example, we posed a simple question to three young boys: What do you think about people who are bossy or try to boss you? First to reply was a five-year-old who, because of developmental difficulties early in life, lacked the emotional pathways that permitted creative and intuitive thought.

"Well," said this articulate youngster, "let's see. Parents are bosses and teachers are bosses and sometimes baby-sitters are bosses." He then tried to list other types of bosses with no other elaborations or discussion. Rather like a living computer, he rattled off a formal classification of different types of bosses, but made no observations that tied these categories to his own life.

A five-and-a-half-year-old without developmental or emotional difficulties gave a strikingly different response. "Most of the time I don't like being bossed," he said, "especially when my parents get too bossy and try to tell me when I can watch TV and when I should sleep, and I'm big enough to decide that myself." This youngster found his answer in his own, apparently generally irritating, brushes with bosses. Rather than simply cataloguing categories or incidents, however, he abstracted a principle from their emotional core ("most of the time I don't like it") and then illustrated with a case in point ("especially when my parents . . .") that he supported with a possibly controversial, but nonetheless reasoned, argument ("I'm big enough to decide that myself.")

A normally developing eight-year-old gave an even more refined answer. "Sometimes I don't like it," he said, "especially when there are things I want to do and they don't let me, but sometimes it's OK because adults know best." He next listed examples of unreasonably bossy parents and teachers, then went on to relate his own reaction to his mood. When he was in a bad mood, he particularly resented being bossed, but at other times he didn't mind so much. He even noted different styles of bossiness. Sometimes people were nice about it; bosses who don't show "dagger eyes" didn't bother him nearly as much as those with a "mean tone of voice." Asked to sum up, he offered, "I guess I don't have just one answer, but there are times when I don't like it and times when it's OK. It depends on how they do it and what kind of mood I'm in."

We see that such an elaborate intellectual activity requires two components: the affectively mediated creation of personal experience and the logical analysis of these experiences.

We have observed that almost every intellectual experience an infant, young child, or adult has involves these two components: an affective one as well as a more purely cognitive one. This process begins early in development. The earliest experiences are double-coded according to both their physical and affective properties. The affects, in fact, appear to work like a sensory organ, providing critical information. For example, the ball is red, but looking at it also feels nice, scary, or interesting. The food is yellow and firm and affectively is delightful or annoying. As a child learns about size, shape and quantity, each of these experiences are also both emotional and cognitive. For example, "a lot" is more than you expected. "A long time" is the rest of your life. The ability to count or formalize these quantities is simply the formal classification of what you already affectively know.

Complex abstract concepts, like love, honor, or justice, are also the products of these same processes. The word has a formal, cognitive definition, but to comprehend or create this definition requires a range of personal affective experience. "Love," for example, is pleasure and excitement, but it is also commitment and loyalty, as well as the ability to forgive and recover from anger.

Taken together, these affective experiences associated with the word give it its full abstract meaning. We have observed that children and adults who remain concrete have difficulty with integrating multiple affective experiences into a word or concept.

Affects are also, as indicated earlier, at the foundation of our most basic ego functions. Our sense of "self" and "other" differentiates out of literally an infinite number of subtle affective interchanges at each of the stages of ego development. In addition, the selection of defenses or coping strategies is often mediated by affects. When a child avoids an angry encounter and becomes compliant and sweet, there is often the affect of fear mediating this change in the child's behavior, feeling tone, and ideas. When an adult avoids intimacy or competition, there are sometimes unpleasant affects associated with these types of interactions mediating the avoidance. As we will describe in more detail later, there is a hierarchy of ways in which the ego copes with underlying affects. These include disorganized behavioral patterns, states of self-absorption, intentional impulsive patterns, somatically experienced affects, polarized, global emotions and beliefs, and represented, symbolized feelings and experiences (from fragmented to cohesive integrated forms).

In our developmental model, therefore, interactions and their associated affects mobilize all aspects of development, emotional as well as cognitive. A wise person is both intellectually and emotionally wise. The two can't be separated. There are, of course, individuals who have isolated areas of cognitive skill (perhaps in science, math, or the arts) and there are other individuals who may have highly differentiated ego structures who lack some of these areas of skill. But overall intelligence, wisdom, and emotional maturity are part of one and the same process. An integrated and differentiated human being is one who can negotiate all the areas of their age-expected functioning, emotional, social, and intellectual.

The affects, as they come into place and as therapeutic experiences harness them, however, not only differentiate and develop our personalities but they serve as the "orchestra leader" for our many ego functions and capacities. When we are trying to remember something quickly or figure out which cognitive operation to use, we don't logically explore all the various alternatives. We quickly come to the strategy or memory through our emotional orchestra leader. The emotions in this sense provide the software programming that organizes and differentiates our intelligence. Similarly, when we automatically use a particular defense coping strategy or regressive route, these same affects are determining the selected operations.

Therapeutic interactions, which generate affects, are at the foundation of developmentally based psychotherapy. In the chapters that follow, we will see how each component of ego development requires certain types of interactions and affective experience. The challenge of the therapeutic process is to figure out ways to harness these as a part of the therapeutic relationship. One must always remember, however, that the therapeutic relationship is only a component of the person's overall set of relationships and, therefore, one needs to help the patient create opportunities for interactive and affective experiences in other sectors of his life. The therapeutic relationship that attempts to provide the critical experiences in the patient's life, rather than assist the patient in orchestrating such life experiences, may limit necessary and healthy age-expected interactions.

SIX LEVELS OF THE MIND (EGO)

In addition to facilitating intellectual and emotional growth in a general sense, affective interactions bring together biology and experience and lead to the construction of a number of basic ego capacities. Observations, clinical work, and studies of infants and young children have enabled us to describe these interactions and formulate six early stages and processes in ego development. In addition, new insights have revealed to us how these stages and processes are formed, including the relative contributions from various sources, biological (constitutional and maturational variations), environmental, cultural, and interactive.

The sequence of intrapsychic organizations that characterizes early ego structure formation includes the organizations that
precede our ability to represent experience. In addition, there is
emerging understanding of how *individual differences,* in terms of
biological aspects of constitutional and maturational phenomena,
contribute to the structure of the ego. This is in keeping with
Freud's goal of understanding the biological aspects of ego development, especially the biological aspects of defenses (see chapter
3). The organizational levels encompass the following six formations:

1. Self-regulation, in which perceptual differences in sensory–affective reactivity and processing as well as behavioral sequencing contribute to the capacity to deal with
   the world and the development of specific types of personality or character structure.
2. Formation and maintenance of relationships as a basis
   for the capacity for object relatedness and intimacy.
3. Boundary-defining,   prerepresentational   interactions,
   which contribute to the formation of discrete wishes, affects, intentional behaviors and the most basic sense of
   reality and a partial self-differentiation.
4. The emergence of a presymbolic complex sense of self
   and "other" through interactive sequences that involve
   behavioral and affective patterns contributes to character
   tendencies around core emotional themes such as dependency, pleasure, gender, assertiveness, aggression, love
   and concern for others.
5. Representational elaboration as a basis for symbolizing
   wishes and affects, creating fantasies and constructing internal self and object, representational elaborations.
6. Representational differentiation as a basis for reality testing, impulse control, stable moods, self-observing capacity and internal self and object differentiations and
   integration.

The different levels of ego organization not only have certain
structural features, but there are certain themes or "content"

that go along with either mastering the stage or having difficulties with the stage. A few examples will follow.

From the stage and processes of self regulation, attention, and interest in the world, children and adults get a sense of confidence in their ability to be calm, regulated, and interested in the world. They also may have a feeling of basic security in the way their bodies work, especially their perceptual and motor equipment. A sense of control often goes along. When difficulties during this stage arise, we not infrequently see themes concerned with being overwhelmed, falling apart, as well as at times, attempts at omnipotent over-control creating order and manipulating selected sensory or motor experiences.

The second stage and set of processes dealing with engagement and patterns of intimate relating can provide the basis for warmth, security with dependency feelings and a sense of optimism and pleasure in relationship to others. In addition there are also themes of positive nurturance. In contrast, difficulties with this stage and its processes can be associated with feelings and themes of isolation, emptiness, greed, preoccupation with inanimate objects, and overreaction to expectable relationship challenges, such as temporary losses or disappointments. At times one also sees compensatory themes centered around grandiosity and the need for unconditional love.

At the third stage and set of processes, the capacity for intentional gestural and affective communication can be associated with constructing more defined affective states such as pleasure, joy, anger, fear, feeling asssertive and confident, as well as developing curiosity about others and the world. A "can do" sense of mastery also emerges from this level. Difficulties with this stage may be associated with the sense that interactions can be chaotic and fragmented, helplessness about one's ability to have impact on others, passivity, fears of unpredictability, and lack of an emerging differentiation of different feeling states, wishes, and intentions.

From the fourth stage and set of processes dealing with a complex sense of self, a number of life's basic emotional needs and themes become defined (not in a symbolic sense, but in the sense of coming together in an organized pattern of behaviors which can be used to negotiate underlying wishes, needs, and intentions). For example, dependency, assertiveness, exploration and curiosity, pleasure and excitement, anger and aggression, a beginning sense of gender and an initial capacity for self limit setting emerge. In contrast, if there are challenges at this level, the child or adult may experience patterns such as narcissistic self-absorption or preoccupation with polarized feeling states and themes such as grandiosity, suspiciousness, somatic concerns, and/or global self-deprecation. One may also see preoccupation with fragmented partial needs and wishes, for example, certain types of limited pleasures.

At the fifth stage (representational elaboration) and its associated processes, we often observe the construction of a rich pattern of imagery concerning inner wishes, ideas and feelings. Fantasies emerge which are part of an elaborate imaginative capacity. Fantasies can embrace most of the major themes of life from dependency and separation anxiety to curiosity, assertiveness and aggression. In short, a rich intrapsychic symbolic life is created. In contrast, challenges at this level can be associated with fears of separation, concerns with danger, as well as tendencies to experience and rely on action patterns rather than ideas and reflection.

In the sixth stage (representational differentiation) emotional thinking and its associated processes, we may see interests in being logical, organized, and reality-based as well as inclinations to construct more complex fantasies, which have their components cohesively and logically tied together. Here too, themes may cover the broad range of human dramas from dependency to aggression. We also may see a more integrated sense of gender emerging along with interests in different aspects of sexuality and pleasure. Often quite prominent are themes of power, being admired, and being respected. Some degree of concern with shame, humiliation, loss of love, fear of injury to self and others is also expected. When there are challenges, one may see polarized rather than integrated themes (preoccupation with things being all bad or all good). We may also see massive preoccupations with order, control, or limited types of pleasure or sexuality. In addition, we may see paralyzing preoccupations with shame, humiliation, loss of love, and injury or harm to self or others.

These stages and processes are described in subsequent chapters and in some detail in *The Development of the Ego* (Greenspan, 1989), as are the types of problems that are related to each level.

There are biologically based constitutional and maturational differences which contribute to ego structure. They are based on differences we have observed in infants and young children, as well as older children and adults. In each sensory pathway, sensory and affective experience can be characterized as hypo- or hyperreactive. In addition, each sensory channel can have differences in the way sensory, interpersonal, affective, and cognitive information is processed (e.g., auditory-verbal, visual-spatial). Furthermore, motor tone and motor planning abilities can vary significantly among individuals. These patterns and the observations they are based on are described in Greenspan (1992). What Hartmann (1939) described as the autonomous ego functions can actually vary quite a bit from person to person, and contribute to character formation and pathology.

When certain biological patterns are coupled with certain environmental patterns, they can intensify each other. We can observe, therefore, what Freud had anticipated: the ways in which the biological influences on character structure and the selection of defenses operate. For example:

1. Individuals who are overreactive to touch or sound and have stronger auditory processing abilities and relatively weaker visual–spatial ones tend toward the hysterical, depressive, and anxiety disorders. Those who have difficulty with movement in space tend toward phobic disorders.
2. Individuals who are underreactive to sensations and have low motor tone tend toward more withdrawn behavior. They tend to escape into fantasy, and, in the extreme, evidence more schizoid and autistic patterns.
3. Individuals with hyperactivity to sensations along with stimulus craving patterns, coupled with high activity levels

and organized gross motor patterns, tend toward risk taking, and, if there is emotional deprivation, antisocial patterns.
4. Individuals with relatively stronger visual–spatial processing and overreactivity to certain sensations tend toward patterns characterized by negativism, stubbornness,
and compulsiveness.

It should be emphasized that when environmental conditions enhance flexibility rather than pathology, we tend to see
healthy character formation, but with a tendency toward one or
another of these characteristics. For example, instead of panic or
anxiety or depression, we see a sensitive person, who is reactive
and alert to others' moods and behaviors.

In this model of development, biological, including genetic,
influences do not act directly on behavior. They influence what
the child brings into his interactive patterns. Cultural, environmental and family factors influence what the caregiver brings
into the interactions. The interactions then determine the relative
mastery of the six-staged process described. Symptoms or adaptive
behaviors are the result of these stage specific–affective interactions.

CONSTRUCTING THE DEVELOPMENTAL PROFILE

Understanding the six levels and building blocks of the mind,
and the related biological and environmental contributions, enables the clinician to construct a developmental profile. As indicated earlier, while the higher levels of ego functioning are
explored and the content of the patient's mental life is being
elaborated, it is especially important to construct a full developmental profile which includes all the mind's levels. This endeavor
is critical to determining the best therapeutic approach and the
focus of that approach. In considering different types of problems
and personalities, one is often tempted to go where the action is,
getting caught up in the conflict of the moment (the family

drama or, understandably, the patient's anguish). However, after one has listened and observed for a reasonable period of time, one should construct, in a systematic way, a full developmental profile so that both the content and structure of mental life is understood.

The profile, which is described in more detail in the Appendix, begins with a description of individuals' regulatory capacities—the ability to remain calm, attentive, and process and respond in an organized way to the variety of sensations around them. Next is a rich description of their style and capacity for engaging, followed by their capacity to enter into reciprocal affective gesturing in a full range of emotional and thematic realms. Then comes their ability to organize their behavior and affects into purposeful patterns that take into account the expectations of their environment. These presymbolic capacities are followed by the ability to represent wishes and ideas, and then to create bridges between different represented experiences.

In each area of the profile, one also looks for deficits (where the ability is not attained at all), or constrictions (where the ability is there but not at its full, robust, and stable form). Constrictions may involve a narrowing of the thematic or affective range (only pleasure, no anger), a lack of stability (the child can engage, but loses this capacity and becomes self-absorbed whenever anxious), or a lack of motor, sensory, cognitive, or language support for that capacity (e.g., the child can be assertive with words, but not with motor patterns).

After an individual's profile is constructed two contributions to the challenges or strengths of that profile are explored. These are the biologically based regulatory contributions, which are discussed elsewhere, and the family, cultural, and interactive contributions.

To illustrate the importance of constructing such a profile, consider the following example. A six-year-old girl presented with an inability to talk in school and only an ability to talk to her mother. She had always been a very dependent, clingy, quiet, and passive little girl, had a lot of separation anxiety in going to school, and had always had difficulty interacting with the other children. However, her difficulties were getting worse over the prior two years. It will be instructive now to look at the profile that had been constructed for this little girl from numerous play sessions. She took a long time to connect with the therapist doing the evaluation each and every session. She would initially fiddle with toys or other objects in a seemingly self-absorbed way and only with a great deal of vocal overtures would she enter into a state of shared attention where she was looking and paying attention to the therapist. The therapist had to maintain a fairly high level of activity to maintain this state of shared attention. Similarly, while she had some warmth and the therapist found herself looking forward to seeing the child, the therapist kept feeling she had to work hard to maintain the sense of engagement. There was some emotional expressiveness and some back and forth smiling and smirking, suggesting some capacity for emotional reciprocity, but often the emotional responses were either very inhibited (lacking) or global, with seemingly inappropriate giggling or repetitive, tense, discharge-oriented play (such as banging a doll). Often the content of the play, such as banging the doll, was not connected to the affect (which might be a smile, as she banged the doll aggressively). She was purposeful and organized in her interactions and play, but during times of transitions, going from one activity to another, she would seem to get lost in her own world again, and the therapist would have to work to regain a sense of organized interaction. She used lots of ideas and was able to build bridges between her ideas (answering "what" and "why" questions), but her imaginative play was focused on only a few themes in a very intense and repetitive manner. She had dolls undressing and had one doll doing aggressive things to the genital areas of the other dolls. In one scene, she had monsters blocking some of the dolls from getting their clothes back, with sadistic fights ensuing. In this profile, then, we see a child who has marked constrictions at the presymbolic areas of development around attention, engagement, and reciprocal affective gesturing and cueing, as well as a preoccupation and constriction at the symbolic or representational level.

In cases like this, with a little child who could elaborate themes, I found that many therapists would focus predominantly on the content of the child's themes (in this case, her preoccupation with sexual and aggressive themes) and obviously want to explore the family dynamics that were contributing, including questions of sexual abuse, sexual play with other children or babysitters, or overstimulation due to exposure to sexual materials or witnessing sexual scenes. But our profile, in addition to alerting us to these factors, also alerts us to the fact that there is a lack of mastery of critical early phases of development, including an ability for consistent attention, engagement, and the earliest types of reciprocity. When, for example, a child can't match the content of her interests with her affects, it often suggests that early in life a caregiver was unable to enter into reciprocal gesturing around certain affective inclinations. For example, the way a child learns to match content with affect is by demonstrating different affects as an infant in association with different kinds of behavior; perhaps, knocking the food off the table with a look of defiance or surprise. In return, they get a reciprocal affect or gesture back from Mommy or Daddy. If the parent freezes or withdraws at that moment, however, there is no return affective gesture and the child's content (i.e., throwing the food on the floor) now has no reciprocal affects associated with it. As a consequence, the child doesn't develop the rich connections between interactive affects and content. Obviously, various types of processing problems can also contribute.

In terms of regulatory patterns in this case, the little girl did have some overreactivity to touch and sound and some mild motor planning problems, but was quite competent in her auditory and visual–spatial processing abilities. There were both physical differences and interactive ones contributing to her profile.

As we look at her developmental profile we are therefore alerted to the fact that there are a number of prerepresentational issues that need to be worked on in the therapy as well as issues involved in her emerging symbolic world. As we are speculating from her profile, we're wondering whether there were some profound difficulties ongoing in the early relationship between this child and her caregivers as well as some current experiences that are leading to her preoccupation with sex and aggression. We are also wondering about current trauma, severe enough to disrupt basic presymbolic abilities (if, for example, they were formerly attained).

As a result of this profile, the therapist who had started with twice-a-week sessions to work on the content of the child's play, and once-a-month sessions with the parents, shifted her approach. It was decided that it was important to develop a deeper alliance with this family to explore the nature of this little girl's preoccupation with sexual and aggressive content and, therefore, they needed to be seen at least once a week. It was also determined that because there were a number of constrictions of the prerepresentational capacities, the therapist needed to work with the parents' interactions with their daughter in order to foster mastery of these basic interactive capacities around attention, engagement, and reciprocal affective interchange. He also began working on the issues directly in therapy, paying more attention to affects and gestures, the tone of the relationship itself, as well as the understanding of verbal content.

A developmental profile systematically done will help the therapist look in a balanced way at the whole individual and, most importantly, it will help the therapist raise hypotheses about where the challenges may lie and even some potential reasons for the challenges. The profile enables the therapist to develop a therapeutic strategy that will further explore the initial hypotheses. Without such a systematic profile, it's easy for the therapist to get lost in the content or symptoms of the moment without a full appreciation of all the areas of challenge and the likely experiences that might be associated with them.

In some respects, the developmental profile, by focusing on the patient's fundamental capacities, may reveal aspects of the patient's developmental history that the patient's "memories" are unable to reveal. The processes that the developmental perspective helps us observe reveals where the patient has been and, even more importantly, where he or she needs to go.

To assist in visualizing the developmental approach to mental health and illness, the following schematic outline may be useful. For each fundamental capacity, there are a range of possibilities from very adaptive and healthy to maladaptive and disordered. This type of approach may prove more useful than narrow-based, symptom-oriented approaches and could even be used for research applications. Each capacity could be rated on a 20-point scale, for example, and the totals summed for a more global picture. Preliminary studies based on rating videotapes of children suggest that these categories can be rated reliably.[1]

Our clinical work with infants and young children helped us understand early affective interactions. We began our explorations of the presymbolic levels of the mind in the early 1970s, observing infants and young children first in a variety of day care settings and then in the context of our studies of infants in multirisk families and infants with biological challenges. Building on the work of pioneers such as Erikson, Piaget, Spitz, Bowlby, Anna Freud, Escalona, Murphy, and Sander, we looked at the different stages infants and young children passed through, the types of adaptive and pathologic patterns that were possible at each stage, and the contribution of both individual biological (constitutional and maturational) and environmental differences. We also formulated models for the relationship between affects and intelligence and healthy and disturbed ego formation (Greenspan 1979, 1981, 1984, 1989, 1992).

In this model, the presymbolic and early symbolic world contains six levels including a number of basic capacities and critical aspects of character and personality. The importance of the presymbolic aspects of the ego have also been emphasized in recent developmental investigations into several aspects of presymbolic learning, sometimes referred to as "implicit learning," "tacit knowledge," or "procedural knowledge." For example, based on experiments where subjects learned the rules of a new grammar (certain sequences of letters), while consciously attending to a

---

[1]For further information on the reliability studies, contact Georgia Di Gangi at the Reginald Lourie Center, 11710 Hunters Lane, Rockville, MD 20895.

SELF REGULATION

0	6	14	20
Attention is fleeting (a few seconds here or there) and/or very active or agitated or Mostly self-absorbed and/or lethargic or passive.	When very interested or motivated or captivated can attend and be calm for short periods (e.g., 30 to 60 seconds).	Focused, organized, and calm except when overstimulated or understimulated (e.g., noisy, active, or very dull setting); challenged to use a vulnerable skill (e.g., a child with weak fine motor skills asked to write rapidly), or ill, anxious, or under stress.	Focused, organized, and calm most of the time, even under stress.

ENGAGEMENT

0	6	14	20
Aloof, withdrawn, and/or indifferent to others.	Superficial and need-oriented, lacking intimacy.	Intimacy and caring is present but disrupted by strong emotions, like anger or separation (e.g., person withdraws or acts out).	Deep, emotionally rich capacity for intimacy, caring, and empathy, even when feelings are strong or under stress.

INTENTIONALITY

0	6	14	20
Mostly aimless, fragmented, unpurposeful behavior and emotional expressions (e.g., no purposeful grins or smiles or reaching out with body posture for warmth or closeness).	Some need-oriented, purposeful islands of behavior and emotional expressions. No cohesive larger social goals.	Often purposeful and organized, but not with a full range of emotional expressions (e.g., seeks out others for closeness and warmth with appropriate flirtatious glances, body posture, and the like, but becomes chaotic, fragmented or aimless when very angry).	Most of the time purposeful and organized behavior and a wide range of subtle emotions, even when there are strong feelings and stress.

THE PREVERBAL SENSE OF SELF:
Comprehending Intentions and Expectations

0	6	14	20
Distorts the intents of others (e.g., misreads cues and, therefore, feels suspicious, mistreated, unloved, angry, etc.).	In selected relationships can read basic intentions of others (such as acceptance or rejection) but unable to read subtle cues (like respect or pride or partial anger).	Often accurately reads and responds to a range of emotional signals, except in certain circumstances involving selected emotions, very strong emotions or stress or due to a difficulty with processing sensations, such as sights or sounds, e.g., certain signals are confusing.	Reads and responds to most emotional signals flexibly and accurately even when under stress (e.g., comprehends safety vs. danger, approval vs. disapproval, acceptance vs. rejection, respect vs. humiliation, partial anger, etc.).

CREATING AND ELABORATING EMOTIONAL IDEAS

0	6	14	20
Puts wishes and feelings into action. Unable to use ideas to elaborate wishes and feelings (e.g., hits when mad, hugs or demands physical intimacy when needy, rather than experiencing idea of anger or expressing wish for closeness).	Uses ideas in a concrete way to convey desire for action or get basic needs met. Does not elaborate idea of feeling in its own right (e.g., "I want to hit but can't because someone is watching" rather than "I feel mad, like I'd want to hit").	Often uses ideas to be imaginative and creative and express range of emotions, except when experiencing selected emotions or when under stress (e.g., cannot bring anger or despondency into verbal discussion or pretend play).	Uses ideas to express full range of emotions. Is imaginative and creative most of the time, even under stress.

EMOTIONAL THINKING

0	6	14	20
Ideas are experienced in a piecemeal or fragmented manner (e.g., one phrase is followed by another with no logical bridges).	Thinking is polarized, ideas are used in an all or nothing manner (e.g., things are all good or all bad. There are no shades of gray).	Thinking is constricted (i.e., tends to focus mostly on certain themes like anger and competition). Often thinking is logical, but strong emotions, selected emotions, or stress can lead to polarized or fragmented thinking.	Thinking is logical, abstract, and flexible across the full range of age expected emotions and interactions. Thinking is also relatively reflective at age expected levels and in relationship to age expected endeavors (e.g., peer, spouse, or family relationships). Thinking supports movement into the next stages in the course of life.

related task, Arthur Reber suggested that "unconscious cognitive learning" was a very important aspect of cognitive development. Others have included in procedural knowledge social conventions, implicit rules, and expectations such as the ordinary rules of grammar or expectations for responses to transgressions (Clyman, 1991; Emde, et al., 1991; Erdelyi, 1985; Horowitz, 1991; Kihlstrom, 1987; Papousek & Papousek, 1979).

Early unconscious and presymbolic learning, however, may be more dynamic than these descriptions suggest. Our work with infants and young children suggests that a number of critical psychological structures involving the formation and definition of the self as well as others are formed through early interactions (Greenspan, 1979, 1989). For example, during a stage of presymbolic learning involving two-way intentional communication (i.e., learning through back and forth [reciprocal] interactions) there is not only the formation of interactive expectations, but an early differentiation of the ego, including, for example, the boundary between parts of the self and non-self and early drive and affect proclivities.

Furthermore, these early-formed psychological structures are based on a dynamic interaction between the infant's early wishes and affects and significant caregivers. Contrary to what Reber suggests, these early-formed capacities are not robust in the face of challenges or insults, nor are they independent of age, intellect or individual differences. In fact, in our work with children with biological or environmental risk (children with pre-autistic patterns and children in multi-risk families) (Greenspan 1987, 1992), we have observed that these early patterns can be easily derailed. In addition, individual differences in motor capacities, sensory modulation and processing and caregiver responses play a large role in determining the character of these early presymbolically-learned patterns. In our view, presymbolic learning is dynamic and interactive. It is sensitive to infant and caregiver characteristics and formative in the building of critical lifelong, psychological structures.

The presymbolic stages and related structures of the ego and personality deal with such basic issues as regulation and security, the depth, range and stability of relationships, and the formation of drive and affect patterns, the early formation and differentiation of a sense of self and the formation of early character patterns (including the negotiation of basic emotional themes such as safety, approval, acceptance, anger, loss, separation, and so forth). In a sense, before symbols are formed to any great degree in the latter part of the second into the third year of life, we have a sense of who we are, what we want and how others will treat us. Symbols and words help us open up this emerging inner world, allowing for more flexible thought, creative excursions into fantasy, imaginative trips into the past, present and future, and elaborate types of logic and thinking. Our capacity for creating symbols is initially simply a shorthand way of indicating and making sense of what we already know at the deeper levels of our mind.

APPLICATIONS OF DEVELOPMENTAL PRINCIPLES TO DIFFERENT TYPES OF THERAPY

In presenting a model for developmentally based psychotherapy, it is useful to be mindful of the traditional distinctions between different types of therapies that use exploration of feelings and

thoughts as a means for facilitating emotional growth or supporting current levels of functioning. Included in the different approaches are psychoanalysis, psychoanalytic psychotherapy, and
supportive psychotherapy. Recent reviews of these point to the
goals, processes, and techniques that characterize and distinguish
them (Allison, 1994; de Jonghe, Rijnierse, and Janssen, 1994). It
is also useful to be mindful of the goals, processes, and techniques
that characterize behavioral and cognitive behavioral approaches.
The principles of developmentally based psychotherapy, while
constituting a unique type of psychotherapeutic process in its own
right, can also enrich the therapeutic approaches of the above
therapies.

In psychoanalysis, understanding developmental principles
at the foundation of developmentally based psychotherapy will
enable therapists to work with prerepresentational transferences.
In addition, it will enable therapists to work with prerepresentational expressions of wishes, conflicts, and defenses. Most importantly, it will guide therapists to examine the structural
elements outlined earlier and discussed in the following chapters.
These structural elements, as indicated, are necessary for any analysis of representational level wishes, conflicts, defenses, and compromise formations. In dealing with these prerepresentational
and structural issues, the intensity of the psychoanalytic situation
makes it possible to use the analytic relationship as the primary
vehicle for exploring experience and constructing new types of
developmentally necessary experiences.

In supportive psychotherapy, the developmental principles
from developmentally based psychotherapy offer explicit descriptions of the types of experiences needed for structural growth. It
allows the therapist to position himself alongside the patient as a
collaborator in the process of helping the patient embrace developmentally facilitating experiences in his or her daily life (e.g.,
maintaining nurturing and supportive relationships, elaborating
and communicating wishes and feelings, etc). This may also include helping the patient comprehend the patterns he or she
uses to avoid or undermine developmentally needed, structure-
building experiences. In supportive psychotherapy, the goal is

to support current functioning and help the patient maintain experiences and relationships that will facilitate gradual emotional growth. The therapeutic relationship itself is not the centerpiece of renegotiating emotional experiences.

Hybrids of the analytic and the supportive approaches, including analytically oriented psychotherapy, would use elements of both of these. In combining explorations of the transference relationship to reveal certain repetitive emotional patterns with growth-facilitating relationships and experiences, analytically oriented psychotherapy can avail itself of the developmentally based psychotherapy principles to more clearly define the patient's developmental needs and the types of intratherapeutic and day-to-day interactive experiences that are likely to facilitate emotional growth. For example, the patient who has difficulty reading nonverbal cues, and therefore distorts experience and fills in with his own favorite, and often painful, fantasies needs to be helped through explicit attention, both in the therapy situation and in day-to-day interactions, to comprehend these types of presymbolic distortions. The therapist needs to know the level of development that is consistent with these types of distortions in order to be helpful in both understanding the problem and assisting the patient in working it through.

Behavioral and cognitive behavioral approaches, because of their lack of a developmental road map, have no systematic theory to determine which behaviors or thoughts should be changed, in addition to the presenting symptom. Similarly, the lack of a developmental road map makes it hard for the therapist to know how or if the symptoms are part of a larger pattern and what new potential patterns, other than simply removing the symptoms, would lead the patient toward a developmentally more advanced psychological configuration. For example, if our anxious, phobic individual has even more significant difficulties with suicidal ideation and a lack of pleasure in intimacy, it is possible that these more significant difficulties, if they weren't explicitly revealed by the patient, might not be included in the treatment program. In addition, in behavioral approaches, there is no systematic developmental theory to help the clinician determine which discriminative and reinforcing stimuli would be relevant to the patient.

The clinician's "green thumb" is often used in the absence of a developmental clinical theory.

The principles from developmentally based psychotherapy can assist behavioral and cognitive behavioral clinicians in constructing the broader behavioral, cognitive, and affective patterns, within which the patient's symptoms reside. Furthermore, it can assist in creating the developmental goals for the patient and in clarifying the types of discriminative and reinforcing experiences that are likely to be relevant to a particular patient.

While not discussed in this work, the relevance of these developmental constructs for couples and family therapies is addressed in *The Development of the Ego* (Greenspan, 1989).

The developmental concepts in this work will, therefore, prove helpful to a variety of therapies that have as their goal personality change and growth. The main goal of this work, however, is to create a set of clinical principles based on how emotional development takes place under natural circumstances. Developmental constructs based on the principles of natural growth and development may provide an especially valid theoretical framework for both understanding and constructing the psychotherapeutic process.

FREQUENCY AND INTENSITY OF THERAPY

Some patients require a very intense therapeutic relationship, which occurs on an almost daily basis to create the circumstances for psychological change and growth. Other patients require understanding of how they avoid growth-producing experiences and how to construct them in their lives. Such understanding often involves deep psychological insights, but this group of patients has the capacity to become involved in growth-producing experiences outside the therapeutic relationship, using the relationship to assist them in constructing such experiences. Traditionally, it has been thought that a certain group of relatively healthy patients with deep-seated, but organized, neurotic configurations, require the intensive therapeutic relationship, where the therapeutic relationship, using especially the transference, becomes the main vehicle for change and growth. Along with this traditional view has been the notion that less well put together patients who have, perhaps, very severe character pathologies or borderline pathologies may not be able to utilize the intensity of an almost-daily therapeutic session and have to settle for a less ambitious therapeutic goal through a combination of supportive and insight-oriented therapy once or several times a week. In this view, then, the relatively healthy individual should receive the most intensive work because a certain degree of health is necessary to participate in the intensive therapeutic process (e.g., the ability to observe one's own feelings and behaviors). The developmental perspective suggests an alternative way of determining the optimal therapeutic program for a given patient. It would suggest that the goal of the therapeutic work is to help the patient progress to higher levels of structural organization and broaden the affective and thematic range and stability at that level. For relatively healthy individuals who can fully engage in many of life's experiences, the patient and the therapist can collaborate in helping the patient understand his or her maladaptive patterns (e.g., patterns of avoidance or patterns of misperception) and construct and stay with developmentally facilitating experiences. Examples might include learning to tolerate the feelings of loss in a relationship where typically one would act out in a counterphobic way, or learning to tolerate the anxiety that arises out of periodically having to tolerate passive feelings associated with being in a relationship with an authority figure. Our relatively healthy individual uses the therapeutic relationship to understand the nature of growth facilitating experiences, the nature of his or her own misperceptions and maladaptive behaviors, and tries to use real life experiences with spouse, friends, or boss as the basis for change and growth. The transference in this context is understood as part of comprehending the patterns in the therapeutic relationship that need to be understood as they play out in other relationships. The working through of the transference in the therapeutic relationship in this context is not the primary agent of change.

Rather, the primary agent of change is the day-to-day coping with a wider range of affects, emotional themes, and the use of developmentally higher structural capacities. These higher developmental structural capacities arise from relationship patterns both in the therapeutic situation and in one's day-to-day life.

Central to growth producing experiences is the experience of affects that are natural and spontaneous. As intense as a therapeutic relationship becomes, for the individual capable of a rich range of developmentally expectable relationships (e.g., marriage, close friendships), the therapeutic relationship can never hope to attain the intensity or saliency of these daily relationships. If it does, it suggests that perhaps the patient's ability to engage in these real daily relationships is not as healthy and flexible as one thought. The spontaneity and naturalness of the patient's affects are perhaps the central feature of his growth. The patient's affects propel him into interactive patterns which, in turn, create opportunities for achieving higher and higher levels of structural organization. It is the patient's ability to abstract from his own affective experience in day-to-day relationships that creates the growth of the personality in the ordinary sense. This growth gets derailed when the patient's conflicts and anxieties or structural limitations derail this process of day-to-day, interactive, affective experience, and the abstractions from these experiences. To get this process back on track, the therapeutic relationship creates the circumstances for change and growth. Therefore, where this can occur in the ordinary day-to-day way, in part guided by the therapeutic relationship, the intensity and naturalness of the affects will be far more conducive to structural change and growth than where these experiences have to occur through the therapeutic relationship. In this context, the use of the therapeutic relationship as the primary vehicle for change and growth is not the preferred choice, because in the therapeutic relationship it is usually not possible for affective experiences to have the same degree of naturalness and saliency they do in everyday life. For patients, however, whose ability to construct day-to-day experiences is necessarily limited by the nature of their psychopathology, the therapeutic relationship must serve a more dominant role, at least initially. With the more flexible, healthier, neurotic patient, however, it may be possible in many circumstances for day-to-day experiences to provide a more optimal medium for change and growth.

Patients, however, with a certain level of character pathology (usually in the moderate to severe range) may not be able to avail themselves of day-to-day experiences that could potentially facilitate change and growth. Their patterns of avoidance, acting out, or misperception are too severe and encompass too wide a range of experiences for them to do anything other than repeat their maladaptive patterns, which pervade most of life's major arenas, including family, friends, work relationships, and the like. In such a situation, the therapeutic situation may be the only relationship where new experiences can be organized and tolerated. The patient initially can only collaborate a little bit in the construction of such experiences and the therapist, in the way he deals with the transference feelings, plays a significant role in creating the circumstances for change and growth. Many of the examples described in these chapters will illustrate how the therapist works with the patient to create circumstances that will support structural change and growth.

Another group of patients who evidence more severe pathologies including various borderline conditions and severe disturbances of affect have traditionally been thought of as too vulnerable to tolerate an intensive four- to five-times-a-week therapeutic relationship. However, such patients may also require the therapeutic relationship to be the primary vehicle for change and growth similar to our patients with moderate to severe character pathology. The greater vulnerability of such patients may mean that the therapist is working with them on more basic and earlier developmental levels. For the borderline patient, for example, issues of preverbal, presymbolic, as well as symbolic self and other organizations may be prominent. For the patient with extreme disorders of affect, regulatory phenomena may be a vital focus. Therefore, such patients may also require intense, almost daily therapeutic sessions and a therapeutic relationship which can be the major vehicle for change and growth, only here the focus becomes developmentally earlier issues.

With the foregoing conceptualization, we would shift the recommendation for the most intensive psychotherapeutic processes to the patients whose disturbances are relatively greater. The relatively healthier patients may be able to use the therapeutic relationship to construct the conditions for change and growth using the real daily experiences of their lives. This approach would alter the recommendations we might make in relationship to current practices. For example, for the relatively healthy neurotic patient with a flexible ego structure, the recommendation might be for the less intensive approach. On the other hand, for the individual whose neurotic structure pervades major and significant areas of his or her life, and where the capacity to construct growth facilitating experiences with the consultation of the therapist is unlikely to occur, intensive therapeutic work may be indicated. Similarly, for the severe character pathologies, the borderline conditions, and severe disorders of affect, the most intensive approaches may be absolutely necessary, with, however, a focus on developmentally early issues and an understanding of the limited structural capacity of the individual. In this way, the therapeutic relationship would not overwhelm an already fragile person, but would initially create the support, regulatory, and interactive experiences for both stability and gradual change and growth. For example, as will be described in greater detail in the chapters on regulatory difficulties and difficulties with engagement and presymbolic communication, many patients will require long periods of working at presymbolic levels. Some patients will require extraordinary patience and flexibility in the development of a therapeutic relationship.

CONTENT AND PRESYMBOLIC STRUCTURES

Certain assumptions from psychoanalytic approaches have influenced the practice of psychotherapy. A particularly important one relates to the central role of verbal discussions of "represented" experience. The following sections of this chapter will discuss this assumption. This section may be of special interest to those with a strong psychoanalytic background.

Psychotherapy which focuses predominantly on discussions of verbal content may only utilize a small part of the human mind. *Developmentally Based Psychotherapy*, in contrast, is based on emerging insights regarding the different levels and processes of the mind and attempts to work with a number of different levels simultaneously.

It is not surprising that most current therapeutic approaches focus only on a small aspect of the mind's capacities. Historically, most therapeutic work has helped a patient with verbal understanding of the nature of their difficulties and the dynamics of their personality. Verbal insight, however, relates to the mind's capacity for symbolic or representational thinking. It deals with the "content" of affects, wishes, fantasies, and thoughts. The level of the mind that deals with understanding, while important, is only one small component of the mind. As will be seen in the chapters that follow, we have learned about other levels and processes of the mind that exert an important influence on our behavior and mental functioning.

The emphasis on verbal content is based on an assumption that most individuals can symbolize or represent wishes, affects and more broadly experiences. While as we will see this assumption may be untrue, the emphasis on using symbolic processes and verbal content is understandable in light of the history of psychoanalysis and psychodynamic approaches. Many of Freud's seminal contributions had to do with certain universal mental contents (e.g., the oedipal conflict, earlier psychosexual fantasies, including oral, anal, and phallic patterns, the castration complex, penis envy, etc). Interestingly, many of the recent critiques of Freud and psychoanalysis concern the fixed or rigid way these mental contents are held onto, and the lack of data to support them.

Different facets of mental content are the focus of different therapies: the affects, underlying wishes, unconscious conflicts, the relationship patterns and/or the repetitive ways of thinking, feeling, and behaving.

The "content" of the mind is the focus even in developmental inquiries, especially when we look at how developmental insights are used in the therapy situation. There are Freud's contributions to understanding psychosexual development and the generic content of unconscious fantasies (1905), and Erikson's psychosocial perspective (1959), which highlights the unconscious themes of mental life. Freud's theory of ego structure (e.g., his work on dreams and mechanisms of condensation, displacement, etc.), early object relationship theories, and Anna Freud's formulations of defenses (1965), in part do focus on certain functions of the ego. Similarly, Margaret Mahler's work on separation and individuation (Mahler, Pine, and Bergman, 1975) and object constancy, her insights into the earliest stages of infancy, including the toddler's struggles to become more individuated and the preschool child's struggle to develop a stable internal image of his loved ones, also relate to certain ego functions. As these insights from Freud (1911), Mahler et al. (1975), or object relations theorists (e.g., Kernberg, 1975) are reworked in adults, they are reworked from the perspective of the content of the individual's mental life. In the actual therapy situation, explorations of these issues are done in the same verbal, content-oriented, self-reflective way as difficulties related to sexual conflicts or conflicts emanating from later stages in development. It is as though the individual already has the capability for representing wishes and feelings and reflecting on feelings; a capacity which itself depends in part on resolution of the very challenges being worked on, such as separation and individuation. Similarly, an object relationships approach might help a patient examine the projections he manifests in his therapeutic interactions and at the same time ignore the fact that he does not have the capacity to observe his own patterns. How one can and should work with such a patient will be discussed in the following chapters.

Advances based on the work of Heinz Kohut and his followers (self psychology and intersubjective phenomena), while extremely useful in understanding narcissistic disorders and the vicissitudes of empathy and of the affective interchanges between parent and child, also utilize similar types of content-oriented self-reflection. The therapist may be sensitive to the lack of (or misguided) empathy in the patient's formative years and in the therapeutic situation, as well as feelings of humiliation and rage. He may understand how these lead to narcissistic character patterns. The intervention strategy, while focusing on the earlier relationship patterns and the empathetic tone of these, nonetheless uses self-reflection and verbal discussion of content to work through different affects, thoughts, and underlying wishes and feelings.

Similarly, the work of colleagues who have discussed the implications of infant research for the psychotherapeutic process (e.g., Emde, 1983; Stern, 1985; Lichtenberg, Lachmann, and Fosshage, 1992), while discussing interpersonal dimensions, have focused mostly on verbal exploration of the "content" of mental life.

At this point, the reader may well say, Of course! What else can be worked with in the therapeutic process, other than verbal exploration of the content of mental life—the patient's wishes, conflicts, thoughts, behaviors, and feelings! It is interesting to talk of the aspects of the mind, but how can you access them if not through the one sector of the mind having to do with verbal exploration? He or she may add, And, it's been very helpful to have even a partial developmental road map, which includes the insights of individuals like Mahler et al. (1975) and Kohut (1971), as well as others such as Hartmann (1939), Hartmann, Kris, and Loewenstein (1946), Spitz (1965), Kernberg (1975), and Fraiberg (1979), to help figure out what type of dramas are being played out in the mental life of the patient. Is it a drama having to do with lack or loss of empathy? Or is it a drama having to do with separation-individuation and object constancy? Or is it a drama having to do with conflicts over sexuality or aggression? In this way, the reader may argue, at least within the in-depth psychological approaches, the therapist is armed with an understanding of aspects of the content of the patient's mental life. But as indicated, what if the individual does not have the capacity to observe or reflect on mental contents? After all such an ability usually suggests an advanced state of mental health.

There is good reason to believe that large segments of the population lack many critical capacities, such as self observing abilities, necessary for mental health, and that even patients who have them, have them only in part. These capacities which can be called "structural capacities" (Greenspan, 1989) have to do with critical abilities such as self regulation, relating, presymbolic-affective communicating, representing and differentializing experience and self observation. These structural capacities make up the stage upon which our psychological dramas can play out. They eminate from the different levels of the mind and are necessary for mental health and overcoming psychopathology.

Using mostly verbal content exploration as a vehicle for psychotherapy as is indicted overutilizes a narrow section of the mind having to do with already represented and differentiated experience. It assumes most patients have abilities which they do not. Understanding the development of the structure of the ego, along with understanding the content of different unconscious or partially conscious themes and dramas, therefore, will provide a more meaningful model for the psychotherapeutic process. In fact, as will be shown in this work, one cannot properly either understand, analyze, or alter a drama without also taking into account the stage upon which this drama is being played out. Structural capacities, when not dealt with directly in the psychotherapeutic process, often result in compromised outcomes or therapeutic failures.

In therapeutic terms how does one build the ego structure, including for example regulation of attention, mood, and behavior; forming, maintaining, and negotiating relationships; understanding the intentions and emotions of others; organizing and controlling one's impulses; and learning to delay, pause, and tolerate frustration? How does one learn to represent feelings, affects, and wishes that have never been represented before? How does one learn to differentiate and build bridges between different wishes and feelings? How does one build bridges between the past, present, and the future, when one's past interactions may have been concrete and grounded in the day-to-day meeting of needs? How does one work on increasing the depth of intimacy and relatedness and overcoming a sense of empty deadness or hollowness, when one doesn't have the ability to represent or abstract the affects associated with these patterns? How does one deal with affects, feelings, and failures of empathy, when there is no ability to represent or put the feelings into words, and when the therapist's attempted verbalization has no symbolic reference point? Similarly, how does one deal with issues of merging and separation-individuation for which there are no verbal or representational analogues in the patient's personality? How does one deal with proclivities for aggression and fears of annihilation, when these potential conflicts exist as fragmented, prerepresentational, behavioral, and somatic tendencies—a series of fragmented, affect, and behavioral discharge states.

At this point, some readers may wonder how an individual could experience mental life without representing feelings, affects, or wishes. Since many therapists experience life via their ability to represent or symbolize wishes and affects ("I feel sad or mad or want this or that"), it becomes difficult to imagine an individual who does not possess this capacity. Interestingly, while most therapists are trained to watch out for projecting their own inner "content" onto others (e.g., assuming the patient is angry when the therapist is feeling angry), they are not trained to be alert to the more profound problem of projecting their own personality "structure" onto the patient. Many of us make an assumption that other human beings are similar to us in certain fundamental ways, including how we perceive sensations, use symbols and representations, and the like. As the following chapters will discuss, human beings vary more than is commonly assumed in these structural foundations of the personality. Individuals, for example, experience sensations such as touch, sound, sight, and movement quite differently. Many individuals do not represent wishes and feelings. This doesn't mean they don't have a wish or feeling, but it may exist more as a somatic and behavioral pattern and not as a representational–symbolic one. For example, instead of feeling angry and being able to reflect on this feeling ("I am angry. I wonder why?''), the individual without the ability to represent anger may simply experience an urgent desire to hit the person next to him at the bar, and will then do it. Later, the person can describe his behavior, but not the feeling that preceded it. Descriptions of behaviors (sometimes after the fact) and somatic states (''tension in my muscles'') occupy mental life rather than what will later be described as abstracted affect states or the representation of wishes and feelings.

Life for many is experienced as concrete, here-and-now behavioral patterns and somatic states. Such individuals can be quite intelligent and use symbolic capacities having to do math, or can figure out a variety of academic problems. They may even discuss, in an intellectual way, many subtle issues about human relations or, in general, people's motivations for doing this or that. They, however, cannot employ these same capacities in their own inner world of wishes and affects.

It is not, however, only our capacity to represent experience that we tend to project onto our patients. We mistakenly tend to project other structural capacities as well, including our capacities to process and regulate sensations, relate, engage, and communicate with preverbal patterns. We tend to assume that people are similar in these fundamental ways; that to most individuals a soft sound sounds soft, a pleasurable touch feels good (unless there is mental conflict), and nonverbal gestures, including looks, glances, affects, body postures, and interactive behaviors are ''read'' in the same way as part of a common biological or cultural set of norms.

Each developmental level of ego structure, however, has different perceptual, relational, interactive, and communicative features. Individuals function at different developmental levels and their conflicts, fantasies, and interactive patterns have meaning only in the context of the developmental level that organizes them. Understanding the structure of these organizations will provide us with a technology for intervention that will lead to interactions that work both with the content of the drama and the structure of the stage. This framework may also facilitate empirical research on the development of ego capacities in therapy that would relate to promising content oriented approaches to the therapeutic process (e.g., Luborsky and Crits-Christoph, 1980; Gill, 1984; Weiss, Sampson, and Mt. Zion Psychotherapy Research Group, 1986; Horowitz, 1991; Miller, 1993; Hartley, 1993; Perry, 1993).

DYNAMIC, DEVELOPMENTAL, AND STRUCTURAL PERSPECTIVES: COMPLEMENTARY OR COMPETING

We have been outlining the ingredients of a developmental approach to therapy and discussing the explication to clinical problems. Many clinicians with a strong background in psychodynamic theory and practice may, however, have many questions about the real differences between developmental, structural, and dynamic perspectives and the degree to which they can truly complement and strengthen each other. The following section will discuss some of the most frequently raised theoretical and clinical questions.

The question often arises whether there is an antithesis between the structural and dynamic perspectives, the latter focusing on unconscious wishes and conflicts. Each perspective is quite necessary, and both can be viewed as essential elements of the multiple points of view necessary for an understanding of the mind. It is easy to focus on only one perspective, such as the dynamic, and lose sight of the fact that every dynamic drama must take place in the context of a particular structure or set of structures. In addition, when focusing on structural perspectives, it is easy to lose sight of the fact that structures provide the housing, so to speak, for different dynamic dramas, each one with its own content or meanings.

Looking at the development of therapeutic approaches over the last forty or fifty years, one can observe a movement from a focus on unconscious wishes and conflicts to an emphasis on current patterns of relationships (in part related to prior relationships and related unconscious wishes) and habitual patterns of thinking and feeling, including specific techniques to interrupt these. In a sense, there has been a movement from approaches that focus on historical and unconscious factors, to those that focus on relationships and cognitive and affective patterns in the here-and-now, with relative degrees of attention to their origins. Yet, in spite of these shifts, the focus on mental content and the emphasis on verbal–symbolic interaction has remained. The point is, early preverbal interaction patterns are thought to be workable with verbal reflective therapeutic strategies even when the individual's early difficulties preclude their having these reflective capacities.

Interestingly, many observations of the psychotherapeutic process suggest a lack of specificity in the most important common elements or active ingredients. For many years now, factors such as the relationship itself, warmth, empathy, acceptance, and understanding have been suggested as being critically helpful aspects of the psychotherapeutic relationship. These types of experiences are based on the tone or affect in the relationship and on many subtle features of the interaction, of which verbal description is only one part. These types of experience, which are related to structural development, have never achieved the degree of conceptualization or centrality as has the focus on mental contents such as wishes, conflicts, or internal fantasies. They may, however, only be the tip of the iceberg in terms of the truly operative elements of the therapeutic process..

Therefore, in attempting to improve our clinical tools, it is especially important clinically to understand the structure of the ego, in addition to the particular dynamic "contents" that the ego is struggling with at any moment in time. Such understanding may enable us to develop a more explicit, systematic, and developmentally based set of therapeutic principles.

It is especially necessary to broaden our stockpile of therapeutic tools because, as indicated, large numbers of individuals who come for treatment, or who could benefit from such treatment, have important structural limitations.

The "ideal" neurotic patient allegedly has intact structural capacities working for him or her, and needs only the therapeutic process, including a transference relationship and the skillful guidance of a seasoned therapist, for opportunities to be made available for new growth. Most patients, however, come into the therapeutic situation with limitations in their ability to represent experience in general or in terms of specific affect realms or with regard to specific wishes. Even those patients who can represent many aspects of intrapsychic experience often have difficulty creating connections or bridges between different aspects of their intrapsychic world.

Furthermore, as indicated earlier, many patients are quite limited in their self-reflective capacities, that is, in being able to observe their intrapsychic world as a dynamic process and as part of the treatment situation. Even more importantly, large percentages of patients who present to us have difficulties at prerepresentational levels, with such basic issues as forming and deepening a relationship, or reading and responding to nonverbal, interpersonal affect cues. In addition, we have discovered large numbers of patients who have basic difficulties in what may be termed *regulatory processes* (see chapter 3). These are the difficulties in regulating or processing sensation or modulating motor responses.

Understanding the structural development of the mind provides us with a way of comprehending how an individual learns to regulate the intensity of sensations, and later, the intensity of internal wishes and affects. It also provides us with a way of understanding how individuals process, that is, comprehend and organize sensations, wishes, and affects and organize both motor and communication patterns.

Furthermore, our structural perspective deals with understanding how individuals learn to become part of a relationship and share a sense of humanity with others. It demarcates the processes involved in early prerepresentational interactions and differentiations. Beginning with part internal object interactions and partial differentiations, it describes how we progress to prerepresentational (presymbolic) whole self and object patterns and further prerepresentational differentiations.. It demarcates how these prerepresentational patterns serve as a foundation for the construction of a representational system, that is, the ability to abstract wishes and affects in a representational form. Most importantly, it helps us understand biologically based constitutional and maturational differences.

Furthermore, the structural perspective seeks to understand how early representational capacities coalesce into internal self and object organizations, and how constitutional and maturational patterns contribute to these early structural capacities. For example, we are able to understand how overreactivity to sound and touch will lead toward one type of organization, while underreactivity will lead to another. It also helps us identify specific interactive patterns that support or undermine particular structural capacities. In addition, it helps us understand how representational, internalized self and object organizations become further differentiated, as a basis for the development of basic ego functions. These functions include reality testing, impulse control, stable mood, stable internal representations of self and object, and stable differentiations between the internal representations of self and object. It also outlines how a differentiated ego structure leads to further growth and development, in terms of shifts from dyadic to triadic structures to those structures dealing with group phenomena as well as more advanced, internalized phenomena.

DYNAMIC CONFLICTS AND LEVELS OF EGO DEVELOPMENT

It is sometimes tempting to explain symptoms or behaviors completely in terms of dynamic conflicts. There are enormous differences in one's approach to conflicts, however, depending on whether this conflict is operating at one level of structural organization or another. Consider, for example, a conflict over aggression, having to do with a wish to hurt the object and, in turn, a fear of being annihilated by the object. If it is operating at a representational level, we may see it reflected in the play of a child, who has one doll hit another doll, followed by a hurricane, where the first doll gets submerged under crumbling buildings.

There may be affects of fear and anxiety. While playing this out, however, the child is using words, maintaining a descriptive or reflective attitude, and, when getting anxious about the hurricane, putting into words aspects of the anxiety and saying, perhaps, "Mommy, I need a hug."

The same conflict played out at a prerepresentational level, where experience cannot be represented, might have the child yelling and screaming at the real object, not the pretend toys, or biting, kicking, or hitting the real object. Following this, in anticipation of severe punishment, the child might experience diffuse anxiety in a more bodily and behavioral sense (e.g., increased diffuse aggressive activity, changes in heart rate and muscle tone, etc.)

A child at the prerepresentational level is unable to represent the expected retaliation. The child is more like a person in a fight who throws a punch, and, simply from the other person's behavioral pattern, anticipates a punch back. Our prerepresentational, conflicted individual, therefore, may pinch, bite, or throw a tantrum and then up the stakes, increasing his own aggression because of the anticipation of counteraggression. Or he may withdraw into a state of unrelatedness. In either case, he does not have the capacity to represent (i.e., create) a multisensory, affective picture of the pattern, which is simply "behaved" out, including expectations of the other's behavior.

What we see here is a drama that is not represented, but a drama played out in the actual reality of a relationship. The content of the drama is not symbolized in representational elements through pretend, or elaborated in words (as in the free associations), but instead is behaviorally enacted in a direct and visceral fashion. The drama is perceived as real, not as a set of feelings or wishes: "He is going to hurt me" rather than "I feel as though I will be hurt." Descriptive words do not reflect on the drama that is part of a "behavioral" pattern. One may further speculate that a drama acted out behaviorally and viscerally might be associated with more primitive and overwhelming fears.

In this sense, the structure of the ego affects the content and vice versa. However, it would be a mistake to think of these fears as having representational forms. Rather, they are experienced in a visceral and behavioral sense (e.g., "My muscles were exploding as I was hitting him").

Using traditional diagnostic thinking, one would see the more representational individual as having a more mature personality structure, capable of more traditional therapeutic exploration, whether it is a child using pretend play, or an adult using words and descriptions, or reporting his or her associations or dreams. The individual who expresses the conflict in terms of direct behavioral phenomena is exhibiting a more primitive character disorder. Such an individual might come to treatment after having been involved in a fist fight or physically acting out of marital problems. We might feel less optimistic about his or her ability to participate in a dynamic therapeutic exploration.

Regardless of our prognostic thinking about these types of individuals, the structure of the personality and ego is obviously critical in understanding the nature of their conflicts and anticipating the type of therapeutic work to come. Helping an individual shift from behaving out their conflicts to representing their conflicts, might be seen, in fact, as the first order of business. Without this step, little growth can occur in the individual's overall personality. One cannot fully understand the drama without knowing the organization within which the drama is being played out. In addition, one cannot fully comprehend the nature of the ego structures without having a comprehension of the drama being played out in it. Both aspects are obviously critical to a successful resolution of a patient's problems.

Structural challenges that are based in early developmental stages are especially interesting. There are many patients who are overreactive to basic sensations, such as touch and sound. They are likely to feel overwhelmed by affects, and in situations involving lots of people or noise, may feel fragmented, fearful, and suspicious. Yet later, in a quiet room with one or two people, they may be organized, reflective, and secure.

In therapy, working with these perceptual differences, and helping the patient understand them and their connection to feelings and wishes, can be critical. Many patients have left therapists who interpret these perceptual differences as "passive-aggressive," and have done well with therapists who explore the physical differences in their own right in a supportive and respectful way. But if the therapist is not alert to looking for these perceptual differences, they are likely to be missed.

CASE ILLUSTRATION OF WORKING WITH DEVELOPMENTAL LEVELS AND DYNAMIC MEANINGS

It is easy to assume that a patient constructs a "meaning" the same way the clinician does. The therapist may be at a different developmental level. The therapist may, for example, "represent" the patient's fear of being hurt, while the patient experiences it as just described as a behavioral expectation, not as a represented or symbolized affect. Furthermore, the second half of the question and its implied answer: often, approaching a structural problem only via its dynamic meaning will not help the person sufficiently resolve the structural difficulty.

Consider the following example: a middle-aged depressed woman had grown up with an extremely intrusive, controlling mother and a very available, but passive father who deferred to mother. As near as can be reconstructed (some of it intellectually from mother's behavior), even as an infant and toddler when this woman was growing up, her every reach for any sort of dependency gratification or for closeness was met by her mother's intrusive, controlling, and, sometimes rejecting responses. Most importantly, the patient later came to feel that her mother's behavior was aimed at humiliating her. Much of her latency, adolescence, and now adulthood were geared to never showing weakness or vulnerability or neediness in regard to her mother.

In addition, this patient had a history from her own recollection, as well as from her parents' descriptions of her, of overreactivity to basic sensations, such as touch and sound. She was gifted in her use of language, but had relatively weaker visual–spatial processing capacities. These patterns continued into adulthood, leaving her prone to feeling "overloaded," "fragmented," or "falling apart." She would, for example, experience "overload" when in a noisy room or when in a group with people brushing up against her, and was much better at recalling details than "seeing the big picture." Her "loud," forceful, "top sergeant" mother, for example, made her "cringe" when she would surprise her and walk into her room.

The patient's tendency to become overloaded and fragmented, and her difficulty in visual–spatial abstracting, in terms of regulating patterns, would have made it hard, under any circumstances, for her to engage in the full range of organized behavioral and emotional patterns as a toddler. Fragmented, piecemeal patterns would be more likely to occur. Likewise it would have been similarly difficult for her to conduct organized and integrated mental representation as a preschooler. Again, fragmented patterns would be more likely from the combination of overreactivity and relatively weak integrating capacities. With an intrusive, overwhelming mother, however, what might have been difficult to master became almost an impossibility. The relationship with the mother, therefore, accentuated her constitutional and maturational weaknesses. A very soothing, comforting mother might have helped her overcome her vulnerabilities. At the same time, the dynamics of her relationship with her mother were intensified by her regulatory patterns. A child with excellent self-calming and self-soothing abilities, and strong integrating capacities, might have been able to deal with an intrusive mother by becoming a little stubborn or negative, or simply, strong willed. This patient's degree of rage and humiliation and sense of fragmentation were all quite intense, in part because of the regulatory pattern.

As she progressed into her representational phases, she was, therefore, unable to fully represent nurturing, caring interactions in a stable manner, since they weren't occurring at the behavioral interaction level.

Contributing to this woman's depression in adulthood was an inability to represent longing feelings for anyone in her life, including her husband, who was thoughtful and very devoted to her; her child; or the therapist. During the therapist's vacation times, the patient would find herself getting agitated and uncomfortable, but could never picture the therapist away on vacation or experience longing or angry feelings. All she would experience was "a vague sense of anxiety, tension in my muscles, and a feeling like I'm going to fall down." Intellectually, being a sophisticated individual, she said, "I'm probably missing you, but I'll be honest, I don't feel a shred of it, although I feel physically lousy when you're away." Interestingly, she felt similarly when she had an urgent work project and needed to talk with her husband when he was away on a business trip. During the day, she would get agitated, headachy, dizzy, and experience patterns of disorganized thinking. When she was having a big meeting with her bosses, she could never imagine being soothed by her husband or calling him up for a pep talk beforehand. "The image just never occurred to me."

This person, like many who are prone toward depression, may lack the ability to represent in the most fundamental sense, wishes and affects having to do with longing feelings. They are, in fact, better at representing anger or aggression than they are at the longing side of life. They have conflicts with aggression, but an even more fundamental issue is the very lack of ability to represent critical affects. This type of difficulty has also been observed in patients with psychosomatic and substance abuse difficulties (Nemiah, 1977).

The ability to represent certain longing feelings can be viewed metaphorically as each individual's ability to create a personal internal Linus-type security blanket. Early in development, children initially are at a level where their own real behavior and the behavior of their caregivers as well as the presence of specific concrete objects serve security and communicative purposes. Around 18 to 24 months, however, under optimal circumstances, they develop the ability to create internal images, as Mahler and others described so well. These internal images become invested with certain wishes and feelings. Once a child can create images, they can obviously be used for self-soothing, as well as for fantasizing about anger. Once an individual has the flexibility of creating representational images, he or she can create a temporary sense of security and experiment with anger, while embraced in a safety of one's real relationships. Many individuals, for a variety of reasons, cannot create aspects of mental representations, often because of early conflicts in their prerepresentational stage and/or certain regulatory patterns. I believe this scenario holds true for the woman discussed here, where the seeking of dependency and support was involved in behavioral level conflicts with her mother. Such people cannot chance creating the representational image of these wishes. This patient may have given up those types of seeking behaviors before she was even 2 years of age. The only memory she had was of things that were told to her; for example, that she either ran around without purpose or withdrew and was sometimes defiant. She never sought out her mother to cuddle or hug. She always treated her mother as a person who could give her things. She was more warm and nurturing with her father, and could seek support from him albeit in concrete ways.

In our developmental model, then, an important aspect of certain types of depression is not necessarily the loss of the real object, but the loss of, or never having the ability to create, the internal representation of the object, particularly in its soothing and dependency-oriented patterns. This leaves the person at the mercy of direct, concrete behavioral patterns. A sense of internal self-esteem, based on representations of the object, in terms of soothing, admiration, respect, and reassurance, is not present. Therefore, it is not the loss of the real object but the internal representation that may be a critical aspect of certain types of depression. Interestingly, the biological components of depression may be mediated through the regulatory patterns (hyperreactivity and/or visual–spatial integration), rather than as a direct effect on mood. Therefore, there is an interaction between experience and biology.

We see a relationship between a dynamic interaction at a critical age of development and an important structural deficit. Here the dynamic interaction may have occurred during the toddler phase of development, and influenced the transition from what I have called the behavioral organizational level (the toddler phase of early development) to the representational phase (from about 16 months to about 30 months). While one cannot make direct correlations between experiences in infancy or early childhood and later adult behaviors and phenomena, one can gain insights about types of structures that did not form optimally in the ordinary sense. When these subsequently have not been formed because certain patterns got set into place and new experiences are not of sufficient quality to alter the early patterns, a structural deficit arises. Obviously, intense affects and conflicts can make these deficits worse.

These considerations would then play out in the treatment of this patient. Simply clarifying and interpreting these patterns would not be sufficient, and might be counterproductive. First, the therapist must always meet the patient at the developmental level of his or her ego structure. For this patient, it meant dealing directly with her regulatory patterns, not only by helping her describe them, but by creating in the office a regulatory environment (e.g., not talking too fast or intrusively and finding soothing vocal rhythms and tones). Second, attention should be paid to the behavioral expectations, which in this case included being intruded upon and the woman's countertendencies to withdraw or become fragmented in speech or behavior. Here, it was insufficient to simply point out that whenever the patient felt needy, she expected the analyst to intrude and overwhelm her as she felt her mother had done in the past. Because this was a behavioral, rather than representational, expectation, it was experienced not as "I *feel* as though you will control me." Instead, it was "You *are* going to control me," or with regard to her withdrawn or fragmented behavior, "You are *overloading* me."

The therapist was verbally very interactive to maintain a sense of relatedness when the patient was withdrawing. His counterbehavior was geared to increase the patient's behavioral and affective range. He attempted to help the patient organize communications when she became fragmented (e.g., "I lost your last idea"). When she became very fragmented, he increased visual and behavioral interchange through gestures, to maintain organization. When there were gestural indications in terms of tone of voice, motor gestures, or affect cues of dependency feelings, the therapist would attempt to maintain and further elaborate these through the interactive dialogue, which would provide an experience of nonintrusive comfort. As the patient withdrew or became hostile, in anticipation of intrusiveness, initially the therapist did not clarify or interpret underlying feelings or wishes. Such comments would have been at a different developmental level than the patient's current level at that point. Instead, the therapist maintained the dialogue with behavioral descriptions: "You see me as doing this or that to you, rather than being comforting, etc."

As the patient became more flexible, the therapist then helped her identify those affects that led to withdrawal or fragmentation, which were initially at a somatic, physical level. "My muscles are tense"; "My heart is beating fast." Detailed somatic descriptions led to abstracted affect descriptions and representational-type patterns ("I feel like I'm falling apart"; "I feel empty"; "I feel lonely and isolated"). Eventually, states of longing and need could be communicated in terms of "missing feelings," and the capacity to represent dependency and longing emerged, perhaps for the first time in the patient's experience.

Once she could represent experience, it was possible to use clarifying and interpretive comments to help her deal with pathologic defenses and work through her conflicts. She could then further develop her capacities for representational differentiation and self-observation. There are a number of representational levels (from concrete to more abstract and reflective) that are described in subsequent chapters.

Some of these strategies are no different from approaches that many intuitive therapists have been following for years. But they are viewed, often, as "intuitive" and not systematic or central to therapeutic growth. The developmental perspective can help systematize them and open up new areas for inclusion, such as constitutional and maturational differences, and the different developmental levels which are not always intuitive. In addition, some will argue that such developmentally guided clinical strategies are part of preparations for intensive psychoanalytic therapy or psychoanalysis. To those who take this point of view, I would suggest that many more patients have these early difficulties than is often recognized, and that for these patients, regardless of the treatment approach, one needs to focus in some depth on these issues as a substantive focus in the therapy. To think of it as preliminary to something else may be a bit like considering the meal to be preliminary to the dessert.

THE DEVELOPMENTAL APPROACH AND PSYCHOPATHOLOGY

The developmental perspective pertains to many types of psychopathologic configurations we deal with, and can help inform our therapeutic approaches for disorders ranging from symptom and character neuroses to character pathology, borderline conditions, and the psychoses. Often, for example, neurotic patterns involve various degrees of circumscribed lack of representational differentiation for certain wishes and affects. Character pathology frequently involves marked constrictions in representational elaboration and in behavioral organization as well. Borderline and psychotic patterns often arise out of significant regulatory difficulties, related to sensory reactivity and processing difficulties, and problems with early presymbolic differentiations of behavior and affect.

It is, as indicated, often assumed that patients with some of these types of psychopathology can participate in the psychotherapeutic process. Such participation can take place through collaborative discussions, self-observation, interest in seeing connections and an ability to make connections between different thoughts, feelings, and ideas, in terms of patterns, and an ability to relate feelings to behaviors and daily events in one's life. In fact, as also indicated, many patients have difficulties with these very capacities that are often thought to be essential for participation in the psychotherapeutic process. The difficulties the patients have cannot necessarily be attributed to motivation or lack of interest. For example, the patient who does not talk, reflect, or make connections may be mistakenly labeled as "resistant" or psycho-logically or unconsciously "disinterested" or consciously "unmo-tivated" due to character pathology. Far from being uninterested, many such patients would like nothing better than relief from their symptoms, and actually do not possess the very capacities that are viewed as essential for participation in the psychothera-peutic process. Furthermore, the very problems patients have and the symptoms they manifest may be related to structural personal-ity deficits that are an integral part of the difficulty they have in participating in the psychotherapeutic process in the ordinary way. Such patients may have difficulties, which are part of their core personality deficits, in the very capacities that we often view as ordinary and expectable in terms of psychotherapeutic collabo-ration. To call such a patient unmotivated is a bit of a tautology. It is a way by which therapists have for years escaped the painful conclusion that the techniques they make available may only be useful for a small number of patients. This is not because other patients are unmotivated, and are therefore inherently incapable of participating, or simply don't want to, consciously or uncon-sciously, but because our techniques are not able to deal with the deficits the patient brings to us. The deficits on the one hand result in their symptoms, and on the other hand result in their inability to collaborate in the ordinary and expectable psychother-apeutic strategies we make available to them.

There are a variety of core capacities that patients often have trouble with, that result both in their symptoms and their diffi-culty in using the psychotherapeutic process as it is usually con-ceptualized. These incapacities include difficulty in representing or labeling feelings along with an inability to construct patterns of feelings, behaviors, and ideas (i.e., building bridges between different internal wishes, feeling states, and behaviors). On an even more basic level, many patients have difficulties understand-ing the meaning of other people's behaviors. Such patients have difficulty understanding the intentions of others ("Did he intend to be mean, or hurtful, or supportive?"). It is not unusual for patients to be preoccupied with trying to figure out what so-and-so meant by their look, glance, body posture, tone of voice, or by the particular way they phrased a word. This difficulty in assessing the intentions of others is far deeper than just understanding the meaning of words. It is not understanding the meaning of peoples' behavior and affect.

On an even more basic level, patients have difficulty with maintaining a psychological boundary, in terms of a sense of self and a sense of the other person. It is hard for them to know which feelings are theirs and which are the other person's, or where their inner reality begins and ends and someone else's begins and ends. We see patients who have difficulty with forming relationships or those who can form relationships, but have difficulty in maintaining a certain degree of stability in those relationships. (The slightest bit of stress, threat of separation, anger, or frustration leads to a breakup of a relationship.) Furthermore, we see patients who can form and maintain some degree of stability in relationships, but who have no emotional depth or range to their relationships, which are shallow and mechanical and concerned with concrete needs, rather than deep feelings of pleasure, dependency, and intimacy. Some patients can tolerate relationships, but only in one area of emotion. They can be dependent or needy, but cannot tolerate assertiveness or explorativeness. Thus we see a range of difficulties just in the ability to negotiate a relationship in terms of its formation, stability, its depth or shallowness, and the range of feelings accommodated. Such difficulties with relationships, at this most fundamental level, are different from the relationship difficulties which have to do with symbolized or represented conflicts or anxieties. A person who is conflicted over sexuality may shy away from sexual intimacy in a relationship, but otherwise experience a broad range of feelings in a stable and ongoing manner. This is contrasted with the more fundamental problem in relationships where from early in life, there is evidence of a pattern of superficial or concrete ways of relating or withdrawing at the first sign of stress or anxiety. In this case, patterns learned in the early years of life are the issue; for example, here what is relevant are the basic ways of relating *before* relationships became represented and symbolized and became affected by one's internal conflicts.

We also see difficulties in individuals' capacities for self-regulation. This involves how individuals respond to and process sensation, noise, touch, sight, smells, and their own movement patterns. Some people are overloaded by information that comes in through sounds and words; others are more confused by information that comes through the visual–spatial domain. Affect expressions communicated through sounds can be confusing to some, while affects that are expressed in visual terms are confusing to others. As seen in our earlier clinical example, simply being in a noisy room will overwhelm certain individuals and make them feel suspicious or paranoid. Being in a crowded room where people are brushing up against them, can lead many people to feel overwhelmed. This difference in physical sensation is common among patients, and challenges the traditional notion that most of us hear, see, smell, and experience touch in similar ways. In fact, we have discovered that there are enormous differences between the ways in which individuals experience basic sensations in terms of reactivity to sensation and the ability to process information through different sensory channels. These "regulatory" difficulties are a very basic level of psychological adaptation and determine how individuals organize their experiences and negotiate many aspects of their psychological lives.

Thus we can see that many patients have difficulties with those core abilities that connect emotions, ideas, and behaviors and that symbolize or represent ideas (i.e., form an intrapsychic, symbolic world). They struggle with their inability to comprehend their behavior in terms of patterns and misunderstand other people's intentions as expressed in behaviors and affects. Patients may lack the ability to form psychological boundaries involving their own reality and someone else's reality. They may be unable to form, maintain, and have deep, wide-range, and affectively ranging relationships. They lack the ability for self-regulation (i.e., regulating and organizing sensations). These fundamental abilities, which clinicians will readily see as an important part of personality structure and an essential foundation for healthy personality functioning, cannot necessarily be taken for granted. Many difficulties are part of deficits in these core abilities, and as indicated above, these core abilities are part of the symptom picture and also form part of the essential way patients relate in the therapeutic relationship. It will be seen later in this work that the relative mastery of various core abilities is inextricably related to the mastery or lack of mastery, of different developmental stages. As the following examples illustrate, core difficulties play out in two ways in the symptom picture and in the way in which the patient negotiates the therapeutic relationship.

Let us consider the example of the person who does not see his or her own patterns of behavior and cannot comprehend the behavior and intentions of others. Such an individual is likely to have a variety of severe character pathologies. These may involve fixed attitudes, such as depressive or paranoid attitudes because, not having the capacity to read others' intentions, they are constantly misreading others' intentions. Closeness may be perceived as hostile; independence on the other person's part may be perceived as rejection; and depressive or suspicious attitudes may be the result.

In the therapeutic situation, such individuals may have difficulty with perceiving the intentions of the therapist. The therapist's fatigue may be perceived as a rejecting or hostile attitude; his apparent neutrality may be perceived as critical. More importantly, such patients who have trouble with perceiving the intentions of others and understanding their own behavioral patterns and those of others, are unlikely to be able to symbolize or represent affects. They are, therefore, unable to label affects in themselves or others and to see emotions and affects as mediators between their own wishes and behaviors. Life for them is a series of interactive behaviors, rather than feelings leading to behaviors. Therapists often wind up labeling behaviors for such patients and giving the patients affect labels, which the patients do not comprehend, but may obsequiously agree to.

Consider another example of patients with regulatory difficulties. Such patients who are overreactive to sound and touch, may, on a physical basis, be prone to anxieties and fears and patterns of avoidance and inhibition. Such patients may develop attitudes and feelings having to do with fears, worries, and anxieties, including anxious, fearful preoccupations, which are derivative from these physical differences and intensified by their interactions with others in their environment. In the therapeutic situation, such individuals may form very dependent and even seemingly symbiotic relationships with their therapists, looking for protection from their fears, worries, and anxieties. They may seem to free associate, often in a fragmented and overwhelmed way, and with rich ideation (particularly if they are bright). They and the therapist may ignore the fact, however, that there is a strong physical component to their difficulties, and that they have a tendency to psychologize their own sensory response tendencies. For example, standing in a crowd packed shoulder-to-shoulder caused such a patient to feel overwhelmed and fearful. Fantasies of intrusion, sexual molestation, or even rape are not unusual. The ability to see that certain characteristic feelings of being overwhelmed and certain fantasies (which have their psychogenic components) are precipitated by feeling physically overloaded, leads such patients into perpetual therapeutic stalemates, where they endlessly review the same feelings with little relief, other than the day-to-day relief of the support of the therapist. Working through such difficulties often requires understanding their own historically based responses to their own physiologic makeup, and how others in their environment dealt with them in response to *their* own physiologic makeup. This helps them, when they're in the middle of a crowded room, realize that the mere brushing of shoulders and body contact overloads them and that going to a corner of the room can be helpful. They can become wary of their own suspicious and paranoid attitudes, with the therapist helping them develop some self-observing capacity, regarding their own physical profile. This then helps them separate out the physical from the psychogenic (i.e., how early in life parents and others may have dug the hole deeper for them by certain ways in which they responded to the child's feeling overloaded or overwhelmed).

The early chapters of this book will further discuss the above examples and difficulties in labeling or representing feelings and making connections between feelings; forming psychological boundaries; and forming stable and deep intimate relationships patterns. Each developmental level will be discussed. Readers unfamiliar with this developmental framework may also want to study Greenspan (1989, 1992).

In each of the following chapters we will discuss therapeutic principles geared to working with each stage of development and level of the mind. We will observe how the principles outlined in this chapter can be utilized in the psychotherapeutic process. Each stage of ego organization will be seen to elucidate therapeutic principles and tactics, which collectively will form the basis for a developmental model of psychotherapy.

Chapter 3

Regulatory Processes

Patients frequently present with complaints of feeling overwhelmed or confused with many of life's routine experiences. Looking, listening, attending, talking, modulating affect and behavior, and feeling calm and collected are not easy. The first core process is the ability to be regulated and to attend to the outside world, taking an interest in sights, sounds, smells, and touches (i.e., balancing, reacting to, processing sensations, and remaining calm and collected and not feeling overwhelmed or needing to shut out input). We can see this process being learned in the first 2 or 3 months of life. You see an infant of this age attending to her mother's sounds, following her mother's face, or examining different visual images. A similar pattern can be observed in an adult patient's ability to listen and comprehend affect cues, sounds, words, and meanings in a busy, noisy setting. With adults, we often lose sight of the fact that many adults, ranging from those with disorders of affect or thought, borderline condition severe character disorders, to those with certain varieties of mild to moderate neurotic problems will have differences in their regulatory patterns.

We first learned about these regulatory patterns through working with at-risk infants and their families (Greenspan, Wieder, Leiberman, Nover, Lourie, and Robinson, 1987). An early observation of our staff, consistent with previous observations by Escalona (1968), Fish, Shapiro, Halpern, and Wile (1965), Weil (1970), and Fish and Hagin (1973) was that infants with severe difficulties, beginning in the earliest months of life, had a range of individual differences in dealing with experiences via different sensory channels. We found, however, that not only severely disturbed infants had these patterns. In accordance with Ayers (1964), we concluded that there were a range of challenges in a range of children. For example, some infants, when presented with high-pitched maternal voice patterns, seemed to over-react. Their bodies became stiff, they turned their heads away from rather than toward the stimulus, and their faces took on a look of panic. It was as though what for most infants would be a pleasurable stimulus (one which they would turn toward, brighten up, and alert to) was, for a certain group of infants, highly aversive. Other infants showed similar patterns with visual stimuli, including bright lights. At a more subtle level, we noticed that some infants were not hyperreactive to auditory information, but had difficulty recognizing a vocal pattern. When mother would talk to them in what sounded like rhythmic, high-pitched maternal vocalizations (which the majority of babies would alert and brighten to), a group of babies would look confused and would look past their mothers rather than orienting to their voices. Other babies could orient to vocalizations, but had trouble orienting and alerting to the presentation of various facial expressions—visual–spatial experiences were not easily processed. We noted that reactivity and processing of information were relatively independent of each other. We also noticed that the early environment could accentuate or ameliorate these individual constitutional and maturational differences. In some families, where the infant seemed to have difficulty organizing auditory experience, caregivers responded with anxiety and talked to the baby very rapidly, overwhelming the system that was having the most difficulty. Their infants often withdrew from the human environment. On the other hand, there were rare caregivers who intuitively slowed down their vocalizations and experimented with pitch and rhythm. They talked, for example, in low-pitched voices and repeated themselves, offering less novelty to the infant who was slow to process auditory information. They also appealed to the infant's visual, tactile, and other senses as a way to communicate information. These infants seemed to do better. They would form an attachment, learn cause-and-effect signaling, organize complex patterns of emotion and behavior, and eventually construct symbols to guide emotions and behavior.

In addition to visual and auditory differences, we also noted differences in tactile sensitivity, sensitivity to movement in space, reactions to odors, reactions to feedback from movement, and differences in motor tone, motor planning and attention, and alertness. Many of these differences were found in different types of infants, such as tactile sensitivity and difficulty in processing sound, or tactile sensitivity, increased motor tone, and visual–spatial processing difficulty. Motor planning differences relate not only to a baby's ability to get his hand to his mouth, but overall sequencing capacities. These include following through on tasks and patterns of social interactions involving sequencing of emotions and behaviors, such as a toddler's putting on socks and shoes and grabbing a lunch bag before heading off to school.

These differences were found in older children and adults as well. Therefore, contrary to early views that sensory differences were only present in very disturbed children, we found that these individual differences in varying degrees characterize many children and adults, in some contributing to psychopathology, in others creating challenges that are mastered. We were able to correlate regulatory problems with behavior and learning difficulties (DeGangi, Porges, Sickel, and Greenspan, 1993).

These observations regarding individual differences in sensory reactivity, processing and motor planning, and environmental patterns, led to hypotheses regarding the relationship between early sensory and affective experiences and specific processing difficulties, and the developmental sequence leading to different types of difficulties.

CLINICAL ILLUSTRATION

Here is a clinical vignette of an adult where this issue of early regulation and ways of attending became the central focus of early therapeutic work, and where the case was actually lost to treatment because the therapist was unwilling or unable to deal with these early regulatory issues.

During several sessions a 22-year-old woman would sit down in the corner of the room hugging the wall. On the floor, the woman would assume a somewhat irregular posture, with her leg up or in a corner where she would have two walls around her. She often wouldn't look at the therapist and went through long periods of silence. She managed to come to each session, however, showed up on time, and got up and left at the end of the hour.

This patient was having numerous difficulties in her life but was an outpatient, a person who managed to take care of herself. She was living with her parents some of the time and on her own some of the time.

Occasionally, she would say just a few words to her therapist, and would describe some concrete details in her life: her work, her parents, her attempts to live on her own. But often there would be long silences, peculiar postures, and averted eyes. When the therapist asked her to look at him, she would refuse to do so. The patient simply clammed up.

After about six or seven months of therapy, the therapist began commenting to the patient that her behavior was passive-aggressive because of her insistence on sitting on the floor, her peculiar postures, and avoidance of the therapist's eyes. The patient would usually look offended and hurt when the therapist made these comments and would up the stakes by doing more of the peculiar posturing. The therapist became very frustrated and eventually began saying: "I guess you must be angry with me.

Why are you so passive-aggressive? Why won't you talk more?'' By focusing on the power struggle and by prematurely going after the affect, the therapist lost the patient, who became more and more paranoid and convinced that the therapist was ''attacking her'' and being critical. The patient eventually left treatment with that therapist.

Now, if one were working with this patient with this kind of pattern, which approach might one have tried to take? One might have asked her why she sat there; and her answer would no doubt have been, ''It's comfortable. I feel better on the floor.'' Would the clinician comment on her being passive-aggressive? What kind of thoughts would be in the back of the clinician's mind? Let's say she exhibited the peculiar posturing more when talking about her parents. She may not have recognized the sensation of anger that these thoughts evoked in her, but continued her posturing any time anger was beginning to bubble up inside of her. What tack should the therapist take?

Fortunately, this patient hooked up with a second therapist who had the wisdom to focus on creating a regulating environment that enhanced her sense of security. This therapist eventually determined that the patient had a history of extreme tactile sensitivity, and she was overly reactive to touch. People who have this sensitivity to touch often feel more secure when there are clearly defined boundaries in their lives. Feeling the pressure of nearby walls and corners can be comforting to some individuals.

Upon further questioning, the therapist learned that the patient had a history of some motor difficulties early in her development. We find that such individuals typically like to exhibit postures that make them feel a little more together or whole. children who have some irregularities in their motor patterns can drive their parents crazy by sitting at the dinner table with an arm or leg propped up over the back of their chairs.

In the above example, the second therapist simply and empathetically explored the ways in which the patient tried to make herself comfortable. He recognized that this was, after all, a person who was adjusting to a new relationship, a new office, and new physical surroundings. In essence, she was coming in and saying, "Here's how I make myself more comfortable." Noticing that the patient was cuddling up against the wall, trying to shut out stimulation, this second therapist inquired: "Does that feel better than sitting in a chair?" Nothing very elaborate, nothing very complex. The patient replied, "Yes," and explained how having her body nestled against the floor and wedged in a corner felt "good." Together patient and therapist explored why hugging the periphery felt comforting—whether it was sitting in a classroom or heading for a corner of the room in the midst of the hubbub of a cocktail party.

From that evolved her history of tactile sensitivity and the fact that her body motorically just felt better when nestled near a wall. That acknowledgment permitted the exploration of how it felt when she didn't do that, and that she sometimes didn't know where her arms were and felt a little depersonalized about her body. The patient was able to describe concrete details of her life that led her to self-regulate when she felt emotionally or sensorially overloaded.

The therapist's inquiry about how the patient experienced touch and sound provoked a lot of discussion about how she reacted to the therapist's voice. When the first therapist got upset, angry, or frustrated, the patient, who also had auditory hypersensitivity, found the therapist's voice to be very intrusive and critical.

The second therapist's main goal was to create a regulating environment that enhanced the patient's sense of security in the office. Together, therapist and patient put some pillows on the floor and discussed whether one rug's texture was more soothing than that of another. They muted the overhead lights, and the therapist even lowered his voice since the patient found that to be more soothing. The therapist wasn't going to refurnish his office for her, but he exhibited empathy with how she regulated herself and how she got herself into an attentive state. Both participants negotiated the regulatory aspects of the therapeutic experiences.

After her confidence increased, the therapist initiated a discussion about when the patient felt able to look at the therapist and when not. He learned that when his voice was too loud or when his facial expressions became too animated, she had to turn her eyes away because she felt a little overloaded or overwhelmed at the perceptual intensity. This very careful, supportive conversation helped the patient feel that the therapist understood her unique physical characteristics and that they could explore the way she experienced and processed sensations.

It is important to assess the patient before deciding on a developmental approach that may be perceived by an otherwise bright adult as being condescending and too intrusive. If the therapist says, "Hey, can I come down here with you on the floor?" the person might find him or her patronizing or overly intrusive. The best approach is to use one's empathetic range to reach the person developmentally at his or her level through emotional tone, tone of voice, interest, and concern, and through the way comments are phrased.

Even in dealing with very regressed, psychotic patients, it is essential to make sure that we are not marching to the beat of our own drummer, rather than attending to the patient's regulatory profile. Become a keen observer; watch how the patient reacts to touch and sound, even if the person is unable to say how he feels. As the therapist's voice modulates in volume, it is important to notice the quality of the patient's attention and regulation. Modulate lighting in the room from bright to dim. In short, begin noticing what tends to help patients form a state of calm, focused regulation where they are maximally attentive and engaged with the therapist. This clinical observation should zero in on each sensory pathway. The therapist needs to think in terms of hypo- or hyperreactivity to each sensory pathway as the way the patient processes information is assessed; how they abstract information by means of sounds, sights, and smells. These sensory clues will dictate how the therapist will most effectively approach patients and help them feel regulated and secure. Thus, in the early stages of therapy, the first therapeutic goal is to help the person feel calm, regulated, and interested in the world around them. For some neurotic patients, that process may occur quickly within the first five seconds. The patient sizes up the room, sizes up the therapist and is ready for the next level. With other neurotic

patients, some very regressed, psychotic patients, or certain borderline patients or with some more primitive character disorders,
there may be a lot of these self-regulatory issues to deal with and
the therapist will find therapy focused at that level for the first
six months or a year, or even two years or more.

The therapeutic value in focusing on regulatory differences
in adults is further illustrated by the following case history.

A 35-year-old woman with a long history of "tensing up and
not enjoying sexual intimacy" had gone to several sex therapists
and participated in five years of psychoanalytic psychotherapy in
hopes of understanding the root of her difficulties. While the
patient felt she benefited from the therapy in terms of improving
her relationship capacities, and gained some useful information
from the more directive sex therapy approaches, she still found
herself feeling tense and only occasionally receptive to pleasurable sexual intimacy with her husband. The marriage grew somewhat sturdier as she and her husband became able to discuss their
feelings around the lack of sexual intimacy.

A new therapist noted, upon meeting the woman, that her
handshake was tentative, as if she were reluctant to cross the
bridge into a personal space. She wore very soft cotton clothing
and sat rigidly in her chair, avoiding contact with the chair back.
After sharing her personal history with the therapist, the therapist
broadened the area of inquiry beyond sexual intimacy to include
her experience with being close in a physical sense. He queried
her about wrestling with other children or her parents as a child,
whether she liked water on her skin, preferred certain kinds of
garments, or whether she enjoyed having her hair or teeth
brushed.

This line of questioning opened up a wealth of clues concerning the patient's pattern of response to sensory stimulation. It
became apparent that she was very sensitive to water and bathing
and experienced discomfort when water hit her body. She seldom
swam in the summer and even showers were difficult for her. She
pointed out that she was careful to wear soft cotton garments or
silks, and shied away from rough woolen garments or those made
with synthetic fibers. As a child, the patient hated having her

parents brush her hair, and as an adult she brushed it herself very gingerly. She went on to add that loud noises often startled and frightened her and that as a result she hated going to cocktail parties. When she did attend such parties, she often sat in the corner of a room where she would feel a little more protected, safe from people noisily bumping into her.

Curious now about her response to basic sensations, the patient spoke to her parents, asking them what she was like as a baby and in the early years of her life. She learned that she was "not a cuddler" like her brothers and sisters (she came from a large family of three brothers and two sisters). She further learned that while she seemed to pull away when her parents tried to play with her gently or tried to tickle her tummy, she would let them cuddle with her if they gave her firm, tight bear hugs. Her parents also recalled that as a toddler, she loved to move around quite a bit. She apparently enjoyed jumping on her bed and any other activity that involved leaping.

As the discussions continued, it became clear that the patient exhibited a pattern of sensitivity to touch, as well as a mild sensitivity to sound, that had existed since infancy. As she discussed her intimate relations with her husband, it became obvious that he was a very warm and romantic individual who liked to use lots of gentle and feathery touches in his lovemaking. His prior experiences with women had taught him that most women enjoyed this technique. He also liked to use his mouth to stimulate all parts of her body. The patient felt embarrassed that her husband's gentle, very involved, and unusually patient approach made her feel such discomfort and even pain. Even though her therapy emboldened her to talk to him about what did give her sexual pleasure, she found that the things he tried had elements of the feathery or wet touches, that made her feel terrible.

Until her association with the new therapist, the patient had never considered the fact that she had a certain type of regulatory sensitivity that influenced her reaction to touch and sound. Upon reflection, she realized that in the past she had fleetingly recognized the fact that she responded to sound and touch differently than her friends and other people, but had always been embarrassed that she had this physical difference. She had preferred to attribute these differences to "psychological causes," rather than physiological sensitivities. Therefore, in her prior therapies and in her own thinking, "conflicts around aggression and fear of getting too sexually excited and losing control" gelled into the notion that there was something different about her.

To consider a physical difference meant to her that "something is wrong with my nervous system; I'm defective." In her family, an uncle who was "mentally ill" became very distinctive and responded in unusual ways to all sensations. In her mind, to acknowledge that something was physically "wrong" with the way she responded to touch meant that she was unbalanced like her uncle. Over a period of time she was able to regard this regulatory pattern as simply an individual difference like shortness or tallness, blue eyes or brown eyes. More importantly, she became curious about ways to work around the sensitivities and began exploring the kinds of physical sensations that were pleasurable for her.

From explorations of her own childhood, she became aware again of the fact that physical activity like jumping, which involves joint compression and large muscle activity, was relaxing and pleasurable. She also reacquainted herself with the idea that firm pressure like bear hugs or deep massage was pleasurable for her. She confirmed the idea that very gentle or wet touches were aversive to her. She even risked upsetting her husband, who took great pride in his gentle physical approaches to her, by letting him know that while his approaches were perfect for 95 percent of women, he was married to one of the remaining 5 percent. She let him know that she enjoyed firmer touching and kisses and "no licking." Over a period of time, her husband, who was reasonably confident in his own sexuality, adjusted his technique, and was soon rewarded by a more responsive wife. The patient found that even with these positive changes, foreplay was not as enjoyable to her as it was to many other women, but at least it was not aversive. Indeed, sometimes it was even pleasurable. She found that she could become orgasmic during actual intercourse, which she never had before. By paying attention to the types of reactions she had to various types of touch, the patient learned to enhance her sexual pleasure. She found that quick movements by her husband were sometimes aversive and always unpleasurable. Alternatively, if she firmly squeezed his penis in her vagina while applying rhythmic pressure to the walls of her vagina and clitoris, she found herself getting more and more excited and had, for the first time in her life, very pleasurable orgasms. She was startled to be able to do this having never "reached a clear peak" before. Her husband enjoyed being able to satisfy his wife and their sexual intimacy improved.

There were related psychotherapeutic issues around her self-perception and what it meant to have these physical differences, and around the renegotiation of how she and her husband communicated during intimacy. It is significant that in this case a regulatory pattern which had been partly obscured by the patient's embarrassment with her "differentness" became a prominent feature in reworking this individual's relationship with her husband around physical intimacy. This awareness helped to put into perspective some feelings of the past, such as "fear of loss of control" and anger at "having to please my husband," and opened up new areas of fear of being defective and anxieties over being in control of her body.

Another example of an unusual regulatory pattern was exhibited by a young man who got very suspicious and anxious, and, as he described it, "somewhat paranoid" in a large group. In a meeting with a large number of people, the buzz of conversation could make him feel overwhelmed, anxious, and worried that "people disapprove of" or that "people are going to attack" me. In a one-on-one situation with his girl friend or coworkers, however, this same man seemed quite trusting and relaxed and able to be close, even optimistic, believing people supported and liked him.

His developmental history suggested an individual who had a long history of close intimate relationships with others. He was quite competent in his work and seemed flexible and open with his feelings. He also could represent his feelings quite easily in a variety of situations. His difficulties seemed to surface in large groups, or small groups that were particularly noisy. Upon further investigation, the therapist learned that this man was sensitive to such domestic noises as humming, vacuum cleaners, and dripping faucets. His parents revealed that flushing toilets made him very agitated as a child.

As a schoolboy, the patient always did best if he were seated in the front row rather than in the middle of the classroom. He said that "the noise would always get to me when other kids were talking; I couldn't filter it out." It became apparent that even during therapeutic sessions he was easily distracted by the high-pitched sounds of birds chirping outside. He said it made him feel as though there were a million birds whirling around his head. Fortunately, this man had had two very gentle and empathetic parents who intuitively modulated their verbal interactions around him in such a way as to make him feel comfortable and secure. He portrayed his mother as a very sensitive person who could be firm, but who rarely had tantrums or yelled. His father, a very passive man, was a bit anxious about competition and aggression and was very gentle with him as a result. In retrospect, the patient felt that his father's passivity served the son well. Even though the patient shied away from competition, he was able to "enjoy a good tennis match and get mostly A's in high school and college." In short, his home environment didn't overload a somewhat vulnerable system.

In his current professional life as a lawyer, however, he found himself feeling overloaded, suspicious, and at times even agoraphobic during large meetings held with other professionals who had booming, competitive voices. He would find himself yearning to stay home in the mornings and not go out, anticipating that he would be feeling anxious during various meetings. As he explored his regulatory profile with the therapist, he could see that he had given a regulatory difference a psychological meaning. He recognized that he would quickly translate an over-loaded–overwhelmed feeling into a fear of being attacked, criticized, or being hurt. This is not a surprising tactic that many individuals unconsciously fall back on when they feel overloaded or overwhelmed. The overloaded feeling itself is somewhat aversive, so there is a natural tendency to try to find reasons for the way one feels and to associate aggressive intent with others. This man's conflicts with aggression, which were mild in a general sense, played into his tendency to project and attribute some malevolence to others who were in the room during those times when he felt overloaded. Understandably, these patterns helped him reason backward from a feeling of "they are going to criticize me, hurt my feelings, or jump on me" to an assessment of the noise level and the amount of commotion and the way it made him feel physically. He became aware that his heart beat faster, his muscles felt tight, and his stomach became queasy. Interestingly, being able to see the somatic aspects of feeling overloaded also helped the patient acknowledge his own competitive feelings in situations where there was a group of lawyers in the room or people who were "working the crowd" at a lively cocktail party. Rather than allowing the patient's newly discovered recognition of his own regulatory differences to obscure the conflictual elements in his pattern, the therapist helped him separate the two insights and appropriately assess the fact that he could simultaneously feel both competitive in these group situations and somewhat anxious as well. He noticed that in other situations where he was immensely competitive, such as when one particular worker vied with him for a job opening, he would not feel suspicious or paranoid, but would be able to engage in some private strategic moves. It was only in group situations that he found himself feeling helpless, overloaded, and suspicious. This gave him a sense of how his inner feelings about competition and anger played out in different social contexts and degrees of regulatory overload.

In developmental terms, the therapist was able to observe that in a large-group situation, there was a regression in ego functioning to somewhat earlier representational levels where the patient was undifferentiated in his perception of the world. In the context of a more regressive ego state, his conflicts around competition played out with more paranoid symptoms. This was based, however, on his regulatory profile which fostered the ego regression—he became overloaded with noise. Alternatively, in settings that didn't overload him and where his ego functioned in a more differentiated way, his zest for competition flourished and he was able to harness his strong intellectual and problem-solving abilities to plan strategies to "defeat my opponents."

This patient learned to tolerate his physical discomfort in groups without attributing the cause of his discomfort to the malevolent intentions of others. At the same time, he found that if he left the room every half hour or so, and walked around and reoriented himself for a couple of minutes in a quieter setting, he could go back in and feel less overloaded. During cocktail parties, he noticed that if he stayed in a corner of the room, or he went out on the balcony or to the bathroom periodically, he could reequilibrate and tolerate the large group a little better without getting overloaded. He also found that by doing exercises with joint compression or applying firm pressure on his arms or legs, he would reequilibrate on days he was feeling overloaded. Furthermore, he noted that getting plenty of sleep on days heavily scheduled with meetings, and minimizing coffee or caffeine products, or anything that had stimulating properties, would also help to reduce his sense of being overloaded.

Over a period of time this individual made an adjustment to his regulatory profile. He accepted it as part of his makeup and learned to work around it rather than let it seed a whole series of maladaptive psychological perceptions.

This case history illustrates that a therapist can give a patient an enhanced sense of understanding of his own self-regulatory and sensory–affective processing system. The patient's ability to put this understanding into practice in day-to-day negotiations with the world further strengthens his sense of security. As the early regulatory stage of ego development becomes better mastered, the patient can eventually go on to work at the representational or symbolic level. There are sensory integration, relaxation, biofeedback, meditation, and other interventions that attempt to enhance self-regulatory capacities. Many medications may work at this level as well.

Many patients seek modes of intervention they feel can regulate affect mood, panic, or anxiety. Some patients seek certain practices on their own, ranging from weekend groups to self-medication with alcohol or drugs. Psychoanalytic inquiry has not had enormous success in helping patients with these early-based regulatory difficulties, in part because often the focus is only on the conflicts that may precipitate the regression or on experiences that can be easily represented. Early somatic experience and somatic differences are not seen as sufficiently important in their own right. The likelihood of the patient improving is enhanced where the analyst or therapist can empathize with this early state of mind, and at the same time collaborate with the patient on self-regulatory strategies.

These illustrations show how selected regulatory difficulties are manifest clinically, and further, how understanding the constitutional and maturational aspects of regulatory problems can facilitate the creation of an appropriate therapeutic strategy.

THE RANGE OF REGULATORY PROBLEMS

Regulatory difficulties in children and adults, however, may be manifest in a variety of symptoms ranging from problems in controlling behavior and mood (including depression) to anxieties, fears, and patterns of avoidance. As indicated earlier, however, what makes a regulatory difficulty unique is the contribution of a clear constitutional or maturational variation to the symptoms. Most typically, the contributing constitutional and maturational variations will be part of one or more of the following patterns:

1. Over- or underreactive to loud or high- or low-pitched noises.
2. Over- or underreactive to bright lights or new and striking visual images (e.g., colors, shapes, complex fields).
3. Tactile defensiveness (e.g., overreactive to changing clothes, bathing, stroking of arms, legs, or trunk, avoids

touching "messy" textures, etc.) and/or underreactive to touch or pain.

4. Under- or overreactive to movement in space (e.g., brisk horizontal or vertical movements such as in tossing a child in the air, playing merry-go-round, jumping, etc).

5. Under- or overreactive to odors.

6. Under- or overreactive to temperature.

7. Poor motor tone (gravitational or postural insecurity, oral–motor difficulties—avoids certain textures).

8. Less than age-appropriate motor planning skills (e.g., complex motor patterns such as alternating hand banging).

9. Less than age-appropriate ability to modulate motor activity (not secondary to anxiety or interactive difficulties).

10. Less than age-appropriate fine motor skills.

11. Less than age-appropriate auditory–verbal processing or articulation capacities (e.g., an 8-month-old imitating distinct sound, a $2^1/2$-year-old following or repeating your requests, or a 3-year-old putting together words and actions, an adult comprehending a complex instruction).

12. Less than age-appropriate visual–spatial processing capacities (e.g., a $2^1/2$-year-old knowing where to turn to get to a friend's house, an 8-month-old recognizing different facial configurations, a 3-year-old putting together certain spaces, such as a room, with activities, an adult being able to construct a mental map of travel directions).

13. Less than age-appropriate capacity to attend and focus without undue distractibility (not related to anxiety, interactive difficulties, or clear auditory–verbal or visual–spatial processing problems).

There are many ways in which these regulatory processes influence development. For example, consider a 15-month-old who experiments with being independent, walking or crawling away from his mother, as well as maintaining a sense of security. The child begins to abstract, in a preverbal way, a sense of who he is as a person, who the mother is, and who the father is. But, if a child is unable to process sounds across the room, and his mother says, "Hey, that's terrific! You're building a great tower," he looks at her face and is confused. He does not get any reassurance, because he cannot decode the rhythm of her voice. He has to come over and cling to her. Meanwhile, she gets upset with his clinging, and without realizing that he can't decode her sound, she ushers him away. The child who can decode the mother's sounds, plays with his tower, looks over, hears his mother's reassuring sounds, and thinks, "Oh, that's great. You like it. I'll do some more." The child who decodes the rhythm feels as if he's in his mother's lap, because he receives her warmth across space. When one talks to a loved one who is far away, one feels warm on the telephone, because one decodes the affect in the voice. The child who cannot decode sound will, therefore, have greater difficulty in developing independence.

The child with visual–spatial processing difficulty may have a difficult time maintaining his internal mental representation, especially under the pressure of intense affects. The visual–spatial vulnerability makes it hard to maintain the internal mental image. If, for example, the representation of a significant caregiver is lost, a child may expectedly experience a sense of loss and even depression or anxiety and fear. An interesting hypothesis regarding depression in children and adults relates to this phenomenon. Perhaps the biologic vulnerability for depression is mediated through a visual–spatial vulnerability which, in turn, creates a vulnerability in the stability of mental representations. The loss of the representation leads to dysphoric affects, which in this model, are secondary.

If motor planning is impaired and the child cannot control his body, his difficulty will affect his confidence in dealing with aggression. He tries in play to touch his father's nose, but instead he hits his father in the eye and makes him mad. The child didn't intend to hit his father; his arm didn't work the way he wanted.

Thus, the child's confidence in his body and his ability to modulate aggression is not going to be optimally established. Motor planning may also influence peer relationships or dealing with colleagues at work. In both these situations one needs to sequence social behaviors quickly, almost on automatic pilot, a capacity that individuals with motor planning problems find difficult.

For the child who is tactilely hyperreactive, his protection from the outside world is overly fragile. How is that going to affect the way he perceives other people's aggressions? How is he going to react when another 2-year-old hits him in the back? When mother tries to hold a 4-month-old who is sensitive to light touch, if she rubs his skin lightly, he may squirm away, and she may misperceive that he is rejecting her.

We studied 8-month-olds (DeGangi and Greenspan, 1988; Doussard-Roosevelt, Walker, Portales, Greenspan, and Porges, 1990; Portales, Porges, and Greenspan, 1990) and were able to further observe how critical the constitutional and maturational factors are to the child's development. In infants with a variety of symptoms, such as eating or sleeping problems and temper tantrums, we were able to demonstrate that a very high percentage had constitutional and maturational differences that were part of the difficulty. The babies were either hypo- or hyperreactive in one or another sensory modality or had sensory processing or motor tone or motor planning difficulties. These differences, in turn, seemed to contribute to a skewing of the parent–infant interaction pattern, which in turn was affecting personality development. These children were also found to have differences in physiological regulation (DeGangi, DiPietro, Greenspan, and Porges, 1991). These differences persisted and were evident at 18 months. There were also signs of family distress at 18 months (Portales, Porges, and Greenspan, 1990). It appeared that the maturational differences were affecting not only the child's personality, but also derailing the family to some extent. A small group of these infants that were followed to age 4 evidenced a greater number of behavioral and learning problems than a comparison group (DeGangi et al., 1993). Therefore, children who have constitutional and maturational unevenness tend to be especially challenging. They have a harder time in their interactions with their caregivers. Family functioning tends to be stressed. Eventually there may be more behavioral and learning difficulties.

Infants and children with regulatory disorders evidence challenges in their constitutional and maturational variations, which in turn create interactive and family challenges. These variations affect how the children perceive and organize experience. For example, a baby who is excessively needy and demanding, fussy, or finicky, intermittently angry, labile in his moods, slow to warm up and adapt to new situations, has an impact on the family, on the nature of interactions between the child and family members, and on the way the child perceives himself and integrates experience. In a sense, all experience is colored in part by the unusual constitutional and maturational variations that infants and young children with regulatory problems evidence.

For purpose of further understanding regulatory problems, and seeing the broad range of clinical problems they may be a part of, we have grouped them into certain patterns based on the constitutional and maturational variations and the related behaviors and symptoms. While each individual should be viewed in terms of his or her unique profile, these groupings (which may facilitate further research and clinical explorations) are suggested both by our ongoing longitudinal study of children with regulatory problems as well as our clinical work. For each type of pattern outlined below, we will describe the typical constitutional and maturational variations, behavioral patterns and symptoms, as well as the types of experiences that worsen the pattern or lead to their improvement. For young children, the presence of adaptive rather than undermining family experience (in relation to the constitutional and maturational variations) can play a significant role in the growing flexibility of the personality. Even for older children and adults, however, these "favorable" types of experience can significantly enhance the flexibility of the personality. For children and adults, the therapeutic relationship can also be characterized either by a more favorable or undermining interactive pattern. Therapists who are aware of the underlying constitutional features will, as the cases described earlier suggest, be more likely to construct an appropriate therapeutic relationship and strategy.

REGULATORY PATTERNS

TYPE I: HYPERSENSITIVE TYPE

There are a number of behavioral patterns seen in conjunction with overreactivity or hypersensitivity to various stimuli. Two characteristic patterns are the fearful and cautious type of person and the negativistic and defiant type.

The fearful and cautious person evidences excessive cautiousness, inhibition, or fearfulness. This pattern is manifested in early infancy by a restricted range of exploration and assertiveness, dislike of changes in routine, and a tendency to be frightened and clinging in new situations. In early childhood it is characterized by excessive fears or worries as well as shyness in relationship to new experiences (forming peer relationships, engaging with new adults). In later childhood and adulthood, this types of person tends to feel anxious or panicky and evidences shifts in mood; he or she may evidence depression or anxiety states. In general, he or she tends to be a sensitive, reactive, detail-type person, who can be overloaded by emotional or interpersonal events. He or she tends toward having a more fragmented, rather than an integrated, internal representational world, and may be easily distracted by different stimuli.

This pattern is intensified by vacillating caregiver or therapist responses (i.e., overindulgent, overprotective some of the time; punitive and intrusive at other times). Flexibility and assertiveness are enhanced by caregiver or therapist patterns characterized by empathy, especially for the person's sensory and affective experience, very gradual and supportive encouragement to explore new experiences, as well as very gentle but firm limits.

Motor and sensory patterns are characterized by overreactivity to sound and touch, loud noises, or bright lights, coupled often with age-appropriate auditory–verbal processing abilities and compromised visual–spatial processing ability. He or she is often overreactive to movement in space, and tends to be easily upset (e.g., as a child, irritable, often crying; as an adult, moody and fearful, anxious or angry), cannot soothe self readily (e.g., finds it difficult to return to sleep), or cannot quickly recover from frustration or disappointment. When motor and sensory patterns are associated with uncertainty in space, one may see a tendency toward phobic patterns.

The negative and defiant person evidences negativistic, stubborn, controlling, defiant behavior and often does the opposite of what is requested or expected. He or she has difficulty in making transitions, and prefers repetition and no change or slow change. This type of person can be perfectionistic and compulsive. As an infant, he or she tends to be fussy, difficult, and resistant to transitions and changes. As a preschooler, there are tendencies toward negative, angry, defiant, and stubborn behavior, as well as compulsive and perfectionistic behavior. Such people can also evidence joyful, flexible behavior at certain times. As an older child or adult, there are tendencies for such a person to be controlling, argumentative, and to frequently engage in power struggles. He or she will often use passive defiance as a coping strategy and will also avoid difficult situations. In the extreme (unfavorable family patterns) this type of person can become more schizoid and suspicious.

In contrast to the fearful–cautious or avoidant type, he or she does not become fragmented, but organizes an integrated sense of self around negative defiant patterns. In addition, in contrast to impulsive / stimulus seeking type, he or she is not generally aggressive unless provoked, and tends to avoid or be slow to engage in new experiences rather than crave them (i.e., is more controlling). In general, he or she seeks to control the amount of stimulation or experiences so as to avoid overload and fragmentation. The need for seemingly excessive control and negativism is an attempt to modulate sensory and affective input.

Caregiver and therapist patterns which are intrusive, excessively demanding, overstimulating, or punitive tend to intensify this pattern. Caregiver and therapeutic patterns which tend to be soothing, empathetic, and supportive of slow, gradual changes (and avoid power struggles) tend to enhance flexibility. In addition, the encouragement of the representation of different affects, especially anger and annoyance, also enhances flexibility.

These people tend to be overreactive to touch, are often overreactive to sound and frequently evidence solid visual–spatial capacities. They may show evidence of compromise in auditory processing capacity. They often have good motor tone and motor planning ability, but may show some delay in fine motor coordination.

TYPE II: UNDERREACTIVE TYPE

There are a number of behavioral patterns seen in conjunction with underreactivity to various stimuli. Characteristic behavioral patterns include the withdrawn/difficult-to-engage person, and the self-absorbed (march to their own drummer) type of individual.

The withdrawn/difficult-to-engage individual evidences seeming disinterest in exploring relationships or even challenging inanimate objects (a challenging game). He or she may appear apathetic, easily exhausted, and withdrawn. As an infant, they may appear delayed or depressed, lacking in motor exploration and responsivity to sensations and social overtures. As a preschooler, he or she may, in addition to the above, evidence a paucity of ideation in terms of diminished range of fantasy and verbal dialogue, or as an adult may appear withdrawn and disinterested, and may look depressed in an apathetic rather than self-condemning way.

This type of person requires intense interactive input from a caregiver or therapist, or high saliency from inanimate objects to attract interest, attention, and emotional engagement. Caregiver or therapeutic patterns that are low-key, laid-back or depressive in tone and rhythm tend to intensify this pattern. Caregiver or therapeutic patterns that are characterized by reaching out, sensitive, energized wooing, and energized responses to the person's cues, however faint, tend to help this type of person engage, attend, interact, and explore his or her environment.

Motor and sensory patterns: These patients are often underreactive to sound, and they may be either over- or underreactive to touch. They often evidence auditory–verbal processing difficulties, though visual–spatial processing capacities may be intact. They often evidence decreased motor tone and motor planning and are frequently underreactive to movement in space.

The self-absorbed (march to their own drummer) type of individual evidences a tendency to be creative and imaginative, yet tunes into his or her own sensations, thoughts, and emotions, rather than being tuned into and attentive to other people's communications. As an infant, he or she can appear self-absorbed. They become interested in objects in a self-absorbed, rather than interactive, manner. As preschoolers, they tend to escape into fantasy when there are external challenges (e.g., competition with a peer or demanding preschool activity). They may appear inattentive, distractible, or preoccupied, especially when not pulled into a task or interaction. They may prefer to play alone when others won't join the fantasy. Their fantasy life may evidence enormous imagination and creativity. As adults, they tend to favor self-absorbed fantasy or reality adaptation which may appear to be idiosyncratic. Depending on intensity of pattern, they may evidence disturbances in thinking.

During the formative years, caregiver patterns that are characterized by the caregiver's self-absorption or preoccupation, or confusing family communications tend to intensify this pattern. Caregiver patterns which open and close circles of communication and evidence a good balance between fantasy and reality, and help the child stay externally and reality-based when he or she is attempting to escape into fantasy, foster flexibility. Therapeutic patterns which are interactive and work on the basic unit of communication (i.e., incorporating another person's thinking and affective presence into a sense of collaborative and shared reality) tends to lead to improvement. Overly passive or interpretive approaches may prove unhelpful.

Motor and sensory patterns: They tend to have decreased auditory–verbal processing capacities (which make it easier to tune into one's own ideas rather than other persons' ideas), coupled with creative and imaginative tendencies. They may be underreactive to sound and may or may not evidence irregularities in other sensory and motor capacities.

TYPE III: STIMULUS-SEEKING, IMPULSIVE, AGGRESSIVE, MOTOR DISCHARGE TYPE

The characteristic behavioral patterns associated with this type include highly active, impulsive, and aggressive behaviors. In such an individual there is often a combination of underreactivity to touch and sound, stimulus craving, with poor motor modulation and motor planning, and evidence of diffuse, impulsive behavior toward people and objects. He or she tends to be active, seeking contact and stimulation; but appears to lack caution. Not infrequently, there is a tendency toward seeking contact with persons or objects leading to destructive behavior (breaking things, intruding into other people's body spaces, unprovoked hitting, etc.). As an infant, he or she evidences stimulus seeking behavior; as a preschooler, there is evidence of aggressive, intrusive behavior and daredevil, risk-taking style, as well as a preoccupation with aggressive themes in pretend play. When unsure of self or anxious, he or she uses counterphobic behaviors (e.g., hits before getting hit). As an older child or adult, he or she tends to be active, risk taking, often aggressive. When unsure of him- or herself, this type of person can also get more depressed and suspicious as adult adaptations do not work. When able to verbalize and self-observe, he or she may describe the need for activity and stimulation as a way to feel alive and vibrant.

Caregiver and therapeutic patterns are characterized by poor limits and boundaries, less than optimal nurturing and over- or understimulation may intensify this pattern. Caregiver and therapeutic patterns characterized by a great deal of consistent nurturing, firm structure and limits, opportunities for consistent, warm engagement, as well as modulation and regulation of activity, and opportunities for sensory and affective involvement with good modulation will enhance flexibility and adaptability. In addition, caregiver patterns that encourage use of imagination to support need for exploration will further enhance flexibility.

Motor and sensory patterns: Such people tend to have poor motor modulation and motor discharge patterns, particularly when frustrated, angry, or vulnerable. They are underreactive to touch (and pain) and crave touch and other physical contact. They may also be underreactive to sound, listening fleetingly, and yet craving loud noise. They may evidence either auditory or visual–spatial processing difficulties, but may also evidence age-appropriate patterns in these areas. They may evidence slightly increased motor tone and subtle motor planning difficulties.

A DISCUSSION OF ATTENTIONAL PROBLEMS

The descriptions of different types of regulatory patterns provide another way of conceptualizing many typical, observed behavioral patterns. While further research and clinical work will refine these descriptions, they offer the clinician therapeutic and research options. Some of these additional options are contained in the foregoing descriptions where the differing constitutional and maturational patterns are the basis for different therapeutic strategies. To further illustrate how understanding constitutional and maturational patterns can enhance clinical options, consider a disorder which is being diagnosed increasingly in both children and adults, Attention Deficit Disorder (ADD). There are two ways to look at ADD: one is as a syndrome where attentional difficulties are the primary component of the syndrome. One works with improving attention, often with medication; one helps the child deal with associated behavioral and emotional issues (e.g., self-esteem challenges) with behavioral therapy, psychotherapy, and/or family counseling. Another way of looking at attentional challenges summarized under the term *ADD* is to consider the possibility that the attentional problems are secondary to regulatory difficulties. Under this hypothesis, each child or adult with ADD patterns would have a potentially different regulatory profile underlying them. One child or adult may be distractible due to overreactivity to noise coupled with an auditory processing deficit, while another might have poor motor planning, coupled with visual–spatial organizing difficulties.

The clinician would then work with these underlying regulatory challenges. Medication might be considered, but only after other educational, behavioral, and psychotherapeutic strategies had been explored. In addition, if one used medication, one would look at its impact, not just on the ADD-type symptoms, but on the regulatory problems as well. For example, we have observed clinically that when a child's symptoms are improving with medication, he or she is often less over- or underreactive to sensations as well.

There are a number of strategies that might be used, based on an understanding of the individual's regulatory profile. First, one figures out which sensory pathways and motor patterns will enable a person to be attentive more easily and which require extra practice. Is he more inattentive when hearing words or when seeing spatial designs? How can the two be used together to foster greater attentiveness? Is he tactilely sensitive, does he have motor planning difficulties? Most importantly, maintaining two way interventions, i.e., opening and closing circles of communication, can be helpful: first on a behavioral, gestural level, then on a symbolic level, then at an internal level where the person sustains his attention by asking himself rhetorical questions. The key is for the individual to use purposeful activity and purposeful thought, and string together these thoughts and activities as a way of sustaining attention. Active problem-solving is better than passive listening for the regulatory-disordered child.

It may be useful to consider an example of how a therapist might use a regulatory perspective in her work with a child with attention difficulties. A 6-year-old comes in. He is there because the teacher said, "Johnny might be hyperactive and distractible; he is not learning in school, and probably should be on medication, so that he will attend better." The child has a history of "spacing out" a little bit in school and tending to get overwhelmed in groups, but when he has a friend over, he plays nicely; with a parent alone, he does well. However, he gets a little "hyper" and distractible in the schoolroom, or if two or three kids come over to play, or if there's a birthday party.

The child comes in and says, "Hi," and he looks warmly at the therapist. They exchange greetings, and he asks where the toys are. The therapist says, "Well, there are some toys over there." "Can I play with them?" "Oh, sure." He goes over to the closet and opens it up. The therapist asks him, "What do you want to play with?" and he takes out three or four trucks and starts rolling and crashing them. The therapist says, "It sure is fun to explore." The child picks up a Transformer truck and asks, "Do you know how this works?" Then the child starts trying to figure out how the Transformer truck works and how the different parts relate to each other. He asks the therapist "Can you help?" "Where do you need help?" the therapist asks. The child might say, "I don't quite know how to change this part." The therapist asks the child if he could show her, then they work on the truck together. As the session progresses and they play out different themes, eventually the therapist asks the child about his family and peers. The child talks easily and says that he has a little sister who really "makes me mad sometimes." "What makes you mad?" asks the therapist. "Well, she bugs me. She takes my toys and stuff." Then the child describes school and says that he doesn't like it when kids "poke fun at me," or when they call him names. What he likes, he says, is to go out with his father on Sundays and he goes on to describe what they do together.

Later on in the session when the child draws, the therapist notes that the child's fine motor control is behind his general intelligence. As the therapist explores what happens in school, she also notes that the child has a difficult time comprehending complex questions, and at times, gives up and seems to favor passivity or avoidance or "escape into fantasy."

At the end of such a session, what has the therapist learned? One-on-one, the child evidences many age-appropriate capacities.

He is attentive and focused, engaged and related. He uses complex intentional gestures and represents his wishes and feelings in an elaborate and organized manner. There are hints that he has some difficulty with competition and aggression (e.g., "The kids poke fun at me"), but further exploration is required to look at how he deals with specific emotional themes. The therapist talks to the teacher, who confirms that the child "spaces out" in class. The therapist obtains a history from the parents; this is a child who has had some difficulties with auditory processing and fine motor control. He also tends to have tactile sensitivity, and gets quickly overloaded with sensory input; when he does overload, he tends to look distracted and withdraw. He seems, therefore, to have some regulatory components to his difficulties.

His parents are warm and supportive; they are able to use the representational mode around complex feelings, as evidenced, in part, by the child's ability to say when he is feeling "needy" or "angry." The clinical sessions, history, and observation of the family lead the therapist to think that there are many strategies to work with. The therapist decides to help the school adjust to the child. The medication issue is brought up by the child's teacher and parents, but the therapist suggests that they put it on hold while they see what can be accomplished in a psychotherapeutic and educational program.

In such a case, the therapist may work on several fronts at once. He will organize a program to remediate maturational differences (e.g., have a speech pathologist help with auditory processing difficulties, an occupational therapist help with motor planning, fine motor regulation, and sensory hyperreactivity difficulties). At the same time, she will help the parents through floor time and problem-solving approaches which help the child learn to attend and focus even when anxious. For example, the parents will work on helping the child break down a task into small parts and find ways of linking one part to another, including helping the child use internal cues (e.g., ask himself questions). Most importantly, the parents will learn about their own feelings and counterproductive tendencies, such as overwhelming or withdrawing from, or being too concrete, with their child.

In her session with the child, the therapist will help the child in two ways. She will help him stay organized at both the gestural and representational levels by helping him learn to close circles of communication. She will also help the child identify and label feelings that lead him to tune out or "avoid" or to lessen his desire to remain focused. Feelings such as anger, humiliation, fear of failure or loss, and fear of success can often trigger regressive patterns. When there are individual differences in ego structure, including processing problems and maladaptive responses to anxiety, both challenges need to be dealt with.

Consider an example of how the therapist might work. The therapist notices that when there is talk about a subject that makes the child uncomfortable, he doesn't close his representational circles. The therapist may say, "Since you were telling me about school, I would like to hear more about what happens." The child says, "Oh, look at this Transformer!" The therapist: "It's an interesting truck, but we were talking about school and your friends." The child: "Oh! Can I play that game over there?" As the child continues to ignore what the therapist says, he evidences his constitutional vulnerability in auditory processing. But he is also deliberately avoiding talking about something that makes him anxious. His problem is a combination of his vulnerability and his way of dealing with anxiety. In a sense he intensifies his vulnerability when anxious. If the therapist then says, "Well, let me get this right. I want to talk about your friends and school, but you would prefer to ignore that I'm even asking you the question and just play the game." The child might confirm the statement and close the circle, but he might talk about the game some more anyhow. The therapist then focuses on a new theme of how the child has a hard time closing a circle and how a complex statement containing three or four sentences causes him to feel lost. "When I ask you a question, what happens to your thoughts?" "My mind is empty. I feel lost," the child might say. As the therapist shifts gears and helps the child look at how he "feels lost," together they can begin looking at situations and feelings that lead him to feeling lost, and the maladaptive patterns of avoidance or escape into fantasy that follow the lost feeling.

The key is for the therapist to shift from a focus on just the content of the child's play or talk about the process by which the child deals with information. They can then look at strategies that the child uses to get "more lost" so no one will find him and make him do his work, and strategies to "stay found." These strategies consist of affective and cognitive efforts.

The therapist should assist the parents in closing circles with the child as well. As parents engage in problem-solving discussions for a fifteen- or twenty-minute period each day and talk about a variety of subjects, they will have lots of opportunities to close circles. The parents' goal is to keep the logic of the conversation going. If the child gets off on a tangent, the parent needs to acknowledge that the child would prefer to talk about another subject or feels lost, then try to bring the child back to the original topic. If the child says, "I don't want to talk about that," he has closed the circle; he is getting practice in being logical, and he is not being "spacey."

The therapist helps the parents determine in which emotional areas the child is more likely to display avoidant behavior—when he is talking about rivalry with peers and aggression, or the teacher's disapproval, or being overloaded by all the noise in school, or writing or math assignments. The therapist, along with the parents, explores what happens when the child is in situations where he gets overloaded. What are his characteristic tendencies? For example, they will try to talk to the child about how he feels when people are making a noise. He may say, as one child did, "It feels like there is buzzing in my head, and I can't hear anything else, and I don't know what I'm doing. It's awful." The therapist may say, "Well, tell me more about what that awful feeling is like," and help him describe the feeling, using as many metaphors as possible. The better the description he is able to give, the more the child learns to understand and anticipate the feeling. He learns to stay with the feeling and not escape from it by withdrawing and "spacing out." Once he can describe his core feeling state, the child will be able to look at how he tends to side-step a feeling with direct avoidance or passivity or aggression or by confusing others (i.e., the "Let's get the adults feeling confused, just like I am). The child's ability to identify his tendencies does not mean they are deliberate or that there is not a maturational component to his difficulty. It only means that he can use his ability to represent and observe feelings to become more flexible in his coping. The fact that the therapist is focusing on the child's coping pattern does not mean he isn't following the child's lead. The child's behavior of avoidance or fragmented thinking is a part of his communication.

One tries over time to help children tolerate the dysphoric affect of confusion by realizing that, because they have a mild processing problem, their tendency is to "play ostrich" and tune out what's going on around them. The therapist shows them that they can learn to become more vigilant. If the parents function well, they can help; at the same time, the occupational therapist or speech pathologist can work to strengthen the child's sensorimotor and language systems. The therapist also works with the parents on their characteristic family patterns. The therapist should also consult directly with the teachers, so that they can work with the child in class. Sometimes a school counselor working with children together in a group can be very helpful. The goals and approaches, however, should be coordinated. The teacher can also work on facilitating ego structure without becoming overly intrusive.

As we consider a coordinated approach to attentional problems, it is important to further understand some of the underlying processes that may influence attention so that they can be worked with in therapy. One such process relates to the child's or adult's ability for self-cuing. A lack of self-cuing is one of the patterns that we have observed clinically with children who evidence attentional difficulties, and especially those who forget their homework, their classroom location, and what they are supposed to do from one minute to the next. Another child, during a transition such as the end of the schoolday, may ask himself, "What is my homework for tonight and which books do I have to take home?" But the forgetful, inattentive child simply walks out of school thinking of the green leaves on the trees outside and the friend he wants to talk to on the way home. The books he needs for homework do not enter his thoughts until his angry parent is standing over him yelling. Clinically, we have also noticed that as children learn to ask themselves these rhetorical questions, their seeming inattentiveness can begin changing. In other words, an aspect of the inattentiveness is a lack of a logical infrastructure of thinking where the child uses self-observation, self-reflection, and most importantly, self-cuing through rhetorical questions to organize his day, and to maintain his concentration. In this framework, attention and concentration are viewed not as a passive or even natural process or ability, but as an active process which rests on active thinking. Since many inattentive children can think quite logically and actively, particularly when they are highly motivated, they may be more capable than we think of applying this same active thinking ability to transitions. Applying active thinking to transition, in terms of self-cuing, would help them stay with a task. In some cases the "forgetfulness" is part of a motor planning/sequencing difficulty. It is helped by the child using verbal cues to maintain the behavioral sequence (i.e., talking oneself through a pattern that is not automatic). In a limited number of clinical cases where this active approach to maintaining attention has been taken, the results have been promising. In such cases, however, in addition to helping the child to think actively, it has been important to also help the child understand his own, at times, latent desire to be forgetful, avoidant, or passive. One child put it beautifully: "When the work gets too hard and too much, I just chuck it over my back by forgetting everything." Family patterns and conflicts over assertiveness and aggression invariably play a role, but the child's tendency, based on constitutional and maturational differences, is not to cue himself with rhetorical questions.

Not only constitutional or maturational patterns, but early learning experiences may create patterns of attention or inattention. For example consider a potentially interesting hypothesis. In operant learning theory, different reinforcement schedules maintain behavior under their control at different rates. Some schedules such as a random ratio schedule (behavior is reinforced based on the number of responses) maintains behavior at high rates and other schedules maintain behavior at low rates (e.g., a fixed interval schedule with long intervals). Early caregiver responses to the infant's attentive behavior may form a pattern which resembles a known schedule. Such caregiver patterns may therefore be studied as a factor influencing attentive behavior.

It is important not to assume that an attentional disorder is a unitary entity. It is useful to assume that every child has some maturational unevenness, which in each child is quite different. Whether the problem is visual–spatial or auditory processing or motor planning will dictate different approaches to the problem. The therapist has to figure out what the maturational vulnerabilities are and what kind of internal experience they produce. He needs to observe how this is experienced one-on-one, and in a group, and with cognitive and affective challenges. The therapist must determine how the child copes with his experience—by thoughtful planning, compulsive planning, withdrawal, activity, fear, ritualistic behavior, or some other way.

Most educators will be very appreciative if a therapist can pinpoint why the child is so difficult to teach, and how he copes with feeling confused. For example, some children with a visual–spatial processing lag have a hard time picturing experience. This difficulty may explain why they find it hard to do math (math has to be pictured). A child has to be able to picture that $5 \times 3 = 15$. For example, ask a child, "How big is 7 if 1 is this big?" Perhaps he cannot represent the proper proportions, he cannot picture spatial entities. If one tries to teach that child the rules of addition and subtraction, "math facts," by rote, he will never be a good math student. If he learns to picture in his mind different sizes and dimensions and develops a "spatial feel" for numbers, he can learn to enjoy and master math. He may need to go from concrete objects to imagination until he has a sense of spatial proportions. As he tries to master a new way of thinking, he may use all his favorite tactics—withdrawal, avoidance, aggression, and so forth. The therapist's perspective can help a tutor recognize the child's unique patterns of regulatory phenomena and work with him more effectively. While neuropsychological testing can be helpful, this is no substitution for careful observation both in the classroom and in the clinical situation. How the child copes with his sense of confusion and either intensifies or compensates for the challenge can best be understood by watching it occur in the clinical situation.

SEVERE REGULATORY PROBLEMS

There are a number of children who come in with severe communication problems, sensory under- and overreactivity and processing difficulties, motor delays, and "autistic" features, with a diagnosis of pervasive developmental disorder or atypical development. Such children often have problems at all of the developmental levels described earlier: attention, engagement, two-way gestural communication, and the symbolization of emotions.

At each developmental level there are problems on all fronts: interactional, familial, and maturational. The constitutional problems with sensory reactivity and processing (of a severe nature, especially auditory–verbal processing), motor tone and motor planning, often so challenge parent–family patterns that there are child interaction problems, family system problems, as well as problems with the parents' own reactions and fantasies about the child. Collectively these undermine attending, forming relationships, being intentional, and using words or complex symbols and gestures to convey needs or desires. Treatment involves a comprehensive approach. Often, however, with these children, professionals may try to work with splinter skills at the symbolic level and not enough with the regulatory difficulties and the early levels of engagement, shared attention, and gestural interactions. Four times a week interactive therapy that focuses on all developmental levels, occupational therapy twice a week (for some children), speech therapy three or more times a week, parent counseling once or twice a week, and a psychoeducational program five half-days a week are elements of a comprehensive program. With such a program, many children we have treated in the last few years have done remarkably well. Within six months, for example, withdrawn preschoolers are comfortable with dependency and closeness, seeking out their parents, and learning to be intentional. Within one year, many are beginning to symbolize affect in both pretend play and with functional language and becoming comfortable with peers. Over time, specific severe learning disabilities become the focus of treatment as the pervasive emotional and communication difficulties improve. Compared to treatment where the focus is on controlling or modifying behavior and working with splinter skills, in our experience working comprehensively on the underlying regulatory difficulties and their associated emotional patterns and the formation of growth producing relationships and interactive patterns leads to children having greater warmth and spontaneity (Greenspan, 1992).

For each case, one must pinpoint the family system dynamics, the parents' fantasies, the child's constitutional–maturational contributions, and the caregiver–child interactions for each developmental level: attention and engagement, two-way communication, shared meanings, and emotional thinking.

GENERAL THERAPEUTIC STRATEGIES

There are general principles that can be applied to children and adults with regulatory difficulties.

The therapist needs to work simultaneously with the child's or adult's constitutional and maturational variations, as well as interactive patterns. In terms of working directly with the constitutional and maturational variations, the therapist needs to find the pattern that will most likely help the person focus, attend, and engage. Before we discuss strategies to work with interactive and emotional patterns, we will briefly discuss some of the ways to work directly with constitutional and maturational variations. To the degree working with these variations can enhance the individual capacity for regulating alertness, attention, reactivity, mood, motor patterns, and behavior, it provides an important foundation for the therapeutic process. To enhance regulatory capacities it is helpful to incorporate practical suggestions developed by occupational therapists trained in sensory integration work (Ayers, 1964). These suggestions can be implemented in daily activities, occupational therapy, or in programs of sports, recreation, or dance. The individual's sensory reactivity in terms of touch, sound, sight, smell, and response to movement helps focus the program. For some individuals, firm pressure, as with rough-and-tumble play or sports, can help to normalize sensory input and foster better capacities to focus and concentrate. Helping adults explore their reaction to different physical activities will enable them to select activities that foster calm attention. In terms of sights and sounds, it is helpful to experiment with different intensities in terms of loudness, different frequencies, and different rhythms. The person who is overly reactive to loud noises will do best with a soft, soothing sound. The person who is underreactive to sound may need a stronger, more dramatic vocal pattern. Some individuals will do better with low-pitched sounds, others with high-pitched ones. The person who has a difficulty with processing, that is, abstracting the sequence of sounds or words, may need simple input. One person, for example, may do better with simple rhythms, which have only one or two variations of sound, whereas the child who processes sound easily may need the novelty of more complex vocal rhythms, with four or five patterns. Observing how the individual attends, whether he has a knowing sense or a confused sense about him, will inform the clinician about what type of vocal rhythm and sequence is more helpful in fostering attention and a sense of engagement. Similarly, the level of brightness or dimness in the room, the intensity of colors used in furnishings and play objects, the complexity of the visual design and even the degree of animation the clinician uses in his own facial expressions will need to vary, depending on the individual's hypo- or hyperreactivity and capacity to process different aspects of what he sees.

Some types of activities can foster calm attending for hours after the activity is over and, therefore, provide a useful component for daily routine. In terms of a person's response to his own movement patterns, some people, for example, focus and attend when involved in slow, rhythmic activities, such as four or five seconds per swing on a swing. Others will do better when moved rapidly, one second per swing. Others will do best when they have opportunities for both fast and slow rhythms.

Some individuals attend and focus better when they are involved in large-muscle activity themselves. Others do best when such an activity is combined with joint-compression activities, where they are getting appropriate receptor feedback. For such individuals, jumping on a bed or on a trampolinelike device may foster their ability to attend and engage.

Many individuals who are oversensitive to touch, sound, light, or who are sensitive to their own movement patterns, attend, focus, and engage best when they can be in charge of the interaction patterns. The more in charge they are, the more they can regulate and monitor the sensory input and the motor control they need.

Young children can be calmed more easily when one understands their unique patterns. An excessively finicky child may calm down most readily when resting on his stomach, over a parent's knees, with firm pressure on the child's back, while being moved in a very slow rhythm, with the parent's knees creating the movement. Another child may do better in an upright position, resting against the parent's chest, with the child's head crooked into the parent's neck. This more typical, upright position is too activating for some children, and a more horizontal position may be more calming, particularly when the child is experiencing some distress. Some adults similarly focus best when moving around, while others do best when still. Some adults can only learn through their own activity, while others can learn in a more passive pattern while they are being talked to.

Many individuals with regulatory difficulties also evidence constitutional and maturational difficulties in the areas of motor tone and motor planning. They may have high or low tone or difficulty with planning motor acts, such as alternating hand movement when drumming on their own legs. As a baby, such a person may have had difficulty getting his hand to his mouth. As a toddler, when trying to grab one thing, he may have knocked over another thing. Practice in coordinating perception and motor acts can be very helpful; it should start with activities a person can master and then work up to more difficult activities. In addition, a person with low motor tone who tends to tire easily because of it, should be understood to require a great deal of effort to carry out routine activities that others perform easily. The person is putting a lot of conscious effort into activities that are more automatic for others. Exercises, such as having the person lie on the floor on his stomach and pretend to be a boat (rocking back and forth, arching his back) or a child playing the bird game (the child scissors his feet around his father's waist, arches his back, and has his arms flap as his father circles around), encourage extensor tone and help with motor tone, strength, and stamina. Such activities, along with certain types of movement patterns, will help individuals gradually learn to enjoy activities around athletics or the playground. Here, too, it is important to remember to take the person one step at a time, to build fundamental abilities by improving motor tone and motor planning, and then to expose the person to activities which, on the one hand, are routine functions, but on the other hand, provide self-support for motor tone and motor planning.

Certain kinds of athletics or play activities per se support more extensor tone and provide practice in motor planning. For example, simple games of putting objects in certain places or taking them out support motor planning. Games that require a child to change direction rapidly, such as a chase game that doesn't operate in a straight line or the bird game, will improve the child's extension and tone. When accompanied by sensori-normalizing activities and interactions, these kinds of activities will foster attention and engagement in both early and later stages of development.

These examples indicate how focusing on constitutional and maturational variations can directly foster engaging and attending. In fostering a relationship, the clinician who is naturally empathetic and flexible will find it easier to engage a wide variety of children and adults, whereas the clinician whose approach is more rigid will find he can work with some children better than others. As a general rule, for the more cautious, hyperreactive regulatory disordered individuals, a very warm and available yet slow step by step approach on the clinician's part is often most helpful. The approach often needs to contain a very gradual, soothing element, together with a dynamic one. Take the example of a regulatory disordered 8-month-old who is especially fearful and cautious when facing new experiences. If the therapist approaches the child slowly from afar, with lots of friendly glances, he often does better than if the child is approached in a more routine way from close up. From across the room, the therapist must look, smile, and vocalize with the child. The child's probable expectation—that the adult is going to approach him and try to pick him up—is not realized, since the therapist moves from across the room only an inch at a time, making interesting facial expressions and gestures. The child often relaxes and begins to gesture back at the adult for a second or two from a distance—looking then hiding his eyes in his mother's chest. As the clinician gets a little closer, he senses when the child starts to become apprehensive and frightened by the changed look in the child's eyes or by the degree to which he averts his gaze. At this point, the clinician should not move closer but should hold his position and continue the gentle signaling. By talking to the mother and only intermittently communicating with the child, the clinician will find that even an infant as overly cautious and sensitive as this 8-month-old will begin seeking eye contact with the therapist and even court him with motor gestures. Once this begins to happen, an important corner has been turned, and the relationship is moving ahead. Soon there will be an opportunity for the clinician to engage the child and foster his attention more fully.

Similarly, in approaching a fearful, cautious adult, simply being overly formal or alternatively getting intrusive too quickly will backfire. A slow, gradual approach, increasing the affective range of the communication with facial gestures and then gradually expanding the range of content, will work best.

Six steps can be identified that often help foster progress in children or adults with regulatory challenges. The six steps work well with problems that do not have a regulatory component as well. The first step involves following the child's or adult's lead in play or talk adjusting to their regulatory and/or interaction patterns and creating an engaging and regulatory relationship and interpersonal environment. This context is used to facilitate the patient's elaboration of their inclinations, including affects, behaviors, thoughts, wishes, etc. The more challenging the regulatory profile of the individual the less intuitive the first step may be. For example figuring out which patients require gentle soothing slow wooing and which ones a high energy, overly animated approach may not be obvious.

Once there is a sense of engagement, the individual can be encouraged toward a problem-solving orientation. This orientation can occur at the gestural and behavioral level, as well as, in the older child or adult, at the symbolic and verbal level. At the gestural and behavioral level, it may involve a simple reality-based, adaptive movement, like rolling a ball to someone or reaching for an object or handing something to someone. For the child with regulatory difficulties, the problem-solving step is oriented toward helping the child anticipate, practice, and master, slowly but surely, those types of behaviors or activities that one would expect the child to find difficult. Children with regulatory difficulties should have extra anticipation and practice in areas where their regulatory system is easily challenged. If they are sensitive to touch, sound, smells, or movement patterns, these are the very patterns where practice and anticipation should occur.

Where words and thoughts can be used to anticipate a problem, a problem-solving discussion between the clinician and the child could, for example, anticipate what will happen at school the next day. The child is helped to anticipate the feelings he is likely to have and the behaviors he is likely to evidence in response to those feelings. He is asked to picture the feelings and other behaviors that he might try or to review similar past situations, as a way of figuring out what he may expect in the future, in order to reduce the sense of surprise or shock and to feel prepared even for uncomfortable sensations. Many clinicians, parents, and educators carry out this exercise, but focus only on the situation and the behaviors. "When you are in circle time, you tend to sit in a corner by yourself," fails to account for the child's feeling. "When you are in circle time you feel . . . how?" The child who can talk about feeling scared, "Like I can't breathe," or "Like my brain doesn't work," will be at a great advantage over a child who discusses only the situation and the behaviors. The child's ability to understand and verbalize how he feels in a situation will give him a great deal more flexibility to cope with that situation.

The adult can be guided by his therapist to use imagination to an even greater degree, to picture, for example, difficult interpersonal situations. Creating internal imagery itself seems very useful for the adult. It serves to organize as well as prepare.

In addition to mental anticipation, with the verbal, thinking child or with adults, actual practice in anticipation can also be helpful. Trial runs in situations similar to the one where the individual is challenged should prove helpful, just as they do for the toddler and infant. For example, a preschooler who is about to experience circle time for the first time and who does poorly in groups because of the noise and the likelihood of being touched needs some careful preparation. He may benefit by playing not just with one child (if he already can do well with only one), but by playing with two or three children. Practice with a small group in the safety of his own house, with his mother present, will expose him to situations where he is likely to bump shoulders, deal with aggression, and hear loud noises. Having the children actually sit in a circle and listen to a story may be a culmination of this activity. Then when the child has to sit in a group of six children at school, without his mother present, he may be more comfortable because he has already had an actual opportunity to practice and anticipate.

If both practice and discussion are modified to be manageable for the child or adult, and gradually increased in level of challenge, they help the individual anticipate situations and provide valuable problem-solving assistance. The adult who practices talking to authority figures or verbalizing feelings of vulnerability, if done in a noncontrived manner, can similarly gain flexibility.

The next step in working with regulatory disorders is to help the person experience empathy for his difficulty and get a sense (particularly if he's verbal and thoughtful) of his basic assumptions about life. For example, the clinician may empathize with the verbal child about how he must feel when he has to sit in a group or hear loud noises. It may be hard for the clinician or parent or educator to imagine how overwhelmed, disorganized, and fragmented a child with sensory overload may be, when they do not have these kinds of sensitivities themselves. The clinician may think that a child just doesn't want to share the limelight with other children in circle time and therefore begins to behave provocatively, when, in fact, the child may feel overwhelmed, fragmented, and "like I'm jumping out of my skin." Feelings like "my brain doesn't work," or "I can't stand it, I've got to get out of here," or "My mind is exploding," or feeling "like moosh," or "like I'm water, like there's no container," are quite different from an adult's ordinary expectations as he tries to empathize with a child about this interaction with his peers. Similarly, adults will have their own special feelings and fantasies which they may keep hidden because they are "embarrassing." Each person will develop his own fantasies that elaborate on sensory and affective experience. When voices are too loud, some may feel that people want to hurt them, and they feel overloaded. Others may feel that people are trying to manipulate or trick them. Still others may believe that people hate them or want to deprive them of something. It is important to help the person sense that one can understand, not just the secondary fantasy that everyone hates him, but also the primary feeling of being overloaded and overwhelmed. The latter feelings are likely to involve emotional and sensory overload in one form or another.

Empathy needs to be gestural as well as verbal. Empathy for the preverbal child, for example, is expressed in the attitude of the parent, caregiver, clinician, or educator. The impatient, critical-looking parent certainly does not calm the overwhelmed, frightened 12-month-old. However, a reassuring, "I-know-it's-scary" look on the parent's part may convey some reassurance to a frightened child. For the younger child, therefore, the parent can convey empathy through facial expressions and gestures, which pick up the child's mood states and convey an expectable understanding of them. There's a difference, for example, in terms of empathetic expectations on the child's part if he is angry and belligerent or frightened and overloaded. Each circumstance requires a different empathetic response. The angry child may benefit from a firm, steady look on a parent's face, a look that says, "You can't do that here, and I'm here to make sure you can't." The frightened child may benefit most from a look of concern for his pain and fear, and a quality of gentleness and tenderness. Even verbal adults, however, require this preverbal empathy along with verbal soothing and understanding.

In addition to demonstrating empathy, the therapist should help the patient identify his core assumptions. Examples of core assumptions are: "I shouldn't have any pain," or "I'm entitled to escape anytime I feel uncomfortable." Characterizing these assumptions helps the patient understand why he's doing what he's doing.

The next step is to figure out a series of small steps to help the individual master new experiences. The person with regulatory disorders requires many tiny steps—one toe in the water at a time. If the first step is not manageable, it can be broken down into ten smaller steps. The critical challenge for the person with regulatory disorders is to overcome his sense of standing still or even moving backwards, and help him achieve some forward momentum, so that he can feel a sense of mastery over some steps. It doesn't make a difference how small the steps are, so long as he can move forward.

The next step requires the establishment of a structure with both limits and incentives. The small steps will work best with the individual who possesses a sense of incentive, as well as a sense of finite structure to operate within. Children with regulatory disorders, for example, may seem so overwhelmed, helpless, and unhappy most of the time, that clinicians, educators, and parents are reluctant to set limits. Yet limits on some of the child's behavior creates a sense of security that his environment cannot be totally manipulated or intimidated by him. Usually the child breaches some behavioral norm, such as not clearing his place from the table, scratching someone, or throwing his food on the floor. It is important to set broad enough limits and set them in areas where one is relatively certain the child has the capacity to keep within them. For example, the child with too little motor control to prevent his food from falling on the floor is not likely to benefit from limits related to eating more neatly. Another child with greater planning abilities and control may be able to minimize the amount of food on the floor with some such limits. Similarly, the child who can control his pinching or biting will benefit from limits having to do with hurting other people. While it is generally useful to set limits on children's capacity for or interest in hurting others or breaking objects, other limits need to be set in ways appropriate to each child's capacities. Moreover, clinicians, educators, and parents should not attempt to fight battles on four or five fronts at once. It is best to establish limits in only one or two areas at a time.

Similarly, adults also need the security of structure and limits. Coming to sessions on time, following the basic rules of not breaking objects and verbalizing rather than acting out feelings can also be used to enhance security via structure. Negotiating the rules can be very helpful for the child or adult who believes being overwhelmed is a license to overwhelm others.

Limits should not, however, compromise the first four steps of the developmental approach to resolving challenges. For example, a limit that isolates a child and reduces the quality of engagement, or that is so concrete as to undermine a child's problem-solving ability, will not prove helpful in the long run. A limit that reduces an adult's therapy time is often unhelpful. On the other hand, useful limits tend to stem from problem-solving discussions, where the individual has been able to anticipate when he will receive limits and what the reasons for the limits will be.

The sixth step involves avoiding situations where relationships become simply a power struggle. Every time limits of some sort are used, there should be increased engaging and empathy. This critical principle is especially hard to establish with individuals who have regulatory disorders because they tend to create a sense of frenzied helplessness with those in their environment. One needs both more limits and more engagement and empathy at the same time.

RESEARCH AND FUTURE DIRECTIONS

The regulatory disorder concept may be especially useful in future research approaches. It provides a construct that can be used to understand patterns that are intermediary between the various causes of problems (including genetic and biochemical ones) and overt symptoms or behaviors. In this model a prenatal, perinatal, or genetic variable may not influence later behaviors directly but instead influence the regulatory profile of the individual. The individual who was exposed to a certain prenatal toxic substance may for example be oversensitive to sound and touch and have poor visual-spatial processing capacities and compromises in master planning. His early experiences and environment, however, will determine how these physical differences translated into behavior or symptoms. Will he be a warmly engaged person with mild learning challenges or a withdrawn, depressed, or antisocial person? Because many children and adults evidence a distinct regulatory profile, an important research question, therefore, is how much of the variation in the designated behavior is related to a particular biochemical, anatomical, physiologic variable or the regulatory profile of the individual. Perhaps biochemical differences, seen in depression, schizophrenia, autism, and other disorders, are related to the underlying regulatory profile rather than the disorder or syndrome.

If this were the case, the different regulatory profiles might prove quite useful in understanding how underlying biological differences express themselves and in what way they interact with environmental influences. At present we often side step looking for appropriate intervening organizations such as regulatory pattern and try to directly study how biological variables affect overt behavior and symptoms. Interestingly our research designs and especially our selection of control groups may contribute to slowing down progress. Many findings relating biological variables to psychiatric disorders do not properly select their control groups. Typically, studies involving a particular biological process investigate differences between a psychiatric disorder group and a normal control group, or other psychiatric disorder groups. At the same time, it is generally recognized that what we are calling regulatory differences, that is, differences in motor, language, cognitive, and sensory processing capacities, accompany many psychiatric disorders (e.g., Vitiello, Alexander, Stoff, Behar, and Denckla, 1989). Many of the functional central nervous system (CNS) differences seen with specific psychiatric disorders (hypothesized to be part of the disorder), however, are also found in nonpsychiatrically impaired individuals (albeit less frequently than impaired individuals). Yet, in explaining a particular biological marker, rarely are the "associated CNS patterns" hypothesized as possible explanatory factors, independent of the psychiatric disorder under study.

The fact that the associated CNS variations are found in nonpsychiatrically impaired individuals mandates that these "associated" CNS findings be controlled for in studies investigating biological correlates of a psychiatric disorder. Only a control group of individuals with the "associated" or accompanying CNS features, but without the psychiatric illness, can rule out the possibility that the associated CNS irregularities (i.e., the regulatory factors) rather than the psychiatric illness's defining characteristics, are responsible for a given biological marker (e.g., children with excellent attention, but with sensory processing, language, and motor irregularities as a comparison group, in addition to "normals," in studies of ADD).

A review of the recent studies (35 articles from three major psychiatric journals), involving biological variables in psychiatric disorders, revealed that none used an "associated features" control group in addition to a normal control group or various psychopathological comparison groups. A few studies used "mentally retarded" children as a general comparison group to control for cognitive impairment. But such a heterogeneous group may have many different subtypes, which can cancel each other out. To control for "associated" CNS developmental patterns, the comparison group must not evidence the disorder, but be relatively similar to the disorder group on variables such as motor tone and planning, sensory reactivity and sensory processing in each sensory modality, and selected aspects of language and cognition (Greenspan, 1989, 1992). Individuals who evidence these variations, but do *not* evidence specific psychiatric disorders (such as ADD, autism, schizophrenia, affective disorder, conduct disorder, obsessive compulsive disorder), can readily be found in the general population.

In addition to serving as a critical control group, using "associated features" comparison groups in biological studies would highlight and clarify patterns of developmentally relevant CNS irregularities, and provide clues about mediating developmental processes (which may, in turn, lead to the identification of especially relevant behavioral and biological patterns). For example, as indicated earlier in studies of 8-month-old infants with regulatory disorders, we have found that infants with difficulties attending, calming, sleeping, eating, and regulating behavior, evidenced subtle irregularities and dysfunctions in motor tone and planning, sensory reactivity and processing, and physiological and psychophysiological organization. Moreover, these differences persisted at 18 and 48 months, and were associated with increased parental stress and behavioral and learning difficulties (DeGangi, DiPietro, Greenspan, and Porges, 1991; DeGangi et al., 1993).

In considering the major psychiatric disorders of children and adults, there is mounting evidence about the nonspecific nature of perinatal, constitutional, and developmental variations, and a lack of specificity to neuroanatomical and chemical studies. There are also family studies suggesting significant overlap in the presence of different psychiatric disorders in extended families. It is time, therefore, to shift the paradigm and use the regulatory disorder concept as part of a biopsychosocial developmental model to understand psychiatric disorders. In such a model, constitutional and maturational variations, that is, regulatory patterns (as expressions of genetic, prenatal, or perinatal influences) interact with family and environmental patterns through child–caregiver relationship patterns. These relationship patterns, in turn, determine the adaptive or maladaptive outcomes for each of a number of specific developmental stages and tasks (e.g., having to do with self regulation, forming relationships, communicating, and representing and organizing experience) (Greenspan, 1992). Specific psychiatric disorders are the final common pathway stemming from these cumulative mediating developmental processes.

Within this model it is possible to hypothesize relationships between specific constitutional and maturational variations and adaptive or maladaptive developmental patterns, as well as to assess, and through intervention, favorably influence the developmental processes leading to adaptive outcomes (Greenspan, 1992).

To illustrate the broader research and clinical usefulness of regulatory disorder concepts, consider the following specific hypothesis.

HYPOTHESIS ON DISORDERS OF THOUGHT AND AFFECT

The concepts of regulatory disorder offer a way to consider the influence of early and continuous constitutional and maturational variations on behavior, feelings, and thoughts. From a diagnostic and clinical treatments perspective it enables the clinician to systematically incorporate important variables into the clinical decision making, planning, and intervention process. From a research perspective it offers a way to study the developmental processes that occur between genetic or constitutional variations, environmental problems, and later outcomes. It provides a potentially useful component in a developmentally based biopsychosocial model.

Thought disorders, in this model are hypothesized to stem from two concomitant circumstances: a difficulty in processing auditory–vocal–verbal information (e.g., may have difficulty with underreactivity or mixed reactivity to sounds and/or comprehending the larger patterns of sounds and words) combined with an environment that tends to operate by confusing the meanings of communications. In this hypothesis the infant at risk for a thought disorder evidences difficulty processing auditory–vocal–verbal information, beginning early in life with difficulty in reacting to and abstracting the sequence of certain sounds. Most infants, for example, quickly become familiar with their mother's and father's vocal rhythms. They often alert and brighten in expectation of the next sound in the sequence. Some infants cannot decode these early rhythmic patterns and look confused in response to a simple vocal pattern. Most importantly, affect, which will further challenge a vulnerable sensory processing system, is conveyed through auditory–vocal–verbal sensory channels. The auditory–vocal channels are important for the gestural level of affective communication discussed earlier and for the successful negotiation of the basic emotional themes of this level (e.g., safety, security, acceptance). We have observed in a number of cases that in such situations there are early compromises in distinguishing and communicating basic affective meanings.

It is further hypothesized that the environment which will bring out this underlying constitutional–maturational deficit early in life overwhelms the vulnerable sensory pathway (in this case, the auditory–vocal–verbal one). In subsequent developmental stages the "high-risk" environment for disorder of thought tends to confuse the meaning of affective communications. For example, in infancy this high-risk environment would tend to speed up rather than slow down vocalizations and increase the variation and novelty so rapidly that the infant would have trouble becoming familiar with any one pattern. In the second and third years of life, this same high-risk environment would keep overwhelming the youngster's auditory–vocal–verbal symbolic ability in other ways, namely, through confusing gestures and meanings. A number of years ago, investigators such as Jackson (1960), Lidz (1973), and Wynne, Matthysse, and Cromwell (1978) discussed schizophrenogenic families and their confusing patterns of communication, but they did not focus equally on the type of child who was vulnerable to such patterns or who might even inadvertently cause the family to accentuate them. Family members can become so anxious with an infant who is not processing their verbal or gestural cues that, in trying harder, they become more overwhelming and confusing. They may vacillate between withdrawal or overly passive approaches and overly intrusive ones. At the gestural and then symbolic or representational level, this may lead to confusion between what are the parent's feelings or ideas and the child's at a time when a representational sense of self and other is in potential formation. One day the child's aggression is aggression; the next day it is love; or one day it is "my feeling" and the next day it is "your feeling." In such circumstances, even a competent child's ability to appropriately label and organize experience along the dimensions of self and nonself, and in terms of different thematic and affective proclivities (i.e., being able to identify dependency, pleasure, aggression, assertion, curiosity, love, etc.) may be compromised. The paradigmatic high-risk environment for a child with an auditory processing problem, therefore, is one that further compounds the child's constitutional–maturational difficulty in abstracting affective meanings. The result is impairments at three levels: somatic–sensory, gestural, and representational–interpretative.

It is not surprising that such a child, as an infant, may turn away from the human world, confused by auditory and auditory–vocal–affect signals. Compromises may follow in pre-symbolic reciprocal cause-and-effect interaction patterns, the ability to organize affect and behavior, and the formation of a functional (conceptual) self (also prerepresentational). If, subsequently, the representational interpretive system is not able to organize these earlier fragmented developmental patterns, the combination of sensory–affective sequencing and representational limitations may result in a variety of deficits in organizing behavior, affect, and thinking.

CLINICAL EXAMPLE

Michael was the product of a seemingly normal pregnancy and delivery; a thin, but otherwise healthy, twenty-two-inch, six-pound, eight-ounce infant. He appeared very competent because of his extraordinary visual interest in the world. He focused on mother's face and brightened to her smiles, even in the first few days. Motorically and physically, he seemed to be progressing. In response to vocalizations, however, he seemed to look blank and confused. Hearing examinations were unremarkable. His visual interest and ability to focus on his mother's and father's smiles, and on inanimate objects, seemed so extraordinary that there was little attention paid to the fact that he was not equally responsive to vocal patterns. In fact, during one of the early assessments, if the examiner tried to gain his attention while he was looking at a bright object by talking to him from the side, his attention to the sound of her voice would only be fleeting, and he would return to his visual interests. If the examiner caught his attention and started making animated facial expressions, however, his interest in the examiner would persist. It seemed clear that he was using vision to an extraordinary degree to understand the world.

His parents were well-intentioned, motivated, successful professionals who were also extremely anxious and controlling. They had little tolerance for anything other than "following the rules." They took great interest in his precocious development, in terms of his ability to examine objects and see how they worked. Frequently, they claimed they had a "brilliant young child."

In the first months of life, mother dealt with his unresponsiveness to her vocalizations by focusing completely on his visual interest in objects. She would try to get him to do exactly what she wanted. She ignored the fact that he had little emotional range, only evidencing shallow smiles now and then, and that she was not getting feedback for her own vocal emotional communications.

This family moved away, but fortunately moved back into the area before his fifth birthday. When we saw him at age 5, he was a tall, thin, healthy-looking child, who scored extremely well on all the intelligence tests. On the clinical examination, however, he related all too quickly with the clinician, putting his arm on the clinician's arm within the first few minutes. He talked clearly, quickly, and spontaneously about school, his parents, and his activities of the day, in a rambling, free-associative style. While he seemed quite sophisticated for a 5-year-old, there was little logic or coherence to his stream of interesting anecdotes. Each one, however, did have a certain internal consistency.

As the interviewer empathized with his verbal abilities and interest in describing his day, he confided to the interviewer that he actually had "more exciting experiences." He then went on to talk about his relationship with "underwater creatures" and his "extraordinary powers," in that he can talk to people through his thoughts without speaking. As his ongoing delusional system emerged, he insisted that this material be confidential. If his parents knew about it, they would think he was "crazy." He did not have friends, felt "different" from the other kids, and related more to his teacher and inanimate objects in the schoolroom than to other children.

The initial impression of this child was that his emerging delusions and intrusion of primary process thinking would be correctable with intensive psychotherapeutic work. This view was supported by his considerable strengths, including his capacity to relate to the interviewer, organize his behavior and aspects of his thoughts, his brightness, interest in talking about his experiences, and, most importantly, his sense of perspective ("I'm different," "My parents would think I'm crazy"). The organization of his representational world was not fully differentiated, according to real–unreal or self–other, even though he had an extraordinary capacity for representational elaboration.

In this case, we were impressed with the fact that an early circumscribed difficulty in auditory affective processing preceded a later difficulty in the organization of thought and affect along self–other dimensions. That the environment accentuated rather than ameliorated the early vulnerability was also of special interest.

In contrast to the high-risk environment for this constitutional–maturational vulnerability, consider the intuitively gifted environment. This environment helps the child organize early experience by using the intact sensory pathways (e.g., vision, touch, smell, proprioception, etc.). It does not overwhelm the auditory–vocal processing capacities. It, instead, provides individually tailored, age-appropriate experiences for developing early regulation and interest in the world, a satisfactory attachment, reciprocal cause-and-effect interactions, and organized functional, behavioral, and affective patterns. It accomplishes this by offering and engaging in experience through the well-functioning sensory pathways. It also intuitively remediates the auditory system by slowing down and offering extra repetition rather than excessive novelty (in essence, it keeps the child at a particular stimulus configuration until the child seems to understand it). Later, at the gestural and representational levels, the family is empathic to the child's meanings, communicates clearly in each thematic affective area (dependency, pleasure, assertion, curiosity, setting one's own limits, etc.), facilitates the child's differentiating feelings and thought of the self and nonself, and sets effective limits. It provides practice, so to speak, in helping the child develop the representational ability that may be especially helpful in interpreting sensations from within, sensations that may be confusing because of the early difficulties in processing auditory information. In the optimal case, the environment ameliorates the early sensory decoding difficulty, strengthens sensory processing in other modes, and supports a representational interpretive system that can use higher level abstractions to make sense, even out of a "somatic underbelly" which tends to send up confusing sensations.

AFFECTIVE DISTURBANCES

It is hypothesized that whereas "thought disorders" emanate from an underlying constitutional–maturational vulnerability in auditory–vocal–verbal processing, affective disorders emanate from an underlying constitutional–maturational vulnerability in visual–spatial processing and integration which has as a feature of its pattern a vulnerability in sensory, affective and behavioral regulation. The child tends to be more reactive to sensations and has a harder time organizing what he perceives.

Visual–spatial processing ability in infancy, it is further hypothesized, is related more to the perception of the intensity of affect than its meaning. Affective meanings in this model are communicated predominately through the auditory–vocal–verbal channel, whereas intensity of affect is communicated more through the visual–spatial pathway. In other words, one understands whether someone is happy or sad through the sequencing of vocal patterns, but one understands the intensity of affect through how one organizes what one sees in space. There is emerging evidence for part of this hypothesis from work with 6- to 8-month olds. The auditory–vocal pathway seems more essential for identifying sad and happy affects than does the visual pathway (Caron and Caron, 1982). Documenting that the visual–spatial pathway is used for the perception of affect intensity requires further research.

Just as a child learns to sequence various auditory–vocal signals and construct a pattern to maintain these in relationship to one another and examine them, the child also learns to sequence and organize visual–spatial experiences in order to make sense of the visual–spatial world. For example, one of the earliest experiences of a newborn infant is to recognize the configuration of the human face and to compare one visual configuration with another. This involves spatial relationships between the mouth, nose, eyes, the differences between a smile and a frown, and so forth (Caron and Caron, 1982).

The capacity for abstracting visual features of the inanimate and animate world is present quite early in the first year of life. By the second and third years, children are able to experiment in space by constructing various simple visual–spatial configurations (e.g., towers, a line of blocks to represent a train, simple closures such as a fenced-in area for the animals), and by the fourth and fifth years, children can construct complex interrelated spatial configurations (e.g., houses which are connected by bridges, drawings of houses with rooms, windows, and interconnecting doors). In other words, children organize spatial relationships much as they organize auditory–vocal–verbal symbols. Some children develop more rapidly in one sphere and others more rapidly in the other.

Visual–spatial capacities, however, may be fundamental for both abstracting intensity and other high-level order pattern abstractions. The visual–spatial domain is a continuous rather than discrete space (e.g., number sequences or various spaces under a changing line representing intervals are on a continuous dimension). Auditory–verbal space, in contrast, tends to be discrete or segmented (e.g., each word has its meaning). Verbal symbols can form classes, but the words and classes are usually still relatively discrete rather than part of continuous categories. In part because of their continuous properties, spatial configurations lend themselves both to abstracting the dimension of intensity, which is also a continuous dimension (as compared to the dimension of meaning which is segmental), and other higher order abstractions or patterns, as in mathematics. It may be that the visual–spatial mode is necessary for constructing higher order organizations of the self and nonself and that without this capacity, the sense of self and other, by necessity, is more concrete and potentially more fragmented.

Consider a hypothetical infant who has difficulty in abstracting the properties of his physical space and finds it difficult to regulate his state, motor behavior, and affect patterns. Although many babies may be labile in the first few weeks or even months of life, our prototypical infant does not evidence increasing regulation and organization. Instead of looking into his caregiver's eyes, and finding solace in her animated facial expression, he continues to rev up when overly excited. He looks left, right, up, and down, often past his caregiver. When looking at his caregiver's face, he is unable to abstract enough of a pattern in the caregiver to use it for self-comfort and self-organization. As he develops he is further unable to determine or organize into a pattern his caregiver's or his own affect and behavioral intensity because of his lag in abstracting interactional spatial–affective patterns. This is an example of an early constitutional–maturational pattern in which the ability to use the visual–spatial system to regulate and organize state, affect, and behavior is not well developed.

What is the prototypical high-risk environment for this type of constitutional–maturational vulnerability? Here the high-risk environment is not one of confused meanings, but one where there is a failure of empathy, regulation, and effective setting of limits. Consider the following developmental sequence. Assume this infant has formed an attachment, be it somewhat chaotic, as he experiences difficulty in calming down and controlling his own affect and motor discharge patterns. Also assume that as he progresses into the 4- to 8-month phase, he learns cause-and-effect communications when not overexcited. There is a blurring of cause-and-effect patterns, however, when he is revved up. He easily become chaotic, and in a sense overwhelms any cause-and-effect interactions offered by the caregiver. In addition he has difficulty abstracting the spatial patterns he does engage in. In the second year, his parents have difficulty understanding the intensity of his affect and motor discharge tendencies. For example, when he cries, he does so inconsolably for a half-hour, and his parents are unsure whether to "ignore him," or "indulge him," and feel a mixture of anger, fear, and concern and also feel overwhelmed. It is not an uncommon tendency, even for parents who feel confident with an easier child, to find it difficult to empathize with such a child's discomfort. There is often a tendency to become mechanical and even aloof. Competent parents who are organized along obsessive–compulsive lines may vacillate; one day they try to wait the child out and not spoil him, hoping the intense crying and discomfort will stop by itself. Another day, overwhelmed and exhausted, they try indulging him. This vacillation may be experienced by the toddler as a lack of empathy, and perhaps at times as a lack of feeling connected to his human environment.

Not infrequently, as with older children and adults, this sense of not being empathized with and feeling unconnected may lead the child to "rev up" even more. It is as though the toddler himself tries to generate the affect necessary to create a feeling of well-being. Initially, this hypomanic style is used partially in the service of reassurance. In a way, the child is saying to himself, "If they can't make me feel good, I'll try to create this good feeling all by myself." A type of denial is operating. The child's own revving up is to create a false sense of bliss and to ignore the lack of appropriate empathy. The deficit (limit-setting) with such a child, which is part of the empathic failure, is related to the expectable inconsistency one often sees when parents try to discipline a very difficult child. Furthermore, his difficulty in comprehending affective intensity and spatial–affective relationships (e.g., dependence and independence) further accentuates this pattern.

The child with a lag in visual–spatial abstracting ability is now in a situation of double indemnity, so to speak. He has difficulty abstracting, comprehending, and organizing affect intensity because of a visual–spatial processing lag. Yet he finds himself in an environment where the shifts in affect intensity are increasingly overwhelming his vulnerable capacity.

If the caregivers themselves have difficulty in modulating affect, the problems are compounded. They rapidly shift from states of extreme indulgence to withdrawal, and from concrete limit-setting to excessive permissiveness, all of which only further accentuate the child's basic difficulty in regulation.

Project this environment into the third and fourth years of life when the representational system is becoming formed. Assume that this child has enough adequate caregiving experiences to form symbolic and representational capacities. One may observe a developmental sequence where meanings are sharply demarcated but where interpretations of affect intensity are distorted. The child who already tends toward poor control of affect expression (i.e., every minor frustration is a major calamity) is now part of a family where distortions of affect intensity are present. His own difficulty is therefore intensified. The child may construct new affect states in order to feel connected and maintain a sense of well-being. At the representational level, the child is able to construct not only new complex feeling states, but to give meanings to these feelings. As a result, he may further distort his own and others' affect intensity.

The deficit in visual–spatial pattern abstraction may limit the child in another way that is consistent with what is observed in affective disorders. The deficit in higher order pattern recognition and organization will limit the formation of representational capacities. This limitation will occur in the organization of an affective self and object. Instead of organized, integrated self and object representations, there may be concrete islands of self and object representations governed by discrete affect states (e.g., the sad or depressed self, the hypomanic self, etc.), each one with little relational connection to the other. In this situation, the self is not fragmented at the level of meanings but in terms of affect proclivities. Clinically, one is impressed that adults with affective disorders are concrete in terms of understanding emotional patterns (their own and others), in spite of their brilliance in other spheres of endeavor.

The tendency of the self to be fragmented leaves the organization of a sense of self vulnerable to affect intensity and stress, especially the stresses of loss or over excitement. In this context it is interesting to consider the etiology of depressive symptoms. Perhaps they are not a direct response to loss or an underlying biological vulnerability which interacts with loss or other stresses. Perhaps depressive symptoms (or even manic symptoms) are secondary phenomena. The symptoms occur because of one internal loss of the self or object representation. Similar to anaclitic depression in a baby who losses its real object, the individual losses the internal representation of an object and then has secondary symptoms. Even when there are biological predispositions toward depression, in this model, the mediating process would be the inability to conserve the image of the internal self or object representation, or self-object representation based on a vulnerability in visual–spacial processing.

CLINICAL EXAMPLE

Molly was a robust, extremely alert, eight-pound infant with good muscle tone, a voracious appetite, an unusual ability to "tune into" sounds, and according to her mother, a "willfulness you wouldn't believe." She was very difficult to console after crying for long periods of time and took little solace from looking at her mother's smiling face. Mother described a pattern where, "I could never get into a rhythm with her"; "When I wanted to hug her, she wanted to pull away"; "When I was busy she would pull on my nose or poke her hand in my eye." By the time she was 8 months old, her behavior was characterized by rapid fluctuations in mood, being upset, gleeful, calm, or fussy. When she was vocalizing or reaching, her behavior was more random than purposeful and lacked a sense of a synchronous fit. Interestingly, she seemed to decode sounds and even words very well. She listened carefully, and by fourteen months could follow simple instructions if they were associated with something she wanted, such as a certain food. For example, when her mother said, "Come into the kitchen for a cookie," she would come rapidly. She had a precocious mastery of simple words.

At the same time, however, she seemed to have difficulty in the visual–spatial domain. Making faces or using motor gestures rarely had impact, as though these were harder for her to decipher. Also she would become confused in new settings about how rooms were connected and frequently would wind up crying rather than being able to retrace her steps and find her mother. Her ability to organize space seemed to lag behind her considerable verbal abilities.

Her father tended to absent himself from the family through twelve-hour workdays, and mother, while very attentive, vacillated between states of depression and frenetic activity when she felt "hyper." With Molly she said, she could never tell "what she was feeling," and always felt "guilty I wasn't doing enough," so she never set limits. Molly by eighteen months was "running the house." There were limitations in both empathy and limit-setting.

After no contact, mother brought Molly in at age $7^1/2$ for a clinical evaluation because of "rapid mood changes," demanding behavior, and problems with friends and with school. At this time Molly appeared to be a healthy, well-coordinated, articulate $7^1/2$-year-old who evidenced an extremely intense quality of relatedness. But she also evidenced a great deal of affect lability, was impulsive, often fragmented in her thinking (staying on each sub-ject for only a few seconds), and deeply concerned with themes of loss, rejection, and humiliation. Dynamically she seemed to operate according to the principle: "I will hurt your feelings and reject you before you can hurt or reject me." A false sense of bravado permeated her words and behavior and only intensified her tendency toward fragmented feeling states, thought patterns, and behaviors. The impression was of primary difficulties in af-fective and behavioral regulation and organization, not unlike affective disorders in adults.

In contrast to the high-risk environment, consider what would be an optimal environment for this constitutionally and maturationally at-risk child. In infancy, the intuitively gifted care-giver uses soothing vocalizations (appealing to the infant's strength) to help calm the infant when he is excessively excited. He learns that affect and motor discharge can be regulated, par-ticularly with the help of auditory–vocal and other sensory path-ways and motor control (e.g., being held tightly and later by working with the child on motor exercises to provide a sense of regulation and organization in space).

The optimal environment balances a sense of empathy (the difficult task of feeling the distress of the out-of-control child when he is excessively excited) with the firm and consistent set-ting of limits. The latter is achieved by limiting disorganized mo-tor activity in infancy and later on by providing an extraordinary affective holding environment and setting firm limits on impulses and excessive demandingness. Therefore, the toddler going out of control may be talked to, or engaged in one way or another, and held when necessary to help him regain control. Sometimes the limit-setting will demand extraordinary conviction and follow-through. Consistency, empathy, and limit-setting take the place of inconsistency, vacillation, and failures of empathy. A key issue is to always increase empathy and limit-setting together rather than the more common practice where one becomes polarized into only giving in or having power struggles. Later on, at the representational level, the same gifted environment places special emphasis on helping the youngster understand the intensity of feelings. Caregivers work with the child through this intact and highly developed auditory–vocal–verbal pathway to understand gradations of feeling intensity through a focus on the subtlety of meanings. For example, they help him describe, represent, verbalize, and play out degrees of feelings (e.g., very upset, a little upset, a tinge upset; pleased, happy, excited; a little sad, very sad; mixed feelings). Even though the sense of continuity of feeling based on the spatial dimension is relatively less developed, extra pretend play can be critical in facilitating this ability. Segmented verbal meanings are used in a novel way to communicate gradations of feelings.

The issue of delay is difficult for a child with an affect regulation problem. Here it might be reasoned that a visual–spatial difficulty (being able to organize the world according to spatial configurations) is closely related to a difficulty in temporal sequencing (how the world works in time). The sense of time is probably more closely allied with a visual–spatial pathway than the auditory–vocal–verbal pathway because the time dimension can be more easily understood along a continuous space than it can with more discrete segmented auditory–symbolic–verbal abstractions. Interestingly, music may have elements of both continuous spatial and verbal meaning. Time and learning how to delay, however, can also be taught in the auditory–verbal mode through creating ordinal sequences (i.e., less than/more than types of perspectives). In addition, visual–spatial configurations can be practiced through interactions and games involving affect intensity, building, drawing, and coordinated motor patterns. While structured activities can be helpful, spontaneous pretend play and verbal–affective interactions often provide the best bases for learning the needed new representational abilities.

The overall goal is to help this type of at-risk child learn how to identify and respond to patterns (see the forest for the trees), because he tends to get overwhelmed by the moment-to-moment meanings. This is no easy task, because over focusing on the "big picture" will be experienced as a lack of empathy. Empathizing with a child's hurt at being rejected by a peer, for example, must come first. But eventually it is important to help that child see the larger pattern of acceptance and rejection that occurs as part of his peer relationships. Helping the child see the larger pattern, even when upset, strengthens the child's capacity to offset the primary vulnerability in visual-spatial processing and construct a stable, affectively integrated internal self-object representation. The symptoms of affective disturbance, be they sadness, low self-regard, and apathy, or agitation, euphoria, and speeded-up think-ing, may, as indicated earlier, be a secondary reaction to the pri-mary one involving spatial processing capacities. As internal representations are fragile (they lack the spatial and temporal stability), there is always a danger of loss and separation, not from an external object, but from the internal representation of one. Of course, real separations or other stresses (loss of self-esteem, anger, etc.) will also undermine a fragile internal structure. The reaction to this internal loss may be dysphoric affect and associ-ated symptoms (depression or mania). In this view, the dysphoric affect is secondary to a primary disturbance in visual-spatial pro-cessing that undermines the capacity to construct a spatially and temporally stable and affectively integrated self and object repre-sentation. It is the loss of the internal representation that then leads to the familiar symptoms. It would be of interest to see if biological findings on affective disturbance could be more use-fully organized in relationship to this hypothesized underlying perceptual difference than in relationship to specific symptoms. It is also of interest that cognitive behavioral therapy, certain forms of dynamic therapy, and biological treatments all do rea-sonably well with certain types of depressive symptoms. Perhaps, in one way or another the underlying capacity to process and abstract a stable, affectively internal self–object representation is supported in all these approaches.

It is interesting to speculate on the milder forms of these disturbances as described in the earlier sections on regulatory types. The milder form of an auditory–vocal–verbal–affective pro-cessing difficulty, it is hypothesized, would tend to be associated with the severe obsessive–compulsive character disorders. The milder form of the visual–spatial–affective difficulty would tend to be associated with the hysterical personality disorders. These character structures are prototypes for a variety of defenses (e.g., isolation of affect from the obsessive–compulsive pattern; overdramatization and repression for the hysterical patterns; avoidance and counterphobia patterns for individuals who are over or under reactive to movements in space) and symptom patterns. As with the more severe disorders, these nonpsychotic disorders may also have prototypical environmental contributions in addition to underlying constitutional–maturational patterns.

These explicit hypotheses, from a developmental perspective, offer a way of understanding the nature versus nurture arguments about thought disorders and affective illness and ego defenses. They take into account the potential for genetic or constitutional proclivities to operate, not directly, but through their impact on sensory processing and subsequent ego structures. In addition, they focus on the role of specific environment experiences in ameliorating or accentuating the maturational vulnerability.

Throughout this chapter, we have discussed the relationship between regulatory processes based on physical differences in the individual and the individual's behavior and symptoms. We have suggested treatment approaches that take into account the child's or adult's unique regulatory profile. Most importantly we have emphasized how the regulatory profile provides understanding which can enable clinicians to foster the patient's ability to be calm, attentive, and organized and to process information. The patient's most fundamental sense of security is dependent on these processes, which are the foundation for the therapeutic relationship and the capacity to engage and communicate.

Chapter 4

Engaging and Relating

Problems with intimacy are among the most common in clinical practice. The second stage and process of development is concerned with the capacity for engagement and the ability to form and maintain an intimate relationship. Just as with sensory reactivity and processing, individuals exhibit an enormous range in their ability to relate to each other.

Normally, beginning at birth and reaching an early crescendo by 4 or 5 months of age, most children show enormous joy, intimacy, and satisfaction in forming human relationships. Of course, this ability continually develops throughout life.

This quality of relating can be enhanced in a number of ways. A middle-aged man seen in therapy recently needed to withdraw every time he experienced some intensity of affect, such as aggression, sexual excitement, and dependent longing. He would become aloof and pull away, and his affect would become somewhat flat and mechanical. This was obviously a chronic pattern, not a temporary regression based on an adult life crisis or a conflict that came up developmentally in adulthood. The therapist had to figure out a way to help this person develop a relationship

135

which was comfortable. When the therapist went back and explored the patient's regulatory pattern with him, it soon became apparent that he would scare the patient away if he sought rapport too quickly, or too obviously. He first noticed when there was a little twinkle in the patient's eye or when a smile lurked in the corner of his mouth. At the same time he tried to notice which affect the patient tended to withdraw from. As he developed this profile, he worked with the patient at a prerepresentational, preverbal level expanding slowly the patient's tolerance for a range of affects.

Family patterns are also important. Consider a patient who had an overprotective, intrusive mother and an emotionally distant father. We don't want to fall into the pattern of inadvertently repeating that experience in our therapy sessions. We don't want to find ourselves one day going after the patient and saying, "Gee, how come you are looking so sad today, how come you're so removed?" and on another day waiting in silence for the patient to make the first move. Not infrequently, these preverbal patterns are reenacted between patient and therapist, and neither has the vaguest idea of the fact that they are locked into this repetitive preverbal reenactment.

Sometimes the tone or cadence of the therapist's voice or the way he greets the patient and says goodbye, or even his body language, may resonate in the patient's mind as following familiar parental patterns. The therapeutic technique may serve to repeat rather than work through critical developmental experiences.

When the patient who has never had the experience of consistency in intimacy is engaged in a therapeutic relationship, that in itself becomes a critical learning and developmentally useful experience. Intimacy is what the patient could never achieve while growing up. He or she would respond to being overwhelmed by withdrawing. Their parents couldn't soothe or pull them into a pattern of engagement. This child requires the sense that even when he feels angry and excited, he can still be part of a relationship.

Parents are a product of their own upbringing and some parents are more intuitively gifted at working with certain patterns in their own children. They may be more successful with one child than another.

It is, therefore, important for developmentally oriented psychotherapists to reach beyond the commonsensical, self-evident tactics that all therapists, and for that matter most individuals, use in forming relationships with other people. Some patients are so challenged in their capacities to relate to others that intuitive, nonspecific tactics are insufficient. Just as many parents find it extremely difficult to engage certain types of children into a relationship, many therapists also experience difficulty when confronted with patients who have a fundamental limitation in relating that has already existed for many years.

This difficulty in relating may manifest itself in a general inability to feel a sense of warmth or trust; it may be evidenced in the shallow depth of such feelings as pleasure, enjoyment, or satisfaction; or it may show up in the limited range of feelings that can be incorporated into a sense of engagement. The therapist may note, for example, whether assertiveness, explorativeness, curiosity, or even anger can be integrated with warmth and pleasure. Limitations may also show up in the stability of the relationship and the ability to experience connectedness with another person. As Mahler, Pine, and Bergman (1975) so well described, many adults, as well as children, lose their sense of relatedness when the other person is out of sight for any period of time or when they feeling disappointed, angry, or ill.

How do therapists assist these patients? Their top priority is to develop their own empathetic range for the kinds of experiences patients are likely to have. What does it feel like to only be partially connected to another person? What is it like to feel disengaged or totally disconnected? Therapists are used to working with patients who can symbolize their distress by saying: "I feel so empty (or alienated) (or want more)," or "I feel so needy." But there are many patients who are unable to symbolically elaborate their relationship capacity. How does a clinician assist such patients whose sense of relatedness is communicated by their affect expression and feeling tone rather than their verbal responses?

The therapist must pay attention to subtle features of relatedness, a lackluster glance, a thin-lipped smile, a rigid posture. As the therapist tunes in to this dimension, he or she begins to look at the types of therapeutic experiences that tend to deepen and enrich a sense of relatedness and the experiences that tend to minimize it. For example, while playing on the floor during a child therapy session, the therapist noted that the child was banging dolls on the floor and breaking off their arms and legs. With an empathetic verbal, "Boy, you're really tearing this doll apart," the therapist extended a bridge to his patient. Though the child seemingly ignored the words, he looked and smiled at the therapist. On an earlier occasion, when the child had behaved in a similar manner, the therapist had firmly remarked, "Why do you want to hurt the dolls?" The child physically withdrew from the therapist, turning away without a glance. The therapist had initially reasoned that it was his job to help the child figure out why he was feeling aggressive toward the dolls, and not just to enter into a state of empathy with the child in terms of sharing his emotional and physical rhythms. He was assuming that the child was representationally differentiated and capable of seeing connections between different types of feelings and ideas. When he realized that the child could not yet operate at the level of affective meaning, could not connect meanings, and could not maintain a sense of relating, he readjusted his approach and sought to broaden and deepen the child's sense of relatedness.

Before continuing with this discussion, further comments on therapists' strategies may be helpful. When a child is withdrawn, the therapist should avoid criticizing his withdrawal by saying, even in a seemingly supportive way, "Why are you withdrawing?" In all likelihood, unless he were already fully differentiated, the child could not answer such a question. The therapist should, instead, maintain with the child a warm synchronism of feeling, while wooing the child out of the state of withdrawal. At the same time, by reengaging the child in the same play theme that was enacted before the withdrawal, the therapist is assisting the child in realizing that he can go back and forth between the behavioral and emotional states of mind while staying connected to another person. The child learns that a behavioral withdrawal need not be followed by a state of complete emotional withdrawal. More importantly, as the patient gently returns to the theme being reenacted during playtime, he starts becoming more comfortable with staying connected and elaborating a theme that was a little bit unpleasant. In short, the therapist helps the child feel safe, secure, warm, and connected, and this feeling of connectedness replaces the feeling of withdrawal. This type of therapeutic playtime is critical for children who tend to disengage rather than use a representational or symbolic type of defense.

Returning to the earlier discussion, the therapist realized that the child became anxious when asked to explain his unpleasant affects. To reduce his anxious feelings, the child reflexively pulled away from the relationship. The child does this because he knows no other way. It is not critical at this point to know whether this is a replay of an already learned pattern. It is not important to know either whether this is in part based on some natural tendencies related to his way of dealing with feeling overloaded or overwhelmed with intense sensation. The child learns that a warm, empathetic relationship can help him negotiate and feel better about an unpleasant affect. He realizes, perhaps for the first time in his life, that this unpleasant affect can be reduced not only by withdrawal from people but by staying connected to people. Another human being can help him feel calm, collected, and secure. Self-absorption or the inanimate world no longer supply him with all the answers anymore.

In the past, the child may, for example, have experienced his parents as further overloading him when he was anxious. He may have withdrawn when they spoke too loudly or in high-pitched voices, or were too intrusive. Perhaps, because the parents felt rejected, they may have become tense and a bit withdrawn themselves. When the child felt isolated or overloaded, to calm himself he focused on objects, such as the floor. In a research paradigm described by Brazelton, Tronick, Lechtig, Lasky, and Klein (1977) parents deliberately refused to return smiles to their

4- or 5-month-olds. Painful affect was apparent on the babies' faces. The infants made overtures and getting no response finally gave up and stared into space.

These parents' inadvertent overloading of their child, or their own tense counterwithdrawal, should be contrasted to the developmental therapist's offer of availability. This availability is geared to the child's unique sensory and affective reactivity and processing profile, and neither overloads nor underloads him. It takes into account his comfort levels in terms of touch, sound, sight, movement patterns, and intensity and style of affect. The therapist subtly communicates to the child that strong affects can be dealt with within, rather than by withdrawing from a relationship. This lesson is profoundly important. A clinician may be faced with a patient who has a primary tendency to withdraw (as opposed to a secondary tendency to withdraw because of representational conflict). If the therapist uses an overly mechanical version of classical techniques—remaining austere, silent, and mechanical—then inadvertently he is setting up a recapitulation of what may have created the original developmental impasse in the patient's infancy.

Let us assume, for example, that an infant is protesting and angry and that his parent shuts down and withdraws. Associated with the child's anger is a feeling of hollowness, emptiness, or nonrelatedness. These are some of the most profound, painful affect states that adults describe in later years. If, on the other hand, the child's parents remain involved with him, trying to comfort and help him regulate and deal with his anger, the child subsequently relates to his angry feelings in a context of engaged connectedness. He intuits that intense affect goes hand in hand with being a part of the human condition and being a member of the human race. Thus, a baby begins experiencing states of relatedness or nonrelatedness with his primary caregivers. These relatedness configurations tend to exist at a prerepresentational level. Without therapy that understands the earliest phases of ego development, such patterns often remain outside the adult's representational realm and are experienced in the most fundamental ways as part of one's inner affective core, instead of feeling states.

As a result, some adults feel completely empty or void of a sense of human connectedness, not knowing that life can feel full, warm, and related.

Later on in the therapeutic process, the patient is able to remain engaged and tolerate unpleasant affect (as opposed to withdrawing), and has progressed to the representational level, where there is some capacity for representational differentiation. Then and only then can the therapist help the patient describe at a representational level the painful affect states and their associated patterns. At that point, the relationship between the precipitating affects of aggression, frustration, fear of loss, and the tendency to withdraw can be explored and understood. The patient may be able to recreate earlier experiences, not so much through direct memory, but through the experiences in therapy in what Hartmann, Kris, and Loewenstein (1946) referred to as the sense of "What Must Have Been." This somewhat intellectualized understanding of "What Must Have Been" in an earlier stage of development helps the person consolidate his new sense of himself. The more critical work, however, is actually the mastery of prerepresentational stages of ego development, which occurred earlier in the patient's therapy.

In other words, when there are structural deficits, the therapist first works with the patient to rework the structural deficit using the intensity of affect generated in the therapeutic situation and the power of prerepresentational transferences. The therapist does not permit himself to become unwittingly involved in reenactment and instead offers enlightened affective and behavioral availability. Traditional insights are only possible later on, when the patient has worked through his maladaptive tendency and has begun progressing up the developmental ladder again, through gesturing capacities into the representational realms, and into the differentiated representational realms. Needless to say, this earlier phase of the work can take a great deal of time for some patients to negotiate. This phase should not be viewed as a poor cousin to the verbal, insight-oriented work, but instead should be viewed as the necessary foundation for therapeutic change. The therapist's own enormous difficulties with early pre-representational affect states can be all too apparent in the way he handles these issues with patients. For example, the therapist may insist on working with a prerepresentational patient at the level of verbal representational insights. He may insist that any deviation from his usually austere affectant baseline will be a countertransference acting out and gratification of the patient's infantile longings.

It should be pointed out that my personal experience has been that I have never met a child or adult who could not be engaged into a relationship, however deep-rooted their tendency to withdraw might be. A therapist may feel frustrated about his abilities to create this warm state of availability and engage a child or an adult in a state of relatedness. In that case he should consider that perhaps he has not discovered the best way to create this availability for a particular child or adult. It may be an appropriate strategy to get some consultation at this point. Otherwise there may be a shift to a more critical interaction with the patient or withdrawal from him or her. Worse, power struggles may develop, which unconsciously give the patient the sense that he or she should look for help elsewhere. Occasionally, there may be a joint decision that the therapeutic working relationship is less than optimum. This is because patient and therapist are unlikely to find the necessary empathetic range to work together. This should be a rare circumstance, however, and not take place until after the therapist has explored his feelings and consulted with other professionals.

RULES OF ENGAGEMENT

The following case descriptions will illustrate the points discussed above. A man who seemed to want therapy and eagerly embraced his therapist as "the right therapist for me" started a pattern of missing every second or third session. He would leave long, complex telephone messages on her answering machine, detailing how various meetings at work or engagements kept him from meeting with her, but he repeatedly indicated he would be eager to come the next time. Sometimes he would show up as promised; other times he would not. When he did appear, he often talked about the events of the day, or the meeting that had so entirely absorbed his energies that he could not break away to go to therapy sessions. Once he even canceled five consecutive sessions.

The patient frequently lamented that people were either letting him down or not meeting his needs in one way or another. He had come into therapy, in part, because he was having difficulties at work, including having tantrums and getting upset in the presence of his boss. He had been told that such behavior would lead to his dismissal if it continued. To his credit, he sought therapeutic help. During each session, the therapist speculated as to why he was missing so many sessions. She wondered out loud whether he missed sessions with her because she wasn't meeting his needs, much like his colleagues at work, his boss, and his roommate. He gave lip service to such interpretations, saying, "Well, maybe there's a point there, but I don't think so because I am very happy with you being my therapist. I look forward to our sessions." Still the patterns continued.

The therapist found herself becoming more angry and frustrated, since his session was the first one in the morning. She had arranged this early session especially for this patient to accommodate his busy work schedule. She awakened earlier than usual to meet with him, and his repeated absences were frustrating her efforts to reach out to him. The patient never demurred about paying for last-minute cancellations, and even seemed good-natured about missing two meetings in a row.

The therapist found herself getting more and more annoyed, and was on the brink of demanding that the patient either participate fully in the therapy sessions or consider quitting. Before confronting the patient, she fortunately sought consultation to review the situation. Her colleague pointed out that confrontation with the patient would be reenacting an experience that this man had had with his own parents. While the patient could not remember his own infancy, he described his mother as a woman who always "became detached and like a rock whenever there were any differences between us." He recollected having "an utter sense of void and fear of her disappearing from the face of the earth whenever I didn't do what she wanted. I was stubborn and I remember that if I hadn't had my older brother who was mostly busy with his own life, I might have been in 'bad shape' as a child." (This man's father had died when he was 4 years old, and he spoke very little about his loss early on in the therapeutic work.) The therapist saw that giving him an ultimatum would in essence be playing the kind of emotional hardball that he had attributed to his mother. With his mother, however, feelings rarely got verbalized, and were expressed instead by her "emotional disappearance."

Before deciding on a strategy, the consulting psychotherapist wondered out loud whether she could gauge this man's overall level of development when it came to engaging with other people. From his history and the sessions that had already occurred, she had a sense that he tended to engage people only insofar as they took care of his concrete needs. He talked about whether girl friends were good cooks or were attractive or whether his male friends were skilled tennis or squash players. He thought of people simply in terms of whether they could hold interesting conversations. His descriptions of other people were concerned with how they entertained him, fed him, or played athletic games with him. There was almost no mention of the emotional feelings that existed between him and other individuals. In the first series of sessions, the patient exhibited no sign of empathy or warmth toward those people he was involved with. He also evidenced very little ability to represent his feelings—showing no capacity for expressing abstract affect states. He never spoke of sadness, loss, anger, or jealousy. Conversations were always at the concrete level, with the people in his life appearing to be somewhat interchangeable.

The patient's associations would range from finding a person who could hold an interesting conversation to one who could play better tennis or prepare a better meal. Ironically, the patient was outgoing and charming, and obviously had a capacity to make people feel interested in him, even as he had already done with the therapist. Historically, this ability to charm seems to have been a recurring attribute throughout his adolescence and the parts of his childhood that he could recall.

With this new perspective on her patient's developmental limitations, the therapist decided that her focus had been developmentally too high with this man. She had mistakenly believed that he was operating at a representational level in which he felt that his needs were not being met, and, thus, became passive-aggressive and, finally, rejected people. The therapist had assumed that perhaps he was replaying the patterns of rejecting others, just as he had felt rejected by his own mother, and even more profoundly rejected when his father became ill and died. It became obvious, however, that this man was not at a level of representational differentiation where he could represent sympathetic states like loss and anger. This man appeared to be most challenged in terms of the earliest stages of the prerepresentational level of ego development, in which his capacity to form a consistent and deep engagement with another person was extremely limited. He seemed to operate at a prereciprocal, shallow level, in which people are viewed as things.

Once she realized that the patient exhibited an extremely primitive pattern of relating, the therapist opened up a different area of inquiry. After the patient once again missed a few sessions, she mentioned that he had missed his appointments. This time, though, she refused to let him go off on a tangent about work and other issues, and focused his attention on the concrete fact that either the time of their session or the way it seemed to conflict with other activities made it hard for him to come regularly. The therapist empathized with the fact that he was a person who took his moment-to-moment comforts very seriously and dealt with things in a here-and-now way. In other words, she acknowledged his view that a meeting sometimes seemed more important to him than his therapy. He similarly would cancel dates with girl friends if they couldn't cook his favorite dish. He lived in a concrete world revolving around who could serve his need of the moment.

It was obvious that the therapist served some need for the patient that had not been fully teased out in their conversations together, but her role would always compete with other more pressing needs in his life. She had not wanted to confront him with this fact because it made her feel unimportant. She had already invested him with significance in her own life as an interesting, charming, and potentially challenging long-term therapy case. Dealing with her countertransference sadness, and recognizing that perhaps she was just another concrete object in his life, led to feelings of disappointment on her part. After dealing with her own countertransference reaction, however, she was able to face directly the fact that he seemed to operate this way. She recognized that he might never understand this pattern unless they found some way of talking more regularly. The therapist said, "Let's be realistic and try to understand how you do operate day to day. What kinds of things happen on days when you decide at the last minute not to come in?" The therapist was aware that the patient might have deeper fears of getting too close and compelling needs to reenact the rejections he felt from his own mother and perhaps his father as well. Exploration of such issues would have to wait, however, until their relationship had deepened and his capacity to represent feelings had further evolved.

The therapist's immediate goal was to facilitate a relationship that would fully foster some deeper sense of relationship and engagement than the patient had ever experienced with other individuals. To do that meant dealing with his current psychic reality, not some hypothetical or idealized state where he would be functioning at a higher developmental level. The therapist, therefore, empathized with his need to be free to make decisions on what was more important to him at any given moment. She accepted his reality that a meeting with a potential new client was obviously more important to him at a particular moment than making a therapy appointment. The idea of delaying or rescheduling that meeting, making therapy his top priority, was obviously not something he was prepared to do. Similarly, an opportunity to play tennis with a partner whom he was anxious to play with might lead him to schedule an early morning tennis match rather than come to his therapy session. His need at that moment to compete on the tennis court superseded his need to work in therapy or win his therapist's approval. As the therapist verbally empathized with the patient's pattern, he suddenly gave a broad, sheepish grin. "No one has ever been willing to acknowledge just how I operate. I always try to keep this part of the way I relate to people somewhat from them." He called this part of his character "my little thief part." He boyishly smiled and admitted, "I like to get as much bang for my buck as I can."

The therapist's empathy, however, did not change the patient's pattern. He continued to play out his little thief part, but there was a slightly deepening sense of involvement as he and the therapist talked about it directly and didn't pretend to engage in some fancy intellectualized interpretive work. This was the beginning of pattern recognition, in which the patient was able to label his desire to always change to meet the needs of the moment as a "little thief pattern." Nonetheless, the therapist continued to point out that the patient's moment-to-moment need to maximize his pleasures and accomplishments directly conflicted with making progress in therapy. She presented the dilemma to him: Was there some way that they could talk or meet that would allow him to come to all four sessions a week? The patient came up with an innovative plan on his own. He said, "Well, if I could call you each morning when I can't make the original time, then I could come in when I had an opening. Sometimes it might be during lunch or it might be the end of the day. I probably could make four or five sessions a week." The therapist empathized with this wish and indicated that it might be a great solution if she had scheduling flexibility, but cancellations were rare. She would certainly try to fit him in, but that plan wouldn't solve their long-term difficulties.

The patient came up with a second plan. "On days that I can't come in, perhaps we could talk on the telephone. That would at least give us a chance to maintain our progress even if circumstances are such that something else has a higher priority. I can usually squeeze in a half-hour in the morning on days when we're supposed to meet. What usually makes me miss my appointment with you is the fact that I have to be somewhere at 8:00 and our sessions are scheduled for 7:15 A.M. If you're willing to talk on the phone with me for a half-hour of our scheduled 45 minutes, I could still make my meetings or other things that sometimes take priority over the sessions."

The therapist's first reaction was that she would have to think about his proposal. She was afraid that she would be getting into a pattern of acting out with him that would be contrary to the long-term therapeutic objectives. Upon reflection, however, she realized that this man had never had a consistent relationship with anyone, and that this linkage was the first developmental milestone he need to accomplish in therapy. Also, she wondered if perhaps talking on the phone and not having to face the person with whom he was growing more intimate would lessen his anxiety about becoming more involved or engaged. Once she got over her disappointment at not being able to have the kind of relationship she was used to having with most of her patients, the therapist realized that this shift in her therapeutic approach was a step in the right direction. While she would prefer to conduct an in-person session with her patient, she indicated that when direct meetings weren't possible they could use the telephone to connect. She added that she hoped that their telephone time would be the exception rather than the rule.

Soon, the patient began to call the therapist faithfully on the days he couldn't come in. They did talk, and over time her ability to empathize with his concrete way of relating to the world and his need to "manipulate people in circumstances to meet his needs of the moment" was examined and explored. For example, he was able to see that his behavior had a pattern which tended to alienate those very people from whom he wanted things. He began to recognize that his short-term needs sometimes conflicted with his long-term goals. Slowly but surely, however, a deepening sense of relatedness began to evolve as he averaged three to four contacts with his therapist each week, rather than one or two. The therapist could sense in his voice and in his facial expressions a deeper sense of longing and unfreezing. He began literally to let down his guard and no longer related to her in a superficially charming and concrete manner. As this began occurring, he explored the theme of how he needed to leave others first, before they left him. His discussions were not expressed at a representational level with feelings, but were concerned with identifying his patterns of behavior.

After many years of therapy, this man was able to deal with some of the deeper feelings around loss and abandonment that he had experienced as a child. Eventually he reached a level of insight where he could represent these affects. The relationship to his therapist was the first relationship in his life that had any degree of depth and continuing feeling tone to it. Upon reflection, a number of years later, the therapist reasoned that he would have undoubtedly left the relationship with her, as he had done with most of the other relationships in his life, but for two factors. Specifically, if she had been unaware of the importance of each individual's varied ability to relate and had confronted him early on at a higher developmental level representing feelings about relationships, his relationship with her would not have survived. The therapist's concrete negotiations with this patient about how she could better meet his needs—in terms of how he perceived his needs—eventually led to a more engaged therapeutic relationship. In order to have an ongoing relationship with his therapist, the patient identified his primary needs as having to maximize the successes of each day, and shared that need with his therapist.

Interestingly, the tantrums and outbursts that originally sent the patient into therapy turned out to be linked to a boss who was very reminiscent of his father. His boss had become ill and the tantrums were a derivative of some of the angry feelings toward his father's illness and death. This awareness—and the ability to work this through—occurred at the very late phases of therapy when the patient had already become engaged with the therapist and learned how to exert some control over the tantrums without knowing their symbolic meaning. Once he had become somewhat representational, he was able to feel the feelings of anger and anxiety, and didn't act out as much.

Similarly, the patient finally came to the understanding that the degree of his concreteness and manipulative style was, in part, related to his mother's tendency to disengage, leaving him to cut his losses early in life. This kept his pattern of relating quite concrete and superficial. As a baby and toddler, perhaps, he learned in some fundamental intuitive sense not to risk deep pain if his mother cut him off at the slightest expression on his part of anger, assertiveness, or excitement, any of which made her feel uncomfortable. He kept this pattern going by finding that other people disengaged from him when he tried to get his needs met in a concrete, manipulative, or somewhat obnoxious manner. By truly renegotiating the earliest stages of engagement with his therapist, the patient slowly but surely renegotiated earlier developmental missteps, and for the first time became capable of higher level insights into his own behavior.

DIFFICULTY OF ENGAGING AND WORKING WITH A CHILD

The following case study further illustrates the importance of staying with the theme of engagement rather than blindly and inappropriately approaching a patient from a developmental level that is too high.

During his sessions a 7-year-old boy played with action figures and dolls. His preferred activity was to break off the legs of the dolls as well as the head, toes, feet, and fingers. He exhibited an aggressive gleefulness and ran in a frenzied manner around the office after he had dismembered one of the therapist's favored dolls. While the child was acting out he rarely looked at the therapist or conveyed a sense of emotional involvement; yet he was not completely detached, either. He gave the therapist fleeting acknowledgment when he walked into the room, and sometimes ordered the therapist to "Get me that toy," if he couldn't reach it. Little depth of feeling, rapport, pleasure, or emotional reciprocity was in evidence.

The therapist felt that this child was not totally devoid of emotional relatedness, but operated on the surface of things in a shallow, concrete way. Indeed, peers and teachers had similar reactions to this youngster. He often hit and hurt other children when frustrated, and engaged in parallel kinds of play or solitary computer games. There was little interest or investment in a best friend or a particular child, although children were not ignored or avoided when he attended a birthday party. Instead, his pattern of relating was becoming more and more associated with episodic aggressive behavior. His teacher saw him as a bright child who could already do complicated math and was also a good reader—way ahead of his age level in both areas. She added that he did not have much of a relationship with other children and occasionally tried to kick her when he felt frustrated. His aggression was the reason for his coming into therapy.

The therapist attempted to interpret his aggressive behavior and began trying to make connections: "You're being mad at that doll. Is one doll mad at another doll? I wonder what is making them so angry?" The child simply gave her a fleeting look in response and continued to pull off the doll's arms and legs. The therapist decided that this confirmed her interpretation and continued remarking on how angry the little boy was and wondered why he wanted to pull arms and legs off. He would only speak to her, however, about getting him another doll, or asking her to hold a doll while he pulled off its leg because he needed to use both hands.

After six months of therapy, there was little change in the child's presenting behavior or his relationship habit. On reviewing this case, a consulting therapist realized that this youngster had an ability to focus and express intent, but had not mastered the second early stage of ego development—the ability to form an in-depth relationship. The child was obviously preoccupied with aggressive themes (mostly behavioral enactments) and had no capacity for labeling angry feelings on the dolls' part. As mentioned before, his verbal interchanges did not involve feelings, but centered on such concrete negotiations as helping him go to the bathroom or holding a toy for him. The first goal, therefore, was to deepen the quality of engagement in the therapeutic session, and to facilitate this at home since he related in a similar concrete manner to both parents as well.

Since the child was so obviously preoccupied with aggression, it seemed like an appropriate avenue to help him learn to relate more fully. The therapist aimed to use his interest in aggression as a way of fostering a deeper sense of engagement rather than having him verbalize self-evident aggressive themes.

When he next played out aggressive themes by pulling off legs and arms, the therapist would engage him by interacting with him to broaden his thematic range, rather than by simply being a commentator on his behavior. She asked, "Well, which doll are we going to pull the arms and legs off?" She would offer, "Could I hold the leg while you work on the arm?" Do you want me to pull the other arm off while you're pulling this arm off?" In other words, she offered herself as a partner in a behavioral sense, following his lead and his themes. She didn't invent the theme. Her comments were not directed toward empathizing with how angry he must feel in a representational manner, but focused more on what he was doing. She would remark, "You're having a hard time getting that arm off; it seems stuck. What are we going to do about that?" The child would then ask for her assistance. The more she empathized with the frustrations of trying to get an arm or leg off, the more she became a colleague and partner in the child's activity.

While the therapist functioned as the child's interactive partner around the theme of aggression, it was very important for the therapist to pay attention to the little boy's regulatory profile. This youngster appeared more relaxed and connected when the therapist talked in an enthusiastic but low-pitched, soothing voice. Since this youngster overloaded easily (which contributed to his lack of engagement), it was important for the therapist to avoid using an agitated, intense voice. Finding the right vocal, affective, visual, and rhetoric rhythms will foster quality engagement within the therapeutic drama.

Over time, however, the child's affects softened; there were fleeting smiles, warmer looks. He would start sessions with "Do we have some fresh dolls for us to maul today?" and she would pull out dolls whose arms and legs had been reconnected and say,

"Okay, let's go to it." Slowly, the sense of involvement between therapist and child deepened.

When the child became frustrated, however, the therapist was in as much danger as others, and received kicks and balls tossed at her head. Firm limits, including clear gestures, loud voice, and physical restraint were needed throughout the early phase of the therapy.

While therapeutic work continued, the therapist urged the parents to avoid being sideline commentators with this youngster. She counseled them to get involved in much the same manner she had, becoming partners who shared the child's natural interests. These half-hour interludes of "floor time" strengthened the child's feelings of engagement, or relatedness, at home as well.

Over a long period of time, the angry ice encasing this child slowly melted. There were islands of smiles, and warmth. The therapist felt as if she were finally a significant person in his life. The boy began relating to her on a more human level, occasionally asking her a question about her office. Why had she moved the chair, why did she have a different vase or lamp in one place or another (he was very spatially oriented and very sensitive to detail, a fact that emerged in therapy). This seemed to be a preliminary step in actually taking an interest in her as a person. After about a year and a half of this approach, the child would make comments about her style of dress, sometimes poking fun at her, other times complimenting her. He even noted that she seemed to have something on her mind because she wasn't holding the doll quite steady enough as he was pulling off the arms and legs.

As time passed, the child's conversational themes broadened into more age-appropriate areas. There were hurricanes, storms, and dangers, as well as themes of more competitive aggression, rather than simple discussions about dismembering dolls. Most significantly, the boy's sense of relatedness began to deepen, not only with the therapist and parents, but eventually with peers and teachers as well. The work was slow and arduous and only after two-and-a-half years did this youngster eventually begin to be able to represent his feelings. First, he had to learn how to simply engage in a relationship. The reworking of this critical early phase helped him to deal with subsequent developmental levels such as his simple and complex gestural systems.

When the therapist became an interactor and modulator of experience, rather than just a commentator on experience, the groundwork was laid for the child's further development.

Many therapists think of relationship building in terms of taking their little clients for walks or playing chess or checkers with them. They regard this as an early phase of ordinary therapy. To be sure, going outside or playing structured games with children can be helpful and affect the overall therapeutic relationship. What is critical, however, is for the therapist to have a rationale for why he chooses one or another option. A well-related, deeply feeling child, who is depressed and upset because of certain family crises or family conflicts over his anger, may be distracted by such games as checkers or chess, or by too much wooing on the therapist's part. He may be ready to get right down to the business of exploring his feelings.

Alternatively, the patient who has never experienced an intense engagement with someone may feel that a therapist who needs to represent or comment on his feelings is too aloof and unengaging, and unable to help him with his primary problem. He may even find the therapist's behavior somewhat aggressive because it is not meeting his fundamental and basic needs. Following a patient's lead and natural inclinations, engaging him around his desires, is a more natural and more emotionally relevant way to build a therapeutic relationship. In this case it meant pulling off the arms and legs of dolls, rather than distracting him with games of checkers or going on long walks.

Engagement demands that the therapist empathize with a patient's wishes and needs through interaction, through being an interactor-modulator rather than a sideline commentator or distractor. Over a period of time, the child discussed above was able to engage in more normal relationship patterns with peers, teachers, and parents. He became an observably warmer youngster who, when treatment ended, could represent some feelings, even though he was still somewhat constricted around the areas of competition, aggression, and feelings of loss. Because he had made so much progress and was operating more like a typical latency-age child, it was felt that further work with his now flexible parents could help him become more wide-ranging in applying his abilities to different feeling states. The child's family was available to him to meet his needs for continuing his developmental progress.

ENGAGEMENT AND THE ANTISOCIAL INDIVIDUAL

Among the most challenging patients to work with is the antisocial individual.

Developmentally, it is observed that the antisocial individual only exhibits a superficial ability to engage other people around concrete needs. His operating principle seems to be, "What's in it for me?" There is little warmth, intimacy, or range of affect, in terms of the quality of engagement. It is also noticed that at subsequent levels (the behavioral and representational levels), the experiences and affects associated with intimacy, warmth, and empathy are not organized or represented. They are not part of the day-to-day experience of this individual, who early on formed a very impersonal way of relating to the world around him.

Such an individual frequently comes to therapy because of getting into hot water with the law, and seeks help from a clinician only because it is a condition for staying out of jail. This is hardly an ideal situation for successful treatment. Developmentally, however, the therapist recognizes that there are significant difficulties in the patient's negotiation of the stage of engagement. Furthermore, this individual shows little ability to represent experiences having to do with intimacy or to represent experiences involving his own rage and sadistic retaliatory desires. The therapist notes that in some instances the patient cannot organize his behavior and plan it, let alone regard the consequences of his actions. Because he has never experienced true intimacy, the patient isn't even able to be organized with this affect at the behavioral level.

Such individuals may be bright, with good intellectual skills, particularly in the areas of math and science, although they may not be very verbally gifted.

The therapist then sets about creating a structure that offers the patient certain developmental experiences that will help him negotiate territory that was never successfully mastered in the past. The patient needs a therapeutic relationship which is characterized by a great deal of intensity and regularity, in the hopes that, for the first time in his life, some feelings of warmth and affection can arise, due to having frequent access to a warm, caring relationship. Either daily therapy as an outpatient, or as part of some sort of residential program will therefore be necessary. Whether this is individual therapy or a combination of group and individual therapy is less important than the consistency and the intimacy of the relationships. The patient's tendency to act out in situations of anger and rage will dictate whether residential or monitored outpatient care is indicated. The need to show up for therapy, to report in, or undergo urine testing for drug use may be part of such a monitoring system.

Once the appropriate therapeutic setting, or structure, is in place and treatment consistency is present, the next challenge with such an individual is to sustain a quality of engagement. This can perhaps be negotiated while the individual is learning to represent affects around intimacy and warmth. Initially, it may involve having the therapist simply be a part of the person's life. One successful program (Shore and Massimo, 1991) with teenagers with antisocial characteristics involved helping them to negotiate with their bosses at work, learn social skills that were necessary for them to make a go of a job, and work though crises with friends. This program, administered through a mentor-counselor, created a nurturing, empathetic relationship that could not be pushed away, and that could celebrate the good or cushion the bad in the teenager's day-to-day life. It helped the individual be soothed when dysphoric affects or uncomfortable sensations were present. The antisocial teenager is unlikely to be able to explore a feeling of disappointment or sadness when something discouraging occurs. There may be a demonstrated ability to verbalize some feelings around humiliation or annoyance, but more likely the sensate world will be described in terms of feelings of tension, and the desire to hit or hurt. A need for soothing around sleeping difficulties or other disorganizations in the somatic organization of the body may also be present. The ability to soothe, to be available for a relationship, and help through the thick-and-thin of everyday challenges, can often lead to new capacities for intimacy, initially defined around concrete needs.

With a group of "multiproblem" families, in which many parents exhibited the same antisocial characteristics as their children did, it sometimes took a year or eighteen months of helping individuals get their welfare checks, assisting them when they got in difficulties with the law, and arbitrating fights within the extended family, before something beyond a self-absorbed level of "What have you done for me lately?" began characterizing the therapeutic relationship. Often the first sign that the relationship was moving beyond the most concrete, need-fulfilling level was the individual's reference to thinking about the therapist over a weekend or when the therapist had been away for a few days, or a comment about the therapist's clothes or some feature of the therapist's body.

In working with very angry, antisocial patients, and individuals who could only relate on a concrete, need-fulfilling basis, we (Greenspan and Wieder, 1987) developed a therapeutic relationship scale that shows how such individuals work their way up the different developmental levels (see Table 4.1).

As Table 4.1 indicates, the therapist must organize the therapeutic approach to begin at the early developmental levels and work up the hierarchy.

In both routine and challenging therapeutic situations, engagement and forming a relationship is a critical challenge. If unattended to or taken for granted, the therapeutic relationship may be constructed on a weak foundation which will undermine real and stable progress.

There are a large range of challenges to engaging and relating. Individuals who can relate warmly but have fears of getting "too close," chronically self-absorbed individuals who have never

TABLE 4.1
Dimensions of the Therapeutic Relationship: Steps in the Therapeutic Process

Regularity and Stability	Attachment	Process
I. Willingness to meet with an interviewer or therapist to convey concrete concerns or hear about services	I. Interest in having concrete needs met and can be provided by anyone (e.g., food, transportation, etc.)	I. Preliminary communication, including verbal support and information gathering
II. Willingness to schedule meetings again	II. Emotional interest in the person of the therapist (e.g., conveys pleasure or anger when they meet)	II. Ability to observe and report single behaviors or action patterns
III. Meeting according to some predictable pattern	III. Communicates purposefully in attempts to deal with problems	III. Focuses on relationships involved in the behavior–action pattern
IV. Meeting regularly with occasional disruptions	IV. Tolerates discomfort or scary emotions	IV. Self-observing function in relationship to feeling
V. Meeting regularly with no disruptions	V. Feels "known" or accepted in positive and negative aspects	V. Self-observing function in relationship to complex and interactive feeling states
		VI. Self-observing function for thematic and affective elaboration
		VII. Makes connections between the key relationships in life including the therapeutic relationship
		VIII. Identification of patterns in current, therapeutic, and historical relationships to work through problems and facilitate new growth
		IX. Consolidation of new patterns and levels of satisfaction and preparing to separate from the therapeutic relationship
		X. Full consolidation of gains in the context of separating and experiencing a full sense of loss and mourning

been in an intimate relationship during their adult lives, and the antisocial individuals described above illustrate the range of challenges we must attempt to meet. The developmental approach enables us to determine the features of the challenge and to construct the types of experiences most likely to be helpful.

Chapter 5

Boundary-Defining Gestures, Behaviors, and Affects

The third stage and processes of development concern the simplest intentional gestures. The exchange of head nods, smiles, smirks, looks, and so on, not only reassures individuals about their mutually familiar, human culturally specific social signals, it also establishes, maintains, and defines the boundary between them. Each of these rapid signals conveys the intentionality of one person (i.e., his or her boundary) to another person, who responds in kind. Children and adults are exchanging this type of gesture most of the time when they interact or communicate with others. The head nods, smiles, smirks, and body posture changes are easy to take for granted. However, they have an important purpose.

We see this capacity emerge in early infancy when the 6- to 8-month-old reaches out to be picked up, the parent nods, picks the child up, and the child responds by smiling warmly and patting the parent's shoulder. The child is not simply synchronously enjoying the warm affect of the parent and feeling a part of and close to the parent, but is interacting in a highly intentional and deliberate way. His need to be picked up, indicated by his gesture of reaching out, is responded to by a logical and causally related counterreaction. The parent smiles and reaches down to the child, rewarding him with warmly appropriate affect and behavior.

The child next responds to the parent's causal, highly differentiated behavioral and affective interaction, with a behavioral interaction of his own—smiling and patting the parent's shoulder. As these interactions occur, we are seeing more than mere playful activity between an infant and his parent; a series of communications is taking place that help the infant define his boundary and partially define who he is. To be sure, the infant's wish is not experienced in the same symbolic verbal form as it is for an adult; an infant does not think to himself, "I want to be picked up," because he does not yet have the words. However, he is feeling a sense of intention, desire, or wish that gets communicated through his motor gestures. When his gesture is responded to in an appropriate way by his parents, the nascent sense of "me," or self, is given a sense of validity and credibility. The "me" begins taking on definition from the feedback it receives from the world.

These feedback loops can be thought of as opening and closing circles of communication. When the infant reaches out on his own initiative, he opens a circle. A parent extends his arms and picks him up in response. When the infant then smiles contentedly and builds on the parent's response, the circle of communication is closed. Obviously, this sets the stage for the opening and closing of circles of communication to continue. The infant's smile may cause the parent to murmur in delight. The infant may then make some gurgling and cooing sounds and reach out to touch his parent's hair, while the parent makes some more sounds of delight. A spiraling sequence of communication circles are being opened and closed in this nonverbal interaction. Thus, we see simple gestures, that define boundaries, occurring in sequence to create a kind of collaborative dialogue.

At this stage, we are not necessarily talking about the child's sense of himself as a whole person, interacting with another person. At a minimum, there is a wish or intention being expressed that is getting a logical and causal reaction leading to another intention or reaction. These circles of communication involve gestures such as looking and counterlooking, smiling, vocalizing, frowning, and/or looking angry or annoyed.

When this early stage of boundary definition is reached involving the simplest interchange of gestures, from the developmental perspective we ask: Are these boundary-defining gestures actually occurring? Are they helping the individual, infant or adult, meet his or her needs? It is interesting to observe in adults and older children how many thousands of times we perform these boundary-defining gestures in any five-minute conversation with another person. It is also easy to forget or not be aware of how important these defining gestures are in maintaining our sense of "primary differentiation," or our earliest sense of differentiation.

Try relating to a person who is stone-faced or completely poker-faced, for example. There is no feedback, and a sense of confusion and anxiety mounts quickly. Try giving a talk in front of a group where the people in the first ten rows look as if their eyes are glazed and their backs are ramrod stiff. In fact, the more anxious one is, the more one relies on such reciprocal, often subtle, boundary-defining cues, as head nodding, facial expressions, and a sparkle in the eye. They create an interpersonal, differentiated context for communication and create a sense of security. Some individuals, of course, are better able to maintain themselves with internal cuing. They can talk themselves through a situation when they're not getting much external feedback. Others are more dependent on the immediacy of moment-to-moment external cues.

In infancy, however, few children can deal for very long with a lack of external cues and with only self-cuing. If the feedback system is lacking for an 8-month-old, for example, the child soon withdraws or becomes chaotic and disorganized. He may become focused on inanimate objects in the environment which provide the feedback of noise or texture. He may bang a block on the floor. As a child gets older, his self-cuing ability improves and he can maintain some boundary definition for short and then eventually longer periods of time. Some children develop this capacity more fully, while others remain more dependent on external cuing. The child's other personality attributes seem to determine his or her reliance on internal and external feedback.

When we think about boundaries in a psychological sense, we focus on borders between the sense of self and the sense of nonself, or the other. We often discuss these boundaries in representational or symbolic terms, such as how one organizes feelings and thoughts about oneself and separates these from feelings and thoughts about another. Such discussions help both therapist and patient avoid confusion over whose feelings are whose. Undermining of reality, projections, and other types of massive distortions are less likely to occur when there are solid representational ego boundaries.

As indicated above, however, an earlier phase in boundary development concerns the preverbal, prerepresentational aspects of relationships. These simple boundary-defining gestures in adults are played out in any interpersonal situation, including psychotherapy. We observe that adults have numerous ways of acknowledging each other in which a respect for each other's boundaries is demonstrated. The glances exchanged between two people are an acknowledgment of their mutual existence.

When a patient looks at his therapist and the therapist looks back with a warm smile, the patient relaxes and a circle of communication is opened and closed. The patient opens the circle by looking and tacitly communicating, "How are you going to greet me?" The therapist conveys a sense of safety and acceptance, and the patient then relaxes, silently communicating that he accepts the therapist's overture. The patient feels safe and secure in the context of having his personhood, or boundaried self, recognized.

Imagine what would happen if one's simplest gesture were ignored. Assume a therapist is preoccupied or busy, or thinking about another patient when his next patient comes into the office. The patient looks expectantly with eager eyes at the therapist, who is distracted and extends a kind of blank, spacey look at the patient. In such a situation, the patient will usually feel momentarily anxious and disorganized. He may withdraw or go into some rote, perseverative-type behavior, such as taking his hat or jacket off, finding his favorite spot on the chair, or lying down on the couch. Alternatively, the patient may up the stakes and try to intrude into the therapist's world by asking, "Is everything okay?" He may increase the level of gestural communication by raising his voice. If the patient has the fortitude and strength to up the gestural stakes again, by speaking louder, repeating comments, shooting penetrating looks, clearing his throat, or otherwise trying to get the therapist's attention, there is a good likelihood that some gestural circles will be opened and closed and the patient will be recognized. Obviously, many patients do not have this fortitude and some will withdraw, become perseverative, self-absorbed, or disorganized in response to a therapist's lack of boundary-defining response.

If the nonverbal communications going on between patient and therapist, or any two people for that matter, are observed, it becomes apparent that an enormous number of these gestures are exchanged, or not exchanged, as the case may be. Greeting and leave-taking are only a few of the numerous gestural negotiations that occur throughout a therapeutic session. It is particularly interesting to observe these communications that are exchanged around the particular themes and affects that the patient is negotiating. Whatever the patient's particular drama, whether it involves dependency issues, sex, loss of love, or aggression, there may be differences in the ability of the therapist and the patient to negotiate the simplest boundary-defining gestures.

Consider the following examples.

When a patient expressed aggression and anger, discussing how he was tempted to hit his wife, the therapist responded to the patient's verbal comments with lots of acknowledging vocalizations like "Aha, aha," or "ah." Or he suggested, "Tell me more about that." The rhythm of the therapist's voice was very responsive to the patient's own vocalizations. Gestural communication was exchanged when the therapist took note of the patient's breathing rhythm and body posture.

This exchange of nonverbal cues can occur with the patient and therapist facing one another, or with the patient reclining on a couch. Even though a visual link is cut off when the patient is lying on the couch, the therapist's and patient's vocal rhythms, body postures, and breathing patterns can still connect. Patients often sense the therapist's movements even when they can't see him or her.

The patient who freely expressed feelings of anger toward his wife spoke about dependency needs and longings, and issues of closeness and dependency; however, he had a great deal of difficulty verbalizing his distress. When it came to those issues, the therapist did not give him acknowledging hums or aha's or the equivalent of "Tell me more." Instead, the therapist fell silent, rationalizing his own silence under the guise of abstinence and neutrality. The therapist was further out of sync with the patient, interrupting in the middle of the patient's stumbling vocalization. The situation was analogous to a baby reaching out to be picked up, and a parent responding by saying, "You've got a spot on your shirt," and then looking at the spot on the shirt. There's no validating, reciprocal response to the child's overture, no boundary-defining response to the baby's initiative. Instead, a distorting, interfering response confuses the baby and redirects his attention.

Similarly, when the patient spoke about "wanting more," and the therapist, in the middle of the patient's vocalizations, began shifting his breathing rhythm and body posture, and interjected his "aha" before the patient had finished his thought, the patient experienced the same sort of undermining and confusing rebuff. These simple boundary-defining gestures can have boundary-confirming and validating effects or, alternatively, can create disorganizing effects that lead the patient to become self-absorbed, perseverative, or involved in patterns of motor discharge and acting out.

Sometimes it is the intensity of affect, rather than the theme, that leads to the disruption of these boundary-defining gestures. A middle-aged man came in and was enraged at his therapist for billing him for a missed session. The therapist, who was easily overloaded with other people's intense rages, froze. He ventured no "uh huh's," head nods, or open-eye acknowledgment of his concern, and instead looked up with a stunned, but flat expression. The therapist's initial gesture, his paralyzed look, offered the patient a blank stare instead of further reciprocity. The patient responded to the circumstances by remaining disorganized and overwrought. His communications became less logical and more disorganized, bringing in associations from the past about various types of injuries and insults. His motor and vocal gestures also became more disorganized. He paced the floor, repeated himself, and became less and less modulated in his vocal tone and motor control of his body.

The original affect overload was now escalated, playing itself out in the context of a system of communication that lacked boundary-defining interactions. Alternatively, if the therapist had not become overloaded by the patient's tirade, he could have responded to him in a variety of gestural ways. It was not so critical which gestural mode he chose to pursue; the key was to validate the patient's sense of self by responding with some boundary-defining gestures. Some may do it with supportive "aha's" or offering an open, responsive, but changing facial expression. Others may choose to get into a more active dialogue, helping the patient examine the issue. The approach that is most appropriate may have to do with the patient's dynamics and the particular stage of the therapy that he has reached. But common to most successful therapeutic approaches will be an ability of the therapist to engage the patient in boundary-defining gesturing.

If such a tirade occurs in the context of a psychoanalytic hour when the patient is not facing the therapist, it is worth reiterating here that gestures can be communicated through vocal tone, breathing rhythms, body posture, and subtle variations of affect. The patient who is not in visual contact with the therapist raises several important technical issues. Which types of patient should always have the visual channel open to them? When is it appropriate to use intensive, in-depth psychological approaches, four and five times a week, including classical psychoanalysis (which by definition involves lying down)? Under what circumstances are parameters, or simply a redefinition of what constitutes analytic technique in developmental terms, necessary? Different patients may require different types of sensory affective regulatory patterns, including various types of engagement and reciprocal gesturing involving the visual modality. A developmentally based approach would gear the approach to the patient's profile, although baseline conditions are always helpful for a particular therapeutic approach. The baseline conditions, however, have to be defined in the context of what is developmentally appropriate. The prerepresentational, ego-enhancing qualities of the interaction between therapist and patient need always to be a key part of the baseline considerations of the structure of each patient's therapy.

The therapist basically uses two technical approaches when dealing with the boundary-defining aspects of the therapeutic process. One technical approach, as has already been suggested, is to make sure that boundary-defining reciprocal gestures are occurring in a general sense, from the patient's opening look to the gestures involved in helping the patient decide where to sit. This, then, establishes the general preverbal, behavioral–gestural pattern of boundary definition. Obviously some patients require focus on this issue more than others. The patient mentioned earlier reached out and pulled the therapist in by raising his voice a little bit or speeding up the rhythm of his vocalizations to draw a response from the therapist. This is a patient who obviously has good boundary definition and can use a variety of motor, vocal, and affective gestures to keep boundaries defined in most settings, even in a setting where the environment is not providing it. With a sleepy, but benign and warm therapist, such a patient may work through a fear of being rejected. The patient only needs the therapist not to act out aggressively or in a hostile, rejecting manner.

Alternatively, there are patients who either become disorganized, withdrawn, self-absorbed, perseverative, or get into modes of behavioral motor discharge—acting out when boundary-defining interactions are absent. Many of these patients cannot easily draw the therapist in. They seem more vulnerable to the vicissitudes of the gestural-defining qualities of their environment. In other words, they organize and differentiate with certain individuals and become highly disorganized with others. Often patients will leave a therapist who does not provide needed gestural support, and this is an important reason for early rupture in many therapies.

For such patients, goals in therapy are to establish these boundary-defining nonverbal communications. One may think about this boundary-defining operation as being similar to Freud's comments about the need for external supports for the superego. In the absence of superego support, he felt, patients regressed in their ability to provide the self-observing, self-monitoring, and inhibiting functions of the superego. Clinically one sees that certain patients can easily find environments that provide this minimal superego support. Others will be skillful at finding environments that do not have this support and therefore they regress more easily. Freud also explored the need for a balance of input from the intrapsychic experience and experience outside one's own person to maintain reality testing. Where feedback is cut off in either direction, the ego has a harder time maintaining the balance between fantasy and reality.

Rapaport (1959) elaborated on Freud's (1905) comments about the need for balanced stimulus nutriment or experiences from inside and outside. In both Freud's original comment and Rapaport's elaboration, there is a recognition that intrapsychic structure is always dependent on a continuing balance of internal and external nutriments. One may think of these prerepresentational ego-supporting types of interactions as falling within the general framework that Freud and Rapaport presented. With a developmental perspective, however, we go beyond a general notion of stimulus nutriment, and specifically define the quality and types of experience that are necessary for each stage of ego development. Therefore, the therapist's first goal is to make sure, particularly for the patients who need it the most, that the general preverbal behaviors and gestures that are necessary for boundary definition are present in the interaction patterns between the two of them.

Second, the therapist tries to make certain that his own personality style is not an impediment, either due to countertransference patterns or to limitations in his own personality. (No therapist is completely flexible, but the more he is aware of his own patterns, the more he can enhance his effectiveness.) The therapist, therefore, needs to be aware of his own response in terms of preverbal gestural ego boundary-defining interactions, different themes and affects the patient communicates, and the intensity of these affects. The therapist needs to know if he is limited in his most basic abilities to enter into these gesturally defining interactions by his own reactions to dependency, aggression, sexual exploration, curiosity, intense anger, or lust. Probably the best person the therapist can check this out with is another colleague and other intimates, particularly his spouse and children, to find out where and when he seems to "be out of it." If he is a psychoanalytically trained therapist, he may have previously ignored this issue in his own analysis because of the focus on symbolic and representational elaboration and the lack of focus on prerepresentational types of experiences.

In addition to attempting, through self-awareness and sheer diligence, to create these boundary-defining interaction patterns as part of the therapeutic process, the therapist has another therapeutic tool at his disposal, a device that is particularly useful for those patients who can identify and possibly represent behavioral patterns and have some self-observation of these patterns. For these patients, where there is an evident deficit in the earliest kind of gestural and interactive negotiations, the therapist seeks to draw the patient's attention to the gestural interactions. He points to the patient's own tendencies to become disorganized, withdrawn, self-absorbed, perseverative, or involved in behavioral acting-out patterns when certain feedback is not present. To be sure, no matter how gifted a clinician, there will be times in which the therapist is not ideally "defining" in such situations and the patient will enter into some of his characteristic maladaptive patterns. This is a golden opportunity to examine these patterns, not only in relationship to internal affect cues, particularly drive derivatives, or particular external life circumstances, but in terms of the here-and-now dynamics of the therapist–patient interaction, and the perception the patient may have about the interaction.

The therapist may review what just happened and realize that he was stone-faced or lacking in his usual responsiveness. This insight may lead the patient to examine how he does in situations with the therapist and with others where this boundary-defining interaction is not present. This second tactic fits into the traditional role of therapists in terms of self-observation and reflection, only here the emphasis is on the actual here-and-now interaction at the very simple gestural level. This becomes viewed as a precipitant of various kinds of maladaptive defensive patterns, many of which are also at the behavioral, rather than representational, level.

As we examine these two therapeutic techniques, it is also important to consider them in relationship to the different challenges a patient will generate for the therapist. For example, what does one do with a patient who offers very little gesturing and easily becomes rigid and aloof? Or the patient who is gesturing so frantically, as part of a verbal tirade, that there seems little opportunity to interact? Or how about the patient who, in a paranoid outburst, distorts what the therapist feels his intention to be? In other words, how does a therapist maintain this sort of boundary-defining gestural interaction with the patient who is throwing up multiple roadblocks? And how does he draw the patient's attention to it, after he has tried to maintain some boundary-defining patterns?

As a caveat, one always should try to engage the patient, help the patient regulate, and enter into boundary-defining interactions prior to helping the patient look at his patterns. It will usually only worsen the situation if the clinician tries to help a patient "clarify" or "interpret" a pattern while the patient is not engaged, regulated, or involved in the simplest boundary-defining interactions that provide validity to the fact that there is a sense of "me" and a sense of "you." The patient may abruptly depart the session, further act out, or become self-absorbed. Clarifications rarely work unless the preconditions having to do with regulation, engagement, and boundary-defining gestural interactions are in place.

Patients who do not have these abilities or who lose them when they are facing such themes as aggression and dependency, or patients who get overloaded, overwhelmed, and then lose the simplest of gestural abilities, will tend to distort interaction patterns to a massive or minimal degree. Either of these situations can be quite challenging.

A patient is likely to distort those experiences that have to do with boundary definitions. For example, such a patient is likely to distort themes and interactions having to do with safety and danger. He often has a distorted sense of intentionality. He asks himself, "Did you initiate it or did I initiate it?" The patient is also likely to distort experiences having to do with the sources of anger or aggression, since those affects are closely related to intentions. He is also likely to distort experiences related to his core sense of self, not being clear about what is "me" and "not-me."

In fact, one can think of reality testing as occurring on two levels: an early, behavioral, gesturally defining level (a core sense of what is "me" as it interacts gesturally with "you"), and a later level having to do with symbolic meanings. One could have a good core sense of "me" and "you," but still get confused about particular symbolic themes and dramas involving sexuality, aggression, or dependency. Such a person, for example, who has problems only at the developmentally more advanced level is likely to behave and gesture appropriately, but talk in a confused manner. The typical well-functioning but seemingly verbally disorganized hysteric would be a good example of such an individual. They behave in an organized, intentional way, give off interactive defining gestures, but talk in a free-associative style. Their problem lies more at the level of symbolic differentiation than at the presymbolic differentiation stage.

Alternatively, the psychopath or paranoid schizophrenic behaves unrealistically and makes judgments about the world based on unrealistic perceptions of intentions ("I have to kill people before they kill me"). He or she does not offer realistic and logical reciprocal gestures, and is likely to have a distorted sense of self at a much deeper level, even though occasionally they may talk logically. Character pathology centering on themes of safety and danger may illustrate a milder form of difficulties related to this stage.

How should one assist the patients who present these special challenges, using the general technical principle discussed above? First, a therapist needs to be aware of his own tendencies to become undifferentiated in his interaction patterns with the patient. The patient may initially, for example, look angrily at the therapist, assuming he or she has somehow done something that is unsafe, or that smacks of betrayal. The therapist is shocked by the patient's facial expressions which radiate anger, annoyance, and suspicion. In the therapist's eyes, this is not a reasonable person trying to discuss whose reality is more appropriate. This is not a person who is coming in and saying, "I understand your perspective about the missed session and the bill, but I thought I gave you enough advance notice, and maybe you should consider my perspective too. Frankly, I'm mad at you." (This developmentally advanced patient is mad, but is capable of maintaining some warm, affective contact and defining gestural interactions.) The person with a more primary difficulty at the gestural level looks suspicious and angry, and the therapist feels that the relationship itself is in danger. The patient's suspiciousness permeates his affect. There is no self-observing capacity; there is only a direct or indirect cry of "You make me unsafe" or "I am unsafe." Here it is important for the therapist to again fall back on his two techniques. The first one is to maintain gestural interaction with the patient as well as engagement and self-regulation. It is important not to fall into the patient's trap, to get into a power struggle with the patient, or into an undifferentiated mode of interaction in which the therapist's own gestures confirm the patient's suspicions. The patient whose furious glare is met with the therapist's own angry tone or heated facial expression (in itself a response to a threatening situation) feels that his own gesturing has been validated. The patient's distortion is thus maintained, or even worsened.

The therapist who is unnecessarily silent or self-absorbed will further disorganize the patient or possibly lead him to intense aggression. On the other hand, rather than offer a countertransference, acting-out, counterreaction in the gestural mode, the therapist who maintains his own gestural integrity and keeps trying to reach the patient will provide a potentially growth-producing therapeutic experience. It is important to underscore that this is not a corrective emotional experience in the sense that some therapists may choose to employ manipulations to bring out a certain affect in the patient. Rather, here the therapist is providing a sense of integrity about the patient's gestural system and maintaining his gestural interaction. The angry glare should be met with understanding, head nods, and vocal tone. To patronize the patient by saying, in a high-pitched, anxious tone, "I understand just how you feel, tell me more about it," conveys a sense of fear, or threat, or an attempt to get the upper hand. The truly empathetic counterreaction at the gestural level is one in which the therapist's open, accepting eye contact, nodding head, and "aha," takes the patient seriously but maintains a respectful, yet accepting, warm attitude. Most mature, experienced therapists will do this automatically without thinking about it. Many, however, can easily get drawn into other kinds of patterns.

The therapist's respect for the regulatory side of the environment is also critical for the patient who is getting more and more agitated. (This respect is made evident by the therapist not raising his voice too much, maintaining a calming, soothing vocal tone, and maximizing the warmth of the engagement.) The therapist conveys, through his gestures, a sense of continuing regulation and acceptance, as well as interaction through opening and closing of gestural circles of communication. The therapist does not avoid sounds, moving his chair if he wishes, nor does he avoid the stares of the patient. He does not invade the patient's space with an angry counterglare, nor does he look down and become evasive. Instead, he responds to the patient's irritated and angry posture with soothing, warm, accepting respectful gestures of his own. Over time, he helps the patient see that his own gestures are met with countergestures which have a different quality and tone to them. The patient learns that gestural interaction can be maintained even under the pressure of intense, angry, and suspicious affect. This is a critical lesson for both therapist and patient. The patient's angry, critical affect should not be met with countercritical affect or with overly patronizing, soppy clichés. Instead, such patients should be responded to with countergestures that convey a respectful, warm, accepting attitude.

Another gestural challenge is posed by individuals who become more silent, withdrawn, pensive, and stone-faced themselves. Here it is easy for the therapist to become involved in a waiting game in which he becomes countersilent, waiting for the patient to come to him. This power struggle and dominating orientation of the therapist is readily rationalized as, "They're not going to manipulate me." Therapists love to dominate patients under the rationalization that the patient is being manipulative. What is needed in a situation where the patient is truly having a difficulty at the gestural level is for the therapist once again to maintain his evenly hovering warmth and attention. He continues to offer welcoming gestural opportunities through his eyes, head nods, and through his desire to understand the patient's plight and offer supportive comments about how the patient might feel. He is constantly trying to woo the patient back into gestural interaction. Facial expressions, more animated than usual in terms of mouth movement, wide-open eyes, and affirming head nods, are ways of urging the patient back into a gestural interaction. Again, this is not a manipulative ploy, it is much the same as a parent's intuitive behavior when a child is momentarily so overwhelmed or angry that they cannot verbally respond.

Sometimes a disorganized person throws so many behaviors, affects, and gestures at the therapist that the therapist, too, begins to feel a little disorganized. He maintains his equilibrium, rather than heightening up his own gestural counterresponses to a manic level, or toning down and being overwhelmed and fragmented by the patient. The therapist tries to help the patient reorganize his gestures. He may speed up momentarily to the person's gestural level with quickened head nods and vocalizations and convey his sense of understanding. Then he may slowly try to pull the patient down to a slightly more relaxed, slower-paced level where he or she can open and close many gestural communication circles. One can picture a skillful therapist doing this, talking rapidly with heightened affect to the patient and gradually slowing the rhythm of his speech, modulating the nodding of his head until the patient relaxes with him. This effort precedes helping the patient look at these gestural patterns. The first therapeutic goal is to help the patient establish or reengage in a baseline of reciprocal boundary-defining gestural interactions. We do this with countergesturing, which, in principle, doesn't offer an acting-out counterreaction to the patient, but rather maintains the integrity of the gestural system, respecting the patient's individual differences. His need to be engaged, his need to be slowed down, and his need to have a respectful attitude exhibited toward his distortions are thus met.

CLINICAL ILLUSTRATIONS

Consider the following additional clinical examples of how one deals therapeutically with someone who has difficulty at this level.

EXAMPLE 1

A 6-year-old child came into the office, sat down on the floor in the midst of some toys, and was completely paralyzed. There were no smiles, facial gestures, or playful behaviors in evidence. His mother came in with him and remained on the couch, trying to give the therapist the freedom to play with the little boy. The child stared off at an object on the wall and appeared frozen with anxiety. The therapist knew he had to tap into the sense of relatedness the boy exhibited in the waiting room where he clung to his mother. In an attempt to get some communication going, the therapist eschewed comments about the boy's apparent fear or "helpful" remarks directing the child's attention to the toys. Such comments would have assumed that the boy was able to represent his feelings. If he could represent his feelings well enough to be relaxed by such comments, the boy would not have appeared to be quite so frozen and anxious. Instead, the therapist recognized that what was missing here was not a state of attention, since the child attended to a spot on the wall; nor did he lack the ability to relate, since he clung to his mother even while in a state of anxiety. The child was neither detached, aloof, nor aimless in the therapist's presence.

The therapist did, however, need to establish some way to interact with the patient using the simplest of gestures. Ordinarily, a child comes into the room and there are little glances and perhaps a silly handshake exchanged between therapist and patient. The therapist may point to a toy and the youngster might smile knowingly, realizing that they are his to play with. This scenario did not occur with this youngster. The therapist picked up a stuffed animal that the child glanced at, and took the toy and held it up to see if the child wanted to play with it. Still, the boy looked frozen and wouldn't even nod. When the therapist held this toy close to the child to see if he would reach out and grab it, as even an 8-month-old infant might do, there was no response. Then the child looked at a car and the therapist raced the car in his direction, moving it closer to his body. Still no response—not even a smile, brief verbalization, or shift in body posture.

Frustrated, the therapist tried to create a circumstance in which the child would have no choice but to gesture to him. He took a toy that the 6-year-old was looking at, building on the child's natural interest, and gently asked his permission to put the toy on his leg. The child was now in a bind, because to do nothing would leave the toy, a stuffed animal, on his leg (which he might not want). To say "No" would be entering into communication with the therapist, which presumably would not be easy to do.

The therapist slowly moved the animal closer and closer, consciously trying not to overwhelm the child. He asked, "Is it okay if I put this little dog on your leg, because he would like to sit right on top of your knee?'' The child sat rigidly, with his legs crossed. He maintained a serious facial expression as the little doggie slowly climbed up to his knee. The therapist reassured him that he would be happy to take it off his knee if he didn't want it there. Most significantly, he used gestures to cue the child in on his options. Pointing a finger at the dog would leave the toy where it was; pointing toward the floor would cause the toy to be removed. All the youngster had to do was to point one little finger to communicate his desires to the therapist.

With that encouragement, the child was able very slowly, and with painstaking effort, to take his finger and point to the floor, indicating he wanted the little dog to be put on the floor. The therapist followed his gesture and took the dog and put it on the floor. The first communication between patient and therapist was thus facilitated by a simple gesture. The pair then continued their game, with the therapist slowly putting the dog on the other knee. He gestured to the child, using facial expressions, pointing fingers, indicating that all the little boy had to do was to point to the floor or his knee to indicate his preference. He pointed and the therapist followed his wishes and put the toy on the floor. The therapist then knocked a toy off his own knee and as he placed it on the boy's knee, the boy knocked it off himself. Pretty soon a little interactive game developed and the boy would start to knock a toy off even before it actually reached his knee.

After a couple of sessions, facial expressions and words like, "No, dog away" were being exchanged. At subsequent meetings, the child would get bold enough to take a toy and begin moving it toward the therapist's toy, exploring a toy-to-toy dialogue using gestures. Slowly but surely the patient and therapist were off and running into more elaborate communications, opening and closing gestural circles. To have persisted in empathizing with the child's anxiety or anger at a verbal representational level, when he was having a hard time engaging at the gestural level, would have been a tactical error.

To summarize: always initially approach a patient from his or her developmental level. If the earlier levels are not fully in place, begin with them and work up. For example, if necessary, foster attention, foster engagement, work toward using two-way, simple, self-defining gestural communications. As the therapist works up the developmental ladder, he or she can reach more representational forms of communication. Some children may only be experiencing a temporary regression due to anxiety and be capable of representational interaction, but still need to be met at the gestural level because of the degree of the regression accompanying the anxiety. Other children may be at that level in a more permanent or chronic sense, if they have never learned to go beyond the simple gestural level. They need a lot of slower-paced, patient work.

The youngster discussed above had capacities to verbalize and use complex gestural interactions, but not represent affects. The anxiety of coming in to see the therapist led him to regress to a level where he was incapable of negotiating even simple gestures. Once he grew comfortable working with simple gestures, he quickly progressed up to the use of complex gestures because this was more a regressive loss of ego capacities, rather than a chronic lack of them. In either event, the therapeutic approach might have been similar, although in this case the recovery to his previous baseline level was rapid once the simple interactive gestures became mobilized.

EXAMPLE 2

The following clinical example concerns a young man whose style of verbal and gestural engagement was a one-way street, which lacked true interactions even at the simplest gestural level. The patient enjoyed coming in. He would make brief eye contact with the therapist, and then look out the window while he talked about what was on his mind. He rarely abstracted affects and related behavioral descriptions of his life. Whenever the therapist commented on these behavioral descriptions with questions, asking for more elaboration, the young man ignored the therapist and continued his own soliloquy. He seemed to enjoy the presence of the therapist, clearly wanting someone to be listening to him, but at the same time did not close any circles that the therapist initiated and instead only closed his own circles.

It was noted that while he smiled, frowned, and changed body postures, which the therapist tried to respond to, the patient almost never responded to the therapist's simplest nonverbal gestures. The therapist would raise his voice or lift his hand as a signal that he was ready to talk, but the patient would continue his monologue, not giving the therapist room to enter into the conversation. Similarly, when the hour was over, the therapist would begin to shuffle in his seat and try to gracefully define his own exit from the session by verbally interrupting the patient and displaying such nonverbal signals as shifting his body posture and opening his appointment book. This patient, however, kept going on and on as though the therapist were an eager listener, and made no gestures to close the session.

The therapist, initially thinking that his patient—who was both a mathematician and an inventor—was quite bright and representational, proffered all kinds of verbal comments about how self-absorbed the patient seemed. He suggested that the patient was impervious to other people's thoughts and comments (this pattern was evident in other areas of his life), and remarked on how passive, aggressive, and angry he must be. None of these comments was particularly helpful. The patient kept right on talking in his own way, following his own agenda.

Interestingly, this young man had lost both his parents in a car accident when he was 9 months old, and had been raised by an aunt and uncle who already had grown children. They were somewhat elderly, and seemed to grant his every whim. He felt they loved him very much, yet they never set any limits or required him to do anything, which ill prepared him for the challenges of later life. He described them as "hanging on his every word" as he would talk to them for hours and hours in much the same way he interacted with the therapist.

Discussing his historical perspective had little impact on the patient and it was noted that he rarely abstracted affects or got involved with very complex comparisons of different behavioral patterns. Concepts such as, "When I do this, someone else does that," went over his head. The therapist came to realize that this person was capable of simple, directed complex gestures, but couldn't fathom the reciprocal nature of either simple or complex gestures. He tried to organize his intervention strategy by meeting this patient at his own developmental level and acting as a modulator and interactor. This meant fostering simple interactive gestures and then eventually moving on to complex gestures.

How should a simple therapeutic interaction be structured? This man liked to command center stage, but was unwilling to assert himself beyond saying what was on his mind. The therapist felt that he could deal with two issues at once: the man's passivity and his imperviousness to another person's side of the simplest gestural communication. When the patient would talk, the therapist would deliberately frame his question, "What did she say after you said that?" The patient, ignoring the therapist, would plow on and continue with his story. Instead of getting frustrated and point out once again that the patient was being self-absorbed, passive-aggressive, or tuning out, the therapist made his remarks more direct. He would say with a direct but gentle, supportive tone, "Don't you want to answer my questions?" The patient tried to ignore that, but the therapist would persevere, gently saying, "Wait, I wanted to hear more of what you were saying, but I noticed you didn't answer my question." The therapist insisted on getting a reply before he permitted the patient to go on. He became a gentle, warm pain in the neck, repeating that simple question like a mantra.

Finally, the patient began saying, "No, I don't want to answer your question. I want to finish my story first."

The therapist would say, "Well, all right. I just didn't know. I need a signal from you."

When the patient looked irritated, the therapist would say, "It seems to me that you are not pleased with my having interrupted you."

The patient would say things like, "Well, what else have you discovered, Sherlock?"

The therapist would then say, "You know, if you don't tell me to shut up or that you want to finish your story uninterrupted, I don't know how to proceed. Is there some way that we can signal to each other more effectively than we have been?"

"What do you mean?" the patient asked.

The therapist explained, "Well, while you are talking about some things that are important to you, I may want to ask a question or clarify or amplify something, but often you will go on without paying attention to what I have said. I don't know whether you haven't heard what I am saying or you don't wish to comment on it, or whether you find the question dumb or stupid. We need to find some way to communicate. I need to let you know when I have something to ask, clarify, or interact with you about. You need some way to signal back to me if it's hard to interrupt your flow of thought. You can do it by answering verbally or finding some other way to let me know."

The patient looked at the therapist and pondered a while. Then, smiling, he said, "Well, how about if I do this. When I put my hand up, like the corner policeman, that means 'no' and I want you to shut up. When I move my hand in a welcoming way, like the policeman does when he wants the traffic to advance, that means 'please continue with your question' and that I want to respond to it. In that way, I don't have to interrupt my thoughts as much and you'll know what I want."

The therapist replied, "That sounds like a marvelous idea. Let's try it."

For the next three months, the patient and therapist utilized this system of hand signals. Accompanying these simple, narrow, gestural interactions were the therapist's vocalizations, shifts in body posture, and responsive facial expressions. This was the beginning of a two-way method of communication and a two-way gestural system with a little more implied self-definition and recognition of the distance of another person.

As this gestural conversation occurred, the patient began verbalizing more details about other people in his life besides himself. Before that, he had always zeroed in on his reaction to others, rather than talking about other people in their own right and trying to describe their patterns. Although this patient never reached the point where he could represent feelings and then make sense of some of his earlier patterns and his need to be one-directional in his interactions, it was clear that as a first step it was important to relate to him at this developmental level in a concrete, here-and-now way. Therefore, the issue of two-way gestural communication was negotiated within the context of the therapeutic relationship, and not bypassed.

Typically, with a patient like this, interpretive kinds of comment will work around rather than on an issue. The gestural facilitating kind of interventions described above helped the patient to deal with the therapist in an interactive gestural mode, giving the therapist clear feedback about the patient's desires. For most patients this would not even be an issue. There would be a natural ebb and flow and an easy rhythm of interaction. But for the self-absorbed, passive patient who doesn't close circles even gesturally, this step must be taken before verbal abstractions and affective elaborations are possible in a meaningful sense.

EXAMPLE 3

A third example, which focuses on the gestural level of communication, involved a middle-aged man who was experiencing marital difficulties. He mentioned that he wanted his wife to finish her studies as a lawyer because he felt she was extremely talented. He was himself a successful attorney. He felt his wife was far more talented than he and looked forward to her becoming a litigator and being the "star" of the family. He had many reasons for admiring his wife and was fixed on the idea that she would be the star of the family and that through her, the family would achieve some special "greatness" that he felt that he, alone, had not provided. They had three small children all under the age of 6. The mother was finishing her schooling part-time and taking care of the children as well. While she was finishing her schooling, she was also getting some work experience in a law office where they utilized her unique talent as a legal assistant.

The therapist empathized with this man's desire to have his wife be a superstar, but added that he could see that she might feel like she wanted to be an at-home mother to their three children. At this the man flew into an agitated rage. He started speaking so rapidly that it would be appropriately characterized as a hypomanic state. His words were spit out; his affect became intense, agitated, and angry; and his thinking focused on the importance of his wife finishing law school and taking on big cases that would help mankind. His thinking became somewhat disorganized although he stayed in his general thematic area. The therapist made the mistake during this state of agitation, which, interestingly, was fairly characteristic of this man whenever he became anxious, of trying to keep the debate at the level of content and at the level of representative affect. The therapist first debated the merits of outside work versus at-home motherhood, and whose right it is to decide.

In arguing the merits of his case, the man simply became more and more agitated and his speech and thoughts speeded up becoming more disorganized. When the therapist tried to shift gears and talk about how angry and agitated the man seemed and how this subject must stir up lots of feeling and anxiety, the patient became even more anxious. In fact he became so disorganized that the therapist had no way to end the session and they continued this dialogue for a full hour and fifteen minutes, instead of the expected forty-five minutes. Finally, the session ended with the therapist having no sense whether the man would return, though fortunately he did.

The next time the patient got agitated around a similar theme, the therapist pursued a different tack, one that would help him deal with the agitation rather than simply get more and more hyperideated, and disorganized. When the patient's vocal rhythm and tone became so rapid that it was impossible to read his signals, he also became incapable of reading the therapist's signals to close off the session when he got out of his chair. This time, as the patient became agitated, the therapist focused on the interactive gestural rhythm, not on the content or the represented affects. As the patient became agitated, the therapist tried to keep closing circles of communication, but first speeded up, along with the patient in his rhythmic vocal harangue, rather than letting the patient simply talk, talk, talk. The therapist briefly matched the rhythm of the patient in a very supportive, sympathetic tone, rather than using an angry, combative voice.

When the patient said, "My wife has to do good; she is so terrific, I know she will do well," the therapist would reply, "I hear that your wife really does accomplish a lot." He didn't focus on the feelings underlying the man's agitation, but let the man know that he was understood. He summarized in detail what the husband said. "Your wife did 'X' yesterday, 'Y' the day before, and got an 'A' on this test and effectively argued a case in moot court—boy, it sounds like she did a lot of wonderful things." As he verbally kept pace with the patient and in a sense communicated by summarizing the behavioral description of the wife, the patient relaxed a little. As this happened, the therapist deliberately started speaking more slowly, particularly about the facts that interested the patient the most: his wife's accomplishments. As the patient talked, the therapist made sure to open and close circles in a slow, rhythmic way.

The therapist realized that the issue here was not one of content and challenge, but was one of maintaining organized communication patterns at the complex gestural level rather than getting disorganized under the pressure of anxiety. The disorganization was not solely a content disorganization, but was a disorganization in vocal rhythm, as expressed by the patient's hypomanic tone. By interacting rhythmically and modulating the rhythm with the patient and making sure that the circles were opened and closed, the therapist was able to help this patient describe the behavioral patterns of his wife and himself. He eventually examined these behavioral patterns as they interacted with one another, focusing on what he did when his wife got an A; what he did when his wife got a B; what he did under other circumstances, all in an interactive, vocal rhythm that was less intense and more in control. In other words, the therapist verbally sped up and slowed down with the patient and maintained the vocal rhythm that was understandable at the simple gestural level.

This was necessary to maintain a self-defining, interactive rhythm in the face of intense anxiety so that the therapeutic process could proceed without each session leading the patient to feel more and more out of control.

Medication had been considered for this patient; he had unsuccessfully tried lithium in the past. Antidepressants led him into a hypomanic and sometimes even manic state. Tegretol had also failed to help him.

Over a period of time, however, the therapist matched the patient's rhythm and slowed the patient down. Thus, he helped him to maintain these self-defining gestures at a level that enabled patient and therapist to keep communication going, and gradually the patient could look in representational terms at this tendency to get agitated and lose the structure of his ideas, as well as his own vocal rhythm.

In this case and the other examples, the goal is to verbalize and maintain the simple gestural system as a self-defining system so that more complex communications can later be built on this foundation. A child frozen with anxiety, a passive, self-absorbed man, and an agitated individual all share the same goal: to mobilize and maintain simple gestural communication as a primarily organizing feature for later and more advanced types of communications.

Before concluding this section, a further word or two is necessary regarding how one distinguishes between the patient who is truly having difficulties at this early gesturing level and the patient who is operating at a higher level but with a manipulative type of regressive movement at this gestural level. This is a key diagnostic question for the therapist because the approach to each patient would be very different. The patient who has mastered the gestural level and is operating in a representationally elaborative or differentiated way, but as part of a defensive maneuver, gets overly disorganized gesturally or withdraws gesturally. He relies on the therapist, as part of an organized transference neurosis, to come in after him and help him out. He expects the therapist to parent or placate him, or to react to him in an aggressive way. These expectations can be part of an organized transference neurosis, a drama that is actually organized at the representational level. When this is occurring and the patient has full self-observing capacities, one can approach with traditional psychotherapeutic methods, in which the therapist helps the patient look at the manipulative or avoidant or escapist-type pattern. Even here, though, one can distinguish between the regression that is under the patient's control versus the regression that started under the patient's control and later slipped out of control. The therapist helps the out-of-control patient get back in control by engaging, regulating, and offering some support for gestural differentiation and then draws out the patient who is under control but is masquerading as out of control. All the work can be done in a solely representational manner.

On the other hand, there are patients who truly have deficits in their self-defining gestural interactive capacities, in which they get disorganized, withdrawn, perseverative, or act out in relationship to the lack of interactive gestural support. They are incapable of drawing the therapist and others in their environments into giving them the kind of gestural support they need. These patients require primary therapeutic work at the early gestural level. Observing such patients over a period of time and assessing their ability to represent affects and their ability to maintain interactive gestures when experiencing difficult affects, will reveal the patients' true developmental level.

Chapter 6

Self- and "Other"-Defining Complex Gestural, Behavioral, and Affective Patterns

The boundary-defining gestures discussed in the previous chapter help a patient define where aspects of his personal self begins and ends, and help him deal with basic issues of intentionality, safety, and danger. In this chapter we will discuss how more complex gestural interactions aid individuals in defining not just parts of their boundaries but the qualities they attribute to themselves and those they attribute to others. The complex gestural patterns that develop between therapist and patient involve a preverbal, presymbolic, and continual defining and redefining of those essential characteristics that contribute to a sense of self. This process takes place in all relationships, and in therapy occurs through an infinite number of microscopic preverbal interaction patterns between the patient and the therapist.

How does this all operate? Let us go back and look developmentally at how this psychological process first occurs. Early on in development, from about 8, 9, or 10 months up through 18 to 24 months, the infant and toddler interacts with those around him in complex and intricate presymbolic ways, long before words are used to any degree. Although a few words are used here and there during this phase, an infinite number of gestures and non-verbal patterns are being displayed. These gestural interchanges reveal how the child is dealing with such major psychological issues as dependence and independence, closeness and warmth, pleasure, assertiveness, anger, approval and disapproval, pride and admiration, and envy and competition.

A toddler who is becoming emotionally and cognitively so-phisticated is capable of taking his mother's hand and walking to the refrigerator, banging on the door, and pointing to the food he wants. When he gestures "come here" to his mother, and indicates he wants her help in getting picked up so he can choose food out of the refrigerator, she may respond to this first overture by nodding with a second look at the refrigerator, and picking him up. As he selects a carrot to eat, the mother will no doubt smile and convey a sense of pride and warm admiration in her eyes, which the child will note. Her words will convey her sense of pride in the toddler's ability to let her know what he wanted.

This little boy is gesturally beginning to get a picture of him-self as someone who can be assertive and inventive; who can figure out a way to get the refrigerator door opened, and who can get his own needs met in terms of arranging for his care. Alterna-tively, his mother may glare at him and say, "I'm too busy," or give him an angry scowl, saying, "You can't go near the refrigera-tor," or shake her head "No," indicating by her look of displea-sure that, "You'll only eat what I tell you to eat." In that case the youngster will develop a picture of himself as someone who has to rebel or become negative to get his needs met, or who is always greeted by opposition if he is assertive or inventive. Even worse, the latter treatment may cause a young child to become extremely negative or disorganized, or withdrawn or aggressive in response to a sense of frustration.

Before we discuss all the different emotional themes that can get communicated through gestures, it is important first to understand how these complex gestures are initiated. In the previ-ous discussion of boundary-defining gestures, the concept of opening and closing circles of communication was explored. These gestural exchanges help the child who reaches out to be picked up realize where his own boundary begins and ends and where the person who picks him up begins and ends. As the child grows older, a complicated set of interactions develops, involving numerous circles of communication in a row. The child looks at the parent, points to the refrigerator, the parent looks back while nodding, but they then exchange ten more gestures negotiating how to get to the refrigerator. The retrieval of the carrot may involve many more looks, smiles, and pointing fingers.

These larger chains of circles of communication constitute the child's way of defining a "complex sense of self." Therefore, the therapist must first determine whether or not these complex chains exist, and then begin looking at the qualitative characteristics that are being negotiated. In the case of the toddler, it is easy to see if these complex chains of interaction are being used to negotiate the relevant emotional themes of life. The clinician only needs to examine what is going on between the toddler and his parents in terms of how they deal with dependency. For example, does the toddler make lots of preverbal sounds, facial expressions, and motor gestures to indicate that he wants a hug or a cuddle? Does he come over and flirt with his mother, using subtle facial variations, and slowly climb up onto her lap? Is he welcomed by a big hug? Or does he simply cry hysterically, hoping she will guess that he wants an embrace? Similarly, does the adult pout or withdraw or wait passively or does he have a complex series of "wooing" behaviors or flirtatious behavior to obtain his dependency needs?

When a toddler curiously explores the house, does she hold her father's hand, pointing in every nook and cranny, babbling about this or that toy, examining it, showing it to her father, getting him to help her climb here or there? Or does she simply run in an aimless hyperkinetic way to different corners of the house?

The child who maintains independent exploration by building a block tower or fitting puzzle pieces together, may from time to time glance over at her mother for nodding approval. Another toddler may cry when not in his mother's lap or within her line of sight. Such a toddler may always need to be concrete in the way he stays "in touch" or may become prematurely "independent" and wary of making contact. Many adults similarly grapple with independence-dependence issues and become clinging and needy.

The expression of anger can highlight differences between gesturally mediated patterns and those which have a disorganized quality. Tantrums, head-banging, and floor-kicking are quite different from angry growls, frowns, and jabbing fingers. In the latter behavior, there may be ten or twenty circles of communication being opened and closed, whereas in the former only disorganized discharge patterns are expressed. Similarly, the adult who walks around with an angry scowl on his face clenching his fist in anger is different from the adult who has tantrums or hits someone while out of control.

The toddler's gestural interactions are limited by the parent's own patterns of communication. A proud gleam in a parent's eye as the child builds a tower opens circles of communication. A preoccupied parent whose nose is buried in the newspaper and who fails to look at the child, cuts off the gestural exchange. The parent who is a willing coexplorer with an adventuresome child, exchanging many gestures in the process, stands in sharp contrast to the overly controlling, bossy parent whose head vehemently shakes indicating disapproval anytime the child wants to flex his muscles.

The parent who only feels good when the child is in her lap may be unconsciously rejecting every time the child ventures off. Such a parent may take the attitude, "If you leave me, I'm going to leave you and become aloof and disinterested and rejecting." The parent may avoid looking at the child by having a body posture that seems walled up or enclosed. Or the parent may become preoccupied with telephone conversations every time the child physically ventures off but gesturally tries to maintain contact.

Many complex emotions can be gesturally communicated. How do these patterns play themselves out in the therapeutic situation? In therapy, the gestural system that develops between patient and therapist is just as active and vibrant as the one that exists between toddlers and their parents. There is one obvious difference: the gestural system is neither the only communication system nor, most of the time, the highest level system operating between patient and therapist. There may be symbolic communication going on as well. If the patient is very concrete, however, the behavioral and gestural system may absorb the lion's share of the patient's communications.

GENERAL CLINICAL EXAMPLES

Before describing the tactics of working with this level in more detail, consider a few general clinical examples.

EXAMPLE 1

A 5-year-old boy, very schizoid in his orientation, entered the therapist's office. He was extremely bright, highly verbal, and already doing fifth grade math. He held himself very stiffly, using few gestures when he spoke. He could talk a little bit about school and playtime, but very little else. From time to time, he would whip out a ball and throw it at the therapist, as if he were overloaded. This little boy came in because he was aggressive at school. His first therapist tried to treat the child by talking about his angry feelings and why he threw balls at other children. The child grew worse. A second therapist immediately recognized that this child had clear deficits. The little boy rarely met the therapist's eyes and looked impassive, or even frozen, in response to verbal overtures. This child probably wasn't differentiating the simplest affects. He was functioning at a prerepresentational, preverbal level, and certainly wasn't negotiating the types of complex interactions in which one reads other people's signals. The second therapist simply aimed at gesturally engaging this child for the first eight months of their sessions together. They next moved up from simple to complex interactive gestures. The therapist tried to open and close circles of communication by trying to get the child to add something to each statement made by the therapist, so that an interactive gesturing system developed. The content of the words was not important, but the exchange of facial expressions, body postures, and motor gestures was key. The looks, smiles, frowns, turning away and reaching toward were the elements of the therapeutic process.

As this little boy learned to interact with gestures, he began to become more secure in his ability to read the therapist's gestures. When the child looked as if he were about to throw something, the therapist could say, "Stop," or "Halt," holding up his palm as a traffic cop would, and the boy would stop and negotiate sometimes with behaviors, sometimes with words. It took two years of therapy before they could move beyond the misreading of gestures to discussions about such feelings as anger. This "higher level" interaction would not have been possible during the first years of the therapy. The little boy would have failed with many therapists who came at him on a higher level because attempts at talking would have replaced the sensitive work of engaging, responding, and elaborating behaviors. It was essential to increase the range of affects at his disposal during communication and deal with prerepresentation fears, anxieties, and conflicts. Gradually this child evolved into a warm-hearted, empathetic youngster.

The same therapist worked with a 5-year-old girl, who similarly had a lot of trouble with her gestural level. Her therapist was getting ready to go on vacation and the child was behaving very provocatively. The therapist kept saying, "I know you are breaking my toys and running around the room because you are worried about my going away. You are already angry at me that I'm going away." The child grinned, nodded, and proceeded to keep breaking toys and throwing them against the wall. This inappropriately abstract interpretation by the therapist, using highly differentiated representations of an affect state, "You are mad at me because I'm going away," demanded a quality of self-observation and differentiation of affect, and representation of affect, that the child was developmentally incapable of having.

This was a child who had failed to master some 18- to 24-month-old level chores, let alone 4- and 5-year-old level ego capacities.

When I was asked to supervise this case, I suggested to the therapist that he employ a gestural communication in his treatment approach that would use words, but only in the spirit of gesture. In other words, a very direct behavioral communication was indicated.

During the next session, when the patient was behaving provocatively, and it was getting closer to the therapist's scheduled vacation time, he very warmly remarked, "You know, soon I'll go bye-bye," and waved his hand in a "bye-bye" gesture. The child looked at him and for the first time dealt with the issue. She stopped her provocative behavior and the play theme shifted a bit, centering around themes of separation. There was an immediate change in her behavior and in her affective tone. What we did was to try to use a gestural, "We are going to go bye-bye," means of communication, and also a direct verbal expression of behavioral intent. In other words, the "I am going to go bye-bye" is a very different communication than, "You must feel sad because you are worried about my leaving." One is focused on represented affect, which might be appropriate for a healthy neurotic patient, while the other is a very direct behavioral negotiation, "I'm going bye-bye. What are you going to do about it?" The latter is a more empathetic line of communication.

Another example of this level occurred with a patient who, after the therapist had been away on vacation, came back and said, "You know, I have been having images of blood spurting from my wrists." The therapist said, "You must be angry at my having been away if you are thinking of cutting your wrists." She said, "You know, I know you want me to say I'm angry and I know that's what I should feel in this situation, but to be honest with you, all I can do is picture blood flowing from my veins. That's the only thing I truly experience." When the therapist tried to explore what the patient's body sensations *felt* like, she expressed a sense of numbing and relief with the blood flowing from her wrists.

The therapist learned to have the woman describe what her different physical states were, rather than merely suggest that she must be angry at his desertion. The patient described many physiologic sensations in her body—numbness, excitement, relaxation, and how the image of blood would affect her skin. She clearly had a lot of somatic preoccupations. Slowly, these somatic descriptions led to some hints of affect. Over a period of weeks and months, following these somatic descriptions of tension, the patient was able to express abstracted affect states. What appears to occur is that the patient, in describing physical states, begins to experience these states as part of a relationship. In early development it is the relationship, the ability to engage a child's interactions around his somatic states, that helps the child abstract the affect. Describing physical states led to the description of physical patterns. The description of physical patterns has certain affective elements; for example, "muscles are tense"; "muscles want to explode"; "explode like a strong volcano." As the affective descriptions are used to describe these physical states, the affective pattern becomes clearer (e.g., "erupt like a volcano and hurt so and so"; "enraged"). Eventually, an abstracted affect state becomes clear. Therefore, the combination of going back and forth between descriptions of physical somatic sensations and reporting of behavioral patterns leads patients to eventually, and spontaneously, abstract an affect state where they will say something that is closer to a feeling of rage, longing, sadness, or despair. The therapist has to *meet the person where they are* and use direct verbalizations of behavioral intent such as, "Going to go bye-bye soon." This approach meets the patient at his existing level of affect organization, which is the most direct route to affective interaction.

TECHNICAL CONSIDERATIONS

It is helpful in the therapeutic setting to consider four questions regarding the gestural system. First, does it exist in a complex form? Second, do the breadth and range of gestures express affects and themes? Third, are the countergestures occurring in which the therapist responds nonverbally to the patient's initiatives, and vice versa? Lastly, when the patient experiences intense affect or stress, does the gestural system remain stable?

While it would seem as if this is a precondition to verbal, symbolic interchange, many adults do not in fact have the system well developed when they speak to one another. Certain adults use words in an impersonal, nonemotional way, rarely representing complex affects verbally and in fact are seldom very engaged, let alone gesturally connected, with others. Such detached adults may talk in a vague, stiff, and mechanical manner. They may not display many gestures. The therapist may, with such an adult, get a look or nod only after a lot of input, but fail to develop long chains of nonverbal dialogue. We tend to describe such adults in colloquial terms as being anxious, uncomfortable, or schizoid, uninvolved, aloof, or withdrawn. The fact may be, however, that as one looks closely, this person may be capable of closing one to four circles in a row, but no more. This disruption in gestural dialogue says something important about the level at which affective communication has gone awry or the depth and degree of regression that has occurred under one or another kind of stress. In normal and healthy development, the gestural system gets very well developed and remains that way except under times of extreme stress and regression. With certain kinds of regression the gestural system may get lost, after some symbolic affective elaborations are lost, and prior to the losing of the affective tie and relatedness itself. Therefore, an adult who has never developed complex gestural interactions or the adult who loses that ability under the power of stressful regression, is revealing something important about his or her makeup and personality.

Often, therapists increase their own use of gestures or subconsciously mirror or model themselves after the patient, becoming a little stiff and aloof and formal themselves. Conversations, to the degree that they exist, become highly concrete, dealing with immediate concerns or become extremely vague, abstract, intellectualized concerns.

When such themes as dependency, assertiveness, aggression, and curiosity are being negotiated through gesturing, in developmentally arrested patients we may see flat affect or stiff and mechanical interaction patterns. More compulsive people exhibit highly perseverative and stereotypical behavior. We are also alert to the paucity of gestures displayed by a person who feels empty, aimless, withdrawn, or depressed, and his or her lack of much interactive ability. We also must look specifically at the number of circles of communication a person can open and close and the richness and feeling tone evidenced by the gestures.

Sometimes we make a mistake and assume a person has little gestural capacity when he or she, in fact, may have a problem with motor planning or communication which uses their motor system. These people may use less posturing and activate fewer voluntary muscles, yet exhibit more twinkle in their eyes, lip movements, and changes in skin tone and texture. The autonomic nervous system may gesturally express what their voluntary system does not. We can, therefore, learn a lot about the preferred modes of interaction. Some people are also more visual and others more vocal in their preferred means of gesturing. For example, some people use variations in vocal tone, while others use facial expressions accompanied by a certain look or body posture to communicate the same message. Indeed, many of these gestures are even culturally dictated, such as the Italian's expressive shrug, or the pronounced use of lips and neck muscles by native French speakers.

After considering the general presence or absence of complex gesturing, the therapist focuses on how wide ranging the individual's gestural communicative capacity is. Does the person gesture, for example, and open and close fifty to a hundred circles of communication when it comes to dependency issues? Do they smile? Do they flirt? Do they have a warm vocal tone? Do they move comfortably close when they converse? Are they flat and mechanical, devoid of affect when they feel anger? Do they use an aloof, mechanical voice when describing how someone mistreated them and they didn't know what to do in return? Do they feel that "other people" might want to hit someone who caused them harm, but they themselves simply feel paralyzed and unsure of themselves? Alternatively, does the angry person who fumes and fusses, making menacing gestures with his or her fists, opening and closing fifty or a hundred circles, only sit passively, looking needy, and showing very little facial animation when it comes to issues involving dependency and closeness?

We could go through the same exercise for assertiveness, empathy, curiosity, and any other affective thematic area that one wishes to categorize. The important point here is to recognize that patients will vary considerably in their ability to open and close fifty to one hundred circles in a row using gestural modes depending on the affective or thematic area. We see the earliest signs of character pathology or constrictions in the range and depth of the person's interactive abilities in this gestural realm. It may be, in fact, that in development, character pathology begins in the early toddler stage when the parents and the child are negotiating which realm of affect and which themes can be communicated. Parents who get anxious around dependency may be communicating to the child that dependency is not a reasonable area in which to interact with parents. It may be felt by the child in a vague, somatic sense. The child never develops communicative intents around negotiating dependence because the parents are either withdrawn, aimless, intrusive or controlling, or are so anxious that they cannot respond in a certain thematic area. A similar pattern can take place with aggression, curiosity, and the like.

Put simply, it takes a partnership between the child and the parent to learn rules of communication around each thematically affected area. When such an area is taboo, it remains relatively undeveloped, leaving the child with only a few rather regressive devices, including aimless and withdrawn patterns, disorganized motor discharge, and perseverative and repetitive motor patterns, and vague somatic sensations.

These are the patterns that exist prior to organized intentional motor patterns, vocal patterns, symbolic labeling patterns, and various affect expressive patterns. They get developed in the context of an interactive relationship between parent and child, and can secondarily be reworked in a therapeutic relationship which fosters gestural communication.

In the therapeutic situation, the clinician fosters the use of complex and simple gestures and verbal symbolic representations, as well as a sense of relatedness and engagement. In other words, the therapist communicates simultaneously on multiple levels. *The earlier levels are not subordinate to symbolic levels and may in fact be far more critical.*

Consider an adult who walks down a dark alley and sees a menacing-looking stranger who says, "I'm a nice guy." She trusts the evidence of her eyes and other senses and reads the stranger's gestures, rather than believing the content of his words. Gestures operate at a visceral and believable level; words can deceive. Even in casual conversation between friends, it is the tone of the affect and the emotional expression that conveys the true message, rather than the words themselves. When the two methods of communication are in sync, words can fine-tune the more primitive gestures.

During the course of therapy, the clinician faces a number of challenges. First, the therapist should be aware of the preverbal transference–countertransference reenactments that are likely to be occurring. Certain themes are being reenacted behaviorally and gesturally and other themes and affects are not being dealt with.

Second, for those patients who give evidence of primary deficits or constrictions at the level of complex gestures, therapy provides gestural opportunities for the patient to break new ground. The therapist helps the patient to develop either the ability for complex gesturing or, in the case of constriction, an increase in the thematic affective range that the patient can organize at the complex gestural level.

Third, the therapist needs to be aware of a patient's representational–symbolic capacities and help the patient look at his or her gestural limitations and the patterns that enable these constrictions or limitations to persist. This level of self-observation and reflection may not be possible until the patient has at least some representational ability.

Finally, to the degree that the patient's gestural deficits or constrictions have become part of the patterns of conflict, anxiety, and therefore compromise formations, the patient will benefit from becoming aware of his own tendencies to maintain certain gestural constrictions and limitations or deficits for purposes of defense. The patient, for example, who associates aggression and assertiveness with loss of the relationship with the paternal object, may be reluctant to extend these gestural interchanges to embrace assertiveness and aggression because it brings forth viscerally painful affects associated with panic over separation and loss. Early on in therapy these visceral patterns may not be available symbolically but may be a factor in the difficulty the patient has in his gestural negotiations. As the patient develops symbolic capacity, he may be able to explore this gestural inhibition symbolically. It is possible, however, as will be elaborated shortly, to explore these patterns even presymbolically at the gestural level.

Let us now examine each of these different therapeutic approaches separately. The therapist must be aware of certain reenactments that can undermine his availability as a broad-ranging communicator with his patient. To the degree that the therapist is locked into a replay of a pattern at this preverbal behavioral level, he may unintentionally maintain the patient's deficits and constrictions. He may, for example, help the patient try to verbalize certain feelings and may raise questions about why the patient did this or that, or looked angry or sad. If a passive and obsequious patient is urged to participate in this typical therapeutic dialogue, he may respond with a very limited repertoire of gestures. He may show no facial affects, body movements, vocal tones suggestive of assertiveness, curiosity, anger, excitement (sexual or otherwise), or even strong dependent longings. The patient is not aware of this at a symbolic level; he doesn't say, "I do what I'm told because I like to be passive and compliant." He has little awareness of a psychological sense of his patterns. He does feel a vague sense of anxiety and fear, a nameless "I must please." The question of *why* he must please may spark an intellectual exploration that is bereft of any affect or emotional involvement. The patient's limited gestural repertoire may consist of submissive

body postures, nervous head nodding, and occasional eye blink-
ing. He uses his few gestures in boundary-defining ways, closing
only three or four gestural circles in a row. He does not use
gestures to further elaborate a more complex sense of self.

One therapist inadvertently replayed a compliance pattern a
patient had previously enacted with his mother. On days in which
the therapist was tired, or exhausted by other patients' aggression,
he enjoyed an "easy session" with the compliant patient. He even
got lost in the patient's intellectual explorations, and relished
hearing about some of the behind-the-scenes gossip at the famous
newspaper where the patient worked as an editor. The patient,
being quite bright, was also skillful in the way he satisfied the
therapist's curiosity.

On reflection, the therapist realized that he enjoyed the
sense of control he had over this patient and the lack of challenge
that the patient offered him. At other times, however, the therapist was aware that he became frustrated with his patient and
wanted to jolt him out of his complacency. His tendency, at such
times, was to be impatient and somewhat provocative and critical.
This was rationalized as "getting the patient going." The patient,
however, responded to the therapist's kick-in-the-pants style with
more passivity and obsequiousness.

Interestingly, the patient's mother had dealt with him in a
similar way. She was a dominating, controlling woman who
seemed to enjoy her son's dutiful compliance. The mother, who
had once come in for a family session as part of the therapy,
remarked that she specifically remembered how "good and easy"
he was as a baby. According to her, he evidenced no "terrible
two's" and was never aggressive. "He never ran away from me at
the store," and seemed to be "my little soldier." The mother also
reported, however, that there were times that she wanted him to
be tougher or "show me his stuff." She also related to her husband in much the same way. He, too, was a passive and compliant
man who was quite afraid of assertiveness. She vacillated between
liking her domination over him and getting "frustrated with his
never getting excited."

As the therapist became aware of the reenactment of these patterns, he also felt perplexed about what to do. He first tried bringing them to the patient's attention verbally, pointing out the pattern that they had become partners in. The patient reacted to this insight dutifully but compliantly, by repeating what the therapist said and trying to find examples of it. The therapist tried various approaches. He commented on the patient's fear of aggression and pleasure in passivity. He interpreted the patient's desire to be taken care of. He focused on the patient's fear of growing up and becoming more independent. He discussed the patient's fear of injuring the analyst by his assertiveness.

Unfortunately, none of these approaches proved in the least bit helpful as the patient compliantly agreed with each and every comment the therapist made. He nodded his assent when the therapist remarked in frustration, "You agree with everything I say and that's an example of your tendency to comply." As the therapist grew more and more frustrated with the patient, he would convey his criticism indirectly, speaking in a tense voice.

The therapist was experiencing a frustrating, albeit common, tendency to interact with the patient in ways that are characteristic of the ways that the patient's parents, caregivers, or other people in close relationships had interacted with him. The patient is usually far more skillful at pulling the therapist into that relationship pattern than the therapist is at recognizing it. The patient is not necessarily going to pull the therapist into making comments that reenact the comments his parents made, because the therapist is usually acutely aware of the power of words. However, his body may betray him; the rhythm of the therapist's head nods and smiles, the tone of his voice, and the frequency of his yawns may repeat certain behavioral patterns that are familiar to the patient. For example, when a patient withdraws, he may seduce the therapist into coming after him or into counterwithdrawal where the therapist stays aloof or stubborn. The therapist will fall into the trap of continuing this counterpattern for a little while until he recognizes it, but then must be sure to avoid the countertransference behavior of acting out or in with the patient.

After a number of years passed with essentially no progress being made with the compliant patient, the therapist sought consultation regarding developmental approaches to psychotherapy. He became aware of the fact that even though he was using ideas that he thought might be helpful to the patient and conveying them in a warm, empathetic way, he was inadvertently facilitating the patient's reenactment of old gestural and behavioral patterns. The therapist was functioning as the dominant person, bossing and controlling his compliant partner. The clinician needed to look at the therapeutic situation from a far simpler, but in some respects more penetrating, vantage point. He had to examine how he and the patient were reenacting this drama not merely with words, but with their vocal tones, facial expressions, and body postures. As he began looking at these elements, he noticed, for example, that when the patient began each session, his vocal tone had a passive, needy quality. It was as though the tone of voice was asking, "What should I do?" Even when the patient was free associating, his vocal tone was tentative, as if asking permission to go ahead.

The therapist, as he watched his own responses, realized that he granted permission by the rhythm of his "aha's" and the way he nodded his head. In the simplest interactions, therapist and patient were maintaining the drama the therapist was trying to interpret and hoped to put into perspective for the patient. This is a familiar situation where routine therapeutic strategies are in fact preverbal enactments. Verbal interpretations only continue the reenactments because they are perceived by the patient at his developmental level, which is a presymbolic one. The therapist made a profound shift in tactics. He decided to create a gestural interaction pattern, not a verbal one, that would cease maintaining the reenactment. He reasoned that his patient could only become aware of a drama that had run on automatic pilot throughout many of his primary relationships by discontinuing that pattern. If the pattern continued, it would become so integral a part of the patient's character structure and sense of being regulated and satisfied, that the patient would have no motive to see it as a separate pattern even in a preverbal intuitive sense.

How not to reenact this drama, however, when every traditional psychotherapeutic intervention seemed only to maintain the pattern, was a challenge. As the therapist focused on small gestural interactions and began thinking about his counterreactions, he first decided to try and resist the tendency (and the accompanying gestural communication) to "grant" permission to the patient. In other words, the patient's compliant, "Can I talk?" vocal tone would no longer be greeted with an "aha" or "yes." Remaining silent, however, would not serve the therapist's purpose as it might only make the patient feel that he had angered the therapist and that he would now need to be even more compliant. Nor would telling the patient to toughen up and talk in a louder voice do the trick. It would tend only to frighten the patient and make him even more compliant.

The therapist decided that two shifts in his approach might have developmental significance and therefore therapeutic value. He tried to be alert to any signs of independence or assertiveness in the way the patient looked, used his vocal tone, or moved. The simplest gesture, such as the way the patient glanced at him, became noteworthy. The therapist noticed, for example, that in the past when the patient came in and looked at him he would look back at the patient and maintain his stare in the patient's visual space until the patient looked down. At this very subtle level, the therapist had been inadvertently emphasizing his dominant position. The therapist realized that this nonverbal behavior was maintaining the patient's subservient pattern as much as verbally granting (with "aha's" and "yeses") the patient permission to talk.

To his chagrin, the therapist realized that he was receiving satisfaction from being in the dominant position. He, therefore, tried at subsequent meetings to return the patient's greeting with a warm look, but didn't wait for the patient to defer to him. Instead, he looked away comfortably rather than waiting for the patient to drop his eyes. The patient initially showed some signs of anxiety when the therapist disengaged his eye contact first. The anxiety was manifested by a little gruffness in the patient's voice and by a clumsiness in his body language. Sometimes he bumped into things as he approached his chair.

The therapist also tried to become more aware of the subtle communications where he could show pride or admiration for the patient without being patronizing or manipulative. In the past, for example, the patient would sometimes strut in with a new jacket or tie and proudly want to show it off. Previously, the therapist had deliberately underplayed his reactions, figuring it would too easily gratify the patient if he showed an interest in his tie or jacket. He would wait for the patient to verbalize his desire for the therapist's admiration. With his awareness of his own countertransference tendency to keep the patient submissive, simple things like a new tie or jacket were greeted with a more open expression and even an admiring look. The patient smiled appreciatively back at the therapist when such gestures were exchanged, even though early on the issue was not verbalized.

Later on in the therapy, issues involving need for approval became increasingly verbalized. When the patient asked for permission to speak, using a whining, somewhat tentative tone, the therapist would neither grant permission with a knowing "yes" or "aha," nor refuse permission by remaining silent. Instead, he entered into a pattern of direct communication, based on both words and gestures. Verbally, he empathized with the state of affect. He didn't try to interpret it and insist the patient form an abstract affect state (which the patient had difficulty doing). Instead, he made a direct *gestural type of comment* (i.e., a comment that operates like an interactive behavior rather than a reflection) and said, "I'm not sure from your tone of voice whether you want to talk further or not." This simple comment about his uncertainty regarding the patient's tone of voice drew the patient's attention to the fact that his own behavior was unclear. The patient then reflected that he wasn't sure what he wanted to do. As he became tentative again, seeking the therapist's guidance, the therapist paid close attention to the patient's gestures (e.g., tone of voice, facial expression, motor patterns, affect variation, breathing rhythm, vocal rhythm, etc.). The therapist responded similarly with an empathetic comment, "I can hear that you sound unsure." The therapist avoided comments like, "I can tell you feel unsure," or "You feel uncertain," or "You feel like you want my approval," because these would focus on abstract affect states, which the patient wasn't capable of fully comprehending yet. By using more direct comments about specific behavioral patterns, the therapist was able to convey to the patient that his "uncertainty" could be *heard* or *observed* and not merely *felt*.

The patient could relate to these descriptions of concrete behavioral and gestural patterns. His therapist's tone of voice was decidedly respectful, neither providing guidance nor depriving the patient of contact. As the therapist empathized with the patient's dilemma, he was being respectful of the patient's existing behavioral pattern, which was one of tentativeness. In this way he was neither reenacting the pattern nor was he trying to interpret it. He was dealing directly with it from a counterbehavioral point of view.

The therapist's new counterbehavioral point of view helped the patient view therapy as a behavioral interaction and dialogue. Such dialogue doesn't ask the patient to look at feelings prematurely when the patient is not yet able to represent or label feelings. The therapist simply counters the patient's behavioral tendencies with a behaviorally direct comment that aims to help the patient broaden the behavioral range of his interactions. Such comments avoid the reenactment of old patterns, and they also avoid what could be termed a reaction formation reenactment. Instead, the therapist directly engages in the patient's behavioral pattern, which inevitably broadens the patient's range. The patient is momentarily somewhat trapped by such a behavioral or gestural comment because it doesn't provide the satisfaction and the guidance he wants, nor does it provide a critical, overly punitive, austere, or abstinent response either.

When the therapist stopped reenacting the patterns of assertiveness and aggression, he began creating a new baseline of therapeutic neutrality that contained elements of experience that the patient required for an expanded behavioral repertoire. Respect and pride replaced assertiveness, and respect, pride, and admiration supplanted bossiness or criticism. Each time the patient engaged in a direct behavioral way around his own behavioral tentativeness or uncertainty, the therapist eschewed such boil-erplate comments as "You want my approval," or "You want me to tell you what to do." Remarks like these would have been counterproductive since the patient was not abstracting affect states nor seeing the connection between different affect states. Later on in therapy he was able to examine how his wishes were part of a relationship with the therapist's wishes, and how he tried to get the therapist to feel a particular way toward him in order to gratify certain wishes.

Another patient had a different character pattern and presented an opposite behavioral challenge for the therapist. This person evidenced a complex behavioral and gestural constriction around dependency and closeness. He used pseudoindependence with bossy, controlling behavior to try to dominate the therapist. This patient came in and took charge of every facet of the session, trying to control the rhythm and tone of the interaction.

The therapist tried a variety of clarifications and interpretations with this patient, but met with no success. Finally, with developmental consultation, he began looking at the reenactments from a developmental perspective. He noticed that, as opposed to the other patient, this patient would stare and stare at him until he turned away. The patient would immediately start talking in a domineering, loud vocal pattern, and would frequently cut the therapist off. The therapist, concerned about appearing competitive with this patient, became somewhat cautious and passive in his own style. On close scrutiny, however, it appeared that the therapist did become competitive from time to time, but in a subtle way. He would insist on things being done *his* way, such as allowing cigarettes to be smoked in the office, but not cigars since "they smell the place up."

The patient kept up this pattern of domination in terms of facial expression, body posture, and subtle affect, and the therapist remained passive. Although the therapist occasionally commented that the patient seemed to want to control everything, these words held little meaning for the patient. Such comments require an ability to represent affect states, which the patient wasn't able to do yet.

The therapist attempted to stop the reenactment and engage his patient in a broader range of ways. He became particularly aware that this patient found it difficult to be close and initiated no gestural interactions around warmth and closeness. There was very little effort to "open up" in a behavioral gestural sense, with warm looks, needy vocal tones, or longing feelings displayed. Since the therapy had been going on for a considerable period of time at an intense level, one would expect such feelings to have already emerged, but they were nowhere to be found in this or any other relationship in the patient's life. When the therapist inquired about whether or not the patient missed having such feelings, he was met with adamant denial and a further tendency on the patient's part to dominate the sessions.

The therapist subsequently decided to try a few new therapeutic techniques. Aware of his tendency to be passive, he tried to maintain a more even vocal tone, facial expression, and relaxed body posture. When the patient came in and looked at him, he would look back without getting too competitive, but tried not to defer to the patient too quickly. When the patient interrupted him, he asked the patient if he wanted him to finish his thought or stop, and that he was also eager to hear what the patient had to say. Interestingly, when the patient first experienced these new overtures by the therapist (as we later found out when the patient became more representational in his abilities) he felt more "viscerally connected" to the therapist at this time because there was "more going on."

In addition to not replaying the passive posture, the therapist also began trying to deal directly with the behavioral level by using counterbehavioral intervention. In the earlier case discussed above, the counterbehavioral intervention focused on empathy with the patient's tentative and uncertain behavior. In this case, too, the therapist tried to deal directly with the patient's behavioral style. For example, when there were hints of dependency or longing feelings (such as following a missed session) the therapist didn't say, "Gee, I noticed that you were trying to dominate me because you missed me so much," even if the patient were more controlling than usual. Instead, he commented more directly, saying, "You just took charge of what we were talking about." The therapist said this warmly and empathetically. The patient indicated that he'd been doing this for some time and wondered why it took so long for the therapist to recognize the fact. He said he liked to be in charge. The patient wasn't inclined to relate this to any particular feeling since he had not advanced to the stage of looking at interactions between feelings. He simply acknowledged that it was his behavioral style to be in charge of the verbal dialogue.

The patient was somewhat disarmed by the therapist's very direct comment about his behavior, "You just took charge of our conversation." A faint little grin played on his lips and revealed his pleasure in taking charge. At this point he didn't evidence any capacity to verbalize such feelings as pleasure, fear, discomfort, or excitement. His pleasure was revealed in his gestures. The beginnings of a broadening of his gestural repertoire were present in this interaction, however. The reenactment had, in essence, kept a certain pattern going. There was little warmth, pleasure, or excitement exchanged between patient and therapist other than that which might be inferred from their long-standing relationship and the patient's reliable record of attending the sessions. The therapist's comments were simple, direct behavioral ones—"You just interrupted me," something that one friend might say to another friend; "You took charge of our conversation." Slowly but surely, these behavioral comments, together with the lack of reenactment and greater assertiveness on the part of the therapist, helped to increase new gestures having to do with warmth or closeness.

For example, when the patient smiled at him with a warm, seductive glance or the therapist mentioned that "you just took over the conversation again," the therapist was careful to see how long he and the patient could maintain gestural dialogue of warm, knowing glances. They nodded heads at each other, stiffened their upper lips, and exchanged a number of smiles. These were quick and subtle interactions—not unlike what might occur in many warm friendships—only they had never previously taken place between the patient and therapist. The therapist had not been particularly relaxed and needed to be aware of the importance of responding to the patient's fleeting overtures. As a matter of fact, this therapist had commented to a colleague that in the past he suspected there were times when the patient had given him warm or dependent glances and he was caught "so off-guard" that he used the principle of abstinence as a defense to explain his lack of responsiveness and his continuing tendency to be passive with the patient. He reflected that this was a "hard patient to read" and he was always afraid that he might overstep his bounds and that, therefore, it was safer to be passive. The therapist, now understanding his feelings, felt comfortable with a different type of baseline for this particular patient. This new baseline was essential to help the patient begin exploring and experimenting with the affects and gestures having to do with dependency and pleasure.

It is important to point out here that it is difficult, if not impossible, to help a patient look at these dependency longings or other abstract feelings without first evidencing them in complex gestural dialogue. It is a frequent tactical error to attempt to discuss feelings ("You never show anger") that are not in evidence yet. These are alien concepts to the patient. The patient who does not represent certain affect states cannot comment on why he does not have them, particularly if he has not yet experienced them even on a behavioral level. The closest thing to an affect state the patient may experience is some vague somatic state (e.g., tense muscles, an ache in the belly). As the patient begins interacting behaviorally with these complex affective interchanges, which are mediated through his gestural system, this vague, somatic affective state becomes more salient. As the behavioral pattern and its affects become clearer, the patient gradually experiences the behavior and affect together, and his natural tendency to abstract leads to a new level of organization where affects are part of the dialogue and eventually become fully abstracted or represented.

As one looks at each thematic affective domain (pleasure, dependency, assertiveness, curiosity, anger, empathy, more mature forms of love), and as one looks at the different fears and anxieties associated with these patterns (separation anxiety, fear of aggression, and the like), it may be that the patient must first progress through a gestural behavioral experience of these thematic affective domains. The therapist's initial tactic in mobilizing this effort is to understand the patient's pattern of reenactment and then to offer gestural counterreactions and support for the formerly unavailable behavioral and affective patterns.

In addition to being more assertive and less passive with the patient just discussed above, the therapist also paid attention to any subtle sign of longing and was especially supportive, warm, and empathetic when these emerged. The therapist was alert to engaging these new gestures and tried to broaden the gestural chain involved with them. Therefore, in addition to understanding the reenactment and the therapist's role in reenactment, the therapist should actively create opportunities for the patient to explore new gestural interactions having to do with the areas which have been constricted or walled off in the development of the patient's personality. Without going through each thematic affective realm, a few general principles should be stated. In addition to not reenacting, the therapist will generate some of the constricted realms by making the counterbehavioral type interventions discussed above. Furthermore, the therapist will be careful to examine his reenactments and their microscopic behavioral gestural derivative interchanges and attempt to find a truly neutral, developmentally facilitating intervention. The therapist will also be especially sensitive to spontaneous overtures on the patient's part and new affect and thematic realms that formerly weren't available to the patient.

The therapist who engages and interacts around the new affects and behaviors is showing empathetic support, respect, and at times even admiration via his looks, body posture, and head nods. Such support for the previously avoided affective thematic realms gradually provide the patient with an opportunity to explore new territory. The combination of support for the formerly warded-off affective thematic realms, with the lack of reenactment and the direct behavioral counterresponses, provides the ingredients for the patient to broaden or increase the complexity of his gestural affective interaction pattern.

One might wonder at this point about the dynamics that drive the patient's limitation. There may be anxiety, defense, and compromise information involved in the patient's constrictions. For example, the passive–compliant patient may be quite frightened over losing the object he depends on were he to experiment with more assertiveness. He does not experience this at a verbal representational level, however, but in terms of a series of behavioral connections and visceral affect states. Assertive behavior is associated with a state of affective and visceral panic and disorganization and actual experiences of loss and separation. In the infancy and early toddlerhood of such an individual there is often a parent who withdrew, not necessarily in person but in spirit. Every time the toddler experimented with assertiveness and curiosity there was a momentary loss of connectedness.

To recover this memory representationally, particularly when the patient does not have such representational abilities, makes psychotherapeutic effort often seem interminable and frustrating, and most important, unsuccessful. At a later phase in the therapy, once the patient becomes representational, he may be able to understand his dynamics from a self-observing, affective representational point of view. This is often not the case when these abilities are not yet present. How then do we help the patient broaden his behavioral affective thematic range in terms of complex gestures, while taking into account that there may be certain dynamics driving the pattern? (Earlier we discussed the association of assertiveness with the fear of loss. The drive to be aggressive and assertive is particularly strong and, therefore, more frightening than otherwise would be the case in terms of the fear of loss it may engender.)

The goal is to build an understanding of the patient's psychological dynamics into the new behavioral negotiations. Let us consider the first patient where there was enormous intensity associated with his internal affect states. Because his mother shut down and pulled away when he experimented with assertiveness, he tended to be afraid of intense emotions. He therefore decided to give up on this side of his nature and become compliant. He did not decide this with logic, thought, or ideas, it was all negotiated as a toddler through behavioral interactions. Anyone who has observed toddlers will see that by 15 months they have already formed complex, repetitive patterns of behavior where they are more compliant and passive, assertive and challenging, or negative. They already have characteristic ways of dealing with their parents and the different conflicts that arise in their relationships with them, as well as their own earlier affective and behavioral patterns, some of which are derivatives of their own drive affect patterns.

As the adult patient becomes bold enough to attempt to be assertive and tries it out during a session, the therapist wants to avoid creating a reenactment by shutting down like the mother did. This would only serve to confirm in the patient's mind the truth of his assumptions. Since these are nonverbal behavioral assumptions, they are harder to shake or disavow. Once the therapist replaces shutting down with empathy and warm support, the patient experiences a different type of pattern.

How does one then deal with the adult's new understanding that their old expectations of another's behavior must change? Not fulfilling old expectation will help the adult eventually learn that his expectations will not be met. Similar to an extinction phenomenon in a behavioral learning paradigm, patterns are given up when certain expectations or reinforcements are not forthcoming. There is sometimes chaotic behavior during the pattern of relinquishment.

Yet there is another aspect to this therapeutic technique that goes beyond not meeting the patient's expectations. The patient's expectations can be built into the therapist's counterbehavioral responses. In addition, the patient's own drive affect tendencies can be factored into the behavioral affective counterresponses. For example, the first patient discussed above is fearful of loss, and this is intensified by the intensity of his own anger as well as his mother's having shut down. If the therapist comments about his tentativeness in a counterbehavioral way, saying that he (the patient) "isn't sure if he wants to talk," the therapist can further add at a later point that the patient expects that the therapist will disappear if he takes the initiative.

This expectation can be explored in a number of steps. The first sign might be a pleading look in his eye, a "please don't leave me" glance. The therapist could say something like, "Your look is to keep me here," or "Your look is compelling; it makes me stay put." It conveys to the patient that his own behavior seeks to elicit other behaviors. In other words, his look is not based on a particular feeling (although we know it is at some higher level that he will achieve later) and it is not based on the therapist's feelings, but is instead behavior geared to elicit behavior on the therapist's part. It won't do any good in the short run to say, "You are fearful I am going to leave," because this will be like speaking Japanese to a patient who doesn't comprehend Japanese; it is at a higher level than he is able to deal with. His behavior is something he can relate to, however, even though it is motivated by a hypothetical fear, which is not yet represented (and, as indicated, may become clear to the patient later). *The first step is to simply alert him to the fact that his look is designed to glue you to your chair.* That conveys to him the intention of his behavior.

Similarly, if one wants to deal with the intensity of his affects (where there is a glimmer of the intensity of the affect that he is constraining and constricting with his passivity because of a momentary annoyed look or facial grimace), one can also comment on his intensity. For example, the therapist might say, "That's a strong look," or even "That's an intense look." That, too, says something about the behavior without trying to convey the feeling that is driving the behavior. It is not always possible to deal with all the different aspects of the patient's dynamics at the behavioral level, but, surprisingly, as the therapist tries to broaden his counterbehaviors through his comments and gestures, he will find he can take many of these into account and set the stage for later therapeutic work when the patient becomes more representational. Here too, just as earlier, the patient cannot deal with a fear or an anxiety or a wish or a drive state unless it is first evidenced and often acknowledged at the behavioral–gestural level.

We have been talking about patients whose character structure is predominantly prerepresentational. But these same principles hold true for the representational patient who has not achieved representationality in various selected areas, such as around certain types of aggression toward authority figures or certain types of dependency longings. These affect patterns may be circumscribed and part of a neurotic pattern. These circumscribed areas will often be part of a pattern where the circumscribed constriction exists at the behavioral–gestural level as well as at the representational level. In such cases the same tactics mentioned above need to be applied to the constricted realm. Obviously, with mostly representational patients the work will go more quickly and the therapist can introduce self-observing tools earlier on. Nonetheless, the general principle holds: the patient must first experience affective states at the behavioral–gestural level before he can represent them. Attempts to represent prior to experiencing will result in intellectualized, therapeutically useless dialogues.

As patients broaden their behavioral–gestural–affective–thematic interactions, with the therapist's assistance they will spontaneously begin abstracting and seeing the patterns of their behaviors. As they learn to observe their behavioral patterns, gradually they will start abstracting affect states associated with these patterns. It is when they reach this representational level that they can begin looking at what they have already learned, which is how they can bring symbolic sense to what they already know to be true at a deeper, more visceral behavioral–gestural level.

THE DEVELOPMENT OF CHARACTER PATHOLOGY: COMPLEX GESTURES, DEPRESSIVE AND PARANOID STATES, AND "FIXED" ATTITUDES

There are many adult patients who have difficulty in accurately reading other people's gestures and intentions. They often assume a fixed point of view. Any facial expression, body posture, or head nod is misinterpreted as, "You are criticizing and disapproving of me," or "You are attacking me," or "You are rejecting me." Some perceptions have more depressive tone: "People don't like me, I'm bad." Others may have more suspicious or angry qualities: "People are critical, angry, or attacking me"; sometimes, it's, "Everyone loves me."

In working clinically with depressed or paranoid patients it is very important to help them deal with the gestural level of communication, which has apparently gone awry for any one of a number of reasons. They may have had difficulty in processing information or interacting in a broad-ranging affective way with their parents. In working with these patients, it is important to separate out symptoms from the more primary issue, which is the sense of confusion over "reading" people. Often, these individuals don't read people well, feel confused, disconnected, helpless, and experience a series of dysphoric affects. Then, to explain the dysphoria, they supply content of a depressive or paranoid nature. The therapist's initial role is to empathize with the patients' general difficulty with reading people and to help them tolerate the discomfort, uncertainty, and confusion associated with somatically felt dysphoric affects.

The difficulty in reading people has its roots in the second year of life, although it may well continue to develop afterward, and is associated with a sense of not being connected with other people. There is an aimless, hollow, anxious, uncertain, insecure, alone, dead, numb feeling associated with the lack of connectedness. The patient needs to examine how confused and uncertain he feels when trying to read the therapist's facial gestures, body posture, and head nods, and how he feels in similar social situations or with intimate acquaintances. The patient can thus begin reworking the foundations for his depressive or paranoid ideation by first learning more about his primary deficits. As he examines his own confusion with the therapist and other people, and becomes more aware of the somatically based affect states (aloneness, emptiness, disconnection) that are associated with the sense of uncertainty and confusion, he will painfully and inexorably begin to interpret his real world more accurately.

The patient will need to avoid the leap into the depressive or paranoid ideation, which serves as a secondary defense by "filling up" the patient and making him feel connected. One characteristic of the secondary elaboration is the sense of being the center of someone else's world: "You don't like me" and "You hate me" imply an intimate relationship with another person. In fact, it is this very quality of intimacy that was often missing in the patient's early life due to his confusion in reading the other person. Often there is some intimacy experienced early in the first year of life that the individual is trying to recapture. This intimacy got lost as life became more confusing and uncertain because of the person's difficulty in reading others and having others read him. Symbolic elaborations in the depressive or paranoid realm serve a secondary purpose of filling up the empty void that was associated with the lack of understanding others' intentions and having others understand one's own intentions.

There are other problem areas involving nonverbal communication. One includes a tendency to "act out" behaviorally, due to the failure to recognize organizing and limit-setting communications; another is the tendency to experience *concrete fixed attitudes* about oneself and others. This is in part due to the lack of being able to enter into more refined reciprocal–gestural interactions that help encourage flexible perceptions. In other words, an accurate, positive picture of oneself as self-assertive, dependent, excited, and lovable comes from numerous, direct, responsive, reciprocal interactions with another person. When this gestural interactive system fails, there is little reciprocity. Flexible affectively mediated attitudes cannot be learned. It takes back and forth interactions of a continuous nature to gain a flexible, accurate picture of oneself or of others. The more interaction we have, the more we abstract general principles that reflect the true complexity of life and our position in it. The more limited our interactions the less we have from which to abstract. When interactions are limited, therefore, the result is repetitive fixed patterns associated with fixed attitudes. There is a constriction at the gestural level of communication. For example, the child, and later the adult, may behave in a fixed competitive way by being only negative, only aggressive, only complacent, only needy, only pseu-doindependent. In the adult, fixed thoughts may accompany them (e.g., "I'm bad," "I'm helpless"). To the degree there are limited interactions expanding these behaviors, they remain rigid and fixed under the pressure of the individual's own fixed, persev-erative tendencies. Interaction leads to flexibility; repetition with constricted or limited interactions leads to further rigidity. The posture of the therapist, like that of the patient, is, therefore, quite significant.

There are many types of constrictions at the gestural level. Behavioral acting out, as described above, occurs when the com-plex gestural system fails to have sufficient patterns that signal limits. The parent who uses just one passive voice or monotone, or who doesn't go up on a one to ten scale in terms of seriousness of their limit-setting intent, gives a child little voice–texture–ges-tural communication. Similarly, facial expression or body posture may be missing in this selective area.

This type of constriction in the gestural system may only re-late to the limit-setting and acting-out tendencies of the child as opposed to across-the-board lack of gestural interaction. The person who lacks a sense of connectedness and is distraught may also evidence a circumscribed limitation. One person may be prone to more depression when his gestural system doesn't work in the context of themes of dependency and closeness. A parent may only react gesturally when it comes to limit setting. Alterna-tively, the parent who is interactive around dependency issues, but not around limit setting, may support acting out. The parent who is confusing to the child around the issues of respect and admiration and certain elements of aggression may leave the child undermined in her assertiveness and feeling overly criticized.

Where the gestural system is not working, there tend to arise a number of fixed belief systems and attitudes. When these atti-tudes occur, however, we see another important phenomenon, the idealization of an aspect of experience. In the absence of a full range of interactions there is a tendency toward polarization and idealization (to fill in the missing experience). Fixed beliefs become more powerful and the belief or carrier of the belief becomes imbued with intense "all good" or "all bad" type polarized emotions. Somatically based affects are also prominent when emotional themes are being negotiated at the gestural level. Somatic affects and idealized or polarized behaviors, and later beliefs, often move into areas of presymbolic confusion.

Certain compulsive rituals and fixed behaviors may also be related to this early stage of ego development, particularly the early part of the gestural phase, when fixed repetitive patterns are more expectable before behavior has gotten interactively flexible. These rituals can be viewed as regulatory or self-calming behaviors. The ritual serves as a "behavioral security blanket," so to speak. Usually these patterns are part of interactive gestural patterns even though there is always a piece of it that is under one's own control. There is a self-regulatory and self-stimulatory component as well as an interactive gestural and representational component. Both play a role in self-regulation.

When interactive gestural components and representational components do not come into play as they should, then the self-stimulatory behavioral component may become more dominant. As one gets older, one may use these in excessive and idiosyncratic ways. Here we see ritualistic and compulsive patterns used for a variety of purposes from initial self-calming and regulation, to coping with different kinds of anxieties, fears, and affects.

While there are probably some individual biological differences in terms of proneness to ritualistic and compulsive patterns, they also may be related to complex difficulties in interactive gestural and representational regulation. In infants and young children, we observe the expression of these biological differences in tendencies to be overly reactive to certain sensations or have mixed reactivity and a tendency toward postural insecurity and motor planning difficulties. These are children who, to remain organized, early on favor shutting out or avoiding or narrowing their range of experience. The interactive component seems to relate to the caregiver's tendency to overload or vacillate and use rigid, rather than soothing, interactive modes of regulation and communication. We have noticed, however, that even children who seemed predisposed, because of their sensory and motor processing profile, to more ritualistic behavior can be brought into more soothing interactive patterns. In fact, caregivers that are naturally soothing and very interactive tend to intuitively assist children in becoming more flexible and less ritualistic. Idiosyncratic and self-stimulatory ritualistic behaviors thus decrease by increasing soothing and interactive gesturing and interactive representational communications.

Often with such children one has to work with the perseverative patterns and various types of individually different sensory processing tendencies. For example, one may have to build on the child's desire to touch a spot on the floor repetitively by putting one's hand on that spot playfully and playing cat and mouse games, thus bringing the very perseverative pattern into direct gestural interaction. Sometimes the therapist can do this by building on the child's perseveration itself. For a child who is opening and closing a door repetitiously, the therapist can get "stuck" in the door. After the child begins to get interactive pushing the therapist out of the door, the therapist can, for example, open and close a door and have a little pretend play with a doll sticking its head out the door and saying, "hello." Either the constructive elaboration of the child's interaction or the obstructive playful interference, if it leads to a gestural interaction, can serve to increase the flexibility of this behavioral regulatory system that may be associated with ritualistic and compulsive behaviors.

With very ritualistic adults, we have noticed as well that soothing vocal tones, increased attention to basic issues of longing, dependency, and feeling connected, as well as supporting expressions of rage and frustration, and lots of flexible interactive dialogue, as opposed to "abstinence" or rigid posture, or overdoing for the patient will decrease the occurrence of rigid behavior and thought patterns.

In summary, therefore, in clinical work we see problems of the gestural interactive level associated with tendencies for depressive or paranoid behavior and later ideation, related to the uncertainty of reading other people's cues. We also observe acting-out behaviors where the limit-setting qualities of gestural communication are not successfully negotiated. We see constrictions in character structure related to the relative degree to which different thematic areas are negotiated at the prerepresentational gestural level. Furthermore, we may see certain ritualistic and compulsive patterns based on the self-regulatory features of the gestural system. These stay fixed at a self-stimulatory level; they are not brought into interactive gestural communication.

In the psychotherapeutic process one needs to recognize the gestural roots of these difficulties. As indicated earlier, for the dysphoric affects associated with depressive and paranoid trends, the therapist needs to help the person deal with the primary issue and rework the secondary elaborations that are attached to it. The secondary elaborations are often like posthypnotic trance states where the person gives meaning to somatically based tendencies.

In the therapeutic process, it is important to separate out two elements of psychopathologic behavior. One element relates the original difficulty with gestural communication that occurs when the person feels uncertain or cannot get certain needs met; for example, self-regulation. Because a patient has failed to master this task, there will be an eruption of either ritualistic behavior for self-comforting, dysphoric affects associated with feeling empty or unconnected, or tendencies to act out. The next step is the secondary elaboration. This may use additional behavior patterns or later representational elements (obsessive thoughts, further ritualistic elaborations, depressive or paranoid ideation). These elaborations are tied to the original state of mind. By helping the person separate the steps in the process of mental construction, they can learn to slowly look at and tolerate the uncertainty of not being able to read other people's gestural signals or the somatic states associated with the need for self-regulation or self-stimulation. As they learn to tolerate these states, and have opportunities for interaction, they can begin to find more flexible, interactive solutions, rather than fixed behavioral or ideational secondary elaborations.

The therapist patiently inquires about the patient's source of uneasiness or lack of certainty or inability to figure out what is going on in their bodies as they work on their somatic states.

In other words, the therapist helps the patient avoid getting lost in depressive or paranoid ideation or in descriptions of acting-out tendencies. Instead the therapist tries to have those individuals describe what their experience was like at the moment they were in the interaction pattern that led to the depression or the paranoia or the behavioral acting out. What were the sensations in their body just before the fixed behavior or thoughts? Being able to describe physical states (e.g., "emptiness," "hollowness," "I've just got to get my muscles moving; just got to touch something smooth or hard; I need a loud noise; I need to squeeze myself") puts such patients in touch with the somatic affect states that accompany the behavioral level of organization.

These somatic affect states are mostly visceral descriptions rather than ideational or representational descriptions of abstracted feelings. As the patient describes these affects, the therapist shows a great deal of empathy for the feelings of discomfort and uneasiness and the desire to escape from them. As the patient experiences this new kind of comforting, interactive relationship around these uncomfortable somatic states, there is a chance to bring them into a gestural communication system.

What was not done in the early original developmental years has an opportunity to be renegotiated now, utilizing the power of reenactments in the transference. In an ongoing therapeutic relationship, these affects may be felt quite strongly. For example, the patient may experience a feeling that the therapist is criticizing him and the patient may act out by not coming to a session or by picking a fight with his spouse. Or, the patient may exhibit paranoid or depressive behavior and ideation. These secondary elaborations are not delved into as issues in their own right (i.e., the therapist and the patient don't get lost in these secondary elaborations). Instead, the therapist empathizes with the fact that there must be a sense of uncertainty about what the "other" person is intending (in this case, the therapist; at other times, the boyfriend, the spouse, etc.). The gestural interaction involving empathetic communication between the therapist and patient creates an interactive gestural system, a new type of interactive, soothing, and explorative experience. The therapist is not directly soothing the person. He is interacting with voice, eye contact, and body posture. He is engaging the patient at the gestural interactive level around painful, somatically based affects—something that may never have occurred earlier in the patient's life. Such interaction brings the gestural system into an interactive pattern. There is now interaction rather than feelings of painful disconnection and isolation. There is interaction rather than the lack of limit setting. Rather than ritualistic self-regulatory experiences, the patient now experiences interactive regulation and interactive gestural elaboration. This enables the patient to gradually and somewhat painfully rework the secondary elaborations of these early somatic states. The patient learns to tolerate them, rather than create behavioral, affective, and ideated elaborations.

As the early somatic states are tolerated, there is a new opportunity to move into the representational level of development in a way that is more open to more new experience. The representational level now will not be at the mercy of early fixed gestural patterns (i.e., as representational elaborations of the problems of the earlier more perseverative gestural level). Instead there will be the opportunity for new experiences to provide the basis for a broader, more flexible representational system, as well as a broader, more flexible gestural system.

Chapter 7

Representational Elaboration

Representational capacities arise out of the ability to form mental images. These multisensory pictures of experience permit individuals to move from merely acting out experiences to mentally representing them. Representational experience occurs when an adult puts feelings or inclinations into words and, in this way, symbolizes affect and wishes. A child may use pretend play as a vehicle for representing wishes, intentions, and feelings.

The symbol, as evidenced by a word or pretend-play drama, replaces the need for direct action, and eventually promotes thinking and reasoning as another way of experiencing important aspects of emotional life. The therapeutic challenge is to help an older child or adult move from a behavioral discharge mode to a representational one. A particular patient's representational mode may not be developed at all, while another patient's is constricted and exists only in relationship to selected emotions or affects.

A clinician may sometimes find it difficult to understand how an intelligent, verbally communicative patient can still be fundamentally operating via a behavioral mode and not a representational mode. It is important to remember that the person who directly acts out his needs (hitting when angry, eating when hungry, grabbing and hugging when needy, rather than saying, "I love you") is putting behavior into action. Even complex social behaviors, such as being charming or dominating, are sometimes only behavioral enactments that are initiated to get certain basic needs met; for example, being admired or being feared.

Such behavior can be quite appropriate, as in lovemaking or enjoying a fine meal. Other times it is characterized by a driven quality, like hitting a person in a bar, acting out a perversion, or indulging in various narcissistic patterns to enhance self-esteem. While there are certainly qualitative and developmental differences between the need to be admired and hitting someone in a bar, these experiences have an important similarity. Both are concerned with direct gratification and behavioral enactment rather than shared representational experience.

While there are similarities, the differences in behavioral patterns should be discussed also. Certain emotional needs and affects may be more primitive than others and come earlier in the course of development. The need to be respected, for example, comes much later than the simple need to deal with frustration by throwing angry temper tantrums or acting out. There are clear indications whether the person is operating at a more primitive or advanced intrapsychic developmental level. Evidence for this includes the relative complexity and sophistication of social behavior that a person can employ to achieve a specific outcome, and the degree to which that person can bring these efforts into accord with the rules of society and his or her own internal rules. Sometimes the patient who is operating with behavioral enactments (based on developmental needs that are more advanced) may initially present a therapeutic face, confusingly similar to the representational patient and only a deep understanding of the patient will help tease out whether or not he or she can truly represent their wishes and affects.

How does the therapist determine whether a verbally adroit patient may yet be locked into a behavior discharge mode? He first must recognize that words can be used in a direct behavioral sense rather than employed in the service of sharing representational experience. Once sufficient language and cognitive skills to verbalize experience are developed (usually between the ages of 2 and 4), we then have two ways of communicating: one is directly through behavior, and the other is through verbalization of affect and wish. However, the verbalization can simply be a cognitive task describing what one does in a situation. For example, if you, as a barroom brawler, are commenting on being insulted, it does not require enormous psychological maturity to remark, "I kick the guy, push him down, and break a bottle over his head." Similarly, if the person who is driven by certain sexual perversions feels that the therapist is both supportive and nonjudgmental, he or she may well describe how they respond to a sexually provocative situation. This does not mean that they are truly able to abstract their feelings in terms of representing wishes and affects. Such patients are merely displaying the ability to intellectually describe behavioral patterns that they tend to reenact. This ability, of course, is an important step toward eventually being able to represent these experiences, but in itself does not suggest full representation. Thus, a patient may display two distinct behavioral patterns: the actual enactment of a behavior and a cognitive description of the behavior. The latter is a step toward representation, but in itself is not a representation.

An important early step in shifting from behavioral to representational capacity involves becoming aware of the affects that accompany or precede the behaviors. These affects can exist in many different forms. There is a hierarchy of such affect organizations which will be described shortly. First, consider the different forms.

Many patients abstract affects in a global way ("I feel bad" or "I don't feel good"). Children often describe these affects using the same words that adults do. Polarized global affect states, attributing vague, all-bad feelings or vague all-good feelings to oneself or someone else is a form of the global use of affects. From these more general verbal descriptions evolve the more truly abstracted affect states. Feelings are described in such terms as *sad, angry, helpless, excited,* and *humiliated.*

Patients also experience somatic based affects (e.g., "tight muscles" "churning stomach"). It should be pointed out, some physical descriptions of affects (queasy stomach) may be accompanied by certain affect descriptions that appear to be high-level abstracted affect states, but are in reality mere derivatives of somatic descriptions that are disguised by flowery language. Patients who say that their "guts were consumed with fire," or that they were "coming apart at the seams in a thousand little pieces," may initially appear to use lots of words to describe their feelings. Such descriptions, however, are so primitive and somatically based in their metaphors that they are simply verbally sophisticated versions of such somatically based comments as "my muscles are tight."

Two tendencies can be seen at the somatic level of description. One involves organized somatic descriptions including organ aches or pains ("my heart hurts," "my stomach feels empty," "my muscles throb," or "I feel empty in the pit of my belly"). The second tendency is revealed by the use of more disorganized, fragmented, and primitive somatic descriptions ("bloody guts all over the place"). One can further subdivide these tendencies in the following ways: (1) the actual physical sensations (pains in the shoulders, back, stomach, and heart), where the somatic pain feels physical and is not a communication about affect states, is probably the most primitive form of description; (2) next in the hierarchy is the use of somatic affects as descriptive of some sensation inside the body, but it does not involve actual physical discomfort or pain to the organs, muscles, or skeletal system of the body. A person might say, "When she looks at me that way, I feel as if my stomach were coming apart and falling into a million pieces, with blood gushing out of my body"; (3) this somatic, disorganized level is closely followed by another level of somatic expression, which is more organized ("my lungs cry out," "my feet are screaming"); (4) one step higher are the general expressions of affects ("I feel awful, hurt, bad"). These are vague, general states of affect.

There is also a hierarchy of behavioral discharge tendencies that are not necessarily parallel to the affect expressions, but also characterize prerepresentational states of mind. First is the direct discharge of behavior (hitting, kicking, biting). Second is the verbalization of the behavioral pattern, a behavioral description of "what I do." Next is the behavioral description of what a person *wants* to do in certain situations. ("I want to hit, kick, bite" rather than "I do hit, kick, bite.")

The most advanced form of representation and expression of affect is where one can talk about affects which have a combined affective–cognitive meaning. The terms used at this level and the emotional expressions which support these terms have to do with familiar concepts of sadness, disappointment, anger, pleasure, excitement, delight, happiness, and pride. These high-level affect states are usually combinations of a set of sensations and a set of symbolic elaborations of these sensations into a combined affective–cognitive construct. Integrated affective structures are present when these affect states are honestly felt and accurately labeled (as opposed to a person who merely says the words in an intellectual sense, but whose demeanor or body posture does not support the expressed words); and when there is a full integration of the nonverbal, affective with the cognitive elaboration. These structures are at the top of our developmental hierarchy.

Not all these advanced affects come in at the same time in development. Affects like empathy and more mature types of love develop a little later in childhood, after earlier affects of rage, anger, excitement, pleasure, delight or happiness, and later, affects around competition. There are also affects related to self-esteem and positive self-regard which come still later in development.

The therapist will often observe that more than one level of affect may be expressed at the same time. Usually, however, the levels that appear simultaneously are adjacent to each other (see Figure 7.1). For example, if an individual is describing behaviors in terms of "I hit," he may also volunteer primitive somatic affects (organized or disorganized), such as "I hit and my heart is coming apart in pieces." A person may have some disorganized somatic affects, even some very vague general affect states accompanying behavioral descriptions. It is less likely that the

Figure 7.1 Hierarchy of affect states

Representational		Examples
		Positive Self-Esteem
		Disappointment
		Mature Love
		Empathy
	• Abstracted Affect States:	Competition
	Words have a combined	Jealousy
	affective/cognitive	Envy
	meaning and refer to	Loss
	specific differentiated	Happiness
	feeling states	Pleasure
		Excitement
		Curiosity
		Anger
		Rage
	• Expressions of Global Affects	"I feel awful"
	• Verbalization of Organized Somatic Feelings	It is as though "my lungs cry out"
		"My heart aches"
	• Verbalization of Disorganized, Somatic Feelings	"When she stares at me it is as if my body's exploding in a thousand pieces"
	• Verbalization of Intentions in Behavioral Terms	"I want to kick her"
	• Verbalization of Behavioral Pattern	"I hit him"
Earliest Representational Behavioral Transition	• Organized Somatic Description	"My heart hurts"
	• Disorganized Fragmented, Primitive, Somatic Pattern	"My blood vessels were going to explode"
Behavioral Level	Complex Gestural Communication	Angry or loving facial
	Direct Discharge of Behavior	Hitting, kicking, biting, hugging, holding, kissing
	Simple Gestural Communication	smiles, head nods, frowns
	Engagement	Joyful relating, self-absorption
Prebehavioral	Regulation and Interest in the World	Looking, listening, or withdrawn

behavioral and the most abstracted affect states having to do with sadness, loss, anger, joy, and pleasure will be involved together. When we talk about abstracted affects, we are referring to the ability to represent a visceral sensation in terms of combined, affective–cognitive elaboration. This is the top of the affect hierarchy. Lower levels in the hierarchy can be associated with behavioral level phenomena and a sort of transition between the behavioral level and the representational level. Pure somatic states and pure behavioral discharge states are transitional between earlier prebehavioral states (the earliest regulatory phenomena) and the behavioral interaction aspects of communication. If we graft our affect hierarchy to our general developmental stages, the rock-bottom base of the structure is the stage of regulation and interest in the world, upon which a sense of engagement and attachment, and a later sense of two-way gestural communication (simple and complex), is built.

In clinical situations it is not always clear when a person is describing behaviors or truly abstracting or representing affects. An indication that the behavioral level rather than the representational level is in evidence occurs when a patient's affective verbalizations concern strategies aimed at changing the behavior of others around them rather than communicating feelings. Such a person is using words to get behavioral goals met, rather than to communicate somatic affect states. In other words, a behavioral negotiation is taking place.

For example, a man who is preoccupied with his safety and security would become preoccupied with whether his wife would be home early or whether she would be working late. This would happen whenever challenging and competitive situations at work became particularly stressful for him. He would call his wife on the phone and complain about how desperate his life was, seeking reassurance that she would remain committed to him. He would also want her there during certain times with the children, when competitive issues were brewing at work. His need for safety and security at times would even take on phobic qualities, as demonstrated by his need to have his wife physically around at certain critical junctures. His entire use of words in these situations was aimed at directly increasing his own sense of security, rather than communicating any feelings to his spouse. In fact, the dramatic nature of his descriptions of his plight at work (being "swamped," feeling "at the mercy" of others) was linked to his desperate, increased need for security.

This situation reveals a behavioral strategy designed to "get her next to me to make me feel better" rather than a strategy of communicating "I don't feel good." Even though the affects expressed by this man may superficially sound representational, his words are simply used as an elaborate behavioral negotiation designed to make his wife act in a way that diminished his acute levels of anxiety. When the goal is representational, the self awareness of "I don't feel good" and the sense of being understood is an end in its own right. Getting the other person to change their behavior is not the primary goal.

It should be noted that sometimes a person has achieved some capacity to represent affects, but is unable to integrate various feelings. In one case, a young woman had to separate any feelings of lust from feelings of dependency. While this patient could experience loving feelings toward her husband and needed him for security and dependency, she was incapable of experiencing physical pleasure when she found herself romantically excited by him. During the course of therapy, it became apparent that earlier conflict with her own mother had led her to mistrust the durability of the pleasure she enjoyed with her mother at certain times, since this enjoyment was often erased by her mother's rejecting and controlling nature. The woman attempted to keep these two affects separate in her most intimate relationships. She could never experience integrated affect states when interacting with her husband, only partial ones. The split-off affects were often in evidence in fantasies of romantic encounters.

In addition, the therapist typically will observe that there are constrictions in the affects displayed by a patient, and that not all affects can be equally well represented or abstracted. Some people are more comfortable revealing feelings of dependency, while others are open with feelings of aggression or pleasure. For example, the child or adult who is passive-aggressive may use such behaviors as avoidance or frustrating others when angry, yet still be able to talk about warm, loving feelings and exciting, pleasurable feelings. In this case, behaviors are used to communicate one affect, such as anger, while abstracted feeling states are used for other affects.

It should be pointed out that when individuals abstract affects, they may in fact also achieve gratification and satisfaction. Sharing meanings, understanding another's feelings, and communicating one's own feelings can be inherently pleasurable.

An individual may, therefore, negotiate a number of steps on the way to representing affects. Enactments of behaviors, the ability to describe one's own behaviors, negotiation around needs and intentions for behavioral goals (e.g., "I feel like I'm falling apart, therefore you have to be next to me all the time"); using general affect states (such as good or bad); and finally, abstracted affect states (feeling sad, happy, excited, or even humiliated) are processes experienced along the way. At the abstracted affect level, two types of constrictions or limitations may occur. One rises out of a difficulty with integrating all of the abstracted affects that an individual actually experiences. Certain elements of a person's feeling may be separated off from one individual and be displaced onto others. The second limitation develops when certain affects are operating at earlier levels so that anger is acted out with passive-aggressive means, while dependency and excitement can be represented. When there is evidence of constrictions or a lack of integration around individual core relationships, the clinician should endeavor to deal with these affects at their earliest level developmentally and work up from there.

HOW TO HELP THE PATIENT SHIFT TO A TRULY REPRESENTATIONAL LEVEL

In helping a patient go from a behavioral or earlier somatic level to the truly representational level, it behooves the therapist to consider what helps children become representational during normal development. If a parent tends to be intimidated by the scope and urgency of a child's needs, it is hard for the child to learn to represent experience. Take, for example, the child who bangs on the front door, wailing, "I want to go outside and I want to go now!" while it's raining cats and dogs. Parent A wants the child to wait until it stops raining, explaining, "No, you can't go outside now." An argument ensues. When the child says, "I want to go outside," the parent replies, "No, you have to listen to me." A power struggle develops and the child has a temper tantrum. The parent may win the fight and not give in to the child, but the child has had little experience with representing his affects in that situation. On the other hand, parent B deals with the situation a little differently. She positions herself between the child and the door so the child can't go outside, and raises the questions, "Why do you have to go outside now? Why can't you wait?" The child then verbalizes that he can't wait because his toy truck is outside, or that he is tired of staying inside all morning. The child is reflecting on his wish, inclination, or affect. He is describing his wish and his related affects rather than acting them out. He is learning to "separate" his feelings. The second parent then empathizes, "Oh, I know how hard it is to wait," and further helps the child talk about his feelings and the sense of urgency he is experiencing in his body. A connecting sense of shared meaning, rather than a power struggle, takes place between the child and parent B. In this second example, and through thousands and perhaps even millions of similar shared connections between parent and child, the child learns to abstract more and more affects, particularly as each need, inclination, wish, or desire becomes part of such a dialogue of shared meanings. Even if the child eventually throws a tantrum, there have been a number of interactions which help the child learn to "reflect" on his or her experience.

What do we learn from parent B, and how does this play out in the psychotherapeutic situation? First and foremost, the therapist should exhibit a nonconcrete or abstracting posture toward the patient. It is similar to the reflective attitude shown by the parent who doesn't get suckered into a power struggle with the demanding child described above. This abstracting posture is harder to implement than one would commonly think. For instance, when a woman complains to her therapist about what an awful guy her husband is, it is very easy for the therapist to get caught up in the woman's attempts to criticize her husband's behavior. A therapist may argue with the patient, suggesting that her strategy is wrong and that the best way to get her husband to love her and act thoughtfully is to not be such a nag, or to try to be more assertive or independent. Each time the therapist joins in the practical, concrete, day-to-day life experiences of the patient, helping the patient achieve a better decision or strategy, he is entering the person's world at the behavioral level. This is much like the behavior of the parent who enters the child's world at the behavioral level and either lets the child go out in the rain or engages in a power struggle.

Typically, therapists will give direct advice to patients about being more assertive, about standing up for themselves, or about not being so passive in their interpersonal relationships. Sometimes they do this by offering direct advice, and other times they more subtly raise pointed questions. By asking, "Why did you say that?" or "Did you consider this?" the therapist is being just as directive as when he says "You should say this," or "You should do that." All therapists will recognize that this is a familiar strategy that they use when they want to be helpful to a patient. They may say, "Well, did you consider a different strategy with your boss?" or "Why were you quiet when he didn't give you the raise?" or "Did it occur to you that you might review for him the highlights of your past performance with the company?"

All these questions are actually directive in their intentions. Why do we do that as therapists? If we are honest with ourselves, we often resort to such an approach in the urgency of the moment. We want to help this patient out of a difficult situation with their spouse, boyfriend, boss, or best friend, and we find ourselves drawn toward acting out the role of a good friend. After all, a confidante of the patient might offer them advice, suggestions, or raise questions, and we want to be at least as helpful as a good friend might be. We then sometimes disguise our guiding hand by putting our suggestions in the form of a question or change our tone of voice or body position. But when we succumb to the urgency of the moment, we are merely helping the person with a behavioral strategy that only helps them improve their situation at the moment. When we do this, we are entering our patients' day-to-day lives at the behavioral level by being so concretely helpful. Patients may desire such direct intervention by a therapist, and often complain about those clinicians who do not give direct advice. *In providing indirect advice, we are not just satisfying the patient's wish, we are compromising an opportunity for more substantial growth.*

If we want to build the patient's representational system, we must take a nonconcrete attitude, and work on helping the person "reflect" his or her experience in the situation. When the patient reports that he or she behaved ineffectually with the boss and avoided asking for a raise, we must explore that experience and foster a "reflective" attitude. They may describe their muscle tension, how their mind was blocked, how they felt tingling in their hands, or what they wanted from their boss. As we reflect with them on their experience and what it felt like in that situation, we are trying to meet them at the level where they are, as well as creating a new shared experience. We thus wind up fostering representational capacities.

In other words, every time we side with the need for discharge, or immediate gratification, even skillfully through a seemingly neutral question, we are inadvertently reinforcing the behavioral level by enacting a pattern to meet a certain need. Even though our goal may be praiseworthy, we wind up shortchanging our patients in the long run, if we seek, for example, only to help the person negotiate a better salary with the boss, to help a woman find the right things to say to her husband, or to help a husband learn to be more understanding with his wife.

Alternatively, however, once we adopt a less concrete, representational approach, our single overriding therapeutic goal is to help the patient understand his or her experiences while under the pressure of some wish, need, inclination, or intention. Following a patient's confrontation with a boss or spouse, we are focused on what their experience was like; we are interested in the patient being able to reflect on that experience. We are less concerned with the particular behaviors that will help the patient achieve certain ends. In other words, we avoid getting caught up in the urgency of the behavioral level, and will bolster the mastery of the representational level instead. The clinician should keep in mind that there are three options available to him when a patient presents him with a sense of urgency. The "yes" option includes coaching the patient on how to achieve a specific end; the "no" option results in power struggles based on thwarting the patient from getting his or her way. The third, "What's your hurry, buddy?" option facilitates the joint exploration of those feelings that the patient experiences while in a state of urgency. This last choice obviously enhances the patient's growth in his ability to represent experience.

HOW TO INTERACT WITH PATIENTS AT THEIR DEVELOPMENTAL LEVEL TO FOSTER A SENSE OF SHARED COMMUNICATION

Developing an effective therapeutic posture in terms of a nonconcrete attitude is only the first step in fostering representational capacity. The next critical step involves assessing the person's true developmental level. Many skillful therapists read and intuit the true messages sent by the patient, but are often unaware of the patient's actual developmental level. An opportunity for fostering the representational mode is missed. The most common error we make occurs in psychodynamic therapy when we routinely ask the patient who operates at the behavioral level to say what comes to mind. When the patient describes his or her situation, we listen to a litany of the many behaviors exhibited by the patient and others. The person may be quite skilled at giving us a detailed commentary on their experiences, and may in fact be comfortable offering up random thoughts as he or she freely associates.

We typically attempt to meet the person empathetically by summarizing what we have heard and acknowledging the implied feelings we think the person is having, and at times, try to ask questions that will lead to insights about the person's behavior. We might empathize with a husband's annoyance when his wife insisted on giving him directions, saying, "It seems as though you were feeling vulnerable when she was telling you how to drive, even though she knew the way better than you since you were going to her friend's house. It sounds like you were feeling emasculated, so you got mad and started yelling at her." This type of insight might be offered to someone who had shown a pattern of sensitivity to being criticized by his wife and revealed a shaky vulnerability about his own masculinity. In offering such a clarification, insight, or summary of a pattern, however, the therapist not infrequently is overlooking the fact that the individual who is talking about behaviors is not yet at the level of representational elaboration and does not abstract affect states. The clinician often does consider the possibility that the patient may be denying or otherwise defending against certain feelings. The clinician may, for example, empathize with the possibility that "no one likes to feel vulnerable" or that the patient feels "it's best to avoid such feelings." But, here too, if the patient is not representational he will not comprehend these concepts. The clinician's comments that the patient is feeling vulnerable, anxious, and emasculated may, thus, be alien concepts. The patient may understand these terms intellectually, and may even enter into a debate, agreeing or disagreeing with the therapist.

The more effective way to approach such a person would be to offer empathy in terms of the behavioral pattern, displaying understanding that when the patient does A and B, and the wife responds by doing C and D, the patient winds up doing E and F. To such a summary, the person might reply, "Yes, of course. Every time we're driving somewhere she tells me what to do. Every time she tells me what to do, I do the opposite. Then I yell and scream at her. She then tells me that I'm mean, and we fight. That's exactly what I'm telling you and I don't know what to do about this." Summarizing and replaying the pattern of behaviors often serves to create a sense of shared experience at the level the patient is at; in this case, the behavioral level. You may perhaps even recap the patient's story in a more cohesive way to show that you are a good listener and that you remember all the elements in the particular drama he or she is describing. You are not, however, suggesting to the patient how he is feeling.

How does conveying a sense of understanding the patient, when you meet the person at the appropriate developmental level, create the necessary second ingredient for fostering the representational mode? The answer can be found in the following discussion of how representations are formed.

HOW REPRESENTATIONS ARE FORMED

Let us begin with the assumption that the individual operating at the behavioral level uses behaviors to meet certain ends or objectives, including the satisfaction of certain needs, wishes, or intentions. The brighter the person, the more intricate and sophisticated these behaviors may be. Another individual who interacts with a person who operates on a behavioral level is not there to be understood or to understand, but only to offer counterbehaviors.

When patients with such an orientation are involved in a therapeutic relationship, they find, often for the first time in their lives, somebody who comprehends their behavioral patterns and how these behavioral patterns interact with those of other people. This can be a profound experience, since such patients have rarely if ever shared meaning at the behavioral level with another person. A unitary individual operates with certain behaviors and experiences certain counterbehaviors with the objective of getting needs met. In a therapeutic relationship this same person becomes an individual who senses that there is a partner involved in an experience of shared comprehension of intentions, and their related behaviors and counterbehaviors. For the first time, a me and a you coexist in a collaborative endeavor organized around exploring interactive patterns.

A key part of this fledgling experience is the new sense of pleasure and comfort within the partnership. This active communication of behavioral patterns creates a relationship with its own emotional tone. No longer is the meeting of one's own personal needs the sole objective in launching interpersonal behaviors. A core need state now operates in two contexts simultaneously: one context is the achievement of satisfaction through behaviors and counterbehaviors. The second context involves a sense of shared experiences around this very same need state and intention. This second context is the pleasure of exploring behavioral patterns with another person.

This newfound sense of another person not simply being a behavioral gratifier or responder but a pattern explorer is a monumental achievement for a person who has been organized at the behavioral level. As the clinician delves into the history of such individuals, she often finds in such families that lots of mechanical operations dealing with food, clothing, and normal security operations may make the children feel safe and protected. They may even be played with, wrestling with their fathers and doing puzzles with their mothers. What is missing in such families, however, is a sense of shared communication around a child's needs or wishes. There are power struggles when the child wants to go outside. There are "yeses" and "no's" to the child's requests for food, excitement, or dependency support. There is, however, little negotiation around these needs, and a lack of exploration of the child's experience. No attempts are made to help the child articulate his or her difficulty in negotiating particular wishes, needs, or intentions.

We mistakenly assume that "reflective" negotiations occur in normal family interactions just as they do when the therapist deliberately tries to help the patient verbalize his or her experiences in life. In some families, it is common for a parent to say to a child who wants to go outside, "What's the hurry? Why can't you wait?" "Come on now, why are you so excited?" This permits the child to talk about how it feels to be frustrated, and why it is so hard to postpone something he or she wants. In other families, however, parents simply respond to the child's importunings with a concrete "yes" or "no." The more there are negotiations, elaborations, and islands of shared meanings, the more likely it is that the child will begin to develop a representational capacity. To be sure, simply exchanging lots of words and dialogues does not mean that these shared meanings will occur. There are families in which the parents constantly misread their children, projecting their own needs and wishes onto the children, and other families where the parents are relating to the child at a developmental level that is too high or too low. In such families an adaptive representational capacity is often not developed and their children grow up fragmented, overwhelmed, or withdrawn as a result. In contrast, in families that "read," respond, and reflect on communications, we see important ego capacities on the ascendancy.

Once pleasure in shared communication in reflecting on interactive patterns is established, the beginnings of new aspects of psychological structure begin to unfold. The goal of the individual is now no longer simply behavioral discharge; instead a complementary goal arises in which shared meanings lead to closeness and some satisfaction in terms of dependency and security. It should also be pointed out that the sharing of meanings need not, and should not, occur only at the verbal level. Sometimes a nod or a certain smile can convey a sense of shared meaning. Consider the therapist who observes a child reenact an episode which involves hitting a sibling. The enactments, which are clearly discharge-type activities, as opposed to true dramas that exhibit themes and feelings, occur through doll play. During this behavioral enactment, the therapist simply nods warmly and assumes a kindly, understanding facial expression. The child glances over as though to say "get my drift?" These nonverbal behavioral patterns can convey this same sense of shared meanings that actually describing the patterns might accomplish with an adult. The therapist might remark to an adult, "I can appreciate that you're telling me that when you do A, B, C, then E, D, F happens." Sometimes the adult who is discussing these behavioral patterns can feel understood simply by an empathetic look in the therapist's eyes, or the therapist's relaxed and accepting posture. Under ideal circumstances with the older child and the adult, both the affects and the words of the therapist reach the person at the appropriate developmental level and are relevant to the particular experience the person is revealing.

This shared experience now creates the basis for the patient to reflect on his own behavior. This ability to take a step away from one's own behavior and observe it is the key to entering into the representational mode. Representational ability initially involves seeing a behavioral pattern, pausing and reflecting, and not feeling immediately compelled to satisfy the goals of that behavioral pattern. Later on this reflective attitude leads to abstracted affect states.

Communicating about behavioral patterns with another person is perceived as pleasurable, and an increased sense of comfort and security are the by-products of sharing behavioral patterns with another person. This interactive pleasure, in turn, provides the bridge or transition to the pleasure found in pondering one's own behavioral patterns. One abstracts from the relationship a new capacity and new pleasure. We have, then, the very beginning of what will later become self-observation, which will eventually lead to the ability to abstract affect states.

As behavioral patterns are identified, the therapist gradually begins to help the patient describe the affects that precede or accompany these behaviors. Initially these affect descriptions may be vague, general, or somatic ("my muscles ache"). Gradually, if the therapist does not make the mistake of verbalizing affects for the patient, which will often be at a higher developmental level than the patient, the patient may progress to more differentiated or abstracted affect states.

As development toward the representational mode continues, we need to consider such postulated psychic structures as the superego and the ego. The latter group of functions of the mind is concerned with self-observation and comparing behaviors to some idealized standards, while the former has, in part, to do with self-observation and inhibitions. Both the ego and superego are elaborations of the representational systems as certain representational capacities become sufficiently organized around various functions to be given their own subidentities in the intrapsychic world. However one chooses to describe these psychological functions, whether one uses classic psychoanalytic terminology or other labels, it is important to note that they have their genesis in the development of the representational system itself. Without representation, none of these advanced functions can come into place, at least not in the form that is associated with adaptive development.

One should therefore resist thinking of the representational system as simply the result of the cognitive capacities to symbolize. One can symbolize impersonal experience without being able to abstract affects or symbolize emotional experience. There are, in fact, many brilliant novelists, physicists, and artists who can symbolize experience in gifted ways due to extraordinary cognitive abilities, but who are quite primitive in their emotional organization and in fact may be functioning at the behavioral or even more primitive levels. The ability to represent impersonal experience should not be confused with the ability to represent emotional experience or abstract affects. This ability to abstract affects and represent experience has its roots in certain types of interpersonal experiences, both in early development and in the therapeutic situation.

The significant other person, whether it is a therapist or parents, can balance empathizing with the individual's developmental level with bringing a sense of objectivity to the patterns being explored. This helps the representational system not just represent internal experience, but also brings in a certain element of reality adaptation. The self-observing part of the representational system should work in tandem with an ability to observe against a background of reality. To the degree that significant others are outside one's own intrapsychic world, yet empathize with one, they wear two hats. They join a person through their empathy and are part of that person's intrapsychic world, yet they also bring with them a certain level of relative objectivity by the very fact that they are a separate person. This then helps the representational system form around the two polarities of subjectivity and objectivity. An individual can reflect on experience against this double set of standards.

What happens, however, when significant others in relationships have distortions in the way they see things? They may project many of their own feelings or wishes onto another person's feelings and wishes, and distort or overexaggerate. Obviously, this can lead to a situation where the very structure of a person's representational system may be influenced by the projections and distortions of the significant other, whether this be a therapist, parent, spouse, sibling, or friend.

As therapists, we often see this situation in individuals who have had a disturbed parent or a troubled therapist, and the reality of their representational system is colored by this experience. There are cetain emotional assumptions that appear to be fixed in these situations whether it is a depressive sense of realiity that people always let you down, or a paranoid sense of reality that people will always hurt and attack.

It should also be pointed out that in psychoanalytic psychology there has been a lot of interest in empathy, and certainly the contributions of Kohut and his followers have emphasized the importance of empathizing with certain affect states of the individual. These significant contributions, however, have been somewhat limited by the lack of a more complete developmental framework. The importance of empathy should be underlined and highlighted. The empathy only works successfully, however, when it is linked with the right developmental level (e.g., prerepresentational, involved in somatic states of organization, representation, highly differentiated representational thinking). For example, if one empathizes with a patient's wish to have and anger over not getting "more approval," a prerepresentational patient may feel lost in terms of the therapist's meaning.

Many aspects of traditional therapeutic theory, such as empathy, have important roles, but when they are viewed as a global ingredient of therapeutic value, misunderstandings can develop. Limit setting, interpretation, clarification, and conflict resolution are all important. Each of these therapeutic options, however, must be seen in terms of the developmental issues and challenges they operate in and must be fined-tuned in terms of their developmental context. For example, clarifications at the representational level are only meaningful for a person who is fully representational. Verbal insights will only be experienced as helpful by the person who is already representationally differentiated. The question still remains: why in the course of normal development or in a therapeutic situation does a person have to share experience with another person in order to develop the representational capacity? Why cannot an individual simply use his or her cognitive abilities to reflect on their own behaviors?

AFFECTIVE AND COGNITIVE REPRESENTATIONS

However gifted a person is cognitively, the first abstractions he or she makes in life are always derived from personal affective experience. They are then explored in terms of general rules of logic. Wish and affect, in a sense, are necessary for adaptive human cognitive operations.

In chapter 2, we discussed the affective bases of intelligence and general ego functioning. The children without developmental challenges as may be recalled had two elements in their abstract thinking. They generated ideas of personal affective experience (e.g., likes and dislikes with bosses). They were then able to reflect on personal experiences, elaborate on them, and finally use their logical abilities to categorize their experiences and compare them with some other experiences.

The more challenged 5-year-old child was unable to start with more personal emotional experience and instead shifted to an impersonal classification. His thinking took on an idiosyncratic and mechanical quality. Simply put, thinking involves affective experience, which is classified or otherwise ordered.

The ability to reflect on and represent experience has its origins in just such affective experience. The therapist and patient experience pleasure in shared explorations of behavioral patterns. As the shared experience is abstracted, the ability to observe one's behavior is formed. Critical to this capacity is the fact that there has already been an experience of conversing around needs without directly trying to satisfy needs. One can never get to this general sense of dealing with wishes or needs within oneself (i.e., beyond direct discharge) to reflection, other than through first collaborating with another person and abstracting the sense of the relationship with that other person, and then having that sense for oneself. Remember, all intellectual activity and abstractions reflecting higher levels of cognitive activity are first and foremost abstractions from personal experience.

CONSTRICTIONS IN REPRESENTATIONAL CAPACITY

Representational capacities need to be considered in terms of specific inclinations and affects as well as general tendencies. First, consider the person who operates at an entirely behavioral level. Such an individual needs to elevate all their experiences, affects, and inclinations to the representational level. As each and every inclination, wish, or need becomes part of a relationship with shared experience, each need or wish becomes elevated to the representational level. The parent is able to engage some inclinations and affects representationally, however, but is unable to enter into a state of shared meaning with all of the child's inclinations, wishes, and affects. Some parents deal better with dependency, entering into a state of shared meaning around a child's loving or warm feelings, but will get into power struggles with the child when it comes to issues involving aggression. With other families, the reverse situation may be true.

In the therapeutic situation, our ideal clinician would have no blind spots and would be able to engage his prerepresentational, behavioral patient in all of the inclinations, needs, and affects in terms of shared experience, and gradually, over time, help elevate each of these needs and affects to the representational level. In the real world, though, therapists have countertransference difficulties, their own personal limitations, and need to ask themselves an important question: In my own life, which affects do I have more trouble with—dependency, aggression, sexual excitement? Which ones am I less representational with? In which one do I tend to lapse into behavioral discharge modes (all-or-nothing ways of thinking)? How do I cope with my own children? How do I relate with my spouse? The therapist can thus become aware of personal blind spots by careful preparation, and be more available to systematically help a patient progress to the representational level, in relation to each wish and affect.

When individuals have a representational capacity for some wishes and affects and not others, it is often challenging to the clinician because he or she expects the person to be able to represent all affects. After all, the person who can wax eloquent on feelings of love and loss and dependency, and mournfully share feelings of sadness and longing, could logically be expected to also talk about rage and anger. Frequently, however, some individuals—poetic though they sound about loss and love—may still be at the behavioral level when it comes to anger, resorting to passive avoidance or discharge enactments. They are unlikely to spontaneously verbalize their rage or their annoyance. Around the dimension of anger, therefore, they may require the therapist to create an opportunity for shared experience through meeting the person at their behavioral level. They help the person recognize the patterns, and then move into this sense of shared experience around a particular affect, which was either never previously elevated to the representational level or which had regressed to an earlier level of organization.

The therapist must profile the individual, trying to determine at which developmental level he or she is operating, in terms of the person's different inclinations, wishes, needs, and associated affects. By dividing up the emotional world into dependency, pleasure, and excitement, assertiveness, curiosity, anger and rage, fears, loss and separation, empathy, and mature forms of love, the therapist can then take a broad look at which areas are at which developmental level and thereby anticipate where the therapeutic focus will lie.

There is another aspect of the therapeutic work that is designed to facilitate the transition from behavioral to representational levels. This aspect focuses on the fact that meeting individuals at their developmental level can work on certain prerepresentational conflicts, which also further facilitates the shift to the representational level. The sense of shared experience and empathy serves to help patients cope with their feelings of being out of control or at the mercy of their own appetites or wishes. Often, individuals at the behavioral, or the earlier somatic, levels can experience a sense of enormous discomfort, which later gets verbalized as embarrassment or humiliation (when they are representational), tied to their inability to modulate or control their own impulses and appetites. This sense of being overwhelmed from inside, which Anna Freud described as being overwhelmed by one's own instincts, is a dysphoric experience for most individuals. When embarrassment or humiliation are not experienced in their abstracted affective sense, dysphoria and self-destructive behavior can result. It is not unusual to see children who are out of control vacillate between appetitive behavior and self-destructive behavior. This seems to be different from conflicts over certain sexual inclinations. The conflicts over being out of control in relationship to one's general state of arousal seem to be a feature of the human organism's tendency to try to stay in some state of emotional and physiologic regulation.

Human beings appear to have two central tendencies that operate: one for taking on new experience in accord with new abilities and maturational capacities, such as to walk, to speak, and in general to broaden the range of experience. The other tendency, however, seems to be the need to be regulated or in control, and not to feel overwhelmed or overloaded. We often see infants or children trying to balance these two tendencies to achieve physiologic and emotional regulation on the one hand, and to take on new experiences in accord with maturational abilities on the other hand. Achieving this equilibrium is difficult at times. The child who is learning to use imagination may have nightmares and scary dreams when the exercise of a new capacity goes beyond itself in terms of the regulatory functions, and the child may need assistance in getting back into regulation. At times, when the desire for regulation leads to perseveration and sameness, as it does with autistic children, new experience is compromised.

In keeping with this basic need of the organism to balance regulation on the one hand and take on new experience in accord with maturational abilities on the other hand, we can look at the role of the therapist in meeting the person at the developmental level and creating a sense of shared experience. Patients experience their appetites, needs, and desires as enacted through these behavioral patterns. For the first time in their lives they now can share (through the therapist's ability to meet them at their developmental level) their inclinations, wishes, and needs, the behaviors that accompany them, and the counterbehaviors they experience from others. For the first time it is not a matter of simply trying to meet these wishes and stay regulated. As the experience is shared, the behaviors, a sense of potential humiliation and embarrassment in their preliminary forms, no longer operate in isolation but come into the context of a shared experience. The empathy, warmth, and acceptance of the therapist softens the intense, often self-destructive rage associated with embarrassment and humiliation. This softening of the needs and wishes on one hand, and the humiliation and rage in relation to being out of control on the other hand, makes the prerepresentational conflicts less intense. These conflicts tend to maintain a system of behavioral enactments and counterenactments. Appetitive need and inclination-oriented behavior and responses are often followed by self-destructive behavior related to rage, humiliation, and embarrassment. These conflicts are softened by bringing the two sides of the equation into some harmony, in the context of a sharing of experience with the therapist.

In place of the behavior and its counterregulatory behavior operating at extreme polarities, we now have a shifting to a representational level, where both sides of the equation can eventually be represented. The humiliation, embarrassment, and rage will have a role in helping individuals at the representational level judge and inhibit their future behaviors. The representation of wishes and needs will help the individual determine different ways to meet these needs. More importantly, the person will be helped to bring these needs into an interpersonal context where the sense of shared experience brings these primitive, discharge-oriented needs into social experiences. These collaborative experiences with other individuals, and eventually with a group, become of value to the person, particularly in terms of enhancing a sense of security, comfort, and pleasure.

Here we see not only the earliest stages of the formation of an individual's representational system, but the birth of true socialization as well. Each time a need, wish, or intention and its corresponding potential for loss of control and self-defeating humiliation and embarrassment becomes part of a shared experience with an empathetic soothing adult (who meets the person at his or her developmental level), there is a new experience of a "me and you" rather than a "me and my appetites and counterreactions." This creates a basis for new social interest because the original need now becomes channeled beyond mere appetitive discharge toward a sense of pleasure in shared experience. The shared experience with another, where one's appetites and behaviors are understood, becomes an end in its own right. This social end, which formed from a person's needs not simply being satisfied or frustrated, becomes the basis for shared social experience, as well as self-observing experience. It is interesting to note that as an individual becomes more representational and more self-observing, he or she also becomes more capable of operating in larger groups. New affects having to do with empathy, concern for others, and more mature forms of love come into being, in part as a result of the shared reflective experiences.

It is important to consider the use of limits in promoting representational capacities. The pressure is strong to try to use direct discharge behavior patterns to achieve gratification, and even empathizing at the right developmental level will often need the additional support of structure and limits. During the course of therapy, the structure of the therapeutic situation provides those essential limits. That structure supports the individual's attempts to verbalize rather than act out. With older children or adults, the basic therapeutic rule is to use words rather than actions, although pretend play in young children is considered communicative-type action. Additionally, behavioral interactions have communicative value when they are of a kind that does not result in breaking things or injuring either party. The need to show up at certain times to respond to the time limits and to deal with the basic rule of communication over direct discharge action furthers and supports the interpersonal aspects discussed above. Sometimes, the therapeutic contract calls for parents to be present to help set limits for their children during sessions.

Some situations arise in which patients test the therapeutic structure by not paying their bills or by coming late or by attempting to physically assault the property or the person of the therapist. These instances have to be dealt with in a way that affirms the value of limits and structure. Some patients can only be treated in inpatient or residential settings because it is difficult at different points in their lives to adhere to limits without the support of extra staff or the physical structure of twenty-four-hour supervision. On the other hand, many patients are responsive to the limit-setting attitudes of the therapist. If the therapist covertly supports the patient's acting out, sends few (or weak) signals regarding the need for structure, and, in general, is not serious about the limits of the therapeutic situation, the patient senses this and more acting out may be likely.

Chapter 8

Clinical Techniques to Facilitate Representational Capacities

In previous pages we have emphasized the need to maintain a general, abstracting attitude, and to meet individuals at their developmental level to create the necessary interpersonal experience, whereby the direct discharge attitude becomes an attitude involved in sharing experiences; that is, experiences around satisfying particular inclinations, needs, or wishes. The experience of sharing brings needs and wishes into an interpersonal context. The security, dependency, and satisfaction involved in sharing takes on meaning that becomes a bridge for the communication of needs and feelings, as opposed to acting on them. This necessary interpersonal experience helps individuals eventually to be able to communicate with themselves and develop both an experiencing part and an observing part of themselves. Limit-setting is an important tool in promoting this process. These interpersonal experiences, in addition to encouraging a sense of shared experience, also help the individual deal with prerepresentational conflicts around being overwhelmed by their own instincts and experiencing shame, humiliation, and self-destructive rage.

How does one use specific therapeutic strategies to empathetically work with patients at their developmental level, capitalizing on a sense of shared experience? Patients who are at the behavioral level will often come into sessions and elaborate different behaviors. They may, as indicated earlier, talk about the transactions between themselves and their spouse, boss, or children. Missing are such statements as, "This made me happy, sad, or excited," because if these statements were spontaneously elaborated with the behaviors, the person would be at the representational level proper.

To help such patients, the clinician does not supply the abstracted affects and remark, as would be common in many therapies (i.e., "It seems to me you're talking about anger, dependency, or love"). Instead, the therapist first helps the patient better describe behavioral patterns. For example, patients may comment on their own behavior and not the behavior of the other person with whom they are interacting. The clinician's role is to broaden the behavioral description by inquiring about what the other person does in response to the patient's behavior.

The therapist can also point out the sequence of the pattern and help the patient focus on what was happening prior to and shortly after the behavior took place. The therapist can also point out how other relationship patterns may bear on the relationship with the significant other. In other words, the first microtechnique at the therapist's disposal involves helping the patient expand the description of his or her behavioral patterns.

Another microtechnique is to help individuals describe the physical sensations they experience within their bodies. If the person says, "I have no feelings," or "There was no experience," the therapist should inquire about what their body felt like. There is always a state of some subjective experience in the body itself—some sort of background bodily tone. There is an underlying physical tone present that individuals describe as feeling "tired," "energetic," "ill," "great," or "my muscles are tight or loose." Such physical descriptions often have a clear somatic, rather than abstracted, feeling tone and quality to them. As indicated earlier, these descriptions may indicate that the person is in transition from the behavioral mode to the representational level.

Patients may not be used to describing the bodily sensations that accompany behavioral patterns; the therapist should assist them in becoming aware that not only are their bodies behaving in a gross motor sense, but their mouths, muscles, voices, and gestures are involved in behavioral patterns as well.

This is a vast improvement over the earlier state of affairs, when such individuals often lived in the here-and-now. Typically they would find themselves behaving in certain ways and then being surprised at the fact that they were embroiled in fights with spouses, or had difficulties with their bosses or their children. They are often reactive, behavioral responders, rather than pondering, reflective individuals.

This microtechnique does not sound so terribly different from the approach a clinician might intuitively follow in many conventional therapies. The developmental emphasis does, however, help the therapist avoid some common errors, such as volunteering certain emotional labels for the person (angry, sad, happy, glad, or embarrassed, for example). Using a developmental approach, the clinician would develop a keen eye and an attentive ear for the person's descriptions of subtle bodily sensations—a tightening muscle, a twitching eye, an itchy nose, or drumming fingers. The therapist would also help the patient see if there are any common or predictable features in their behaviors and the behaviors of the other people, in terms of the configurations they get involved in.

For example, one woman, whenever she was in a situation where her husband was working late, would find herself complaining a great deal, citing all of his shortcomings, chapter and verse. She would rarely do anything for him during these times. Her pattern under these circumstances was to complain and insist that he direct his attention to her. He, predictably, responded to this by working later and later, and becoming more self-absorbed. When the woman first described this behavioral pattern to the therapist, all she could see was that her husband didn't do anything she wanted him to. He didn't help her take care of the children, do housework, or show her affection.

The patient didn't connect this behavior pas de deux with any sensations in her own body; she was only aware that she felt "depressed." As she talked about the situation, however, she began to see that there was a pattern to her behavior of complaining and self-directed interest. She saw that there was also a pattern to her husband's behavior. After further exploration, she was able to see that when her husband was working a lot, the physical tone of her body was directly affected, and that her muscles were "tight and tense." As she described it, "It's as though my body were getting ready for an attack . . . as if I felt scared." General somatic and affective descriptors began emerging—"tense," "panicked," and "scared." No high-level abstracted affects were volunteered at first.

A broad pattern became evident to both patient and therapist, in which tense muscles, vigilant anticipation of danger, and scared panicky sensations accompanied by complaining and self-directed focus were not really involved with the husband's response of working more and more and directing attention to himself. As the woman talked about this tense, panicky, scared state, she saw that her behaviors were directed at getting her husband to be home with her more. She thought if he were home to protect her, her muscles wouldn't be tense, and she wouldn't have a sense of looming danger. It was not clear to her, however, why having him away meant that danger was impending.

The therapist next asked how the husband's presence fended off danger, and in what other ways the woman thought about the husband when he was away. The therapist silently mused about whether this woman ever missed her spouse, or felt a sense of sadness or longing for him, or even allowed herself to rage when he didn't call her. Was the absence of these feelings in some way related to the physical sensation of danger and panic, and the associated behaviors?

In the past, the therapist had made the mistake of offering too much clarification and interpretation, and a previous patient had been overwhelmed. No matter how accurate an interpretation may be in relation to the patient's history, it has no real value, and may overload the person even more, if the individual is not yet able to represent such affects as sadness and rage. The patient would be incapable of detecting the connection between these represented affects and associated behaviors or related affects, like panic or tension. Although it was tempting, the therapist refrained from calling the patient's attention to her current sense of panic and the desperate feelings of impending abandonment felt by her when she was a little girl forced to rely on a depressed, erratic mother.

It is common therapeutic strategy, though, to try to offer such clarifications, which indeed many patients buy into intellectually. Rarely do these interpretations help to any significant degree, however. Sometimes, the patient may be reassured to think that the therapist at least has a working hypothesis, and the person tries valiantly to repeat the explanation word for word to the therapist or their best friend or spouse. Rather than offering facile clarifications of the woman's behaviors, the therapist aided her in elaborating the behavioral pattern, helped her describe the somatic states in detail, and tried to empathize with what her sense of danger felt like. As the patient explored her somatically experienced state of panic, she spoke more and more about being left all to herself, feeling abandoned and completely alone. It turned out that her mother was a very rigid person, who when challenged would shut down and emotionally leave her daughter. She recalled feeling panicked as a young child whenever she made demands or confronted her mother. She, too, was very stubborn as a little girl, as her mother was as an older woman. The patient and the therapist wondered why she and her mother always got into confrontations. Was it because they were never able to compromise with each other, or work out some way to mutually nurture one another? It turned out she couldn't stand to "give in" to her mother. During one session she said, "To give in to her would have been to be her lackey, to be totally dominated and controlled by her. I could never do that. I'd rather die than do that." Here too, this woman didn't elaborate on the feelings, but hinted that there was something overwhelmingly distasteful about capitulating to her mother. It was significant that this woman never shared any feelings of longing for or missing

her husband, and she had no recollection of any feelings of longing for or missing her mother, or even vaguely positive feelings
for her. To this day, however, the woman is quite sensitive to her
mother's paying her brother more attention than her, suggesting
there are still attentions she wants from her mother.

As the sessions went on and the explorations and plot thick-
ened, it became apparent to the woman that she was panicked
about being alone, and this reminded her of feeling abandoned
as a little girl when her mother would shut down. It seemed her
dilemma with her mother was that she could not bear to give in
to her mother and do things on her mother's terms. She could
not explain the physical sensations or emotions associated with
her position.

Over time, the patient described her wish to have her husband home, and her belief that only he could make her feel less
tense, scared, and panicky. Patient and therapist were able to
begin looking at what her body sensations would feel like when
he was home with her. What happened when he did spend more
time with her? What did she experience when he had time off
from work during weekends or vacation time? The woman described her body as feeling more relaxed and protected; her muscles seemed less tense. She recalled a four-day weekend when he
had helped her out with the children, and how she was aware
of feeling more physically relaxed. These were the first positive
sensations she had described during the therapy. The behavioral
patterns and the behaviors in her body were now broadened.

The therapist went on to empathize with the patient, remarking that there seemed to be a lot that her spouse could do
for her in terms of the physical sensations in her body. The patient looked at the therapist, her face crumbled, and she began
to cry. As she heaved with sobs, her tears seemed to visibly dimin-
ish her tenseness; even her posture seemed more relaxed. For
the first time, she revealed, "I need him. I'm in little pieces unless
he's there." This was the dramatic beginning of her ability to
express (with some undifferentiated somatic affects) what would
later become an abstracted affect around longing, missing, sadness, and even some rage and anger, as well. The critical linchpin

in this process, however, was to foster a broadening of somatically experienced affects so that the tension and panicked sensations broadened to include sensations associated with feeling secure and comforted, although these were not the terms used by the patient.

Being able to describe the sensations in her own words at her own developmental level enabled the patient to feel her own connection between her physical sensations and their associated behaviors at a deep visceral level. This broadening of sensation could be felt in her own body, and this led to the dawning awareness of wanting and needing her husband to make her feel "whole," rather than "in pieces." Over time, the woman could talk spontaneously about wanting him home, not just about falling apart, being panicked, depressed, or even suicidal when he was not at home. She could finally discuss her need for her husband.

After a number of months, the patient spoke one day about missing and longing for her husband. This might be considered a truly abstracted affect state. Around this time the patient spoke about feeling panicky and scared, particularly when her child was being very competitive with her, wouldn't listen, and insisted on playing with his genitals in a provocative way. She was anxious to know what to do and did not want to undermine his growing masculinity (he was now 4 years old), yet she also did not want to support what she thought was inappropriate behavior. The patient came in and spoke about these circumstances and talked about wanting her husband to come home soon. The therapist inquired, as he had other times, what the physical sensations were like when she was aware of wanting her husband. He reminded her that she and her husband had not made love in some time. Because the patient seemed ready at this point to handle a question about yearning (because of her prior descriptions of somatic states of wish, desire, and longing), the therapist asked if she could actually picture her husband in her mind when she wanted him. She said that she never did picture her husband, nor did she even look at his picture during these times. When asked what would happen if she closed her eyes and tried to imagine her husband, the patient complied and said she just saw a blank and couldn't picture him. She then told the therapist that it would be hard for her to imagine anyone at all, even a good friend. The capacity to picture an absent loved one or significant other was not present. Many such individuals who are prerepresentational lack this ability. In fact, many of the assumptions therapists make about standard intrapsychic tools and capacities have been often assumed to be part of the apparatus of every individual's ego structure; yet these capacities are not present in a vast majority of patients and have to be learned.

Both patient and therapist were now impressed by the fact that she could not picture her husband when she wanted him home. When asked what aspect of her husband she could sense if she simply tried to imagine him as though he were there, the woman reported that she had an auditory impression of his voice. She could almost hear him telling her that, "You are melodramatic and worry too much." She could even imagine hearing the mild irritation in his voice. Just the imagined sound of his voice, however, did lead her to feel less tense and panicked.

As the woman focused on the voice and the feeling it created for her, the therapist wondered if there were other sensations associated with the husband, such as smell or touch. She nodded and quickly said, "There is a distinct smell about him that I can sense." She said she should have mentioned it, but it never occurred to her to think about smells in terms of her sensory and affective experience of him. Once she focused on the voice and the smell during the session, she was able to close her eyes and imagine different physical features. She was first able to picture his hair, because he had beautiful wavy hair which she liked to fondle. She realized that stroking his hair made her feel less tense, especially when they were cuddling together. Eventually, she could mentally piece together different facial features to go along with the voice, smell, and hair, although a total visual sense of him was never as vivid as the auditory impact of his voice, the impression left by his distinct smell, and the tactile sensation of stroking his hair. A sense of her husband was emerging, however, and she could imagine at times that this new presence would make her feel less scared.

There were spontaneous verbal expressions of missing her husband and longing for him. She also noted that picturing him helped comfort her and soothed her when she waited for him to come home in the evening. Interestingly, when she recalled the times he would call and say he would be two hours late, the patient was newly able to feel rage and could picture herself yelling at him to get even. But these were also experienced as more abstracted affect states, particularly the expressions of anger and rage.

With the experience of these more abstracted affect states (particularly feelings of longing, but also the angry feelings), less panic, tension, fear, and depressive symptomatology were in evidence. The patient somehow seemed to be more "there," more substantial, as if the creation of intrapsychic structures literally shored her up.

What happened during the course of this woman's therapy can be looked at in two ways. On the one hand, one can say: Aha! She had an insight about the connection between her mother and her husband, and recognized that she never could tolerate missing her mother because that would be putting herself under the domination of her mother. As she worked that out, she was able eventually to long for and miss her husband, and therefore, felt less panicky when he was away. He became a reachable presence in her sensations and her body even when he was away, so she wasn't all alone anymore.

From a traditional psychodynamic viewpoint, this interpretation sounds plausible. As mentioned earlier, however, what was actually occurring here was the step-by-step building up of the psychological structure of a representational capacity—the capacity to go from more primitive behavioral affect states and states of behavioral enactment to a truly representational mode. In this case, the patient's achievement of the ability to represent was linked to the set of affects associated with her husband and his being away, and her resulting panicky and tense feelings. In many patients like this woman, such dynamic insights reached in therapy merely serve to reinforce concrete attitudes and result in direct discharge-type behavior. As this patient went from acting-out behaviors and experiencing vague physical sensations, she became aware of undifferentiated somatic states (a feeling of "falling apart") with her husband putting her back together when he reentered her life. She went from needing him to wanting him to make her feel better in very general, vague ways. Finally, these general, vague affect states gave birth to more specific abstracted affect states.

What mediates and allows the developmental process to occur (or reoccur) during therapy are conditions that are similar to those occurring in normal childhood development. The empathetic availability of a significant other person who meets the individual at his or her developmental level is a prerequisite to the growth of ego capacity. Helping the person to experience a shared sense of a "me and you" creates a bridge from direct discharge (delaying gratification) to two-way interior communication; the ability to communicate within oneself. This communication within oneself then becomes the basis for experiencing and observing the sense of self, which allows a person to reflect on and begin to represent experience. Once the individual begins to represent experience, even at the level of undifferentiated somatic affects and very general diffuse affects, empathy and self-examination will lead to more specific abstracted affects, if these same interpersonal processes continue.

Of course, the therapist must be keyed into the nuances of what the patient is saying, if he is to continue to help with pattern recognition and assist patients in their self-observing capacities. By noting physical sensations in their patients' bodies, and eventually becoming aware of the abstracted affects associated with these inclinations, and being scrupulous not to project his own needs and wishes onto the situation, therapists can be effective in helping patients represent affects.

Thus far, we have considered both the general tactics for fostering representational elaboration, and the specific microstrategies for fostering representation. Another microstrategy that should be considered has to do with the clinician's therapeutic activity. In traditional psychodynamic therapies, clinicians may limit their role to facilitating the patient's free associations and clarifying and interpreting what the patient communicates. This therapeutic posture, however, is only useful for the small percentage of patients who are already able to represent experience, and can, in fact, self-observe and build bridges between different representations. Clarifying or interpreting comments help the bridges be more complete in areas where defenses are operating or anxiety makes it difficult for the patient to connect certain wishes and feelings to fears and anxieties.

The majority of patients, however, have a more fundamental challenge facing them. They are not yet able to represent certain experiences. Some patients cannot represent experience in an emotional sense at all; others are unable to represent experience in certain emotional areas, such as around dependency, excitement, sexuality, or aggression. With such patients it is important for the therapist to help expand the drama. Patients will generally verbalize either the behavioral patterns or the beginning representations in those emotional areas in which they are comfortable. There is a massive avoidance of other emotional areas, though, because the individuals haven't had the experience of representing those experiences, or because the experiences are fraught with anxiety and the representation of them feels more dangerous than simply behaving them out.

In the developmental approach, the therapist is an active commentator and questioner with regard to the drama that the patient is communicating. The therapist wants to know, for example, about the patient's physical sensations and feelings. He raises questions that the patient does not raise, or wonders aloud why the patient has not asked certain questions. This tactic of being an active questioner, commentator, and broadener of the drama is one utilized in other conventional psychodynamic, psychotherapeutic approaches.

The developmentally oriented therapist has an additional microstrategy at his disposal, however, and that is to become a part of the drama. He does not accomplish this by participating in the patient's life. He does this by being a constructor of the drama with the patient, much like an adult engages in pretend play with a child. Remember that in normal development, representational capacities first become learned through make-believe play, as well as through the use of words to express feelings and to negotiate around feelings. When a little girl stages a scene where she assigns the role of the wolf or the three scared little pigs to the adult, the adult's playing of that role—in response to the child's cues—will help the child elaborate his or her drama. The adult may pretend to be a little pig and wonder why the wolf thinks it's so much fun to blow the house down. The wolf might say, "I just love to scare little pigs," or the angry wolf might ask the pigs if they're scared enough and ready to surrender. The adult pretending to be a little pig may say that he's scared, but that he'll never surrender.

How does this representationally expanding dialogue occur between two adults in therapy when the therapist similarly joins an unfolding drama? In the adult drama, the therapist becomes a part of a hypothetical or dramatic situation that the patient is describing, much as a child's make-believe is not a real situation. When an adult does similar hypothetical work with another adult, the clinician should be willing to imagine what the boss might feel like or say, if the patient were unable to express this. The patient may be talking, for example, about going in and asking for a raise, and be considering various strategies and how he or she imagines their body will feel when the strategies are implemented. The patient may be blind to what is going on in terms of the boss's own agenda. The therapist in the drama might inquire, "How would your boss be playing his part in this role?" The patient might volunteer, "Well, he tends to be very aggressive and tries to intimidate people." The therapist would then wonder out loud what the boss might think: "Where do you come off asking me for a raise! What have you done for the company lately?" The therapist thus picks up a cue from the patient and dramatizes it, much as he might play the role of the big, bad wolf in make-believe play. The patient might add, "Gosh, I can feel my muscles tensing up already." "But what are you going to say?"

the therapist might prod. "I think you're an SOB" the patient would blurt out. Back in character as the boss, the therapist might shake his fist and say, "You're calling me an SOB when you never turned in your last three reports?!" The patient would reply, "What are you talking about? Those reports have been on your desk for two weeks and you haven't even taken the time to glance at them!"

After amplifying the drama together, the patient and therapist can examine the broad elements in the pattern. Their behaviors and counterbehaviors and the physical sensations and emotions can be explored. The point is that the therapist's goal is to broaden the drama in collaboration with the patient, and simply to sit on the sidelines encouraging free associations is an insufficient tactic to broaden the drama of patients at this representational level. Some patients only associate in a narrow realm of experience, such as, "Look how everyone has been mean to me!" or "See how everyone admires me!" This sort of constriction can go on for years, even with perfect empathy displayed by a therapist. On the other hand, by expanding the drama as commentator and questioner, as well as by being an active participant in the make-believe or hypothetical realm of the drama, the therapist can help the patient see the forest, and not just the trees. The therapist's involvement in the drama is essential to the patient's seeing the connection between the somatic affects within his body and his behavioral patterns, which eventually leads to more representational capacities and to truly abstracted affects.

It should also be reemphasized that patients whose development has passed the point of representational elaboration, and who can elaborate different themes, dramas, and feelings, may be able to do all the aforementioned work on their own, such as picturing the boss and examining their own feelings. They may simply have problems in understanding certain connections because of anxiety or conflict. They may want the therapist's assistance in helping them understand why it is that they are passive and compliant with the boss, rather than motivated to build their own case with a coherent and assertive argument. Such patients

with representational capacities may be able to effectively associate to this tendency to be passive and compliant in terms of their
own family patterns. With the therapist's clarifications and occasional interpretations, these patients may be able to see why it is
so hard for them to carry out something they want to do. Such
patients experience a narrow band of limitation in their representational elaboration, and this narrow band is constricted due to
certain dynamic reasons arising out of conflict and anxiety. Remember, though, that such patients are the exception to the rule.
They are the prototype upon which traditional therapies have
been built, but unfortunately, such prototypes are a rarity in today's world.

To further illustrate how the therapist acting as commentator, questioner, and cocreator of experience might operate, consider the following example of a patient who was struggling to
deal with the loss of a friend.

A therapist saw a young man who missed an absent friend.
Instead of talking about his "missing" feelings, all he could do
was talk about how he had gone to an X-rated videostore and
rented a lot of X-rated videos, allegedly to deal with his feelings
of loss and hunger. But he distrusted that and went on to pick
up a girl in a bar. That girl talked with him about some of his
sexual exploits. He communicated all this in a barrage of words,
without a mention of his missing the absent friend. When the
therapist said, "It sounds like this behavior has increased dramati-
cally since your friend went away," the patient replied, "Well,
maybe so," and retreated back to describing his escapades.

The therapist realized, after a number of attempts at clarification and interpretation, that the patient wasn't broadening his
ability to experience loss, mourning, and feelings of missing his
friend. The therapist asked himself, "How would I play with a
child on the floor if that child set up a situation where one doll
left another doll, but then, without exploring that theme further,
moved on to having the dolls hit one another? What would I do
to help the child broaden her ability to represent the experience
of one doll missing the other?" The answer revolved around the
therapist's ability to thicken the plot of the pretend play, perhaps

by saying to the child, "I wonder what the Daddy doll is doing off in California" to see how the child would react. If the child reacted by avoiding the doll in "California," the therapist would move ahead anyway, pursuing the matter. This technique was easily transferred to the treatment of this adult patient.

The therapist took an active hand in the conversation, and said, "I wonder what your friend is doing on the Riviera." The patient did not want to think about that. He was the kind of person who avoided visualizing what people were doing when they were away, because that would obviously bring him in touch with uncomfortable affects. The therapist became more provocative in his comments (as opposed to just clarifying), and remarked, "I wonder what he's doing or if he's having a good time." Together, then, patient and therapist faced the whole difficulty the patient had with imagining what people were doing when they were not with him. The patient preferred to live in his concrete, here-and-now world.

Provoked by the therapist's comment, the patient was able to take a chance and let himself speculate a little. He got in touch with a lot of sadness created by his friend's departure. Once he imagined that the friend was not thinking about him, and was, in fact, having a better time than he was, two issues emerged: a competitive edge to his friendship (the patient wanted to have more girls than his friend) and a latent negative, oedipal longing with homosexual themes in his friendship. These themes became apparent only when the therapist became an interactive partner in the representational drama that was unfolding. The therapist did not take the conversational lead, nor did he insert his own thoughts on the subject into their discussions. Instead, the therapist copied a pattern he had set up for pretend play with a child, followed his patient's lead, and helped him expand his internal world.

In this example, the questioning therapist actively helps the patient create experience by imagining what the patient's friend might be doing. The patient is not permitted to simply describe what pops into his mind. He is urged by the therapist to look at what is not coming readily to mind, as well. The therapist treats the absence of certain associations as a critical association in its own right, and then works around it by helping the patient picture what is going on with his friend. This is not unlike working with a child who is worried about an absent mother yet makes no references to her and behaves aggressively. The therapist might suggest, "Let's picture what your mother is doing right now." Or, she might pick up a doll and say, "Let's pretend this doll is mom and see what the other dolls are up to." This creates an opportunity for the child to "picture" the feelings having to do with the mother's absence in the child's visual, auditory, or affective space. Even though the child is not consciously thinking about the mother, she usually is very much present in the child's emotional life.

Thus, the therapist as a collaborative constructor of experience employs a number of microtechniques to create those experiences that are necessary for the patient to expand the range and depth of his representational life. It is important to keep in mind that only real-time experience, which is abstracted, is able to become internalized. Similarly, a person's ability to self-observe is abstracted from the ability to observe oneself in the process of communicating with another person. When communicating with a significant other, an individual comes to the recognition that representational life goes beyond one's own immediate sense of equilibrium. No doubt such a person previously found it easier simply to think about day-to-day issues and wonder who would provide him or her with the next source of satisfaction. Only when this perspective gets broadened in the active experience of the therapeutic situation do patients develop an internal sense of how to look at experience through the process of abstracting off their experience. They now have a sense that part of one's experiences now include considering people who may not be present in one's life in a concrete sense but who are a part of important feelings of the immediate past. It might appear to many therapists that such issues could be dealt with by simply pointing out to the patient that he does not like to think about his friend who is away. But the concrete behavioral patient will respond to such a clarification with, "Yes, you're absolutely right. Why should

I?" To them, out of sight literally means out of mind. Some therapists then tell such patients to get their head out of the sand and stop being an ostrich. They insist that these patients are denying their true feelings and that they really miss the person. That can lead to an intellectual battle of wills and even result in the patient's virtual surrender ("Well, I suppose you may have a point there"). Clearly little real emotional elaboration and representational growth can occur in such an atmosphere.

On the other hand, helping a patient imagine what his absent friend may be doing creates a bridge to a new way of thinking, new sensations in the body, and new affects. Once such a bridge is built, the issue of whether the patient likes to use this bridge or not will surely come up at some time during the course of therapy. A patient who has finally constructed such a bridge may run away from it and not want to talk about an absent friend or lover. In later sessions the same patient may come in and want to talk about an exercise class, a cup of coffee, or some new friends. At this point, when the therapist wonders if this banal conversation is more comforting to talk about than the absent friend, the patient who has had his representational perspectives broadened will probably be able to use the traditional therapeutic tool of free associating to understand his preference for living in the here-and-now, rather than considering the affects associated with the immediate past. Exploring this particular preference and the anxiety and defenses that may be associated with it are finally possible, because the representational capacity is already present. Prior to helping a person expand their representational range, however, the very representational capacities that one hopes would emerge after clarification may not have been intrapsychically present, and therefore, could hardly emerge. In fact, when representational elaboration is built up first and then defenses against it are explored (although sometimes these can be done simultaneously), one often sees greater representational elaboration develop in therapy. Therapeutic approaches, which assume the presence of representational elaborations that are not really present, often disintegrate into endless power struggles and intellectualizations with little real representational growth. It is a mistake to assume patients have a range of ideas and feelings but that they are simply defending against them. While sometimes patients are simply avoiding, repressing, or denying certain ideas and feelings, many patients have never had the experiences that would allow them to have such feelings and ideas in the first place.

As indicated earlier, the clinician's role is to help individuals broaden and elevate their representational capacities to more sophisticated levels. The microtechniques discussed in this chapter need to be employed for each level of the hierarchy (see Figure 7.1, p. 230) to help the patient master the next higher level. And at the same time that the therapist employs these techniques to go up from level to level, he or she is also using them to broaden the range of experiences that are considered and representationally elaborated at each of these levels. So, for example, when the patient is still at the level of using very general affective expressions (such as "I like that" or "That's unpleasant"), instead of talking specifically about disgust, anger, rage, humiliation, love, excitement, or pleasure, the therapist tries to expand the range of experiences the person can describe in terms of liking or not liking. An attempt to expand the range should be made because these general affective expressions may still be an advance over behavioral descriptions, and they should be broadened to include all the emotional themes (dependency, anger, love, pleasure, excitement, disgust, sadness, loss, and longing). The clinician is, therefore, always trying to move the patient up the hierarchy and broaden the range of the patient's emotional themes, which occur at each hierarchical level.

Sometimes certain emotional themes, such as dependency, may move up the hierarchy more quickly than others having to do with aggression. Using such a framework the therapist can profile where the patient is at any particular point in therapy. Do not make the common mistake of assuming that the patient who has gotten better at being assertive and expressing his anger is therefore, by definition, going to be more representational and operate on this level when it comes to longing or feelings of dependency, loss, and missing. Do not assume that such emotions also operate at a representational level until direct evidence indicates this. The same caveat would hold true for feelings of competition, humiliation, shame, and even certain fears.

CLINICAL CONDITIONS RELATED TO REPRESENTATIONAL ELABORATION

There are a number of common clinical conditions that can be more fully understood in the context of the patient's ability to elaborate his or her representational system. Let us first build on earlier discussions and further consider a developmental understanding of certain types of depression. A traditional psychodynamic perspective describes depression as involving a loss of self-esteem or hatred directed against the self. Sometimes the dynamics involve self-hate because of internal conflict. The wrath of those experiences, organized under the umbrella of the superego, rain terror on the ego because of certain drive derivatives that are found unacceptable. Other models of depression have to do with the loss of a loved object, or a prolonged grief or mourning reaction turning into melancholia. The loss leads to feelings of being unworthy or bad, and depressive affects follow. Biological models of depression postulate a biological shift leading to a depressed mood. These biological reactions can be triggered by reactions to the loss of a loved one, loss of self-esteem, difficulties in work or marriage, or even conflicts, as defined by the more classic psychoanalytic models. The biological predisposition toward depressive affect and the biological reaction to depression may be triggered by psychosocial factors which are often responsive to biological treatments. Biological models also postulate subgroups of patients who become depressed almost solely for biological reasons, having to do with biological cycles, with only minimal impact by dynamic or interpersonal events.

Let us take a closer look at the model that involves loss of love or object. In normal development, as discussed earlier, the loved one is retained through the representational capacity. At around age 18 months to 3 years, the child gradually learns to organize an image of his most loved caregiver, as well as other caregivers, which he can then call on to give him a sense of comfort and security even when the caregiver is out of sight. Thus, even when displaced by time and space, the child can conjure up the image of the caregiver. The younger child's situation is far different. A baby may recognize the caregiver and show an emotional response of warmth or love or excitement or dependency, but does not have the ability to form comforting mental images of the caretaker. There may be a feeling tone in the body which can survive for a period of time, but as Bowlby (1969, 1979) pointed out in his studies on hospitalized children, young children go through phases where they become angry and protest, and then eventually become despondent. Even children who are prerepresentational seem to be able to hold onto a sense of their parents in some prerepresentational form, but only for a brief period of time; then they begin losing hope and become despairing. The anger and protest phase they experience suggests an aggrieved sense of something missing or taken away. The representational child can hold onto this image longer, and when a parent is on vacation, for example, can be reminded of the parents through chats on the telephone or seeing family photographs. In this way, much like adults who stay in emotional touch with one another through periodic phone calls or visits, the representational child can keep the image of the loved one alive, though not glowing very brightly, over a period of time. As we picture the child using representational capacities, it is clear that the ability to represent the loved one becomes a way for the child to hold onto an internal sense of security, warmth, and comfort.

This ability to represent the object goes through a series of interesting stages where children can initially tolerate parents outside their visual space, but only in another room where they can still hear them. They permit their parents to be physically separate but not temporally absent. As children emerge from the behavioral level they can tolerate greater displacements in space, such as having parents be in an adjoining room, but still need, at least periodically, to sense the presence of their parents by hearing their voices. They gradually can begin to tolerate a displacement in time when the parents are not there, but they know the parent will be back, and they can picture them in their minds. This ability to "see" the parent in their minds results in a multisensory picture composed of voices, smells, affects, and perhaps visual images. A sense of time is involved because such children expect (within their own primitive perspective of time) that their parents will return at some point within their psychic time expectations. In other words, it is not a "never" or "forever" but often a promise of "soon" that keeps this internal picture aglow.

What happens when this representational ability is lost or so vulnerable that it easily disappears? This may be similar to the loss of a real love object, such as when a parent disappears. The mental picture of a loved one is the mediator of the warm, secure, and comforting feelings that the original parent maintained. When this image fades, it may lead to the same types of anaclitic affects which have to do with hopelessness, helplessness, lethargy, and general shutdown that are evidenced in primary anaclitic-type depressions when there is actual loss of a loved one.

In the developmental model, depression is seen as a breakdown of the mediating role of the representational system. The loss of the capacity to represent, or not developing a stable capacity to represent the warm nurturing side of primary relationships, can leave one vulnerable to depressive affects because the loved objects and the comfort, security, and dependency gratification that they bring are easily lost.

How does this line of thinking fit in with other models of depression? In the conflict model, the ego, in a sense, surrenders under the attack of internal anger against instincts; depressive affects develop. The stronger the representations—warm, secure, loving, and reassuring love objects—the better the individual can mediate and synthesize the demands of the supergo and his or her instincts. Similarly, demoralizing experiences at work or in marriage lead to a loss of self-esteem. Thus, the inner source of self-esteem, which is based on the representation of experiences of love and maintained through the ability to represent such experiences, becomes an important buffer for day-to-day ups and downs, and the even more profound crises that involve family, marriage, and work. To the degree that these representations are weak or vulnerable, an individual finds himself dependent on daily external experiences to maintain self-esteem. Thus, when a temporary loss of self-esteem occurs, the ability to bounce back, go out and find a new job, hang in there and work out the marriage, or settle the divorce, may be very dependent on the strength and integrity of the original representational system. Here, too, vulnerability and the ability to represent loving feelings abstracted from relationships with loving caregivers is a critical variable. We can see the importance, therefore, of strengthening the representational capacity and increasing the range of experiences that can be represented in the therapeutic situation. Bypassing the representational capacity and trying to deal with conflicts or only changing behaviors, may leave the individual's personality vulnerable to the types of difficulties we are describing here.

Now let us consider biological aspects of depression. Is there a direct chemical effect on the brain, and therefore, the mind, leading to depressed affects? Or do the biological variables that make one individual more vulnerable to depression than another indirectly create their effects by the person's ability or inability to organize aspects of his or her representational system? Perhaps the biological effects are not as direct as has been assumed, but are actually influenced by certain perceptual and processing capacities, which are in turn linked with the ability to organize and maintain certain representational capacities. It may well be that vulnerability to depression manifests itself through these mediating structures. In this model, there are two ways in which biological variables affect the central nervous system. One type of vulnerability is tied to an inability to abstract visual–spatial information and at the same time regulate sensation, affect, and experience. Such combined regulatory and visual–spatial processing difficulties, it is suggested, are related to the biological profiles found in certain anxiety conditions. It is hypothesized that this spectrum of disorders, including panic disorders, depressive reactions, separation anxiety, and bipolar disorder, has as a common feature difficulties with regulation springing from over- and underreactivity to certain kinds of sensations, as well as visual–spatial processing difficulties.

In this model, therefore, certain biological variables seem to cause depression by making it constitutionally difficult to organize the very basis of the representational capacity. Regulatory dysfunctions, including visual–spatial processing deficits, make it hard to stabilize and organize experience in such a way that it can be easily represented. The visual–spatial dimension is critical for being able to hold onto and "see the big picture."

Certain physical vulnerabilities caused by processing and regulatory difficulties may impede the representational system from fully organizing itself. For example, due to the processing difficulties, it cannot easily hold onto an internal sense of being loved or admired. Due to the overreactivity to sensation it is at the same time bombarded by overly intense and/or labile affects. When interpersonal difficulties (which are often caused in part by poor regulation leading to unstable relationships) are yoked to biological issues, the difficulty in organizing representations becomes obvious. As suggested earlier, certain types of potential environments, in which the child is extended neither limits nor empathy, further prevent him or her from seeing the big picture. Thus, biological variables and vulnerabilities are accentuated by environmental ones and the organization of representations remains an elusive brass ring. This difficulty then serves as the critical mediator for a variety of clinical conditions, of which depression is a very useful model. In this model, therefore, depression is not a direct result of biological vulnerability nor of a loss or conflict, but is related to the impact of these experiences on the ability to represent comforting, nurturing, and dependency aspects of experience. As long as the representation of these types of experiences remains unstable, the individual may be prone to depressive affects or symptoms.

Another aspect of representing experience commonly seen in clinical conditions has less to do with difficulty in organizing representations or experiencing the representation in a salient, affective way. Some individuals, as discussed in the chapter on regulatory patterns, characterized most obviously by those who are isolated from their feelings, tend to organize the big picture, but in a highly cognitive or intellectual sense. They lack sensitivity to subtlety, nuance, and emotional detail. These individuals see a big picture, but it is faded and lacking in affective detail. It is as though they see the forest, but cannot quite make out the size and shape of the trees. The more obsessive–compulsive (in the old-fashioned psychoanalytic sense of this term) and schizoid individuals share this characteristic. In comparison those individuals who tend toward depression, anxiety, and hysterical personality patterns share the pattern, described earlier, involving sensitivity to emotional details and a tendency to become overloaded or fragmented rather than organize the "big picture" perspective.

It is important to note that a full representational system has to involve both the ability to organize the representational system across a broad range of affects in a stable way, as well as the ability to experience the subtlety, detail, and emotional saliency of one's representational capacity. The picture in one's mind, in other words, has to be rich in color and detail. As we did in our discussion of depression, when we consider compulsive or schizoid patterns, it is important not to think of experiential or biological variables as having a direct impact on certain end behaviors, but instead note that the effect is felt on certain mediating structures, including the representational system.

It is also interesting in this perspective to consider certain compulsive rituals, which we alluded to earlier, in terms of the behavioral–gestural stage of development. It has been hypothesized elsewhere that compulsive rituals are related to grooming behaviors gone awry. It is thought that this has a direct biological antecedent which can be observed in current primate behavior. However, if we think of the behavioral–gestural level of development (having to do with the stage at which communication is organized largely around prerepresentational behaviors), we can see that at this stage there are two ways in which gestures can be used. Gestures can be employed in a broad, flexible way, where all the emotional themes of life, including dependency, assertiveness, happiness, excitement, pleasure, and sadness are conveyed and communicated. Sometimes, however, gestures may be constructed and not embrace the full range of emotional themes. The most extreme form of constriction would be in evidence when gestures become increasingly repetitive, and even perseverative. The more ritualistic and perseverative the gestures appear, the more inflexible and constricted is the gestural system.

Compulsive rituals, which are not flexible in their adaptation to the demands of the environment, could be viewed along with the perseverative qualities we see in autistic individuals as one end of this gestural continuum.

We have seen that the interpersonal experiences that lead to flexibility in the use of gestural communication are keyed to responsive parenting that responds to the child's needs and wishes with accurate and responsive reciprocal reactions as well as empathy and understanding. On the other hand, parents who misread signals, and are not reciprocal (e.g., withdraw and shut down, are overly punitive or frightening, fail to meet the child at his or her developmental level, or infantalize the child) may increase the tendency toward ritualistic behavior. Certain biological variables, which may be manifested as difficulties in auditory processing, play a role as well. Processing difficulties conspire to undermine the toddler's ability to flexibly interact with others. The child who cannot comprehend what he hears or sees will tend to communicate more with him- or herself or impersonal aspects of his environment. The expanding flexibility-building aspects of interactions will be relatively less available and fixed, rigid patterns may take over, in part also fueled by the need to shut out experience which is confusing or overloading.

The child who has trouble with visual–spatial processing experiences difficulty with reading and initiating signals, and as a result remains dependent on concrete objects to supply a sense of comfort. Such a youngster is likely to be anxious, particularly if the processing difficulties are severe in the auditory area and the child is unable to decode the rhythm of the mother's voice as well as the meaning of her facial expressions. The child's fears and anxiety prevent him or her from successfully mastering the behavioral or gestural stage of development because the child does not have the security of moving independently away from, yet remaining emotionally close to, the parent. Such a child resorts to maladaptive strategies at the gestural and behavioral levels.

The child who can communicate across space when separated from a love object seems to be wrapped in a flexible emotional security blanket. When such a child attempts to communicate across space, he or she can read the look in the mother's eyes, or register her nodding approval, warm smile and glances, and feel close to her. Being able to receive such signals feels almost as satisfying to the child as sitting in the mother's lap, touching her, or sniffing her scarf or hat and being comforted by her familiar scent. The more flexible child begins at the age of 12 to 24 months to employ a wide range of behaviors and gestures to negotiate emotional interactions. The child may woo the parent with smiles, respond to the parent's smiles with another smile or with a frown, may point and take the parent by the hand to look for a favorite food in the refrigerator. The antithesis of flexible, wide-ranging behaviors and gestures are ritualistic, repetitive, or compulsive use of gestures. Thus, an anxious child may use repetitive behavior and gesture as a way of trying to feel secure. The compulsive and ritualistic acts become a maladaptive type of self-comforting that provides the child with a flimsy sense of security. The child falls back on these behaviors as a way of withdrawing from relationships with others. This regression to self-stimulatory behavior is reminiscent of the behavior of infants, who engage in such behavior when they are neglected in the first year of life.

A certain sequence of behavior generally unfolds when a child feels emotionally deprived. Usually (and in keeping with Bowlby's original description of hospitalized children), the latency-aged child will show anger and protest, while the toddler may exhibit impulsive and aggressive behavior. For the toddler who is hindered by low motor tone, and tends to be more lethargic, the expression of anger may be veiled. There may be evidence only of more passive–aggressive behavior, such as defiance, more negativism, and less cooperativeness. Often, a mixture of both impulsive and negative–defiant behavior will be observed.

When the child's anger or defiance fails to change the behavior of the parent or caregiver, or to create an enhanced sense of security, the child tends partially to give up on the world and to try to comfort himself. An infant will regurgitate feedings or rock rhythmically, sometimes resorting to head banging and other kinds of self-stimulatory behavior. In the toddler phase, ritualistic, gestural behaviors are added to self-stimulatory actions. Doors are opened and closed and objects are spun. Sometimes ritualistic behavior involving the vestibular and proprioceptive systems (spinning oneself, moving and rocking rhythmically) is displayed. It is useful to see those behaviors as a coping strategy and an attempt at using ritual and repetitive behavior patterns to achieve some sense of security and homeostasis that is independent of the disappointing caretaker. The child who partially gives up on another human being as a source of comfort and security begins to rely on his or her own body and behaviors. In addition to self-stimulatory behaviors, certain mechanical patterns may develop such as rubbing a silky piece of fabric, or making various sounds or tongue clicks. Older children may rehash certain stories or watch the same TV programs over and over and over again.

When a child engages in mechanical patterns such as the opening and closing of a door, the therapist has a golden opportunity to subtly foster the child's ability to socially interact. The therapist may get conveniently stuck behind the door, forcing the child to start dealing with an adult. The adult's hand may get stuck on the rug with a child who is perseveratively trying to remove a spot. The adult may interact verbally with a child who likes to tell one story over and over again, by asking lots of silly questions. This may initially annoy the child, but is nonetheless a practical way to draw the child back into seeing that pleasure and silliness—and not merely discomfort—can characterize human interactions.

These ritualistic patterns involve strong motivation and do assist children in achieving some sense of temporary stability and security, but at the expense of continuing to learn how to relate and interact. Given that such children have partially given up on interactions and relationships, it is understandable that they then try to achieve security without becoming tangled up in relationships. Therefore, in the second year of life when gesture and behavior become important, it is likely the child will use these in his ritualistic and perseverative patterns. One can think about ritualistic behavior and obsessive–compulsive patterns as having their origins in the self-stimulatory and ritualistic maladaptive responses which occur in the person's second year of life. In part, such children give up on aspects of human interactions having to do with the more joyful and nurturing themes because their own processing difficulties in the auditory or visual–spatial area have made it difficult for them to use human interactions for self-comforting. Similarly, their sensitivities in the area of reactivity (in terms of touch and sound) may make it difficult for them to gain a sense of physical comfort from human interaction.

Not infrequently, however, chaotic, intrusive, or abusive environments can lead children who do not have a marked processing or reactivity difficulty to the same sort of reliance on ritualistic behavior. Spitz (1945) studied children who did not evidence severe organic pathology at birth, but who later fell back on self-stimulatory and ritualistic behavior because of severe deprivation. He found that under extreme stress, many children will increasingly rely on ritualistic and perseverative mechanisms. The obvious therapeutic goal for the ritualistic child or adult is to help them use gesture and behavior more interactively and flexibly, and then to graduate to representational ways of dealing with affects. If these individuals are feeling insecure or deprived, the therapist assists them in using interactions, words and/or pretend play to communicate those feelings. The therapist also helps the patient achieve a sense of security by developing the ability to interact flexibly with and envision or mentally picture the loved one. This representational capacity is a much more flexible tool than simply using behaviors to achieve a sense of comfort and security. The tendency to fall back on ritual is less likely then, unless the environmental challenges are extremely severe and a loss of representational capacity results. Occasionally, however, representational images do get caught up in the ritualistic pattern itself, as it does with obsessive types of ideation. This occurs most frequently when ideation is being driven by ritualistic intentions, rather than flexible age-appropriate needs.

THERAPEUTIC STRATEGIES FOR CONSTITUTIONAL AND MATURATIONAL VARIATIONS IN RELATIONSHIP TO GESTURAL AND REPRESENTATIONAL LEVELS

In general, as discussed in the chapter on regulatory patterns, when an individual suffers from overreactivity or oversensitivity to a particular sensation, there is an increased likelihood of sensitivity to affects associated with those sensations. For instance, although tactile sensitivity may lead to a disproportionate reaction to being physically touched, it also leads to a certain reaction to affects communicated through touch, like warmth or pleasure, or issues around dependency. Also, since touch is involved with the negotiation of hostility, it may lead to a heightened or exaggerated reactivity to other people's imagined aggressive intentions. A variety of affects around comfort, dependency, pleasure, and aggression may, therefore, be more intense when an individual is overreactive to touch.

Similarly, a variety of affects are associated with an overreactivity to sound. The key therapeutic goal when treating patients who are overreactive to touch and sound involves increasing and enhancing the sense of self-regulation and regulation as part of the interpersonal relationship. (Chapter three's discussion of regulatory processes presents a number of examples which illustrate how to regulate the interpersonal relationship and pay attention to the reactivity theme that unfolds during therapy.)

The clinician may also treat individuals who are underreactive to sensation. Here the goal is to help the person more fully experience the sensations and affects associated with relating. Such individuals can often appear to be apathetic or withdrawn, because relationships do not have saliency for them, and the affects that are part of the relationships are similarly dulled. Or we may see, as described earlier, stimulus-seeking behavior, where patients try to correct their own sensory environments by seeking out stimulation. They may resort to self-stimulatory activities such as spinning, rocking, running or fidgeting, constantly holding onto things, rubbing against people, invading other people's body space, or being very aggressive. The therapist tries to help such patients achieve adequate levels of sensation (and therefore adequate experience of affect) which should make their relationships more salient and meaningful. The clinician accomplishes this by creating a more compelling interpersonal environment. They may for example energize their voices and up the intensity of expressed affect to involve the other person more fully in verbal interactions. The therapist should also provide the patient with developmentally appropriate ways to self-stimulate, so that the individual creates enough physiologic "background noise" to feel in balance. Certain types of exercise or athletic approaches, involving a lot of joint compression, large motor activity, rhythmic movement, and deep tactile pressure are often helpful in creating a sense of physiologic equilibrium or engagement in both under-reactive and overreactive individuals.

Other patients, however, experience difficulty in processing information through visual–spatial or auditory–verbal channels. These problems usually stem from difficulties in discriminating incoming information, storing incoming information (in terms of short-term memory), and being able to abstract and categorize information. Sometimes one modality is stronger than another. Occasionally children are weak in both the visual–spatial and the auditory–verbal areas, as we have observed in some autistic and borderline children. Surprisingly, many autistic children are reasonably strong in the visual–spatial domain, but are particularly weak in auditory–verbal processing and abstracting. The clinician should avoid inferring that because a patient has a weak ability either to absorb information or for short-term memory, or to discriminate inflowing data, that the ability to categorize and abstract is equally weak. If the information doesn't come in, there is nothing organized to categorize or abstract. Sometimes the abstracting ability is surprisingly strong but cannot be evidenced until the child masters the first level of taking in information and being able to exchange it with others.

Since many adults and children are relatively weaker or stronger in one domain or another, and since relative strengths in visual–spatial or auditory–verbal abilities tend to be associated with certain types of psychopathology, it is useful to think of different general therapeutic strategies for each category of patient. When the primary difficulty lies in the visual–spatial area, associated with the affect disorders, anxiety disorders, and depressive and manic–depressive states, a major goal of the therapeutic involvement is to help individuals maintain the integrity of their representational capacities. Such individuals have a tendency to become fragmented, and under stress or anxiety lose the "big picture" and see mere trees instead of a forest. Working with these patients and helping them to picture their feelings and important individuals in their lives, for example, can be a helpful therapeutic strategy. Such individuals may talk, as in the case of the depressed woman mentioned earlier, about their need for security and wanting their husbands or children near (this is true for anxiety states too). They rarely focus, however, on the fact that they cannot visualize the picture or hold the important people and associated affects in their lives close to them when those people are out of sight.

The ability to hold the person close who is displaced in time and space by creating a mental image of them in one's mind—a visual, tactile, olfactory, auditory, and affective image—is a significant challenge. Making this challenge explicit to the patient, rather than simply concentrating on better strategies designed to keep the person close in a concrete sense, is a key goal for the therapist. Typically, patients complain that another person is absent from their lives. Although there may be some truth to this fact, the more important psychological issue for such individuals to face is their inability to keep the absent person alive in their hearts, by mentally representing them.

We previously described how one woman was able to experience the sound of her husband's voice, but was incapable of creating a visual image of him. Over time, however, the recollected sounds led to a sense of him interacting with her, and eventually she could build on her visual experiences with her husband as well. As this case history demonstrates, a person whose visual–spatial system is weak may be very capable of sensing the voice of a husband, child, or parent when they are not near them. By building on the sensory and affective experience that the patient can mentally recreate, and then focusing on this, rather than escaping into the more manipulative desire to bring the absent person close in a concrete sense, the therapist can assist these patients in piecing together their fragmented representational images. For instance, when a voice is close and available to the patient, the clinician focuses on the affects associated with the voice. Once the affects can be recalled by the patient, the therapist asks the patient to imagine what it would feel like when such affects were present.

For example, the therapist may explore a patient's feelings about her employer in the following manner, asking, "How do you feel when your boss orders you around?" The patient replies, "I hate it when he barks orders at me. I can feel it in my bones." The therapist might say, "Can you picture it also? Can you see what the situation might look like?" If the person says, "No, I can't," the therapist might continue with, "What can you picture?" The person might then say, "I can just feel a sense of his yelling and criticizing me." The therapist might ask, "Was there a time when he did that recently?" "Yes, yesterday." "What happened?" The person will then describe behaviorally what happened when the boss criticized them. "Can you draw pictures for these behaviors you're describing?" "I think I can." Now it is easier to draw the picture of the behavior, since the person has actually articulated and detailed the behaviors. In other words, although the visual image could not be summoned quickly, when the person actually has to verbally describe behaviors, she can then go on to form a picture of those behaviors. Following this the affects that are part of that picture can be explored. This becomes a kind of representational shorthand method of recalling an interpersonal situation.

Interestingly, and not infrequently, it is the person's negative experiences with the loved one that, in part, intensifies their inability to conjure up a full, rich multisensory image of them. Because such experiences are associated with ambivalent or hostile affects, the therapist must empathetically help the patient explore these feelings as they come up. First, however, the therapist aids the patient in creating their representations by breaking experience down to the sensations and affects that are available. Then the patient recreates his or her behavior, based on prior experiences, trying to picture those behaviors and their related affects in a fuller, multisensory way, and then finally attempts to project those into the future by imagining an upcoming interaction or challenge.

Once the patient is able to conjure up a multisensory image of the person, the therapist expands this newfound ability to other situations with multiple feelings such as longing, disappointment, anger, excitement, and pleasure. Obviously, the therapist needs to help the person create representations in relationship to all different feeling experiences in the absence of the actual presence of the object. In addition to picturing the object in a full, multisensory way, however, the patient must become aware of his or her tendency to become fragmented, seeing each unit of representation as an isolated entity, rather than as part of a larger whole. A patient with a tendency toward visual–spatial challenges and difficulties is unlikely to see how a relationship with her husband fits into the larger relationship with her children and family, and how that fits into her own family background. She is more likely to see each relationship and each set of feelings as an isolated entity, and is likely to look for a quick fix or temporary solution, based on this more fragmented view.

On the other hand, we have individuals who experience difficulty in the auditory–verbal area rather than with visual–spatial processing. They are often good at seeing the big picture, and even pretty good at representing people. They can actually picture their spouses or friends, showing a good ability to represent important people in their lives. What is lacking here, along with the auditory–verbal processing difficulties, is an abundant sense of emotional detail and specific affects. Just as a person with a tin ear may not hear subtleties in music, the individual with verbal processing issues may be "deaf" to the subtlety of character formation in novels, because such people are not sensitive to the nuance of words and the affects associated with those words. Simply put, the affects in words come through auditory–verbal channels. To the degree that one has a tin ear, one is not likely to pick up the subtlety or the detail in either the meaning level or the affect level of sounds and words. Thus, such individuals tend to lack emotional intensity or saliency.

A good example of this is the person who has a lot of isolation of affect, is very good at abstract thinking and spatial concepts, and may be a great scientist but misses subtle interpersonal cues at home. Often such an individual may be married to a person who has great auditory–verbal and affect sensitivity, but who lacks the stability and big picture abstracting abilities of the spouse. The two, if they don't get into difficulties, can complement each other. The absent-minded physicist professor is a good example of the former type of individual, while the emotionally overreactive, gifted poet, author, or writer may be an example of the latter.

The therapeutic challenge here is to help such individuals figure out their feelings. They see the big picture, observe patterns, and may even know intellectually how they should feel, but their feelings are devoid of subtle sensitivity. Alternatively, at the more severe end of the continuum, there are individuals who routinely misperceive the intentions of others and confuse meanings, in part because of this difficulty in experiencing subtlety in meaning.

The general strategy with such individuals is to increase the sensitivity to nuance and detail, quite the opposite of the strategy employed for the individual with visual–spatial processing difficulties. When individuals have both difficulties, the therapist may be working simultaneously with seeing the big picture and with sensitivity to affects and verbal cues. With individuals having visual–spatial processing problems, the therapist should try to work up the developmental ladder, as described in earlier chapters. The auditory–verbal processing difficulty may manifest itself clinically when individuals try to rely less and less on their "tin ear." The therapist should attempt to reverse that sequence and help them focus more on the subtlety of the message and affect.

Take, for example, a child for whom picking up subtleties in affect and message is difficult. Such a child starts marching to the beat of his own drummer more and more, retreating into fantasy rather than attending to the affect and verbal cues supplied by others as a way to orient himself. When the clinician tries to have a normal conversation about school or friends, the child intrudes with silly behavior or make-believe play, talking about fighting Ninja turtles or about a silly joke. The child easily gets lost in make-believe play or dissolves in giggles. The therapist has a hard time figuring out whether the child is sharing reality or fantasy. Such children find it easier to listen to their own thoughts rather than another person's because they don't have to work as hard at picking up the affect and verbal cues coming in from the outside. The comments of others have to be processed through the "tin ear" that they are handicapped with.

Adults, too, will evidence this same tendency to escape into fantasy or toward what appears to be more idiosyncratic and tangential thinking. The therapist may set out to discuss subject A, but before he knows it, he is talking about subject B. It may appear that such patients are manipulative in always interjecting their own agenda, but many of these people really do have a genuinely hard time paying attention to a script other than their own, because of their relative difficulty with auditory–verbal processing.

There are two simultaneous approaches to such individuals. On the one hand, the therapist tunes them in to cues in their environment, paying attention to details, seeing the "leaves" on the trees that make up the forest. On the other hand, the therapist helps them focus on their own reactions to the new varieties of "leaves" and "trees" they are recognizing, beginning with physical sensations and working up the hierarchy to abstracted affect states.

Let us consider the first approach and how it operates in a clinical situation. It is commonly observed that both adults and children may appear to be at ease when they are free associating. It is noteworthy, however, that the therapist's clarifications, comments, or questions rarely become the stimulus for further relevant associations. The individual sticks to his or her own track of associating regardless of what the therapist says or does. The therapist who has the same tendency to withdraw or live in his own world, may miss this nuance and both patient and therapist may continue to talk at cross-purposes, each one playing out a different drama. There is activity, verbalization, and even affect expression in evidence. On the surface it looks as if something's cooking, but in fact, there is little relationship between what the patient says and what the therapist says. The patient goes on associating to his own ideas and thoughts, and the therapist occasionally makes a comment, which is largely ignored by the patient.

The first therapeutic strategy, therefore, is to help such patients attend to the existence of the other person in their presence and the person's verbal and affective communications. In the here-and-now of the therapy hour, the therapist is obviously the significant "other." This sometimes runs contrary to the basic rule in psychoanalytic or psychodynamic therapy of having the patient only say what comes to mind and wanting patients to do all of the talking, and to reveal their own associations. The clinician should be sensitive to the degree to which the patient's associations are utilizing the comments and affect cues of the therapist. When the therapist asks a question such as, "Why do you think you did A, B, and C?" does the patient logically answer the question or are the free associations that follow at least related to answering that "why" question? When the therapist offers a comment or interpretation, linking some piece of historical information with something current, does the patient go on to amplify that idea? Or does the patient continue to march to his own beat, ignoring the verbal rhythm established by the therapist?

The therapist helps the patient open and close circles of communication that are built on the therapist's comments. He also will make such comments as, "Wait, I lost you. I was wondering out loud about A, and now you're talking about C, D, and E. I missed the connection." This forces the patient to recall what the therapist said or ask for clarification, and thus increases the patient's concentration and ability to pick up on other people's interpersonal cues. Often in such patients' lives, parents and family members collaborate with them and let them escape into their own thoughts, rather than helping them attend to the affect cues of the other. Their maturational tendency is thus exaggerated rather than modified. As the therapist insists on opening and closing circles of communication, the patient is actually free associating in a more relevant context and the therapist's supportive but persistent attention to the circles being opened and closed helps the patient pay attention to the therapist's cues. At some point the therapist may wonder out loud how hard it is for the patient to build on the therapist's words or communications, and how the patient tends to find it easier and more pleasurable just to become involved in his or her own thoughts. The patient might then be led to reflect on the fact that it is not always easy to understand what the therapist is saying and that he or she is not always clear about the emotions or feelings evoked by the therapist's words.

With a child who escapes into fantasy, the clinician patiently, but very persistently and supportively, helps the child open and close circles of communication. Such a "spacey" child often loses track of what the therapist says. When the therapist points out that he does not follow what the child is saying, and asks how the child's response relates to what the therapist just said, the child is forced to come to grips with the therapist's statements. When the child shakes his head or looks confused, the therapist can then explore which word or meaning was baffling. If the child can learn to express his or her confusion about the therapist's emotion or about the meaning or sequence of the therapist's words, then a collaboration that focuses on the subtlety of two-way communication is underway.

It is important to remember that the patient's ability to feel and experience a reaction to the therapist's communication is hindered by processing difficulties. The therapist needs to be extremely patient and not expect ordinary or expectable responses on the patient's part. Do not assume the patient is able to represent annoyance or happiness or experience it in the ordinary emotional way just because he or she looks annoyed or happy. The therapist should painstakingly inquire about the patient's feelings in response to the therapist's statements. For instance, one therapist remarked that he thought his patient was about to run away, and asked him how the patient felt about that remark. The patient angrily replied that he was not sure what he felt. The therapist rejoined with, "I can well understand that. Let's see if we can figure it out together. Do you have any cues or clues to your feeling?" The patient said, "No." The therapist then offered, "Let's take it step by step. What was happening in your muscles when I made that comment? Did you feel tense or relaxed?" The patient replied, "Well, I felt my arms and legs tense up a bit, in fact. I hadn't realized that until you asked me that question. . . ." "What was that tension in your arms and legs like?" The patient then described the sensation as feeling like a rubber band was about to stretch and break. "That sounds like an important sensation in your body," the therapist commented. Over time, by starting from physical sensations, the therapist led the patient to descriptions of behavior. "It felt like I had to get up and leave, so that the rubber band wouldn't stretch so far that it would pop." Eventually, the patient was able to associate the physical sensation of the rubber band breaking and muscle tensing with behavior having to do with avoidance or running away. The therapist was able to help the patient further describe what those behaviors would be like ("I would run away, and you would run after me. You would call me back and you would comfort me and you wouldn't make me feel tense anymore").

As the therapist heard the patient describe those behaviors, he empathetically remarked, "Gee, if you want to get away, there must be a sense in your body about that." The patient responded, "Well, yes, it does feel unpleasant." This general "not feeling good" was the beginning of the patient's ability to represent affect. Over time, the therapist discussed behaviors of wanting to get away and not feeling good and somatic affects were expanded, such as, "It feels like that rubber band is going to break and my body will be coming apart if I don't get away. It just feels no good." Later, the patient even remarked, "It feels terrifying." Thus, we can see the beginnings of some abstracted affects developing. Later on, angry feelings and feelings of rejection were associated with terrified feelings.

The key point here is that along with helping the person open and close circles of communication so that they are taking into account the comments and affects of the other person, the therapist should also help the affect system be more sensitive and experience the meanings of the other person in a more salient way. What the patient experiences as "nothing" going on inside may in fact have some elements of affect, at least at the physiologic or physical level. The therapist helps the person who is insensitive to their own internal cues and the cues of others because of a processing problem, become more aware of the comments of others and more aware of their own internal responses.

Unfortunately, for many, many years it has always been assumed that patients can both see the forest for the trees if only the therapist clears away anxieties and conflicts, and that they can experience their own affects, if only the therapist dismantles the operating defenses that lead to isolation or denial of affect. What has been missing is the awareness that many of our patients have never had, and now do not possess, the intrapsychic structures necessary to perform these seemingly routine tasks. Our ideal model of the patient unfortunately does not fit the way in which individuals are constructed in reality. Understanding these structural features of the personality leads to new strategies to enable our patients to develop those intrapsychic structures necessary to understand their own emotions and the emotions of others, and to see how they operate and form patterns.

COMMENTS ON INTENSITY OF AFFECT AND THE REPRESENTATIONAL CAPACITY

An issue alluded to earlier involves the ways in which intensity of affect is handled in a therapeutic situation. All therapists are aware of those trying times in the therapeutic situation when the patient's affect intensity becomes compelling. When a child desperately wants to take a toy home or wants something to eat, or when an adult insists that the therapist made a mistake and becomes enraged, or is overwhelmed with a sense of betrayal by a good friend or spouse, the therapist usually finds herself treating the communication in a literal or concrete way. The therapist can either be supportive, trying to help the patient feel less intense, and in a sense nourishing the individual back to a usual state of affect intensity, or sometimes lock horns in a power struggle, saying, "No you won't go outside" to the child, or to the adult, "You're definitely wrong about your bill."

In these situations, it is important to realize that the representational attitude requires helping patients further articulate the sensations or feelings that they are having. If they are out of control with rage, the emphasis might be on the therapist listening and then helping them calm down through his or her soothing voice. The focus here would be on what it feels like or what the sensations are like when they experience such intensity, and how hard it is for them to calm down or return to their baseline. In other words, the therapist might focus on the patient's difficulty in self-calming, and the experience of feeling so enraged and out of control, rather than the idea of placating or being "firm" with the patient. The clinician avoids taking a literal attitude toward the patient, and resists treating the patient's content as though it demanded counteraction from the therapist. It is not a question of whether the patient is accurate or inaccurate in his or her perceptions; the key point is whether the patient's communication, which really consists of words used in the spirit of behavior, shares meanings or merely demands counteraction. If the therapist responds with counteraction, rather than interaction to elaborate shared meanings, a concrete behavioral, rather than a representational, attitude is facilitated.

There are many episodes of intensity or crunch points which occur in the therapeutic situation. While tough therapists may develop power struggles, and more nourishing or compliant therapists give in, neither stance is the effective one. The attitude of helping patients reflect on their experiences, sometimes in a soothing way and sometimes in a firmer way, with the goal being a reflection of experience, is the proper attitude to foster the representational mode.

Limit setting should also be discussed in this context. Limits are only necessary when the rules and structure of the therapeutic situation are challenged, such as when a child tries to break a toy or hit the therapist, or when an adult refuses to leave a session or consistently arrives late. In such situations, limit setting is quite important. If the structure of the therapeutic relationship is not protected, the patient will often experience unnecessary, frightening, or disorganizing anxiety, or may maintain the behavioral mode of interaction. When the structure is challenged, a certain kind of behavioral communication is taking place that is not unlike the situation caused by a child who challenges the structure of the family in such a way that creates a lack of security.

Therefore, when the structure of the therapeutic situation is being challenged, the counterbehavioral attitude associated with setting limits and then exploring meanings is necessary. This would be an exception to the general rule of responding to the patient's behavioral communication with reflection. The clinician must maintain the boundaries, security, and structure of the therapeutic relationship and then explore various meanings.

CASE ILLUSTRATION OF PROMOTING THE REPRESENTATIONAL CAPACITY

An example of the subtle issues involved in intervening at the correct developmental level, in terms of the behavioral or the representational, is illustrated by the following brief interaction.

A patient who had recently experienced some losses in his life, including the death of his best friend, was mostly concerned about security issues during his therapeutic session. Who would he rely on? Who would give him advice? Was he all alone in the world? He also spoke about "maybe switching to less frequent sessions—I need to learn to be on my own now. I've been doing okay, I don't need so much therapy." As the patient argued for less therapy, the therapist was tempted to comment on the obvious fact that the patient was experiencing a profound sense of loss and perhaps feeling that he couldn't trust people he had formerly relied on, and therefore, wanted to fire, or at least lessen his time with, the therapist. After all, his friend was no longer available, and he had relied on him. This would have been a representational level intervention, however, because it would have tried to tease out feelings of trust, disappointment, or loss, and with persistence even get to some feelings of anger at the loss.

On the other hand, the therapist recognized that the patient was communicating at a behavioral level by saying, "I should see you less frequently," describing a behavioral pattern, rather than saying, "I feel like I can't trust you." The patient was also dealing with his experience in a concrete, behavioral sense, wondering where his security would come from, rather than talking about loss, disappointment, or sadness. Before even considering what comment to make, the therapist tried to help the patient elaborate on what the experience of not having his friend was like. Two associative trends emerged; one was about increasing the patient's own security by having people available to ask for advice, and the other involved distancing himself more from the therapist.

The therapist then chose to try to reach the patient at his developmentally appropriate level. The goal here was to build a representational attitude, which would eventually lead to an exploration of feelings, rather than try to circumvent this by coming in above the patient's ability to emotionally comprehend his words. The therapist commented in the form of a question, "Is it your belief now that no one, including me, can provide the security you're talking about, and, therefore, you figure that the best way to be is on your own?" The therapist deliberately avoided comments about trust and deep feelings, and kept his comments at the behavioral level. The patient was concerned about security and distancing himself from a person who had been providing some security for him—the therapist—and the therapist tried to combine these two concerns in terms of a behavioral level question.

The therapist's question led to a look of recognition in the patient's eyes and a begrudging "yes." The patient then reflected, "I guess life is telling me I'm on my own." As he said this, there was no reflection on feelings, but there was a decided annoyance and anger evident in his voice. When the therapist proceeded to inquire what that sensation was like the patient said, "I have no choice but to be on my own." Gradually, the patient began associating to some general affect states, using beginning affects such as, "Well, you know, I don't like it." In a petulant, almost childish way, he began to get outraged about how he liked to have people around that he could rely on and he wasn't going to like this new, unfair situation. As he expressed more of these general "I don't like it, it makes me feel bad" affects, there were also associations to memories of being ill, where the basic theme was that his body didn't work. This came out in the form of recalling the time he was sick and he didn't have a girl friend, and there was no one there to take care of him. Fear and outrage were expressed in both general affective terms and some undifferentiated, somatic affective images.

Over a number of months, in talking about his dislike and his fear of being alone, he was able eventually to talk about how angry he gets when people are not there for him. After the patient was able to abstract being "angry-feeling," which had to occur spontaneously, he was also able to associate to deep feelings of "emptiness and aloneness inside."

This brief clinical example illustrates the subtle differences between the typical way of commenting to such a patient about his feeling a lack of trust or feeling angry or sad about a loss, versus the above therapist's care in meeting the patient at an appropriate developmental level. At this patient's behavioral level of development, he was incapable of focusing on affects. Instead, he was thinking, "I will distance myself and no one can take care of me." He had some reflective capacities; the patient was aware that he was at a lower developmental level, saying, "I sound like a spoiled brat, don't I?" He would have been willing to indulge the therapist in discussion of feelings that perhaps he thought he should have, but this would have taken on the intellectualized tone that it had on prior occasions, when the therapist made the error of not meeting him at his true developmental level. Therefore, it was important to search carefully for the patient's present developmental level and find a way of phrasing therapeutic comments that was truly empathetic and developmentally appropriate. This approach allows the patient to eventually make progress and move up the developmental ladder. The other approach of suggesting the affects the patient might be experiencing usually leads to intellectualizations or rationalizations, which sound good to the patient temporarily, and may even sound good to the therapist, but often do not yield substantive therapeutic progress.

CLINICAL VIGNETTE DEMONSTRATING CHANGE FROM BEHAVIORAL TO REPRESENTATIONAL MODES

Another recent clinical example of shifting from a behavioral to a representational mode occurred in the following therapeutic interaction.

A young woman was upset with the therapist because, in her view, he had crudely and with a rough voice pointed out to her that she wanted "to have her cake and eat it too." His comment followed her statement that she wanted to keep her marriage intact, but also to have a liaison with a man who fit her romantic, idealized image of what an exciting man should be like. For a long time she had been unable to find both sources of satisfaction in what, by all objective standards (including her own), was a reasonably good marriage with a man who was attentive, supportive, a good father to her children, and with whom she also enjoyed lovemaking. She loved him and felt secure with him, but he didn't provide that extra romantic excitement that only more emotional men could provide (her husband was a more stable, unemotional type, as she described it, but not without warmth).

Her anger at the therapist for being crude in his comment (which made her cry for a number of days) led her to consider leaving therapy. Instead of examining the correctness or incorrectness of his earlier comment, or the patient's denial of her own inner dynamics, the therapist focused with the patient on where she was at the moment. She was greatly disturbed at him because of his "not operating like a perfect therapist" as she put it. As she talked, she readily admitted that most of the time, the therapist was quite warm and empathetic, and it was rare that he had "lapses." The therapist wondered why such an infrequent lapse would be the cause for her considering saying goodbye. This then led to her talking about her need for him to not make mistakes.

After many discussions, it turned out that the dynamics behind the need for perfection were as follows. The patient experienced a "deep wound" inside herself, related to an angry, depressed mother, who would withdraw rather abruptly whenever there was any intense affect in their relationship, especially expressions of anger. This sense of a deep wound was exaggerated by certain medical problems she'd had as a child. In order to dull the pain of the deep wound, the patient fantasized about a perfect knight in shining armor who would take care of her, and shield her from the angry, depressed mother and the inner wound. As an adult, she had been able to tolerate neither a sense of disappointment in herself nor in the person who was cast in the role of her "knight in shining armor."

While her father had represented the "knight in shining armor" to her, the nondepressed side of her mother's personality also served as a "savior" knight to some degree. She could never bring the two together, the defective mother and the "knight in shining armor" mother, who apparently did give her some nurturing, since the patient was a deeply feeling and warm person.

In her relationship with her husband, she found it difficult to integrate the exciting part of the "knight in shining armor" with the security side. When her children or the therapist behaved imperfectly, she not only had thoughts of leaving them, but also felt that she was a bad person. In order to get away from suicidal images in which she would be hurting herself, she had to reconstruct significant others in her life as perfect. Sometimes leaving them would be the only way to maintain their perfection. She would rationalize, "They have a problem with me because there's something wrong with me," so her associations in therapeutic sessions weren't so much "why you made a mistake" or "why you were gruff," but instead "I must have done something to get you to be more crude or gruff than usual." This type of reenactment would occur anytime someone she was very close to acted out of the bounds of the role she had constructed for them. In this case it was the therapist, but it could have been her children or close friends in other circumstances.

For many months the therapist tried to interpret these patterns at the level of feelings—the rage, disappointment, the need to split her objects into the idealized one, and the tendency to incorporate the badness into herself to protect the idealized other in her life. The pattern kept repeating itself, though the patient did get some benefit from just the ability to come in and talk, and experience the closeness and security that are involved in the supportive atmosphere of the therapeutic relationship. The clinician finally changed tactics and began focusing on this pattern more in its proper developmental context, not assuming that this patient's rich description of life and its pattern meant that she could represent the affects. In fact, she rarely talked spontaneously about her anger, sadness, or loss, and instead talked about how people had to behave and how she would behave if they didn't behave that way. When the therapist recognized that their dialogue was characterized by behavioral interactions, he realized that there were certain scripts for him to behave out or else, and that there were certain scripts that she would behave out. The affects mediating these scripts were not as available to her as the scripts themselves.

The therapist began systematically commenting on the script she had for him and herself. He was to behave perfectly or else. If he behaved imperfectly it was because she had done something wrong to make him behave that way and she would then leave so as not to soil him anymore. Her leaving also included her suicidal images. As the therapist shared his insights about this behavioral drama, the patient had a look in her eyes which seemed to express, "Finally, you understand me!" Being an extremely bright person and a person with some intuitiveness, she wondered aloud what her feelings were. All she could experience was a tremendous sense of "There's a numbing of my body when I feel like escaping." She described many physical and somatic sensations around body numbing associated with the escapist behaviors.

Over time, she was gradually able to move up from these vague, numbing affect states to more undifferentiated somatic affects and general and specific affects having to do with an expected sense of disappointment and sadness, as well as outrage. These feelings were related to her experiences with her mother and now played out in relationship to her therapist and family members. The point to be made here is that this patient, bright and gifted as she was, had developed complex reenactments having to do with her own despair. These reenactments were related to those times when the therapist or one of her children did not play out their role as the perfect other in her life, which would help preserve her from having to make herself into the bad person. Another example of this linkage occurred when her child had been ill and she had become quite suicidal again, because the child's illness meant there must be something fundamentally bad about herself.

The ways in which the perfect others in this patient's life could protect her from certain aspects of her relationship with her mother, became the source and the focus of the therapeutic work. The work could only occur when these behavioral enactments were understood. As complex as they were and as psychodynamically loaded as they appeared, these enactments were still operating at the behavioral level. Once this was recognized, and it was recognized that the affects in their abstracted form were not there, both patient and therapist examined how these intricate behavioral patterns operated. The therapist stopped feeding her with his empathetic summaries of what she must have felt like—enraged, despairing, a sense of loss, all of which were hinted at by her facial expressions and certainly indicated by her behavioral descriptions. The lack of certain affects become apparent only when her behaviors were comprehended in terms of which patterns led to which other patterns. The woman would experience only a numbing feeling and nothing else, and would intellectualize, "I must be enraged, but I don't feel it." Instead of joining in with a, "You must feel something, let's see if we can find it," the therapist helped her focus on the numbing sense, a feeling she could readily experience. This allowed a gradual process to occur in which the patient became more aware of the need she had for people to operate in a certain way, and the numbness she felt when they didn't. In time, this led to "I can't stand it when you don't do what I need you to do," which in turn eventually opened the door to some undifferentiated somatic rages and then more abstracted rage. This finally led to a feeling of disappointment and sadness.

Not infrequently, behind a tenacious, complex behavioral pattern there exists enormous, frightening rage. The rage, however, may never have been experienced at a representational level. Far from being a regression from a representational form to a defensive concretization, which is acted out behaviorally, many of these patterns may have first been experienced by the individual during the toddler phase of development, before representations are possible. That rage operates in its behavioral derivatives with fixed, constricted ritualized behavioral patterns, rather than a repressed representational pattern. What was a fixed, unexamined pattern, now becomes a fixed, reflected-upon pattern which eventually becomes more flexible, just through the reflection of the fixed behavioral pattern. Other options are considered, in part because of the warm empathy of the therapeutic relationship. By way of contrast, the patient's own mother had countered the patient's behavior with behavior of her own, and was part and parcel of the fixed pattern. In this case, the patient would become assertive or challenging and the mother would withdraw. The patient would then become either disorganized in her behavior or run away from the mother. Even as a toddler the patient refused ever to become compliant, needy, or vulnerable to her mother.

The therapist did not reenact this pattern quite in the same way the mother did. The therapist brought a reflective attitude and through his empathy remained engaged with the patient when the patient expected a shutdown. This brought flexibility to the formerly ritualized pattern. The flexibility broadened life at the behavioral level, coupled with the reflective attitude and the focus on sensations in the body, which also broadened the understanding of the pattern and facilitated movement, as described earlier, up the ladder to more representational modes.

Interestingly, the inappropriate representational or pseudo-affect approach to these patterns in some respects repeats the pattern, because when the therapist failed to meet the patient developmentally, the patient experienced the therapist as not being with her and not being empathetic. This is similar to the mother's shutdown. Even when a therapist thinks he is in tune with the patient and correct in his interpretation, if he approaches the patient at the wrong developmental level, the patient experiences familiar patterns of rejection since her signals are misread. The therapist is actually reenacting the parental pattern, and inadvertently continuing a certain ritualistic set of behaviors. In this case, the therapist broadened the pattern by not reenacting as the mother had, and thereby helped a ritualistic pattern become more flexible. He was empathetic to the sensations and emerging affects and helped a progression occur, which eventually produced more abstracted affect states and a true representational capacity.

FIXED ATTITUDES AND CHARACTER CONSTRICTIONS AND THE TRANSITION FROM BEHAVIORAL TO REPRESENTATIONAL LEVELS

We have discussed some of the types of experiences that promote representational capacities and the challenges of elevating selected affects to the representational level. In this section, we will further explore how certain fixed attitudes about oneself, often associated with depressive or other contents, are related to the inability to represent certain affects, and how the ability to represent certain affects can be helpful in reducing these fixed attitudes. A clinical vignette which illustrates this point is as follows.

A bright young woman, with two young children, was recently offered an exciting position at work. The new position, however, would have involved her shifting from part-time to full-time, which she was reluctant to do, since she had two young children. After hearing of this potential new job, which she quickly, almost reflexively, turned down, even before it was formally offered to her (because of her intuitive concern that it would overload and overwhelm her and she couldn't be home as much as she wanted to with her children), she came into a session. (She had turned down the job through a third party, who was exploring her potential availability for the new position.) She began her session with:

> I really blew it. There I am, a failure again. I can't hack tough jobs and I'll never amount to anything. I'll always be mediocre. I'll never be able to progress. I guess I'm just not cut out for professional life. Maybe I should just chuck all those years of education. Getting A's in college and graduate school doesn't amount to a hill of beans. I can't even have an intelligent conversation about politics anymore, my mind is so bad.

She went on and on criticizing herself in a negative, depressive tone, explaining in bits and pieces that she "blew her one opportunity to have a position with some responsibility and upward potential." Nowhere in her associations were there any references to the more intimate details of her decision—her struggle about wanting to be home with her children and not wanting to work full-time—other than some brief mention ("Well, there's no way I could have done it anyhow, because I have to take care of my kids, etc."). These were just passing comments, though, and her main focus was on how much of a loser she was.

What seemed to be missing from her associations were certain emotions or affects. There was no sense of disappointment over what she had to give up because of her choice to spend more time with her children. There was no mourning over the loss. There was no subsequent planning for how she might be able to regroup in the future, when her children were older and she was able to work more hours and take advantage of such opportunities. In addition to there being no emotion of loss, there was no annoyance or anger at the fact that one can't do everything in life—one can't be home with one's children and still have a full-time career. There were no feelings of unfairness expressed that maybe her husband should stay home part-time so she could increase her hours at work.

A range of expectable feelings was not present. In lieu of all these expectable feelings was a fixed set of ideas; that is, a lot of depressive ideation. Key among the various missing affects was the affect of loss or disappointment which is often useful in working through a situation like this. Here the person in some way recognizes that life is full of choices, and even when electing among good choices, one is, nonetheless, often compelled to give something up.

The ability to abstract the affect of sadness, loss, or disappointment and experience them in a representational form, is a critical aspect of resolving the tendency to have fixed, rigid ideas. Sometimes these fixed ideas are more of a depressive nature, other times they can be more of a suspicious or externalizing nature. Resolving the related affects of anger (that the young woman has to make a choice, that she can't have it all, that it's unfair, that her husband won't stay home) is also based in part on the ability to experience a range of affects, especially sadness or loss. At times, the patient experienced affects of outrage and blaming others, but with a sense of "this is the way life is and I'll have to accept it, but I'll be damned angry at him for the rest of his life for it," that goes along with negative and depressive fixed attitudes.

In a pattern such as this, the person who is unable to utilize the representational level, where affects can be abstracted and deeply felt, instead falls back on the prerepresentational modes of coping, which have to do with behavioral enactments (using behaviors instead of affects), or uses fixed, polarized attitudes or beliefs. It is suggested here that fixed, polarized beliefs, including beliefs about oneself, depressive or paranoid ideation, is a partner to the behavioral mode of coping with wishes and conflicts. That is, one either behaves it out or one uses fixed, ritualized-type of thought patterns. Recall that when we discussed the behavioral level of organization, we pointed out that at the behavioral level, one can increase flexibility and range of behaviors to cope with a wide range of situations, including internal states of wish and affect, or one can develop fixed rituals—repetitive behavioral patterns. Similarly, as one begins using ideas and thoughts, the fixed behavioral patterns can give birth to fixed ideation. If thoughts and ideas are available, fixed ideation can be used instead of fixed, rigid, ritualized behavior. In this sense, the ritual is the maladaptive side of a continuum, with flexible behavior and thinking at one end, and ritualized, fixed patterns of behavior or thought at the other end. The inability to experience loss or disappointment partially determines whether or not one uses fixed behavior patterns in situations like the one described.

Interestingly enough, this is observed when some types of animals are placed in a situation where a difficult choice is to be made, and there is obvious ambivalence demonstrated by the animals going back and forth between the possible choices; one sees the animals scratching or touching themselves a lot. This behavior is similar to what is observed in humans in an ambivalent situation. It would seem that a perpetual state of ambivalence is related to this same inability to experience disappointment and loss. If one cannot let go and experience loss or disappointment, one holds onto all possibilities, and in doing so, one remains perpetually ambivalent, searching for a seeming perfection where nothing has to be given up.

Looking at the difficulty in representing certain affects as a critical contributor to certain fixed beliefs or attitudes, such as depressive ones, is somewhat different from, and yet complements, traditional ways of looking at the nature of symptomatic behavior. Traditionally, one would look for the unconscious wish and affect behind the behavior or symptom, with the goal of helping the individual become aware, often through verbalizing, of the hidden wishes or affects and then working them through. Thus, aggression might be behind certain compulsive sets of ideas or behaviors. As one becomes aware of the aggressive wishes, the need to defend against them through some sort of symptom, such as cleansing oneself with hand washing or thinking "only good thoughts," may not be necessary and there is increased flexibility in the personality.

From our developmental perspective, however, we are looking at certain structural capacities of the ego in addition to unconscious wishes, the defenses against them, and compromise formations. Can the patient, for example, abstract certain affects such as loss? When the individual is incapable of utilizing certain developmentally more advanced ego mechanisms, such as the ability to abstract certain affects, it leaves only certain primitive strategies available to the ego, including behavioral enactment or fixed, inflexible beliefs or ideation.

The content of these fixed beliefs or behaviors is in part determined by experience and unconscious wishes. The need to use the primitive defense or coping strategy, however, may be determined, in part, by the lack of more mature ego mechanisms. Let us continue our example, for instance, of the person using hand washing or thoughts about cleanliness to defend against unconscious aggressive wishes.

This same situation could occur at a stage of representational differentiation where there is a tendency to wash one's hands a few extra times when one is angry, or to focus on certain religious themes in terms of goodness, when one is feeling enraged. Given this general ability to reflect on such a trend, the individual, while not aware of the angry feelings, wonders to himself why it is that at certain times he is more concerned with clean hands or clean thoughts. This exists as a narrow band of circumscribed painful experience in an otherwise healthy personality, with some reflection on the driven nature of this particular circumscribed piece of behavior.

On the other hand, when these same conflicts over aggression exist in an individual who is at a primarily behavioral discharge level of organization, and where there is a global impairment in the ability to abstract or represent affects, then we may see global fixed beliefs or attitudes instead of circumscribed obsessive behaviors and thoughts. We may also see very ritualized behavior that characterizes almost the entire, if not the entire, personality. There is little ability to represent a range of affects.

It is the inability to represent the affects that is responsible for the fixed, massively negative beliefs that are part of a global, depressive character disorder (as opposed to, in the other case, a more narrow, circumscribed set of symptoms in a rather healthy, flexible personality organization).

In essence, the developmental perspective alerts us to an aspect of the solution of the problem, as well as its genesis. If the individual is basically at a primitive level of character organization, it does little good to simply help him or her to achieve catharsis of a particular set of unconscious wishes and affects. Here the main goal is to improve the individual's ability to make use of more advanced ego mechanisms, which, coupled with self-awareness, lead to ultimate flexibility. Awareness in an otherwise inflexible, rigid, immature personality organization often has, at best, the benefits from temporary relief. It is a little bit akin to an individual with a severe back problem due to a fracture of a bone, getting momentary relief from some applied heat. It feels good for the time being, but it doesn't deal with the underlying structural vulnerability.

Another case will illustrate this same developmental process, that is, the difficulty in making the transition from the behavioral level, including fixed behaviors or attitudes, to the representational level. A child who was in late latency was of concern to his parents because, "He yells at kids a lot. He doesn't understand subtlety and nuance. He takes casual statements as major insults. For example, if you say, 'Your hair is short,' he'll say, 'What do you mean?' and then accuse a person of hating him." When he was upset, he would utter such extreme statements as, "I wish I weren't alive," which greatly worried his parents. In addition, with slight provocation, he would hit and push other children and generally act out behaviorally. In other words, he had both fixed ideas which were polarized in extremes, such as, "I wish I weren't alive" or "Everyone hates me," and he also had fixed impulsive behavior patterns—hitting or pushing—when frustrated.

His parents were perplexed about this and spoke about the way they were trying to help him put limits on his behavior. Father described a sequence where his son had collected some bugs from the backyard and was trying to keep them in an enclosed area, a sort of makeshift cage. Mother was upset, however, because her son wasn't putting enough dirt in and, therefore, the bugs wouldn't have enough to eat and she was afraid they would die. Father also got frustrated with him and was tired of hearing Mother complain. Father said he warned the child for several days in a row to take better care of his bugs, and finally, without further warning, and without previously telling him what the punishment would be, "threw the bugs out into the backyard because the boy didn't take care of them. But then he ran away without his shoes on, and I had to go out after him. I finally found him and he asked me, 'What would you do if I ran away?' to which I replied, 'I'd cry a million tears'." The child then said, "I'm a shit. I wish I weren't alive."

These parents didn't realize at first that their own behavior was very similar to that of their son. Both sets of behaviors represented a certain concrete way of coping—their son either hurt other children or failed to take care of his animals (i.e., acting out certain wishes); the parents dealt with their frustration with their son by using a behavioral discharge mode (i.e., throwing away his bugs). The child then responded, after feeling guilty because his father said he would cry a million tears for him, with, "I'm a shit. I wish I weren't alive," another polarized concrete orientation.

The parents felt that they had warned their child and that they had done what they could to be reasonable. They did not immediately see the similarity between their concrete way of behaving and their child's concrete way of behaving. The therapist went on to wonder hypothetically how this situation might have been handled differently and then explored the reasons why the parents handled it the way they did.

An alternative therapeutic mode would have been to establish empathy and support to help this child identify his behavioral pattern of not taking care of the insects, and then set up in advance limits related to his not taking care of his insects, and perhaps his feeling about caring or not caring about his insects. The limits would not, however, be something that had an impulsive, behavioral, acting out quality, like throwing the insects away. Instead they might be that he wouldn't be allowed to bring new insects or pets into the house until he demonstrated some responsibility by perhaps caring for something living that was less demanding, like flowers or a plant. The boy would have to first show he could water them and put nutrients into the soil, before being permitted to work his way back up to being responsible for insects or perhaps fish or some other small animal. During this process, his parents would be talking to him about how hard it is to take on responsibility and what feelings are associated with sometimes wanting to have pets and yet not wanting to give them the time they need. They would provide a lot of support to help him care for the pets through understanding the feelings that sometimes led him to ignore the pets and other times led him to want the pets. For the child who magically believes the pets will be okay, even if he fails to care for them, such an approach helps him to understand what pets need and why sometimes he has a hard time providing it. One is still firm around the boundaries of setting limits, however, in terms of not allowing future insects into the house until the child demonstrates more sense of responsibility with simple life forms.

To this suggestion, the mother's first reaction was, "But I didn't want him to let those insects die, and I was frustrated and mad that he wasn't listening to me! I had to do something right away, something immediate, to get his attention." Here we see a very good example of a mother who feels the need to discharge her frustration quickly and rapidly. She could not stand taking a longer term strategy, where her son would be prevented from bringing future pets in and be educated gradually. The parent's need for immediacy only compounded the child's sense of immediacy. Both were operating with a short fuse, little tolerance for frustration, and the need to discharge frustration into action very quickly. This was the cornerstone of their similarity.

There are many families who cannot understand how such "good citizens" like themselves can produce children who are impulse-ridden and make trouble. They fail to see, often, that their "good citizen" posture may be a very concrete one, whereby they deal with frustration by rigid rules and behavior discharge, even though their own behavior discharge mode is more in the enforcer style of a policeman while their children act out in the delinquent mode. Sometimes, children who are compliant and have certain approaches to processing information that enables them to easily take it in and comprehend it, will be rigid and concrete like their parents, but also in the mode of being obedient to authority. Other children who are physically different, or whose early experiences have created a lot of anger, may utilize a rebellious strategy. The interesting irony is that both the compliant and the angry child have certain similarities, in terms of having short fuses and responding to frustration with a need for immediate behavioral actions; one to become passive; the other, impulsive. Neither child has an ability to reflect his or her own feelings, plan and anticipate the consequences of his or her actions, and take the long-term perspective.

As the parents in the anecdote further explored what made it hard for them to take a long-term perspective and why they had to be concrete like their child, the father's association was, "I don't recognize feelings of anger. I dumped the bugs because that's it, but there was no feeling. I didn't feel angry before I dumped the bugs. I just did it. In fact, I didn't feel anything." So here we have a father who is carrying out an angry behavior, and who was obviously frustrated, but who dumped the bugs in a matter-of-fact way. He wasn't warned by his own angry feelings that he was capable of doing something that his child would perceive as sadistic, and, in all likelihood, was sadistic. The father, however, reported, "But I never am aware of many of my feelings, especially angry feelings or competitive feelings. I am in situations where I know that's what most people would feel, but I feel nothing inside. Sometimes I take a little delight in watching people suffer, but that is the closest I come to intellectually knowing I must be angry."

Interestingly, as both parents looked at their own patterns, the father described himself as a person who had, "infinite patience, but no feelings." Within his infinite patience, he was clearly capable of acting out his anger without awareness, passive aggressively, under the umbrella of being a placid, complacent sort of person. Mother described herself as "angry, easily frustrated, and impatient." The child was caught between these two concrete patterns, father's passive–avoidant and passive–aggressive mode and mother's frustrated, somewhat more belligerent, intrusive style.

Another situation, somewhat similar, occurred in the context of a family session with a 10-year-old boy and his parents. The child was functioning at a higher developmental level than the boy in the previous example. The parents complained that their son talked out in class, often made fun of the teacher, and occasionally got carried away when he was with other children, and could push and shove. They were annoyed with him for not "sizing up situations better." This was an extraordinarily bright youngster, and they felt he needed to set himself limits, because he was getting into mild hot water in school. As the discussion evolved, the therapist asked the youngster what he thought about his parents' challenges. The boy pointed out that Mother yelled too much and Father was too critical. He said he didn't like it, especially when they yelled at each other. The therapist remarked that the boy's parents wanted him to be more considerate of the teacher's and other students' feelings, and wondered whether did he think that his parents were considerate of each other. The boy said flatly, "No, hardly at all."

Both parents looked stunned, since they both considered themselves to be thoughtful and empathetic people. But on reflection, it became clear that Father often was impatient with Mother if she hadn't done routine things like getting the outside of the house painted or hadn't picked up something from the store he wanted. She was equally impatient with him if he disagreed with her over a childrearing issue. Upon further exploration, the child persisted in the view that the parents did not take each other's perspective.

As the discussion continued, it became clear that in this family, no one was particularly adept at empathizing and truly seeing life from another's point of view—not the child at school, nor the parents with each other. The parents both wanted to empathize with him more, but he was "closed" and would never tell them much about what happened in school. After observing the dynamics between the parents, the therapist was not surprised that the child elected to "stonewall" them in his family, and, furthermore, that he wasn't developing a skill that the whole family had failed to develop. Where else could he learn it, but in the family? Various representational capacities, including especially the capacity for empathy, can only be learned interactively. If relationships are devoid of empathy, there is no experimental basis for a child learning how to represent it.

Yet another case, and a more dramatic one, involved a boy who had made enormous progress, after having been diagnosed with Pervasive Developmental Disorder as a 2-year-old. Now he was a fully related, warm, youngster, using language and having logical conversations and even a sense of humor with parents and peers. What he did, though, was to often act as though he were king of the universe and no one else existed, particularly when he felt like grabbing people or mussing their hair or making funny noises to mock them. His parents were annoyed that he wasn't developing a new level of ability.

I pointed out to the parents that there comes a time when the child may find it hard to develop a new ability, because the ability isn't present in the family, and the parents are unable to interact with him around this new ability, as easily as they could around prior ones. It was easy to get his attention, to form a relationship with him in terms of emotional warmth, to teach him to use words and gestures to communicate feelings, and even to be logical. These were skills they had mastered well as a family. But as a family unit, it was clear to the clinician that the parents had very little ability to size up each other's needs or to empathize with or see the other one's perspective. I pointed out that this capacity might be, in some respects, harder, even though it is a more subtle capacity and hardly seems as challenging as learning how to relate, talk, and think. But feeling empathy, rather than operating by being demanding and selfish, posed a greater challenge for these parents and this family.

Within this family, Father perceived Mother as being emotional, opinionated, and demanding, and incapable of understanding where he was coming from. Mother viewed Father as rigid, controlling, critical, and bossy; never understanding where she was coming from. It was not surprising, therefore, that this child might have a hard time developing the needed ability to put himself in someone else's shoes, to size up how they were feeling, and adapt his behavior appropriately.

The child requires relationships where the recognition of certain core aspects is substituted for either direct discharge behavior or fixed belief systems. When feelings are not abstracted for the self they often cannot be easily understood in others, and this then leads to difficulty in a continuum of dealing with one's own and other people's emotions. The individual is then left to a direct discharge mode of interacting, behavior to behavior, fixed attitudes and beliefs to fixed attitudes and beliefs. This makes for battles in families, results in concrete and primitive attitudes in growing children, and can even lead to volatility between larger groups of people, or wars between nations. This family had to work on learning empathy, as a more general challenge, before this child could experience it enough to abstract it. Over time they were able to accomplish this goal and the child began also to be able to put himself in the emotional shoes of others.

We have seen, therefore, that the transition from behavioral and somatic to representational levels is a vital aspect of the psychotherapeutic process. It involves interaction patterns which in their origins lacked representational forms, either globally or around certain affects. In the therapeutic situation these interaction patterns become the basis for growth. Identifying the patterns, exploring the different levels of affect associated with the pattern, and most importantly, making available interactive opportunities which can serve as a foundation for representational experience are the steps of building representational capacities.

Chapter 9

Representational Differentiation (Emotional Thinking)

Representational differentiation occurs when an individual can represent experience in the form of a multisensory image and categorize it. This ability to categorize experience is the first step in the differentiation process. The second step involves building bridges between various categories of experience.

A person may, for example, categorize a realm of experience having to do with closeness and dependency. All the different feelings, behaviors, and experiences having to do with closeness form a category in the individual's mind. The person may then link this category with another category of experience based on aggression or anger. Not infrequently, such an emotional bridge may arise out of a fantasy or belief that angry feelings lead to loss of dependency or closeness.

Categories of experience are formed around such different feelings as dependency, pleasure, aggression, and assertiveness. They can also occur when a person organizes experience according to what's "me" and what's "not me," or the self and nonself, or object. Another level of categorization occurs when

313

experience is broken down into what is subjective and what is objective, what is fantasy or make-believe, and what is reality. Experience can also be categorized in terms of the dimensions of time and space: What's happening now? What's in store for the future? What took place in the past? What's happening here? What's going on in the next room? The emotionally salient aspects of time and space are experienced by the representationally differentiated child or adult and readily expressed. When will mother be back—in ten minutes, or an hour? Is she next door—or far away in California?

At the level of representational differentiation, the therapist helps the patient accomplish the goal most often set in therapy: to form connections between different affects, themes, and areas of representation (connections between aggression and loss; dependency and withdrawal). The therapist deals with conflicts between different representational dramas and tries to help the person find connecting bridges. One caveat is that in some discussions of the therapeutic process, including the "good hour" described by Hartmann, Kris, and Loewenstein (1946), the model described is of the therapist being very active in making connections. The patient shows his acceptance of the therapist's comments by a deepening of the associative pattern. Developmentally, however, it makes more sense to help the patient be active, with the therapist juxtaposing the different conflicting dramas and asking the patient to form the connecting bridges. Often, when this is done, some very interesting patterns emerge.

Many patients who seem to be using insights in therapy really are not. They escape into fantasy. They use fantasy to avoid rather than elaborate on wishes or painful affects. Some patients, while the therapist tries to draw their attention to a connection, become more representationally elaborative, but only in one direction. While some individuals relate more with free associations and fantasies, they often fail to integrate them with their daily challenges. On the other hand, other patients may stick only to their real lives and avoid depth of fantasy.

The following exchange between a therapist and his 6-year-old patient is illustrative.

Therapist:	What's going on with your friends at school?
Child:	Look at these dolls fighting!
Therapist:	Well, that's interesting, but what did Johnny do to you today at school?
Child:	Look at the wrestler! He's going to jump on the house and crush it into pieces.

This seems like rich material, imaginatively filled with wrestlers and aggression. This child has a difficulty with talking about what is happening with his best friend at school, and instead keeps escaping into fantasy about the fighting wrestlers. While aggression may be quite relevant to school relationships, many children use the fantasy to escape from the daily world of intense affects and avoid trying to create bridges that would link the two.

A lot of adults have the same difficulty. Therapists, however, often persist in making bridges for them, never saying, "I can see it's hard for you to go back and forth between your wife and your associations (or your boss at work and these feelings you have about your family, or your dreams)."

In a developmentally based therapy, the therapist lets the patient do the construction of his own bridges. The therapist looks for those areas where the patient avoids making connections and lets the patient do the work. With patients who are representationally differentiated, earlier difficulties in the depth of relationships or affect-cuing can be brought into representational awareness.

Traditional psychodynamic approaches to therapy have heretofore been based on the assumption that just as the capacity for representational elaboration is present in most people, so the capacity for representational differentiation must similarly be present. The therapist's chief role has been seen as analyzing conflicts, helping individuals deal with their defenses in order to handle the anxiety which stems from these conflicts, and then assisting the patients to reintegrate and, if necessary, redifferentiate their experiences. The tools of free association, listening, empathy, clarifying, and interpreting, serve this purpose.

In this chapter we will reexamine the traditional psychodynamic model and step by step build a case which supports the
notion that the capacity to integrate and differentiate experience needs to be developed in many patients. We will take
the position that there are many different elements to the
capacity to differentiate experience; that most patients come
into therapy without some of these capacities, and that the
therapist needs to understand that helping the patient to
analyze conflicts, anxieties, and compromise formations needs
to be done in the context of building up these differentiating structures.

Attempting to help an individual who lacks a particular
differentiating structure by using insight and clarification can
be likened to building a house without first laying a stable
foundation. Such a patient may have some intellectual awareness of what the therapist says, but has no ability emotionally
to process the words. Structure building is thus a critical therapeutic goal for patients who lack full differentiating capacity.
Furthermore, the therapist's understanding of the content of
the patient's productions must occur in the context of structure building.

Therapeutic rules and strategies for dealing with patients
who lack some element of differentiation will be detailed later in
this chapter. In addition, there will be a review of the different
problems that patients have that involve a lack of differentiation.
It will be suggested that the majority of patients lack some elements of differentiation and that the classical model of neurosis
and the notion of character neurosis, as a basis for understanding
psychopathology, is inadequate. Understanding how many of the
patient's presenting problems involve subtle aspects of lack of
differentiation will make available a more general and systematic
model of therapy. This model enables the therapist to work on
building up those structures that patients have deficiencies in.
Patients can then learn to differentiate and integrate their internal worlds in order to deal with conflict, anxiety, and compromise.

REPRESENTATIONAL DIFFERENTIATION AND THE BASIC FUNCTIONS OF THE EGO

During this stage of representational differentiation the ego is characterized by its ability to abstract patterns along dimensions of self and object meanings, drive affect dispositions, affective tendencies, and the dimensions of time, space, and causality. These include reality testing (a representational "me" separate from a representational "other"); impulse control (a representational "me" has an impact on and elicits consequences from a representational "other"); mood stabilization (a representational "me" and "other" becomes organized along a dominant mood as affects are abstracted into larger affective patterns); focused attention and a capacity for planning (a representational "me" causes events to occur in a temporal context); and a more integrated body selfobject representation (the parts of "me" and object are abstracted in spatial contexts).

Ego functions include representational differentiation characterized by:

1. Genetic integration (early somatic and behavioral patterns are organized by emerging mental representations);
2. Dynamic integration (current drive–affect proclivities are organized by emerging mental representations);
3. Intermicrostructural integration (i.e., affect, impulse, and thought are integrated);
4. Structure formation (selfobject representations are abstracted into stable patterns performing the ongoing ego functions of reality testing, impulse control, mood stabilization, etc.);
5. Self and object identity formation (i.e., there is an emerging sense of self and object which begins to integrate past, current, and changing aspects of fantasy and reality).

Or alternatively the ego may be characterized by:

1. Representational fragmentation (either genetic, dynamic, or both);

2. Lack of, or unstable, basic structures (e.g., reality testing, impulse control, etc.);
3. Defective, polarized, or constricted (global or encapsulated) self/object identity formation.

For the child to meet the challenges of organizing and differentiating his internal world according to self and other, inside and outside, dimensions of time and space, and affective valence, he is, in part, dependent on the integrity of the sensory organization that underlies his experiential world. Now, even more than earlier in his life, the capacity to process sensory information is critical, including sequencing auditory–verbal and visual–spatial patterns according to physical, temporal, and spatial qualities in the context of abstracting emerging cognitive and affective meanings. The child is challenged to understand what he hears, sees, touches, and feels, not only in terms of ideas, but in terms of what is me and not-me; what is past, present, and future; what is close and far, and so forth. These learning tasks depend on the ability to sequence and categorize information. Therefore, if anywhere along the pathway of sensory processing there are difficulties, the subsequent ability to organize even impersonal, let alone affective-dynamic, information will likely be compromised. For example, if sounds are confused, words will not be easily understood. If spatial references are confused, spatial configurations will not be easily negotiated. If short-term memory for either verbal or spatial symbols is vulnerable, information will be lost before it can be combined with, and compared to, other information (to abstract meanings). And if higher level auditory–verbal symbolic or visual–spatial symbolic abstracting capacities are less than are appropriate, the very capacity to categorize experience will be limited. Perhaps most importantly, if sequencing capacities are vulnerable, the ability to form patterns of thought and behavior, a critical building block of an integrated sense of "self" and "other" as well as one's intentions will be compromised. When one considers that the child must now learn how to process and organize not only impersonal cognitive experiences, but highly emotional, interpersonal experiences (which keep moving, so to speak), this challenge to the sensory system is formidable. Furthermore, categories such as "me," "not me," "real," and "make-believe" are high-level constructs. Not surprisingly, learning difficulties often are first evidenced in emotional functioning.

In contrast to earlier views by Freud (1900) and Mahler, Pine, and Berman (1975), our clinical observations suggest that a parallel path of differentiation exists simultaneously with the onset of the representational capacity and its elaboration. The child appears to use his representational capacity to simultaneously elaborate and differentiate experience. There does not appear to be a period of magical representational thinking followed by one of reality thinking. The child continually differentiates affective–thematic organizations along lines that pertain to self and other, inner-outer, time, space, and so forth. This differentiation is based on the child's capacity to experience the representational consequences of his representational elaborations with the emotionally relevant people in his world, usually parents, family, and friends. The parent who interacts with the child, using emotionally meaningful words and gestures, and engages in pretend play in a contingent manner (offering, in other words, logical representational feedback) provides the child with consequences that help him differentiate his representational world. In this view, reality testing—the capacity to separate magical from realistic thought—appears to be a gradual process beginning with the onset of the representational capacity proper and stabilizing prior to the child's formal entry into school.

One observes the child's elaborate representational themes along two dimensions. In one dimension, the child broadens the range of emotional domains or drive–affect realms, including closeness or dependency, pleasure and excitement, assertiveness, curiosity, aggression, self-limit-setting, the beginnings of empathy and consistent love. For example, not infrequently one observes repetitive pretend play of a feeding or hugging scene suggesting nurturance and dependency. Over time, however, the dramas the child may initiate (with parental interactive support) will expand to include scenes of separation (one doll going off on a trip and leaving the other behind), competition, assertiveness, aggression, injury, death, recovery (the doctor doll trying to fix the wounded soldier), and so forth. At the same time, along another dimension the logical infrastructure of the child's pretend play and functional use of language becomes more complex and causally connected. The "Power Ranger" action figure is hurt by the "bad guys" and therefore "gets them." After the tea party, the little girl doll goes to the "potty" and then decides it is time to begin cooking dinner. In discussions, the $3^1/2$-year-old sounds more and more like a lawyer with "buts" and "becauses"—"I don't like that food because it looks yucky and will make me sick." There is, therefore, both thematic elaboration and differentiation. Even though the themes may be pretend and phantasmagoric, the structure of the drama becomes more and more logical. A "Power Ranger" may have a run-in with a villain who is trying to poison a town's drinking water.

As indicated, representational differentiation depends not only on a child being representationally engaged in thematic–affective areas but experiencing cause-and-effect feedback at the representational level. Parents have to be able not only to engage but also to respond to and interpret experiences correctly. The parents who react to play with a gun as aggression one day, as sexuality another day, and as dependency on a third day, or who keep shifting meanings within the same thematic play session, will confuse the child. This child may not develop meanings with a reality orientation. Parents who confuse their own feelings with the child's feelings, or cannot set limits, may also compromise the formation of a reality orientation.

The child needs to learn how to shift gears between the make-believe and the real world. Ordinarily, we see this occur gradually between the ages of 2 and 4. As part of this process, we see more planning in children's play, as Piaget (1962) highlighted (e.g., going upstairs to get just the right cup for the tea party). What happens if there are failures of development during this stage? Earlier it was suggested that if representational elaboration is not occurring, the child is left with a preideational or prerepresentational, somatic, and behavioral orientation. If there are limitations in representational differentiation (confused meanings), a child's self and object differentiation at the representational level may be compromised. It is interesting to consider those people who can engage others warmly (have mastered attachment) and organize their behavior, but who have "crazy" thoughts. They often cannot separate their own thoughts from someone else's; they may have organized delusions, but are extremely warm and can relate to others (they are not autistic or schizoid).

These individuals have an adaptive sense, a type of behavioral reality testing even though their thoughts may be illogical. In contrast there are individuals who have illogical thoughts who are also able to organize their behavior and participate in intimate relationships. These individuals have difficulties at multiple developmental levels. They not only think illogically but behave illogically as well. Reality testing can be thought of in terms of realistic thoughts and realistic thoughts and realistic behaviors. Impairments of both thoughts and behaviors are more challenging.

One may also see constrictions; that is, people who cannot represent or differentiate aggression or sexuality and are left only with the behavioral–action mode, or who are confused about their own and others' ideas or feelings in these thematic areas (but not in other thematic areas). Constrictions at this stage may be associated with relatively more differentiated and internalized conflicts (i.e., between opposing differentiated tendencies in relation to relative degrees of undifferentiation).

It is also interesting to discuss psychosexual trends at this stage. The phallic trend is clearly present beginning at age $2^1/_2$ to 3. Kids love to build towers, pretend to be Superman, and undress to show off their bodies. In our clinical practice, an equal preoccupation with the anal concerns (eliminative or retentive patterns) has not been evidenced. It seems reasonable then to wonder if the anal body interest is elaborated as much in the representational sphere as in the phallic one.

It may be useful to consider the oral, anal, and phallic stages of psychosexual inclinations in terms of observable thematic–affective inclinations. There may be a sensory, tactile, or oral mode early in life. The oral stage may be more usefully thought of as part of a broader, sensory, tactile motor stage. Between the ages of 1 and 2, muscle control may predominate (better gross and fine motor coordination, including anal control by the end of the second year). Here, the general trend is toward motor modulation and exploration. There is a great deal of exploration of assertive curiosity and aggression. Then, by 2½ years, one sees the phallic inclinations as part of the ever-increasing body control and investment in the body and its parts (which begins at 17 to 18 months). The phallic inclinations become part of an emerging, more differentiated sense of childhood sexuality, as the interest in the genitals becomes integrated with the overall emerging sense of the body as part of an internal bodily representation. In summary, even though there is fascination with feces, we have not observed the representational derivatives of anal body interest in normal children to the same degree as phallic derivatives. On the other hand, where development is not progressing optimally, either exaggerated phallic trends or excessive anal preoccupation is not uncommon.

To return to the earlier discussion, inclinations that do not have access to the representational mode and its differentiation, even in mild degrees, are perhaps sowing the seeds for severe character pathology and/or neurotic conflicts. What is often referred to as magical thinking is more probable where representational elaboration and differentiation have not fully occurred. Later on, in the triangular oedipal and latency phases of development, earlier patterns obviously are reenacted and reworked.

In summary, it is useful to clinically observe and assess the representational capacity along the two simultaneous dimensions of representational elaboration and representational differentiation. Clinically one observes defects and constrictions in both domains. These are evidenced by the child who:

1. Remains concrete and uses behavior rather than representations to deal with wishes, affects, and inclinations. Never learns to use the representational mode to elaborate "inner sensations" to the level of meanings;

2. Is severely constricted and is only able to represent a few of the affective–thematic domains characteristic of human functioning (i.e., uses behavioral discharge for dependency or aggression rather than representational modes);

3. In order to differentiate experience, avoids affective–thematic realms that are potentially disruptive (character disorders) (i.e., may avoid dependency or anger or assertiveness in order to protect the differentiation that is already present. Trying to engage too quickly in these warded off areas may be associated with compromises in reality testing);

4. Demonstrates representational affective–thematic life but remains undifferentiated along one or another dimension. These may include ideas or thoughts (thought disorder), affective proclivities (mood disturbances), self and object organizations (reality testing and "self" and "other" boundary disturbances), intentionality (impulse disorders), or sense of time and space (disorders of learning, concentration, and planning).

Contributing to the genesis of these limitations during childhood is the caregiver who cannot engage representationally in all domains because he or she is fearful of certain affective–thematic realms and therefore withdraws or becomes disorganized. Then there is the caregiver who engages in all realms but has difficulty operating at a representationally contingent level. The child's own limitations from earlier maturationally based processing problems and psychosexual difficulties also contribute to representational disorders.

One can also see more subtle limitations or difficulties related to the stage of representational differentiation. As one observes both healthy and disturbed children, it appears that each category of experience can undergo relative degrees of differentiation, depending on the appropriateness and adaptiveness of environmental–representational feedback. As indicated earlier, the areas of pleasure, dependency, assertion, curiosity, anger, self-limit-setting, love, and empathy may be seen as a way to categorize experience (e.g., separation anxiety would be a feature of dependency). As realms of experience are defined and differentiated, each affective–thematic domain becomes a basis for further interaction and more refined meanings.

During this stage, ambivalence can be dealt with in a new way and an integrated representational self can be organized, or one may observe a lack of integration. Different selfobject representational units may exist, depending on interpersonal factors or maturational factors, at various degrees of differentiation. The sexual selfobject, assertive selfobject, dependent selfobject, and so on, may each achieve its own relative degree of differentiation. As indicated earlier, sensory processing difficulties may undermine differentiation in auditory–verbal or visual–spatial modes. Or a lack of representational feedback or distorted or illogical feedback in certain realms of experience will tend to leave those areas of representational life relatively undifferentiated.

As is well known, anxiety and conflict now tend to play a key role, but perhaps earlier than often thought. With growing representational capacity, anxiety can be interpreted via the emerging representational system. Conflicts between selfobject representations can occur in terms of an "internal debate" at the level of ideas (e.g., the good me and you versus the angry, evil me and you). Conflicts between selfobject representations and external expectations can also occur (the "greedy" me and the "strict" limiting other). Therefore, while anxiety and internal conflict have been thought to be dominant in the late oedipal and postoedipal phases (because of the necessity of internalized prohibitions, i.e., superego formation), our clinical observations of young children supports the notion that representational differentiation alone may be a sufficient condition.

What operations are available to the ego to deal with anxiety and conflict at this point?

Observations of both normal and disturbed young children suggest that the approaches available to the ego include:

1. Global lack of differentiation (reality and the object ties that provide reality feedback are too disruptive or "scary").

2. Selective dedifferentiation (blurring of boundaries and changing meanings, as with "my anger won't make mother leave because we are the same person").

3. Thought–drive–affect dedifferentiations ("I can think anything, but I won't have feelings so I won't be scared").

4. Thought–behavior (impulse) dedifferentiation ("If I do it, it's not me. Only when I think and plan it is it me").

5. Selective constrictions of drive–affect–thematic realms (areas such as anger or sexual curiosity are avoided and may remain relatively undifferentiated, often due to being associated with disorganizing interactive experience such as withdrawal, overstimulation, etc.).

6. Affect, behavioral, or thought intensification ("If I exaggerate it or its opposite, it can't scare me").

7. Differentiated representational distortions (changing meanings along lines of drive–affect dispositions—"I am supergirl, the strongest." But basic reality testing is maintained; e.g., "It is only pretend").

8. Encapsulated distortions (dynamically based, conflict driven, highly selective shifts of meanings; e.g., "I am the cause of mother's anger").

9. Transforming differentiational linkages. This is an early form of rationalization. As the child's capacity to connect representational units is forming, he or she can elaborate. ("I like Mommy because she is home all the time and I am mad at Daddy because he travels a lot.") These logical links can undergo subtle shifts to change meanings for defensive purposes. ("I like Daddy to travel a lot because he brings me presents. I am mad at Mommy," etc.)

10. Compromises in representational integration and representational identity. The integration of somatic, behavioral (and representational selfobject organizations),

and associated drive–affect proclivities are not fully maintained, as evidenced by the irritable-looking 3-year-old who "feels fine" or the belligerent 3-year-old who "loves everyone."

We have considered how the ego grows in its ability to organize experience. Somatic and behavioral experience is now abstracted to a higher plane, that of representation. In addition, somatic and behavioral patterns are interpreted or labeled. Most importantly, new experience is now organized and elaborated in representational modes. Representational elaboration and differentiation creates the basis for internal life to be symbolized and categorized along dimensions of self and nonself, affective meanings, time, and space. The categorization of experience in turn becomes the basis for fundamental ego functions, new relationship patterns, relatively more differentiated and internalized conflicts, higher level defenses, and psychosexual and psychosocial advances.

ADDITIONAL STAGES IN EGO DEVELOPMENT

Thus far, only the early stages of ego have been described. Ego functions progress to make possible triangular patterns and higher-level transformations of meanings, including the development of new structures such as the superego and ego ideal (i.e., new representational capacities are constructed).

As the foregoing has described in some detail, a variety of capacities are involved in representational differentiation. In addition, understanding how it continues throughout childhood and into adolescence and adulthood gives us a more complete model of the levels of differentiation.

The initial level of differentiation, which occurs in childhood, involves patterns that are mostly dyadic (self/nonself), with different affect proclivities, and dimensions of time and space that are experienced in the sense of a "me" and a "you." The next level of differentiation occurs as these various capacities become applied to triadic situations. The oedipal triangle leaves its mark on internal structure formation as surely as dyadic relationships do.

In the oedipal triangle, the bridges built between different categories of experience are more complex than those linking dyadic experiences. In this situation, the bridges occur within a three-person matrix. A child's construction of a triadic bridge may be along the following lines: "If I get mad at Mom, I'm not just worried about whether or not she will reject or attack me. I also wonder whether or not Dad will support me because he's mad at Mom, too. Will he be my ally?" The child might alternatively speculate, "If I'm nice to Mom, Dad will be jealous of me or he'll pick a fight with me," or "If I'm bossy with Dad, Mom will admire me because she loves it when I keep Dad in his place." The latter hints at some awareness of competition between the parents, with the mother using the child to further her own competitive assertiveness. One can imagine very many different triadic bridges, based on the experiences that the child constructs for himself. The key point here is that the system is now more complicated, with the behaviors of one person always having implications for the other two involved in the triad. In this triadic model, every behavior between A and B has implications for C, and every interaction between A and C has implications for B, and every interaction between B and C has implications for A. So there are no strictly dyadic patterns within the triadic structure. This is not to suggest that dyadic patterns cannot coexist with a triadic pattern, but it does suggest that within the triadic structure, there is always an implication for the three aspects of experience involved.

Obviously, this is a more complex cognitive and affective structure to operate in. Many intrigues of adult life in organizations, as well as in families, involve triadic kinds of thinking. When school-aged children are unable to be involved in triadic thinking, they often get into hot water. As the following example illustrates, they may involve themselves in dyadic thinking when triadic thinking is needed. Take, for example, John, who is friendly with Brian and David, and David who is similarly friendly with John and

Brian. John calls Brian for a play date while David is there and proceeds to negotiate about getting his needs met, even though he is aware that David is overhearing the conversation. John is shocked the following week when David doesn't invite him to his birthday party. "How could he do that to me? I was nice to him and invited him to my birthday party last month," John says. He is further shocked that David might have feelings about the fact that John excluded him when he called Brian the previous week. In short, John had tried to keep his relationship with Brian and David as two separate dyads, without realizing that a triangle was already in place. He was unaware that David would have feelings about what happened between him and Brian and that those feelings would come back to haunt him. Had John been able emotionally to integrate the concept of the triadic level of differentiation, he would have understood that his behavior with one person had implications for another. Like feelings of dependency, aggression, assertiveness, and a sense of me/not-me, dimensions of time and space will also operate at a triangular level. *Where* Brian is in relation to John *when* David overhears the conversation has reverberations among the members of the triad.

All the differentiating capacities we discussed above—dependency, aggression, assertiveness, the me/not-me—are now experienced at a higher level, in triadic configurations as well as dyadic ones. If I am angry at Sally, it may make Mark more dependent on Sally, because he will become worried that my anger is going to destroy Sally, and therefore he is going to be more clingy, for fear of loss. This kind of theme may occur in a family where a child sees rivalry and becomes more clingy because he is scared of losing one parent because of the anger of the other parent.

The next level of ego structural development takes place when the child moves from the triadic to the group situation. During the latency years, children typically move out of the family triad into the peer group, where they learn to negotiate even more complex relationship patterns. Pecking orders are established. Affects are experienced in gradations: "I like Megan first, Anne second, Michael third, and Jeff fourth." "I'm the best at soccer, the second best at softball, the third best at hockey."

Within the peer group, children learn how to form many categories among various people, and also form several gradations of feelings. They also learn how to integrate different feelings and see that those feelings can exist simultaneously. So, for example, a child comes to understand that he can be competitive with Matt and struggle over who's going to claim Robert as a best friend this week. And yet, while being competitive on the one hand, that same child can also respect both Matt and Robert and be friends. Children learn that they can compete on the soccer field and still not be enemies. Healthy, constructive competition, in fact, is the ability to feel aggressive and want to win and still feel warm, caring, and respectful at the same time. Many younger children will enter into all or nothing patterns. If they are competing with another child for a third child's attention, they may experience that as a "hate" relationship, rather than one of healthy competition, because they cannot tolerate both warm and aggressive feelings toward the same person at the same time.

The ability to see shades of gray, to integrate a variety of feelings toward the same person, and the ability to see feeling operate in the peer group, becomes yet another level of differentiation.

When her mother was away for an extended period of time, an 8-year-old schoolgirl would spill boys' secrets to girls during recess and let slip girls' secrets to boys. This gave her enormous attention, which filled her up while she missed her mother. On the other hand, her behavior annoyed both the boys and the girls and made the 8-year-old feel that even though she had created a satisfying stir, she had lost all her friends and "allies." The girl then complained that everyone hated her. In reviewing the situation, it became clear that she was being provocative to get everyone to pay attention to her, much as she had at home. This behavior arose out of a long-standing dyadic pattern with her mother. The child would become provocative, receive a lot of (negative) attention, and feel filled up. She would often reveal secrets at home to get some attention for herself. She was shocked to see that her friends at school were angry with her, since no one at home got mad at her when she behaved in a similar fashion. In fact, it took many months for her to understand the nature of how her peer group operated. Emotionally, she was unable to truly grasp the intricate nature of different subgroups within the larger group: Ruth, Sally, and Ann were the children who liked her, some boys wanted to use her to ferret out information about the other girls, but didn't particularly like her because she was a girl. Some girls felt competitive with her and didn't mind relating to her, but didn't particularly like her. Still other girls were shy and did not feel included in the different "warring factions" on the playground, and saw her as someone who rejected them and therefore they tended to be aloof from her.

The young girl came to understand these different groups of peers and saw her own objective of needing to feel close to someone while her mother was away. She figured out that the best thing to do was to play with the girls she was most friendly with and who liked her, and perhaps she could feel close and warm with them when she felt "lonely and sad." At a subsequent time when the girl's mother went away, the 8-year-old was able to reach out to the girls who liked her and who were a part of her more intimate network. She also understood in a general sense why some children would sometimes be hostile and competitive with her, or why some children were aloof, and she didn't take these things so personally anymore. For the first time she became aware of the politics of the playground, and saw the value of negotiating a new strategy among her peers.

Toward the end of the elementary school years, the child develops the ability to move beyond the peer group, although he or she is still heavily dependent on the peer group for a sense of self and identity. The sense of self begins to have some tentative independence from the group context, the triadic context, and the dyadic context. There are now internal values and standards, such as the wish to be a good or bad person, a nice or sweet person, or an angry or hostile person. These values exist to some degree in time and space, and offer a sense of stability to the preadolescent. In a sense, a child can now construct two internal realities simultaneously. One internal reality has to do with the social context in which the child finds himself (the dyad, the triad, and the group). The child feels defined by such experiences as whether or not a friend likes him, whether he is being nurtured or not, whether the rivalrous, jealous, competitive foe is going to undermine his relationship with his best friend, or whether he is the first or last picked for the baseball team. At the same time, there is a stable set of attitudes that are coalescing into a sense of self that exists independently of what is happening on any given day in school. Therefore, this second sense of internal reality survives the vicissitudes of daily life and has some stability in time and space. When a child is away from a best friend or from mother or father, he or she may still feel similarly about themselves even though they may simultaneously have feelings of missing the particular people. This stable sense of internal reality prevents one from feeling as if one is falling apart or is an entirely different person.

Simply put, the self is defined by the social reality of the moment (the dyad, triad, and group) and the inner sense of a stable "me" that operates independently of social dynamics. ("I tend to be nice to people, therefore I am a nice person, even if my best friend doesn't like me and I'm at a competitive disadvantage in soccer.") As one looks at the different ego capacities for differentiation, in terms of building bridges between experiences and categorizing experiences, it becomes apparent that a sort of internal dialogue is going on. How do I feel about myself when I am angry or needy, or when I tell a lie or act supportively? Bridges are built between an individual's standards and values and his or her desires and wants. It has often been thought that this sort of internal debate exists during the preoedipal and oedipal phases, in terms of superego interjects and valuing oneself. In these early developmental stages, however, this process is not the conscious dialogue it becomes at the end of latency. The values which later become the ego ideal and the superego are not as organized or explicit as they are at the end of latency, when the child can be consciously aware of two realities and feel a sense of stability. The oedipal and preoedipal child, and even the latency child, is still largely a product of day-to-day experiences with the dyad, triad, and group. Even the superego values require almost daily nourishment by the reality of the external objects. Put a child at age 7 in a group with certain values, and the child's alleged superego standards will rather rapidly drift toward the values of the group. This is less likely with a 10-year-old. These three levels of ego differentiation characterizing middle and late childhood are discussed more fully in *Playground Politics: The Emotional Life of the School Aged Child* (Greenspan, 1993).

A still higher level of representational differentiation occurs throughout adolescence and into adulthood. This higher level keeps developing long into adulthood. Adolescents begin contemplating themselves as part of a larger societal and cultural reality, rather than merely as a part of a peer group. The older child is also better able to define himself in terms of his past as well as his future. The latency-aged child can integrate and form bridges with the past, but only to a limited degree. The 10- to 11-year-old forms a more stable sense of self that is based for the most part on day-to-day realities and the short-term immediate past, although traumatic experiences from the distant past can still have powerful emotional effects.

The adolescent and young adult, however, can integrate a broader range of past experiences, but more importantly can do so in the dimensions of time, anticipating the future. The child of 10, 11, 12, and even 13 still lives pretty much in an immediate past, present, and future context. Studying hard to qualify to go to a good college does not yet have the same emotional meaning it does for the middle to late adolescent and the adult. Anticipation of a career or a family can provide the contextual defining points for the sense of the future that now is a part of the internal reality of the child. Much of this has been beautifully described by Erikson in his descriptions of adolescence and early adulthood.

As the child moves out into a larger social reality, this greater mobility in time and space further defines a sense of self. In addition, changing biological functions, leading to new feelings about pleasure and sexuality, further increase the types of experience the adolescent is capable of categorizing. New types of intimacy become possible because of sexual experiences. Closeness and friendship patterns are also changed, and in a spatial context the teenager now operates more as part of a culture, rather than connected to just an immediate family, local school, or neighborhood.

Adults progress through additional stages of ego development as they experience new types of relationships, feelings, and challenges. New levels of ego differentiation are evidenced in such capacities as the young adult's ability to separate from his family and carry the nurturing functions of his nuclear family within his growing sense of self; the adult's ability to carry the limit setting and judgmental functions of his family within him; the adult's ability to enter into truly stable intimate relationships, which capture the wishes and feelings of intimacy from earlier stages into a new pattern; the adult's ability to expand one's sense of self to encompass one's own children and yet at the same time respect their individuality (the ability to find pleasure in their delight, satisfaction in their growth and pride in their ways of being different from you); the middle aged individual's ability to see themselves on a new time and space continuum in the middle of their own life cycle (no longer looking up an infinite mountain), and feel not only a part of and leader in their own family but in their community and the world at large; and the aging individual finding new meanings in their pasts, integrating changing bodily functions into their still-changing sense of self and growing into a yet new time and space perspective as a part of the larger universal policies of nature.

These new levels of differentiation reflect changes in relationships, emotional themes, perspectives of time and space, and one's relationship to one's own body. If the fundamental capacity to categorize and integrate experiences is not present, however, these higher levels of differentiation are not going to be possible, or are only going to be possible in highly fragmented or constricted form. The basic ability to categorize experience and build bridges between experiences is fundamental in creating the architectural structure that supports the ability to make all these newer levels of experience meaningful and organized. The social, historical, future-oriented, role-defined, and sexual realities of the adolescent and adult have to be far more synthetic and integrating than the simpler bridges that simply pull together the relationship between anger and dependency for the 4- to 5-year-old.

It is important to remember that when those initial bridges which relate basic feelings like anger and dependency are not fully differentiated and integrated, the application of these basic tools to the triad, the group, the two internal realities, changing bodily functions, new relationship patterns, and the larger social structure are not going to be possible, or at best will be fragmented or overly vague. In fact, we often see this in adolescents who are not succeeding; they are either overly fragmented or too diffuse and vaguely abstracted.

Such patients raise two questions. How do we profile the differentiating capacities in our patients? What do we do to help build these structures when the patient is not functioning at the age-expected level?

A 35-year-old adult may operate much like a latency-age child, worrying in a here-and-now sense about getting his needs met. He may be able to differentiate reality from fantasy, self from nonself, and even categorize some affects, such as anger and dependency, and perhaps even have some bridges between those feelings, but is incapable of integrating or building bridges with a sense of his own history. He is unable to anticipate the future, does not take into account the larger group he operates in at work, and deals poorly with close relationships (which create feelings for prior relationships in his own family), sexual intimacy, or his present and future work roles. Here we see an example of a person who can differentiate simple experiences at the level of a 10-year-old, but who operates concretely and cannot differentiate at the more advanced levels of his ego organization.

On the other hand, another adult who operates more fully at the 35-year-old level is able to categorize different emotional experiences, build bridges between them, intuitively comprehend how the bridges work at the dyadic, triadic, group, new family, and wider social levels, and successfully deal with sexual intimacy and work roles as well as the more basic earlier emotional issues. Such a person can anticipate the impact of his feelings and behaviors now and in the future, as well as understand them within the context of the past. This person may, however, experience some mild anxiety about applying some of his emotional capacities in certain contexts, so that when he is assertive within a sexually intimate setting, he finds himself anxious and more passive than he would like. He may well be constructively assertive at work and in the womb of his own nuclear family. Finding a limitation in integrating assertiveness with sexual intimacy (a frequent adult issue) suggests that the man has not fully constructed integrating bridges and perhaps has some trouble fully differentiating experiences in this narrow band of experience having to do with early adult issues. This is a very different challenge than the more global problems faced by the first 35-year-old. Having a road map of the new levels of differentiation and integration required at each stage of development, including the later childhood, adolescent and adult stages, helps the clinician look beyond the particular disturbances in affect, mood, behavior, or thought and observe where the individual is in terms of age-expected psychological structures. The therapist must determine whether there are only circumscribed conflicts in an age-appropriate structural capacity, or whether these are structural limitations which require therapeutic work.

As the therapist begins to profile such patients, he or she wonders whether they have some deficits in their ability to differentiate their egos, and whether they require structure-building work as a result. Do the majority of these patients just experience some anxiety related to conflict, and, therefore, circumscribed compromise formations? Or do they experience any structural limitations in terms of their ability to differentiate experience?

It has been our experience that most adults and children who are presented for therapy, have subtle, if not gross, deficits in their ability to fully differentiate or integrate experience. The clinical situation of a "healthy" individual presenting with simple neurotic patterns is a rarity, and represents at most only a very small part of the patient population. Our traditional psychodynamic way of thinking often leads us to assume that there are differential ego structures present in many of our patients but that conflict is interfering in their being used. We often postulate that a relatively differentiated ego structure experiences conflict between wishes and fears and prohibitions, and that as defenses are brought in, compromise formation occurs. So, for example, when a person feels anger, and there is a prohibition against the anger, the defense may be a reaction formation in which the person acts nicely toward the person who is the source of the anger. As part of the compromise formation, while the person behaves nicely toward this other individual, he or she may continually forget to show up for appointments with this person. Such forgetting and accompanying passive–aggressive behavior toward a certain type of authority figure is obviously regressive behavior. This is an instance in which an encapsulated fantasy guides certain behaviors but does not represent a lack of differentiation within the broader structure of the personality. Thus, this angry individual could also be a deeply feeling, warm, empathetic, yet assertive and flexible person who has some difficulties with certain types of authority figures when he or she is angry at them.

The model of psychopathology which stems from conflict theory is based on this basic paradigm of conflict, anxiety, defense, and compromise formation. The particular nature of each compromise formation and the accompanying and regressive behavior characterize a variety of problematic personality profiles, including hysterical, compulsive, and depressive patterns. According to this model, character pathology is thought to have a similar dynamic to symptom neurosis. Character pathology though is reflected in repetitive behaviors, more global use of defenses, and often more regressive enactments, including replacing certain patterns related to internalized self and object representations.

Under this view, ego defects or deficits are reserved for borderline pathology and psychotic level pathology, where defects in reality-testing, impulse control, or mood regulation may predominate and result in a psychotic or borderline-type thinking or modulation of affect or behavior.

This traditional model of psychopathology may be based on mistaken assumptions. The model's most significant flaw may be the insistence that in most cases of psychopathology (other than the psychotic or borderline pathologies), the personality can (or potentially can without direct work and structured building capacities) differentiate and integrate experience, and that the pathology primarily results from regression along dimensions of drive and affect rather than a weakness in structure. Our developmental model of psychopathology suggests that the differentiation of the ego is a complicated process, going on through early childhood, but also into the childhood, adolescent, and adult years, as described above. As part of the formation of psychopathology, there are either global or subtle deficits in one or another aspect of the ego's capacity to differentiate. Maladaptive patterns involve behavior, affect, fantasy, and ego structural components. Furthermore, most psychopathologies involve the ego structural component, not merely the most severe psychopathologies. As an extension of this position, the chosen therapeutic strategy must deal with these ego structural deficits, as well as with the accompanying behaviors, affects, and conflicts.

The following examples will discuss how characteristic types of psychopathology stem in part from a lack of structural ego differentiation. The individual with a narcissistic personality disorder, for example, is described as being self-absorbed, defensively reacting against early lack of empathy and loss, as well as having conflict with aggression (Kohut, 1971; Kernberg, 1975). When we examine the narcissistic disorder in terms of a deficit in differentiation, however, the narcissistic individual's self-absorption is seen as arising from a lack of capacity to truly appreciate the affect, wishes, and intentions of another person. Other people are not seen as full human beings with wishes, intentions, and affects in their own right. They are taken into consideration only as potential satisfiers of the narcissistic individual's own needs of the moment.

This inability to appreciate the affect of the other can be viewed as a deficit in the ability to categorize experience. In other words, the affect of other individuals in the dyad, triad, group situation, or larger social reality is not adequately represented or categorized in the person's internal affective world. Not represented and not categorized, this experience of the other does not become part of the experiences for which bridges are built, and is not part of an integrated personality structure. There is thus no reasoning possible along the lines of "What I feel and do will have an impact on X, Y, and Z in terms of how they think and feel." There is no ability to actually appraise how others think and feel in terms of their real affects (as compared to what they might do to me) because the appraisal reference point is only oneself. An individual may be intellectually able to appreciate another person when he or she reads about a character in a novel, for example, but never grasp the nuances of another's personality in an intuitive, emotional sense. The narcissist, therefore, has a deficit in differentiation in terms of being able to differentiate the affect of the other person. The other person in essence is viewed in a limited way in terms of what they will do to me if I do this or that to them, and as a result, is not differentiated off sufficiently in terms of affective proclivities.

Narcissistic individuals who have a narcissistic character disorder are not psychotic; they do not confuse the content of their thinking with the content of someone else's thinking and they do not confuse elements of social reality. They are not hallucinating or delusional, or think people are about to attack them, so they are not projecting gross contents from their minds onto someone else's mind or incorporating someone else's thoughts and making them their own. They are, however, unable to appreciate a key dimension of the other person's persona: the individual's affect and emotional needs and wishes. In this sense, the narcissistic inability to affectively appreciate another's affects indicates a subtle deficit in a narrower band of experience than the deficit we see in the psychotic individual who cannot differentiate the other person as a global experience. A narcissist experiences boundaries between people, and can appreciate the other's thoughts and contents in a general sense, but lacks a full appreciation of the other person's affects.

The antisocial individual has no capacity to empathize with another individual in the most global sense. Individuals are viewed as things to meet needs or else are ignored or pushed aside. Extremely antisocial individuals, as exemplified by delinquents who shoot or kill people they hardly know, but who otherwise operate in a seemingly realistic way (certainly in terms of their cunning and ability to circumvent the law), evidence a deficit in their ability to empathize with other human beings and picture them as fellow travelers in the human race. This deficit is marked by an inability to appreciate the human nature of other people's experience and to fully differentiate the distinctly human qualities having to do with empathy, nurturing, and caring of the self and nonself. Instead, only survival-oriented aspects of experience are differentiated ("What do I need to do to get money to buy food to make it to next week?"). Life is experienced in a here-and-now, dog-eat-dog manner, absent the experiences of nurturance, empathy, and concern for others. A whole realm of experience is neither represented nor differentiated, and consequently there are no bridges being built between this human side of experience and other aspects of experience. As a result, aggression and competitiveness, which can be healthy and coexist with compassion and empathy, now exist in isolation.

The antisocial individual is thus lacking any sense of appreciation of a whole area of experience having to do with human warmth and empathy. When anger erupts, it exists in isolation since there is no bridge in place between the angry, competitive "I need that fur coat" and the compassionate, caring side—"But someone else is wearing it and they would feel terrible if I took it from them, and I would feel bad also." The antisocial person is incapable of making a mature judgment, because he cannot bridge various aspects of experience and synthesize his many needs.

When whole realms of experience are not represented or differentiated, extreme primitive behavior can emerge in an otherwise seemingly clever individual. A whole realm of experience remains unintegrated with the rest of the personality. (One could say that the problem with differentiation should be reserved for those conditions where there is fragmentation in thinking, but this would be too narrow a definition, in terms of the ability to differentiate, at least from the developmental perspective.)

Difficulties in differentiating experience and integrating experience, also underlie the more traditional hysterical, obsessive–compulsive, depressive, and anxious personality patterns. As was described in chapter 7, "Representational Elaboration," individuals with hysterical personality patterns tend to have difficulties with visual–spatial integration and, therefore, tend to get lost in the "trees" and fail to observe that they're actually in a "forest." They are unable to mentally construct the forest; they are incapable of building higher and higher level bridges between different categories of experience. One way of visualizing this concept is to imagine that the individual forms not one bridge between such realms of experience as dependency and anger, but instead forms many superordinate bridges, linking the larger spans that connect broad categories of experience. So, for example, an individual may have a bridge between aggression and dependency ("When I get angry, I get scared I'll lose my sense of self"); that may be a fundamental bridge. Another bridge may be, "If I keep them feeling sexy and excited, even if I get angry at them, I won't lose them." That's a further defining bridge between those two categories of experience. A superordinate bridge might be one which integrates those two bridges: "There's danger in losing people when you are angry at them, but not if you can keep them involved with you in one way or another." The "one way or another" may involve sexual approaches, or it may involve simultaneously nurturing others while you are angry at them, or making other people feel like they need you for safety. The ability to see the overall picture is something we have hypothesized is not as easy for a person with hysterical patterns, because of the difficulty in higher level abstractions (due to a relative visual–spatial deficit). When it comes to differentiating experience, there is a tendency for the person with hysterical patterns to form simple differentiations, remaining concrete. Therefore, forming higher level abstract categories may not be easily done by a person who sees only "trees" (e.g., it may be hard for them to move from the dyad to the triad to the group to the larger social reality and the challenge of integrating sexual, occupational, and family inclinations and interests into a differentiated personality structure). Such a person will exhibit lots of tendencies to operate naively or concretely in the more fragmented patterns characteristic of school-aged children, rather than evidence the behaviors of a mature adult personality. The degree to which this pattern is more global or related only to specific affects will in part determine the severity of the disorder. Against this backdrop we often see various symptoms having to do with anxiety or depressive-type symptomatology—sometimes in the extreme, even disassociative patterns. The subtle ego differentiating deficit is related to an inability to organize thought and affect while building bridges between different realms of experience, due in part to visual–spatial limitations and in part to the way that limitations are part of early personality patterns.

Other disorders are similarly related to processing limitations. As was discussed earlier, auditory, rather than visual–spatial processing, underlies difficulties in abstracting the meaning affectively from words and auditory communication. This then makes it hard for the individual to perceive and interpret affective signals coming from another person. An understandable preference for listening to one's own thoughts and ideas thus can develop. Because of this preference for the internal world, the differentiating experiences that ordinarily occur at the dyadic level on up, may not occur as regularly, and, therefore, will tend to lead to more idiosyncratic, subjective thinking. There is a tendency to form an ego structure that does not have sufficient representation of external objects, and, in a sense, has excessive representation of one's own inclinations, wishes, and ideas. As a result, an undifferentiated sense of the world, based on subjective reality and not infused with representations of what is coming from the outside, distorts the individual's thinking. Normally, the most important element in normal growth and development in forming differentiated structures or differentiating one's ego structure, is the ability to interact with significant others around all the relevant emotional themes of life. This is the basis for differentiated experience.

One form of this pattern readily observable in children is their frequent escape into fantasy. Young school-aged children will respond to a therapist's question about what they did in school with descriptions of how two dolls were fighting, or get lost in the saga of Superman saving the dolls from a dragon. The child begins to describe something in real life and almost seems to stop in midsentence and go off on a tangent. There are often two aspects to the escape into fantasy. One is anxiety, other dysphoric or disassociative affects, or traumatic experiences. The other is the individual's constitutional-maturational pattern in terms of processing different sensations. One child seen recently in therapy beautifully illustrates this pattern.

The child spoke at length about a "story of an evil woman who wants to find out about something," and made funny sounds, mimicking the evil woman. When the therapist picked up on the content of evil ("This is a person with evil abilities?"), the boy replied, "Yes, she wants to control the earth." When the therapist asked how she would do this, the boy regressed into simply making more noises. Whenever pressed to continue, the boy would complete half a thought and then go back into acting out in a fragmented way. He would make noises and sounds while imitating one or another character, losing the cohesiveness of the story. Even while participating in fantasy play, he could not elaborate in a sustained manner. He would withdraw into his own idiosyncratic world, ignoring input from the therapist.

As time went on, the therapist helped him build bridges between his ideas in discussions about fantasy or reality. He asked him more about school and friends, restructuring questions to keep the child focused on the task: "Now I didn't get the answer to that question. Don't you want to answer it?" The boy would indulge the therapist more and more, but the interaction demanded a lot of energy and effort on the clinician's part. The child wasn't being stubborn; his history of auditory processing difficulties explained part of his insistence on marching to the beat of his own drummer and ignoring the conversational rhythm offered by others, especially when anxious. It is important to note that for many of these patterns, anxiety or feelings of uncertainty will intensify the pattern. At age 9 it required enormous focus and concentration on his part to understand the therapist's questions, and he simply found it much easier to withdraw into his own fantasy even when not anxious. When anxious or feeling helpless or conflicted, his tendency toward fragmentation was fueled even more by its defensive goals. Although he would escape into fantasy in preference to relating to the therapist, and he showed no inclination to take the therapist's affective interest into account vis-à-vis fantasy or reality discussion, the child still managed to project a warm, though muffled, sense of engagement. So many differentiating experiences were thus beyond his reach, since two-way interactive experience around his affects was so obviously limited. Some children are slow to develop their ability to construct bridges between their ideas.

For example, Linda, a nine year old girl, loved to become enthusiastically involved in different make believe dramas using organized sentences and responses. She would, however, go from one scene to another, one drama to another, just as though she were switching the dial on an internal TV monitor without letting anyone know that she had changed the channel. For example, she might start off orienting her mother or father to a particular upcoming scenario, such as "I'm going to be Cinderella," but after a few lines of talking to the fairy godmother, all of a sudden, Linda would switch to talking about Snow White, without saying, "I'm now going to pretend to be Snow White." The listener would become confused because the scene was changed and suddenly he was hearing very skillful imitations of all the dwarves, including sneezes, grumpy moans, and happy giggles. The listener initially didn't know where these new sounds or lines were coming from.

Also, as Linda made these station changes without informing anyone, including herself, there was a change in her vocal tone, emotional expressiveness, and subtle emotional interactiveness. The knowing look in her eye, the reciprocal nodding, and vocal rhythm that was reaching out to the listener and was responsive to his or her nods and vocalizations, now became more of a monotone. It looked like Linda was lost in her own internal landscape.

What started off as a shared experience, with connectedness, affective emotional gesturing, and shared ideas now became a self-absorbed, monotone. Fragmented pieces of scripts were being played out without any obvious context or reference points.

In essence, Linda was temporarily "lost" to the listener and she was also temporarily lost to herself. The affective glue that held her personality together—the bridges that have been discussed—were missing and, along with them, the affective ties that connected her to others.

It was as though Linda operated with islands of organized images and ideas, but that these islands had not coalesced into larger countries or continents. The self was, thus, a piecemeal self. Groups of symbols connected together were floating around quite separate from other groups of symbols or images. Some of these groups which were tied to affect (which, in turn, were tied to interaction, purpose, and goals in relationships) had the feel of the real Linda. Others existed in the seemingly affectless monotone of mindless repetition.

In working with Linda, and many children like her, it has been seen that they often have an auditory processing problem and some motor and verbal sequencing problems making it harder for them to organize a structure of logical bridges between their images. To assist them in mastering the new ability, her therapist attempted to accentuate a process that goes on in ordinary development (which can easily be overlooked in this type of circumstance) and which reveals how the bridges defining an organized sense of self get laid down in the first place.

In Linda's case, her parents were falling into the trap of going along with her fragmented thinking and often supplied the bridges themselves. After starting out with Cinderella, Linda might jump into Snow White and the parents tended either to join in making additional sounds for the dwarves or asking Linda questions about how many dwarves there were and how many she could name. Linda, in turn, might answer partially and then turn the dial on her internal TV set to play out a commercial involving GI Joe. Her parents would again jump in either with academic type questions about GI Joe (e.g., what color his shirt was) or simply reenacting elements of this new drama with her.

What her parents weren't doing was helping Linda find Linda after she had lost her. The challenge existed at two levels. On the one hand, Linda was getting lost within her own ideas, but at the same time, she was losing the emotional or affective tie to her parents. Remember, reciprocal gesturing, smiling, and head nodding—that is, emotional cueing that all individuals do with one another when they are in some contact—was lost. First, therefore, was always to try to find the affective or emotional Linda (and facilitate affective gesturing again). She couldn't be permitted to get lost.

Even before the parents were helped to recognize that they lost track of Linda's stream of ideas, they had to realize that they had more profoundly lost the emotional connectedness, as Linda went into her monotone voice and more global, affectless looks. To "find" Linda, as the parents sensed this shift, they would reestablish their emotional contact with her by increasing the expectancy in their voices and increasing their own emotional tie through the looks in their eyes, body posture and the way they emphasized their sense of confusion. In other words, they, through increased animation and the sheer intensity of emotion and expectation on their parts, maintained an emotional give and take.

Often, simply getting more animated and compelling with voice tone and facial expressions will pull a child back in. If necessary, intruding a bit in a playful way by either having a doll try to sit on their doll or by simply saying, with great enthusiasm, "Hold on! I have to ask a question!" or "Wait, wait" until they look and re-engage.

Then the parents would immediately, and with lots of emotional expressiveness, let the child know that they lost track of what she was saying. Rather than join the new drama or ask academic questions about it, they would wonder what happened to what they were talking about first. "Where did Cinderella go?" Alternatively, they would point out that she had gone from Cinderella to Snow White without telling them why or how the two were connected. If Linda didn't respond to their general confusion or question, they might go to a multiple choice-type question, wondering out loud whether the new thing being talked about was something she saw on TV, a movie, or a commercial. If that didn't work, they might go to even a simpler "yes" or "no" kind of question. The key is that they were working with her like a detective to "find" her and maintain the affective contact.

It was less important that she identify exactly where the new scene was coming from than that the two were *working together* to try to discover where it came from. The working together maintained the affective interaction and, in essence, discovered and reconnected with the real Linda.

Working in this way has helped children like Linda go from a kind of fragmented, piecemeal type of thinking to a cohesive pattern of thought. However, underlying a cohesive pattern of thought is a cohesive sense of self. This cohesive sense of self is formed only through the maintenance of emotional bridges with the caregiver as images and symbols are being shared or discussed. In other words, by constantly searching for the real Linda, the existing islands of her emotional self, symbols and images were being added on to the emerging sense Linda had of herself as an intentional person with desires and wishes that define her. The more children like Linda go off into unrelated islands of images, the more their language is structured for them, or the more they are involved in rote, academic exercises to keep them organized, the more their sense of self remains fragmented and concrete. What's necessary is a give and take across many emotional themes where the give and take occurs through facial expressions, gestures and emotional looks and the content of the conversation.

Like the child who escapes into fantasy patterns, adults who are characterized by a great deal of self-absorption, also lack the ability to a greater or lesser degree, to differentiate their experience of the world representationally. In the schizoid pattern there are constitutional issues at work also, including sensitivities to routine types of sensation, which make it hard for the person to become fully engaged with others. Withdrawing into a shell becomes a way for such individuals to find comfort. Here, too, the avoidance is also fueled by painful affects related to difficulties with intimacy. Constitutional vulnerabilities increase the likelihood of painful affects, and painful affects, in turn, intensify the manifestation of these vulnerabilities.

Depressed individuals often have difficulty modulating certain affects, particularly joy, pleasure, and various aspects of aggression and assertiveness. There is a tendency to have depressive ideation and feelings around low self-esteem, including apathy and self-degradation. There has often been a developmental difficulty early on in integrating assertiveness, pleasure, and excitement with loss and disappointment. Such individuals usually have a difficulty, as described in an earlier chapter, with holding onto a representation of the nurturing sympathetic side of the significant other in their lives—forming a representation of a nurturing, loving, or warm mother or father. They can experience them in the moment, but not in an ongoing, continuous sense. In the absence of this internal representation, there is a sense of loss and depressive affect, particularly under pressure, as well as a missing realm of experience of ongoing pleasure, joy, and stability that the ego cannot integrate. Such a person experiences enormous rage, but the rage cannot form a bridge with nourishing comfort that can balance the rage and create a sense of well-being. That inner sense of comfort and security is not present unless it is present in the external environment in an ongoing sense. Therefore, depression may result not just from the inability to represent the nurturing experience. There may also be an inability to construct bridges between an ongoing, nurturing presence that a person can internalize and the anger and rage that naturally develop when needs aren't met in the real world. For the representationally differentiated individual, however, bridges to a sense of more nurturance are already in place. Under the pressure of loss, such people recall the warm presence of a mother, father, or significant other and derive a sense of hope. Under the impact of intense rage, they have a bridge to the fact that life can be nourishing and that they can feel better and move beyond a sense of rage.

On the other hand, if the sense of ongoing internal nourishing experience is not present in the depressive configuration, due in part to earlier experience with caregivers and in part to some of the visual–spatial difficulties described earlier, it is as though the depressed individual walks over a bridge in search of nourishing experience, but finds nothing on the other side except an empty void without pleasure and hope. In this sense, depression occurs not only when there is actual loss, but arises when certain representations are activated, and the bridges to compensatory representations are not present. To reiterate: this results from a deficit in representational differentiation, as well as representational elaboration.

The above examples illustrate the general thesis that many types of problems involve some relative deficit in an aspect of ego differentiation. Profiling various clinical problems in terms of their ego structure may help clinicians focus on what types of subtle or global deficits exist for different kinds of problems. Many of the classical disorders—depression, anxiety states, phobias, compulsive patterns, hysterical patterns, borderline, and even psychotic patterns—could be profiled in this way. This may tease out gradations of psychopathology, heretofore unidentified. These nuances may involve subtle deficits in differentiation, where the individual operates more like a school-aged child or young adolescent, rather than an adult, at least in certain domains of affects. In other words, the egos of such individuals are only partially differentiated so that when it comes to dependency or sexuality, they operate concretely in the here-and-now, but cannot take into account the future or the past or new relationships or the larger social context. This is usually understood in the give-and-take of the therapy situation, but is not present in standard diagnostic thinking. Sometimes therapists use the terms *good hysterics* or *bad hysterics* or *advanced obsessives* or *primitive or immature obsessives*. But these are vague general terms that try to grapple with what the therapist intuitively feels to be an immature or more mature personality pattern. To be able to love and work, as Freud said, are very good general descriptives, but hardly adequate to narrow down the personality into a profile which can be related to certain age-expected attainments and achievements. One way to picture our profile, then, is to have the various stages of ego differentiation on one axis, and the different basic capacities that are involved in a differentiated ego structure on the other axis. The personality can be viewed in terms of what level of differentiating capacity an individual can bring to different affect proclivities.

DEFICITS: CONSTITUTIONAL, INTERACTIVE, AND FANTASY COMPONENTS

What implications does formulating such a profile have for the treatment process? What can the therapist do that will enable the individual to develop these ego structural capacities? How does the therapist take into account the fact that these relative deficits are part of an interactive process and also relate to wishes and fantasies? The deficit and related fantasies may have certain shared features.

In general, the clinician looks for three components to a structural deficit in ego differentiation: the constitutional, interactive, and dynamic fantasy. First, constitutional and maturational variations are observed, usually in terms of visual–spatial processing, auditory–verbal processing, under- or overreactivity in sensory, affective dimensions, such as touch, sound, and light, and motor tone or planning or more generally sequencing difficulties. These variations can, as explained earlier, undermine the ability to represent and differentiate experience, because these basic maturational capacities are necessary for healthy differentiation. For example, the child who is overreactive to sensation will almost certainly have a tendency to be more fragmented. It is consequently harder for him to organize bridges between categories. The child who has auditory or verbal processing difficulties is also going to find it harder to represent auditory–verbal affective experience in a clear and salient way. He will, therefore, find it more difficult to create a differentiated, representational system. Similarly, the child who has visual–spatial processing difficulties will find it hard to form the abstract categories needed for building superordinate bridges between categories of experience.

The second feature to look for is the interactive style that is in place between the child and the parents. Does it create a deficit in differentiation such as, for example, the caregiver who is unable to help the child represent anger or dependency or who operates in a fragmenting manner? It is especially important to look at how interactions and maturational factors work together. Does the interactive pattern accentuate or ameliorate the child's constitutional and maturational variations? An intrusive, fragmented, or unpredictable parent will make a child with visual–spatial processing difficulties more fragmented. A parent who has idiosyncratic verbal meanings for things will make the child who tends to have auditory–verbal processing problems find it hard to process information, rather than less hard, and will tend to permit that child to withdraw more and more into his own world.

A good example of just such a situation occurred in therapy when the patient, a very bright child with auditory processing difficulties, turned out to have elaborate, yet creative, fantasies. Her mother thought of her child as a poet and, therefore, given her own poetic bent, talked to the child in vague, abstract metaphors. The girl never understood her mother, and the mother only partially understood her child. The little girl became more and more absorbed in her own world, and the mother tried to make poetic, metaphorical meaning of the child's various pretend play productions and communications. When seen in therapy, the girl would build elaborate fantasies in pretend castles and houses, and the mother recited poetry to the child, but there was also no organized, logical communication between the two of them. This 3-year-old girl had difficulty handling most simple, reality-based conversations, even though she was, in many respects, quite creative and obviously had potential to be quite bright.

The therapist ascertained that this mother and child had to be helped to open and close circles of communication. The mother was urged to tune into her daughter's communications, build on them, and help the child in turn build on her mother's communications. The mother learned simple ways to engage her daughter. When she participated in her child's fantasy play, she became a character who would ask concrete questions like, "Why are you putting me in jail?" or "Why do we have to have our tea party now?" Over a period of a few months, the little girl became more differentiated, holding reality-based conversations and separating fantasy play from reality demands.

As an example of an amelioration, consider a family where the child had an auditory processing deficit, but the father was very gentle and persistent in making sure that he and his child understood each other. He would patiently remark, "Let me see if I understand. Raggedy Anne is about to pull off the leg of Raggedy Andy, right?" When his daughter would ignore him, he would look perplexed and say, "Wait, I didn't get that. Is she going to pull off his leg?" The daughter would just nod her head, but this gesture communicated to her father that a real interchange was operating. The father would then jump into the character of one of the dolls and cry, "Please don't hurt me! Please don't hurt me!" After ignoring him the first two times he said this, the child would gleefully say, "I'm going to pull your leg off because you've been bad." "What did I do?" the father would ask, and after the third or fourth time he asked, the little girl would respond. By patiently joining her play and making sure that any discussion they had about the play involved opening and closing circles of communication, this father facilitated the child's exposure to differentiating experiences. He made sure that she always responded to his comments, after he responded to hers, even if he had to gently repeat himself four or five times and literally insert his face between her and her toys. He helped her become a very differentiated little girl who learned to respond to the outer world, even though it required a good deal more attention and effort, given her auditory processing difficulties.

In another case, a mother came into therapy with a very finicky, overreactive son who was diagnosed with visual–spatial deficits. The child threw tantrums, and was always fragmented in his thinking and affect. Over time, she learned how to become exceedingly empathetic, firm on limits, and exude a dependable sense of calm. These three traits helped her son become consistently more integrated. Rather than joining in the boy's overreactivity, the mother empathized with his feelings, aided him in seeing the big picture, and helped him realize that she could help him set up a secure, calm environment that would not make him feel more fragmented. Slowly but surely, the child became more and more cohesive and organized.

As the above examples demonstrate, each constitutional and maturational variation displayed by children (and adults as well) can be met with a behavioral pattern that can either accentuate or ameliorate the problem. In addition, the interactive pattern, if sufficiently intense, can in itself create the basis for a representational differentiation deficit. Thus, a highly fragmented and chaotic set of interactions can lead any child to feel fragmented and chaotic. When the "other" in a dyad, triad, or larger social group doesn't communicate or is very withdrawn or unavailable, or very idiosyncratic or preoccupied, a child will tend to withdraw and live in his subjective world. A caregiver who becomes sullen every time her child is angry or assertive is likely to lead to the child inhibiting his anger and assertiveness and having a tendency toward depression and for clinging neediness. Often, however, children and adults have some maturational and interactive reasons for their particular structural challenge.

The third element to look for, as indicated earlier, are the evolving fantasies of the child. As children become somewhat representational, they increasingly evolve content in fantasy. A dynamic picture of the world begins to take shape, in which a child and his family are players in the drama. There may be sadistic, excited, or masochistic fantasies, or fantasies of intrigue. The nature of the fantasy itself may contribute to the deficit, or may reveal an aspect of deficit. For example, a child who has a visual–spatial deficit and does not modulate his impulses well, will tend to get overloaded by affect and then become somewhat impulsive. Such a child may fantasize that he or she is a space ship that is constantly misfiring and falling to the ground with a thump. This picture may, in part, stem from the fact that the child is anxious about being assertive and feels defective when he or she is angry or assertive. But it may also be equally related to the fact that the child's sense of lacking regulation, of being out of control, is based on the reality of a deficit in ego differentiation which gets represented in the fantasy of the space ship that keeps crashing. This fantasy illustrates the child's picture of his own structure. While the fantasy does not show evidence of an understanding of a structural deficit, the vivid picture of a crashing space ship does portray the child's unconscious awareness of his own limitations and his fears surrounding these. For example, the child with motor planning problems may be representing his own deficit when he or she draws pictures of rats in a maze constantly banging into obstructions.

What is particularly interesting, however, about the content of organizing fantasies or personal narratives, is how it reflects preverbal and presymbolic patterns, which have come before it. Like explaining a confusing dream or some earlier behavior, the content of an organizing fantasy may not be an accurate reflection of prior patterns. Rather, it often serves as an explanation to people of who they are. It is an explanation which is constructed, however, with the purpose of helping to understand wishes and feelings as well as thoughts and behaviors. For example, a person very early in life, for good reason (perhaps a frightening mother), gave up overt aggression and assertiveness. Way before he could think, he adopted passive, avoidant behavior patterns as a safe solution to many of life's conflicts. When those who follow patterns like this are finally able to create a self-image, they may persuade themselves that they are a calm, sweet person who abhors competition, violence and all forms of aggression. They may adopt values and even political beliefs to support this self-image. Their avoidance of anger never finds its way into the content of their personal self-view. This anger is not unconscious either because the passive pattern was adopted before unconscious symbols were formed.

Like our passive person, many individuals who have challenges in the four presymbolic stages of development need to find ways of creating a self image which explains both who they are and who they are not. It is impossible initially for a person to know who they are not or what they are missing. If the person lacked early nurturing (the "chicken soup" of life) they may adopt a self view where they feel, "I like to make people feel good. I have a talent for making people happy. It makes me happy to make them happy. I'll say anything to them—even make up things—because we both feel good and that's more important. Yes, I can do this with new people who I hardly even know because it's important for people to connect."

However transparent a person's underlying needs, for example to please others so he can feel filled up, may be to a therapist or even a friend, it's difficult to know what's missing, what's buried even more deeply in his personal history and makeup than his deepest unconscious symbols. Instead, his initial definition of who he is is an explanation of who he is in terms of what he wants and desires. Just as it was impossible to know about TV when all that was heard was the radio, similarly it's nearly impossible to know what we're not when all we are is what we are.

Perhaps the clearest example is the person whose prior experiences, in part because of processing difficulties coupled with certain family patterns, failed to establish a firm grasp of the difference between what's real and not real. The person believes that "Others are out to get me. I have to be cautious and vigilant." It's nearly impossible to help that person see that it's just a feeling he or she is having. There is a huge difference between the truly suspicious person and the one who says, "I don't know why I all of a sudden feel like I can't trust people. I wonder why I'm in this mood." The former person lacks the ability to separate real from non-real while the latter not only appreciates the distinction but can also observe themselves and ponder their own feelings and patterns.

Our initial picture of who we are is, therefore, not accurate. It's a first attempt at creating a content, a story or an image of what we know about ourselves. It must deal with what we are and what we're not. But because what we are not is hidden in lost opportunities and unmastered challenges, it remains a deep, illusive core of our ego, which underlies the image, storyline, and even values that feel compatible and reasonable to our construction of who we are. It is an image of convenience with only relative degrees of accuracy. Yet, if we can create an ability for self-observation, we can begin to explore the limits of our consciously constructed and unconsciously organized self-image. In therapy, for example, patients who have missed out on mastering relatively fully the challenges of the early states of the ego, must first be assisted in developing new capacities such as, for example, stronger reality-testing and the ability for self-observation before they can be assisted in attempting to understand the limits of their organizing fantasies and personal story.

The clinician must, therefore, understand the dynamic meaning of a fantasy in the context of earlier stages of development, missed opportunities, and maturational strengths and vulnerabilities. Sometimes a deficit will lead to representational fragmentation, making the elucidation of the fantasy difficult. The existence of a deficit may make the child more afraid of his own inclinations than would otherwise be the case. Children who are in the oedipal phase, for example, and who feel they cannot modulate their impulses for good reason (because they have a motor deficit) may be more afraid of punishment than children who feel secure in their ability to modulate their impulses.

IMPLICATIONS FOR THE THERAPEUTIC PROCESS

How does the therapist use this understanding of the child's ego differentiating capacity in the treatment process? First, he avoids making the assumption that the child develops these ego differentiating abilities just by being listened to or by having clarifications or even insights given to him by another person. In fact, most individuals have some degree of character pathology, and often character pathology involves some degree of a lack of differentiation of a core element in ego functioning. It is reasonable to assume, therefore, that many treatments are particularly unsuccessful from a structure-building point of view because a systematic way of understanding the intervention process, in terms of its structure building, has not been established.

Kohut's work with narcissism is of interest in this regard. He emphasizes how some of his patients' feelings about the lack of being properly understood and empathized with (even for negative displays of behavior like aggressiveness or greediness), affects their self-esteem regulation. Cognitive behavioral approaches advocate forming certain images to help patients correct or change certain perceptions of themselves. Thus, cognitive behavioral therapists focus on the construction of the representation as a vehicle for therapeutic help. Examining how representations become constructed can be an important part of the therapeutic process. But representations need to build on wishes and affects, and it can be counterproductive to create representations that are inconsistent with underlying affects.

Some of the work on transference (Gill, 1984) stresses the immediacy of the transference and the importance of dealing with the here-and-now affects, as they are mobilized in the transference. The implications of this research may be especially valuable for patients who have trouble representing the affective component of experience. These patients have trouble with subtlety and nuance when dealing with the affect of saliency. Certain narcissistic individuals will have trouble with affective saliency in a different way; not so much in identifying the meaning of the affect, but in experiencing the affect of the other person. For both these types of individuals—the person with processing difficulties as well as the narcissistic person—the therapist can offer real help by focusing on the specificity of the affective experience in the here-and-now, and its meaning and affective intensity, and helping the patient pay attention to these experiences.

A few characteristics of the proverbial elephant have been perceived by different therapists and schools of thought. A coherent therapeutic strategy is needed. A systematic approach to therapy must involve elements that have been discovered intuitively and that are elements in the developmental process. It must also include characteristics that may not have been discovered intuitively, but are part of the developmental process. Understanding the developmental progression also helps us see those elements that are counterproductive.

Many traditional psychotherapeutic techniques are useful in helping to differentiate experiences and build bridges. Asking patients how certain experiences are connected, for example, helps the patient build bridges between certain domains of experience. If the therapist does do the work of providing insight, and instead helps the patient construct insights by reminding the patient of certain things he or she has said, the therapist can actually facilitate integration or the building of bridges across different internalized experiential domains. Behavioral approaches often help patients look at the prerepresentational behavioral type interactions, insofar as they tend to help patients analyze their behaviors in terms of the patterns, including the effect that their behaviors have on others, and the effect that other people's behavior has on them. Some of the elements of supportive therapy having to do with comfort, support, and nurturance help deepen the quality of engagement and relatedness that is necessary for most therapies.

Most therapeutic approaches do not to any great degree use the notion of individual differences as they play out in the constitutional–maturational tendencies (i.e., sensory reactivity, processing, or motor planning or sequencing). In addition most approaches do not attempt to pinpoint the developmental level of the patients in terms of his or her functional ego development and then build systematically the needed ego structure that may have never been attained.

Developmentally based therapy must systematically create the opportunity for the patient to develop differentiating capacities. Certain ego functions may have never been attained. At times there may be a regression in ego functions as well, in which case these same principles would hold, although one might see a more rapid progress because the level had been attained once before.

It has been thought that either basic ego functions are attained or not, but as we observe developmental progress, we see that structural growth in terms of representing and differentiating experience is a gradual process that can be partially attained. Each affect realm may have different degrees of representation and differentiation. These partial structural achievements have to be worked with.

The treatment approach chosen by the therapist has to use the relationship and the transference relationship to foster differentiation and integration. For example, when the therapeutic relationship fosters the saliency of affective experience between the therapist and the patient, the latter is helped in terms of recognizing the meaning of affect, as well as the experience of the self and the other in an affective interaction. To the degree that the relationship provides opportunities to differentiate experience, it fosters categorization. To the degree that the therapeutic relationship promotes building bridges, it fosters integrating and affect regulation. The question then becomes: How do we most effectively use the therapeutic relationship and the transference relationship? We will see later how the therapist can systematically assist the patient in integrating and dealing with experiences that will promote structural growth. For each type of neurotic or characterologic pattern, the therapist focuses on how the patient maintains his or her avoidance of certain affects and, at the same time, uses the therapeutic relationship and the transference to create opportunities to differentiate these affects and inclinations.

If the therapist believes the differentiating ego structure is present and all that is needed is insight and awareness of the defenses and the underlying wishes and feelings and working them through to foster growth, he may simply clarify and offer insights. The clinical route may, for example, involve the clinician sharing a complicated insight, with the patient responding by freely associating, even in a fragmented way. This can provide a false sense of mastery and wind up with the patient doing poorly after therapy stops. This is not surprising since the therapist has been lending his ego strength to the patient, rather than helping the patient learn how to differentiate and perform these differentiating functions. Therapists wind up making the clarifications, arriving at the insights, and the patient is left merely confirming the therapist's insight with free associations. Even the process of relating these insights to the patient's daily life as well as past experiences may do little other than temporarily relieve some of the patient's internal pressure, because an affect finally became represented or expressed. If the patient is in a representationally differentiating experience with the therapist and from this experience actively constructs representations and actively creates bridges with other representations, the impact on ego structure is more stable and growth producing.

Chapter 10

Tactics to Foster Representational Differentiation

The basic therapeutic principle in fostering representational differentiation is to create interactive experience between the clinician and the patient. The therapist functions as the object outside the patient and helps the patient relate to the object in such a way that various aspects of experience are differentiated. The clinician often must focus on those aspects of experience that have not undergone representational differentiation.

The developmental model of differentiation is based on the hypothesis that differentiation occurs through interactive experience in the normal course of growing up. In normal development, the object of the person's affect has to be interactive with the individual in such a way that a basic unit of experience occurs. A unit of experience involves opening and closing representational or symbolic circles. In other words, the therapist follows the patient's lead, in response to the patient's representations, in terms of affect, intention (drive derivative), and meaning. The patient is then inspired to build on the therapist's communications, and when this takes place, symbolic circles of communication are opened and closed. Experiences become differentiated

361

when many hundreds, even thousands, of these circles are strung together. When the patient does not build on the therapist's communications, differentiation is not achieved. Such an individual may be capable of elaborating representational experience, but only in an idiosyncratic and subjective way. In such an instance, the clinician must attempt to guide the patient into opening and closing circles of communication.

Sometimes when treating a highly differentiated patient there may be reason for fostering regressive, representationally elaborative experiences without the differentiating influence of the therapist. In such instances, as when a patient is free associating to a dream, the therapist may elect to remain quiet and passive.

It is important to remember that symbolic circles of communication between patient and therapist are being opened and closed simultaneously at a number of different levels. These levels involve the patient's intentions, or drive derivatives, affect, as well as meaning or content. The therapist who uses a monotone deprives the patient of experiencing the full range of affective response. Thus, the patient may build on the therapist's responses, but will be unable to fully differentiate experience in terms of affect.

The therapist who correctly identifies the content, but is limited in his own affective range or misempathizes with the affective valence of the content, also does not provide a differentiating experience for the patient. The therapist who misses the meaning, but is correct on the affect and the valence, provides only a partially differentiating experience. Only by tuning in to the patient on many levels at the same time can the therapist inspire the patient to open and close a full range of communication circles. It should be noted here that encouraging the patient to build on the therapist's comments does not imply agreement with the therapist. The patient who says, "Where do you get off saying that?" or "Don't sound like such a jerk!" is building on the therapist's comments. As long as the patient's communication is not independent of the therapist's communication, a differentiated system is operating.

As was noted earlier, the focus of the differentiating experience that occurs in a therapeutic setting may have a different emphasis for different patients. Some aspects of the differentiation may occur quite readily. For example, therapist and patient may tune in to each other at one level of meaning quite easily, whenever they talk intellectually about the patient's life, work, and loves, or about baseball or football. The therapist's comments to the patient are built on by the patient's remarks, and both individuals seem to be involved in a differentiated conversation. Suppose, however, the patient, due to narcissistic difficulties, never considers or consciously feels the affects of another person including the therapist. The therapist may need to go beyond simply commenting on what the patient seems to experience. He may need to energetically point out the patient's lack of interest in his reactions. In doing this, he not only clarifies or identifies a pattern, he creates an affect state in the therapeutic relationship. This affect state in this instance is his own affective presence. He is creating a differentiating interaction around this dimension of expression. Over time, this awareness may enter into the spontaneous considerations or free associations of the patient. In other words, the therapist focuses on a selective aspect of the differentiating experience, because that is where the primary deficit is. One may choose to view such an intervention in terms of being a "real object" or simply interpreting a defense such as avoidance or self-absorption. Such an explanation for this type of intervention, however, may miss the essential goal of the intervention, to further differential experience. At times interventions may be justified for many different reasons. A developmental explanation, however, has the best chance of generating a consistently growth facilitating therapeutic relationship.

Let us examine another example. A patient who operates in the dyad exhibits a deficit in awareness of triadic relationships. He is very detailed about how his love or hate causes someone else's rejection or overcontrol. The therapist realizes that the patient's attention should be directed toward the area where the differentiating deficit exists. Some readers of this example will, at this point, jump to the conclusion that such a pattern of inability to deal with the triad is by necessity a reflection of conflict and anxiety around oedipal dynamics. A minute's reflection, however, will reveal that it is a mistake to assume conflict, anxiety, and regression as the *only* explanation. Many difficulties may be related to structural limitations as well.

For example, the patient may remark, "I know my wife will hate me because I was mad at her earlier today." In the process he may be ignoring the fact that the wife may be worried that the children heard him yell at her, and is primarily concerned about the effect this has on the children. Her concerns are clearly more triangular. The therapist, aware of this issue from previous knowledge about the family, and aware of the patient's ignoring it, may raise a question with the patient, "You don't seem to consider the possibility that your wife may be concerned about more than just the two of you." This discussion may naturally lead to an observation that in the therapeutic situation, the patient seems to assume that the therapist is late because he dislikes him, ignoring the possibility that perhaps the therapist is late because he was involved with his children or his spouse. When this issue is raised in the heat of transference, it may come as a shock to the patient, who is only accustomed to thinking in terms of the dyadic system.

Let us take a look at another example of a person who thinks dyadically and who never considers his impact on the group. At work he plays all the angles, trying to get the most important work for himself, aiming to be the office star. He ignores the impact of his efforts on the morale of the larger group. He may even understand triangular intrigues but has no comprehension that his own affects, wishes, and behaviors impact on the dynamics of the larger peer group. The therapist may attempt to direct such a patient's attention by saying, "You know, you talk a lot about the relationship between you and your boss, but you never talk about the impact on your peers of your trying to take all the firm's important cases from all the other attorneys in the firm." Such a person, who is not used to thinking along these lines, and who shows a predilection for thinking in simpler dyadic terms, may be shocked, surprised, and even angry that the therapist raises such questions. The patient may also, however, be intrigued and begin to think in a new way.

Similarly, an individual who is arrested at the early adolescent level of ego differentiation is not yet taking into account his own internal standards. But he *is* caught up in how he manipulates and is manipulated by other people, and may be helped when you ask him about his own standards of behavior or lack thereof. Furthermore, the individual who does not think in terms of the larger cultural and societal impact of his or her behavior and affects, or in a historical and future context, may be helped when the therapist speculates about the impact of various feelings or thoughts in terms of the future, or on how this reverberates with who he or she was in the past.

These types of interventions may appear to be similar to the kinds of comments clinicians often make during therapy, such as, "What impact will that have on your spouse or your children?" or "How will that affect your career?" or "How does that fit in with your picture of yourself in the past?" The important point here is that we may often ignore where the patient is developmentally because we do not have a developmental map of the ego in mind. Rather than helping a patient go from one level to another, we may inappropriately ask patients who function at the dyadic level what the future impact of a certain behavior or affect will be on themselves. Such a question assumes that a very advanced adult level of ego differentiation is already in place. This type of comment may have little meaning for the person, because he or she may not have achieved the triadic, smaller group, or internal value level of ego differentiation.

It is often falsely assumed that therapists can do certain psychological work involving differentiated ego functions with any individual who is above a particular age and functions above a certain level of cognitive ability. What the therapist first needs to consider, however, is the patient's level of ego development. The therapist should then systematically focus his or her differentiating comments on the next level of ego differentiation the patient has to achieve. This may involve affective saliency (in the case of the narcissistic person), or affective meaning (in the case of an obsessive or schizoid person), or bringing cohesion to fragmentation (in an affective disordered person or one who is visually and spatially impaired).

The therapist systematically helps patients to first experience and then comprehend their own structural deficits. While doing this, the clinician provides the patient with repeated interactive experiences that create or strengthen certain structural capacities.

How should the therapist view his own role in this interaction? Is the therapist simply a real object to the patient, or is he or she a transference object? Is the therapist both? Are insights regarding transference or aggression useful here?

The clearest way to think about the therapist's role in this process is as a developmental object in the patient's life. To the degree that transference distortions are present and that the patient has some yearnings and longings for the therapist, the saliency and the affective field surrounding the therapist will increase. Therefore, the therapist should attempt to gain a sense of what meaning he or she has in the patient's life. Is the therapist experienced as nurturing, hostile, suspicious, or dependent? Is the therapist experienced representationally or prerepresentationally? Does the patient experience the therapist in a differentiated way or as an extension of him- or herself?

As the clinician gets a sense of how he is experienced by the patient in this therapeutic context, he is better equipped to further help the patient differentiate experience. Assume, for example, that the therapist is somewhat represented, and will be experienced, because of the transference, with certain affective and drive-derivative intensity. Aware of that, the therapist makes himself useful to the patient in terms of opening and closing representational circles of communication. For example, the therapist cannot simply prescribe in a structured way that the patient is now going to work on pleasure and excitement, dependency, or aggression and differentiate these realms of experience. The patient will experience the therapist as aggressive or nurturing, depending on the issues of the moment (particularly if transference has heated up).

Let's say, for the sake of argument, that the therapist is experienced as a highly nurturing object. Because the therapist functions as an interactive differentiating object, the patient experiences and understands feelings of dependency and nurturing in a more representationally differentiated way. The clues to this are revealed by the patient's affects and representational associations. Therefore, the clinician approaches developmental therapy in much the same way as a routine therapy, asking the patient to say and communicate whatever comes to mind. In this case, however, the therapist looks at all kinds of communication, both verbal and nonverbal, and how it is expressed at all levels of ego development. For example, when a patient talks about his wife or boss and their lack of nurturing qualities, the therapist recognizes that his own nurturance or nonnurturance of the patient is a simultaneous, if unspoken, theme. The therapist is also aware that he is a differentiated interactor, and builds on the patient's comments and inspires the patient to build on his comments. To the degree that patients get lost in their own associations and become fragmented, the therapist helps them to come back to close the circle of communication by remarking, "I'm lost here . . . You said A and then you said B, but I don't quite see how they go together." In that way, the therapist fosters the patient in actively doing the work of differentiating. When a patient subtly ignores particular affective dimensions of the therapist (such as the therapist's affects or motivations or the possibility of alternatives concerning why the therapist did something), the therapist will deliberately mention this, rather than keep it as a private thought for days or weeks at a time. These comments by the clinician create differentiating experience, because the patient is then expected to build on those comments in one way or another (either arguing why it is not the case, or at least elaborating on it affectively).

For example, the patient who easily closes symbolic circles around competition, but can only communicate dependency with a longing look and associations to "an ideal mate," would not be allowed to endlessly repeat this pattern. While the pattern was being pointed out, the therapist would remind the patient that he or she hadn't remarked on the longing look, and would directly address the issue of whether the individual's "ideal sexual mate" would take care of his or her "chicken soup" needs. Needy feelings would be responded to with empathetic vocal rhythms. A differentiating interactive experience is thereby mobilized.

The heat of transference provides an intensity factor which can be particularly helpful. In addition to using the heat of the transference in an experiential and reflective way the patient becomes able to grasp the issue at hand as he or she experiences it. (The use of the transference is experiential in the sense that one is opening and closing circles of communication; reflective insofar as one reflects on what the therapeutic challenge is.)

Countertransference tendencies are significant here, as they would be in any dynamic psychotherapy. These tendencies will interfere with an accurate perception of the themes as well as the therapist's ability to exercise his or her good judgment about how to create differentiating experiences for the patient. When not understood by the therapist, countertransference will cause the therapist to inadvertently act in, rather than constructively help the patient to work through, a particular drama.

While the clinician is creating these representationally differentiating experiences, he or she is also simultaneously caught up in exploring the dynamic meaning of the patient's behavior. The therapist may be cast as a nurturing mother or protecting father, or a monster who inflicts damage. Take, for example, the patient who says he feels like a spaceship. He fantasizes that he rises majestically in the air, only to plummet, damaged, back to earth with a thump. The therapist is aware that the patient's "damage" is caused in part by a visual–motor processing difficulty which is intensified by certain family dynamics. When the theme of nurturing comes up in the context of this fantasy which was explored during therapy, however, the therapist is clearly labeled by the patient as the cause of his "engine failure," or sense of damage. The therapist is thus cast in a complex role that goes beyond merely serving as a differentiating object.

In situations like the above, the therapist must resist exploring dynamic meanings until certain structural capacities are in place. For example, to discuss various dynamic meanings with a person who is basically not representationally differentiated may be little more than a self-indulgent, intellectual exercise. On the other hand, as the person's representational differentiating capacity becomes more solid through interactive experiences (and this may be area by area, rather than all or nothing), the therapist can begin to take a look at dynamic meanings and the configuration of specific fantasies that have in part stemmed from particular structural deficits. For example, after the above patient learns to differentiate nurturing experiences and look at the relationship between nurturing and aggressive experiences without getting overly fragmented or lost, the therapist might well wonder aloud why the therapist is responsible for the crash of the patient's spaceship. The patient may be able to reflect on the notion that, like his parents, the therapist has exacted a big price for the nurturing he supplies. The patient may verbalize a feeling that both his parents and the therapist want to rob him of his masculinity, undermine him, and not permit him to be powerful as a "price" of providing dependency support. Although the boy's mother was in fact emasculating, the therapist did not behave in a similar way. The patient tarred both authority figures with the same brush, though, due to transference. Clarifying such feelings provides the patient with a chance to analyze and work through these issues.

If the patient cannot differentiate historical experience from current experience, however, or separate therapist from parent, or build bridges between aggressive and dependent experience, such analytic work cannot occur. Therefore, the therapist must always first provide differentiating experiences for the patient who is undifferentiated in certain domains.

For example, it may seem that the patient can differentiate all realms of experience, but he evidences a subtle deficit in constructing bridges between aggressive and dependent feelings. Endless interpretation won't change this. But interactive experiences where aggression and dependent longings are experienced and are part of circle-closing dialogues, will facilitate further differentiation.

Therapy ultimately is only a small portion of the patient's total experiences. So, in addition to discussing the dynamic significance with patients, the therapist also assists the therapeutic process by trying to help patients create situations, in their experience outside the therapy, which will be differentiating, particularly in those areas of ego structure that are deficient. For example, a clinician may try to facilitate differentiating interactions in the marital relationship or in relationships with good friends and with colleagues at work. Let us take as an example the narcissistic individual who stays at work as a result of becoming self-absorbed, and in order to support his self-absorption whenever he is in conflict with his wife around issues involving dependency and nurturing. The individual can then spend long hours at his desk staring into space. As he avoids family life more and more, he rationalizes that he is a busy man with meetings to go to and phone calls to make. When narcissistically injured, he becomes increasingly self-absorbed.

Besides becoming a developmental object, working on issues that arise during transference, and helping the patient differentiate the therapist's affective experience and experience it, the therapist can also make forceful, developmentally facilitating comments to the patient. The therapist can straightforwardly remark that by staying away from his wife and children when he feels frustrated, the patient is furthering his self-absorption. When he has strong feelings during these stressful periods, he avoids attempting, as he did with the therapist, to understand the motivation of others. The therapist thus helps the patient experience those affective situations that are likely to be differentiating. The therapist cannot literally hold the patient's hand and facilitate a differentiating experience with the patient's wife, but he can in a sense make the escape routes difficult to use and, therefore, help the patient to repeatedly expose himself to those kinds of useful experiential opportunities.

There is a risk, however, of the patient then experiencing the therapist as a savior, parent, or all-knowing guide. In intensive analytic therapy this may distort the transference. The fantasy that is constructed can be analyzed if the ego structure is sufficiently differentiated. If the therapist is too careful, trying to keep the content neutral, he or she may never succeed in creating a differentiated ego structure in the patient, and may never be able to analyze the patient's fantasies. Freud (1911), in dealing with phobias, underscored this point. Here we are extending this approach to structural ego development.

Most people who have ego deficits have constructed their lives to support those deficits. They avoid experiences that will remediate or help correct the deficits. Patients have a vested interest in continuing to avoid experiences that may be differentiating, because the original reasons they never differentiated those functions had to do with family interaction patterns which are associated with painful affects. It is understandable that on their own, patients don't want to experience those painful affects. As the therapist comes to appreciate the content and historical context for the patient's original departure from ego differentiation, he or she can constrict opportunities and encourage the patient to permit situations where he can experience some of those affects.

The therapist faces a losing battle if he or she tries to wait for the full historical context to be understood, analyzed, and used, since the patient is *not* motivated to put himself back in a situation where his ego can differentiate. The lack of differentiation itself will limit the patient's ability to reveal and understand his own historical context.

Patient and therapist thus progress in a "two steps forward one step back" approach. Differentiation is the first step forward. The patient will then understand more of the content, fantasy, and historical perspective of his or her experiences, gaining strength to take another step forward. Often, the patient's differentiating experiences with the therapist and with real life experiences have to lead the way to understanding the historical perspective and content. With the encouragement of the therapist, the patient may take a half-step forward, even without a full understanding of his or her patterns of avoidance. Patients can then understand why they are avoiding certain experiences, and perhaps fully involve themselves in those experiences. Waiting for full understanding through the free associative process rarely works well, and fails to mimic the natural developmental process. As the patient becomes more differentiated and engages nore fully in a range of age-expected life experience, it often becomes possible to observe and deal with intrapsychic conflicts more directly and fully.

RESOLVING CONFLICTS

When patients are reasonably differentiated, the therapeutic situation creates opportunities for resolving conflicts and increasing new capacities. The transference relationship, over a period of time, brings into stark reality the nature of the patient's wishes, fears, and prohibitions. These play themselves out in the therapeutic relationship. The therapist first, inadvertently, engages the patient in his old patterns because of the patient's greater skill at creating the transference and bringing the therapist into it. Initially, the therapist joins in and colludes with the patient due to countertransference problems. Together, the therapist and the patient replay the old object ties which contain defenses against both wishes and prohibitions. As the therapist comes to understand these patterns, he refrains from replaying them and, instead, substitutes a broad support for representational elaboration and differentiation across the full range of themes. In other words, he offers categorization, clarification, and interpretation as a way of broadening the base of representational elaboration and differentiation. The formerly warded-off themes (in the patient's elaborative and differentiating structures) now begin to find representational access through consistent scrutiny. At the same time that he is technically facilitating the formerly avoided areas, the therapist is refusing to reengage in the old defensive patterns, that is, the archaic patterns, that conspired to keep the patient from moving into a broader range of elaborative and differentiating experiences.

Facilitating this process is the fact that the transference occurs at a level of relative lack of differentiation. This lack of differentiation fosters generalization in terms of the hierarchy of behavioral and affective patterns in the patient's personality structure. The relatively undifferentiated experience of the transference, combined with the intensity of the transference (because of the ambiguity of the therapeutic situation), permits a profound learning to occur.

What must not be forgotten, however, is that ultimately the patient's boldness in jumping into the water, to embrace new thematic–affective realms in more differentiated ways, requires a great deal of security in the therapeutic relationship. This boldness is encouraged, in part, by the prerepresentational experience of constant engagement and prerepresentational reality-based communications which convey safety, acceptance, and respect (from the mutual reading of preverbal signals). These two foundations create the necessary security (which often was not completely available as the patient grows up). This security, in part, helps the patient tackle new affective–thematic domains at the level of representational elaboration and differentiation. The inability to retrieve the old object tie (i.e., the therapist will not reenact the old patterns) and avoid these new patterns, as well as the continuing interest of the therapist in engaging the patient in new thematic–affective areas, provide the ingredients for further ego growth and development. In this way, approaches to conflict resolution work synergistically with the experiences which support ego development.

In summary, our general developmental model explains how insights into behavior and feelings work together with the experience. The psychotherapeutic situations provide critical learning ingredients in addition to insight. They are:

1. Baseline security through engagement and preverbal cuing.
2. An opportunity to engage in and describe the pathologic configurations.
3. An opportunity through the therapeutic dialogue to engage in the neurotic or problematic patterns at an undifferentiated level.

4. The opportunity to relinquish this pattern at this same undifferentiated level. This creates a tendency toward learning with *generalizations*. It also creates an opportunity for relinquishing these patterns at a similar level of generalization as they were likely learned in the first place.
5. The therapist's true neutrality facilitates the patient's relinquishing of old patterns. The therapist does not engage in these patterns once he is aware of them. He substitutes clarification and interpretation.
6. The avoidance of new age-appropriate patterns are dealt with via clarifications and interpretations of the fears of engaging in a broad range of age-appropriate feelings and behaviors. The security of the therapeutic situation and the lack of engagement in old patterns provide the patient with the necessary motivation to try out new patterns.

In this model, we see the complementary roles of insight and transference interactions in the context of a developmental model of learning (Greenspan, 1975, 1989).

STRUCTURE BUILDING AND CONFLICT RESOLUTION

Therefore, while resolving conflicts can be very helpful, they are not the central feature of psychological growth. Structure building, a critical aspect of psychological growth, for example, does not occur, as often postulated, out of resolving conflicts; it occurs from certain features of a relationship that are ongoing in nature. These are the same relationship features that lead to proper structural growth during development. They have to be in place for structural growth at any age or stage of development. Conflicts have to be analyzed so that individuals will be amenable and accessible to the type of relationship that will build structures. The resolution of conflict in itself does not strengthen structure; rather it reduces the need to reenact and reduces inhibitions. Individuals are then available to opportunities for developmental experiences. These, in turn, build structures to resolve the conflict.

The following case illustrates the interplay of structural and dynamic issues in a partially representationally differentiated patient. A youngster at age $4^1/_2$ entered treatment because he was "confusing fantasy and reality," according to this parents. It will be seen that at a crucial structural developmental stage involving fantasy–reality differentiation, he had a strong desire to confuse his parents. Family conflicts were confusing and angering him, and he was, in turn, using confusion as a weapon.

In preschool he regaled his teachers and classmates with stories about how wolves were chasing him outside and how he saw a clown around the corner. He related these tales in such a serious way that no one was sure whether he was fantasizing and knew he was fantasizing, or whether he was in fact distorting reality. He was having trouble with his impulses, often hitting and taunting the other children. He exhibited some fine-motor delays, but was otherwise gifted in his language skills and seemed to be a bright child. Psychological testing revealed some worrisome questions about the age adequacy of his reality testing and whether this youngster was going to be vulnerable to a psychotic decompensation.

The little boy's relationship with his parents was characterized by lots of power struggles and fights, in which the parents accused him of lying and making up stories. The father and mother were often angry, annoyed, and protective of him, although there was clearly an intense relationship among the three of them. Significant marital conflicts existed between the parents as well.

While the therapy involved helping stabilize the family and helping the parents deal with their conflicts, a very interesting dimension emerged about this youngster that revealed an important aspect covering content and structure. During the course of this boy's therapy, the warmth and support of the therapeutic relationship helped him settle down and learn to shift from behaving out his conflicts by hitting and pinching to talking and representing more of his affects. About eight months into the therapy he was still spinning tall tales during the therapy session. The therapist sought consultation with a supervisor who alerted him to the patient's structural developmental issues. The therapist, instead of following his usual practice of looking for the themes of sexuality, aggression, preoedipal and oedipal themes so evident in the child's whoppers, focused on the difficulty this child had in structurally separating the tall tales from reality. The therapist said, "We have been talking about the anger or the excitement in your story; now I want to ask you to look at something else. What do you like best? Do you like making up a story the most or do you like it more when you tell me about what happened at school or between you and your parents?" The child gave a broad grin and said, "You know what? I like making up stories." His therapist said, "I don't even know sometimes whether you are making them up or not." The little boy once again broke into a big smile and said, "Well, sometimes I get confused. It's so exciting once I start that I can't be sure whether it really happened or not." His therapist empathized with the child, saying how exciting it must feel and how sometimes stories seem to take over the real world. The therapist wondered aloud about what made the story-telling so exciting. At the same time, the therapist helped this child close his symbolic circles. Whenever he got fragmented, the therapist intervened with, "How did we get here?" helping the child fill in the missing bridges.

As he became more differentiated, the boy could focus on the structural issue of making up the story (Why did the youngster prefer fantasy as a category in itself rather than reality?), rather than why he preferred to whip up feelings of anger, excitement, or sexuality. The child responded by starting to associate to the fact that he liked to "confuse" people. The associations circled around how he liked to "keep his parents guessing" and also confuse those "dumb teachers." As he was talking about confusing people, he started making clay dolls and sticking sharp objects into them. It was clear that his wish to confuse was associated with sadistic impulses. He talked about liking to see people's faces as they looked scared and anxious when he spun his yarns. The therapist empathized with the fact that he probably even liked doing this to the therapist, too. With this, the boy smiled broadly and then started banging into things and slightly injured himself.

The child was obviously showing some of the anxiety he felt when directly dealing with this issue with his therapist. The therapist empathized with the fact that the little boy was uncomfortable thinking that he could be that angry with the therapist and that sometimes he wanted to fool him the same way he wanted to fool other people. The therapist also made a comment that maybe sticking pins in the dolls made the child feel as if he were taking the hot air out of people. He went on to speculate that maybe confusing the therapist and others was like letting their hot air out.

Another line of associations became clear over the next few months. This child did, in fact, frequently get lost in fantasy and wasn't sure sometimes when he thought about wolves whether in fact there were real wolves outside or not. He could scare himself with his stories. According to the parents and to the youngster himself, the telling of these tall tales had started about a year and a half before the family entered therapy. It became more and more evident that this child for dynamic reasons within his own family had chosen to use fantasy and tall tales as an aggressive weapon against his parents to confuse them. Perhaps they had confused him first with all the family chaos and anger that was aired during marital conflicts. This had occurred in this very bright, imaginative child just at a time when he was structurally learning to differentiate his representational system; that is, to distinguish reality from fantasy and connect up different thoughts, ideas, and feelings in terms of their thematic, temporal, and spatial characteristics, as well as the qualities of real versus unreal and self versus nonself. During this critical phase of structure formation, the child was busy using the more primitive form of structure, the representational–elaborative form, as a weapon (which suggests some differentiation). This weapon was wielded so successfully, however, that it undermined the very process of differentiation. The serious look that he showed on his face when he was talking about the wolves, the clowns, or other figments of his imagination was alerting the adults around him. Since he scared himself as well as others, the weapon that he was using against others was cutting both ways. It was also undermining his own structural development. This was happening, in part, because of the phase of development at which he used this weapon. Had he been a child of 9 or 10, he might have been aware both that he was fabricating and that he was using the lie as an aggressive weapon.

By focusing on the patient's structural capacity, the therapist helped this child take a look at the dynamics that were underlying his desire to use fantasy as a weapon against his parents, teachers, and even the therapist. The therapist might have continued to follow the usual lines of inquiry concerning aggression, sexuality, or excitement from a content point of view. This youngster probably would then have gradually continued to better represent his thoughts and feelings in terms of the representational phase, but not have gotten a full understanding or full resolution of his representational differentiation capacity.

In much theory underpinning psychotherapeutic capacities, structural change is a by-product of insight. According to the classical model, structural change occurs as the unconscious becomes conscious, as conflicts become more clear and conscious, and give the ego a chance to reorganize itself. There are *alleged* tendencies within the ego that help a person reorganize at a higher level of development; that is, experience structural change. But many patients have long courses of treatment without attaining full structural change, although they get symptom relief and may have some modest increased flexibility in their character structure. Perhaps this is because the issue of structural change is left to informal, intuitive processes and is a by-product of content-oriented dynamic foci. If the foci on structural change were systematically approached as the content is approached, and if our theoretical model could focus on issues of structural development as well as it does on dynamic issues, we would have a more complete model of the therapeutic process.

The structural issues were clarified in the case of the 4-year-old discussed above, by focusing on his inability to separate fantasy from reality and his desire to use fantasy at a critical age.

The previous case highlighted the family's inability to represent certain themes and affects, which represented their structural limitation. Moving beyond concrete ways of representing affects made it possible for the father to recover the memories of his own father and brother which were limiting his greater structural flexibility. Making structure explicit to the patient allows an individual or family to enter into relationships in such a way that structural growth is possible. In the first case, the family was able to represent affects more fully in a less concrete way and was slowly engaging in structural growth in much the same way it occurs in normal development. Once the 4-year-old teller of tales understood his wish to use fantasy as a weapon, he was more comfortable in separating fantasy and reality, and he could fully begin differentiating his representational systems. There was no longer a vested interest in using undifferentiated thinking for dynamic purposes. Both he and his parents were able to represent affects and feelings more fully and he was able to move into the different levels of structural differentiation.

In cases such as these, it may seem obvious that therapy should focus on the broader structural components of defenses as well as the underlying contents. Indeed, many intuitive and skillful therapists would do just this. But without a good map of structural developmental levels to go along with a knowledge of psychosexual and object relations developmental levels, there is a tendency to get lost in the content or the object relations dynamics or miss the structural issues. Monday morning quarterbacking makes the process seem easy, but without a structural road map, the therapeutic process can be frustrated.

Most importantly, the structural road map provides opportunities to evolve new therapeutic strategies. For each capacity from building bridges between different groups of affects and ideas in early childhood to integrating and reflecting on one's own and one's families' needs and desires as an adult, there are certain types of experiences that are formative. For some individuals these formative experiences are present in their ongoing relationships, once maladaptive patterns, anxieties, and conflicts are worked through. For many individuals, however, their personality structures, family or relationship patterns obstruct their participation in these formative experiences. The therapeutic relationship, in such cases, must provide structure-building experiences and assist the patient in constructing ongoing relationships that will further this process. For example, in the discussions of representational differentiation, it was discussed how the therapist challenges the patient to build bridges between different affective realms, construct links from fantasy to reality and appreciate the nature of his own physical makeup and presymbolic character structure.

Conclusion

Different therapies look at different aspects of the proverbial elephant, whether from a psychodynamic, object relations, self psychology, behavioral, or cognitive-behavioral point of view. A comprehensive cohesive developmental framework integrates elements from these approaches with a broader understanding of the developmental processes essential for emotional or mental health. It formulates series of principles that our understanding of human development tells us are essential for emotional growth to take place.

Developmentally based psychotherapy constructs its therapeutic strategies from these principles of human development and growth. The clinician first determines the level of the patient's ego or personality development and the presence or absence of deficits or constrictions. For example, can the person regulate activity and sensations, relate to others, read nonverbal, affective symbols, represent experience, build bridges between representations, integrate emotional polarities, abstract feelings, and reflect on internal wishes and feelings?

After determining the developmental level, the clinician looks for constitutional and maturational contributions, the presence of difficulties with sensory processing, modulation or motor planning. The clinician looks for interactive and family contributions. Each of these is explored in the present and the past as well as the anticipated future. The patient's fantasies and sense of self and others, as well as conflicts are understood in the context of all these influences. They are the patient's way of making sense of his ego structure, physical makeup, family patterns and interactions with others. The developmentally oriented therapist does not permit him or herself the luxury of over-focusing on one set of variables such as inner fantasies, family dynamics, biological proclivities, or prior experience. Similarly, the formulated therapeutic strategy cannot deal only with one or two factors. It must deal with all the critical factors that influence the developmental process. As a collaborator in the construction of experience, the therapist uses his or her understanding of the patient's development to assist the patient in constructing interactions that will provide growth and overcome difficulties.

Often it is assumed that critical aspects of development occur through the maturation of the nervous system along with routine, expectable experiences. It is also assumed that from these routine, expectable maturational sequences and experiences, certain psychological structures having to do with the ability to regulate, engage, interact, represent (symbolize) experience, and reflect and compare experiences, are present in most people. With these capacities in place, it is believed that the therapeutic process can focus on conflicts and anxieties and selected maladaptive behaviors or thoughts. We have observed, however, that these core capacities are present in only a small percentage of individuals. For most, such capacities have to be learned as part of the therapeutic process.

The developmental perspective shows us how we learn these capacities during development. It suggests strategies that can be employed in the psychotherapeutic process, so that adults and children who have not achieved these capacities can learn them. From a developmental point of view, the integral parts of the therapeutic process include learning how to regulate experience; to engage more fully and deeply in relationships; to read and respond to boundary-defining behaviors and affects; to perceive, comprehend, and respond to complex self- and object-defining affects, behaviors, and interactive patterns; to represent experience; to differentiate represented experience; and to form higher-level differentiations, including the capacity to engage in the ever-changing opportunities, tasks and challenges during the course of life (e.g., adulthood and aging) and, throughout, to observe and reflect on one's own and others' experiences. Mastering these core developmental processes makes dealing with conflicts, anxieties, maladaptive behaviors and thoughts possible.

These processes are the foundation of the ego, and more broadly, the personality. Their presence constitutes emotional health and their absence, emotional disorder. The developmental approach describes how to harness these core processes and, in this way, assist the patient in mobilizing his or her own growth.

Appendix: The Clinical Assessment of Developmental Levels

A developmentally based conceptual framework can alert clinicians to the different dimensions of functioning that can be observed in the clinical setting. Noteworthy contributions to understanding the development of different areas of personality functioning have been made by a number of authors. Anna Freud (1965) delineated a number of developmental lines, dimensions of behavior, and experience. Erik Erikson (1950) formulated psychosocial stages. Margaret Mahler (Mahler, Pine, and Bergman, 1975) discussed the development and individuation of the self and the role of early object relations. Jean Piaget (1962) studied cognitive developmental stages. More recently, clinical research studies of infants and young children have made it possible to formulate in greater detail both affective and cognitive components of the early stages in development and to observe how constitutional–maturational and experiential factors interact and resonate throughout an individual's lifetime.

In using the developmental structuralist approach to understand early development (Greenspan, 1979; Greenspan and

Lourie, 1981), experience is broadly defined as encompassing interactions with the inanimate or impersonal world, as well as emotional intercourse. The person's experiential organization is the final common pathway for the multiple environmental and biological determinants that influence behavior (Greenspan, 1989, 1992).

AN OVERVIEW OF THE DEVELOPMENTAL–STRUCTURAL APPROACH AND THE STAGES OF EGO DEVELOPMENT

In an attempt to understand early development, we undertook a clinical descriptive intervention study of multirisk infants and their families as well as normal infants and their families (Greenspan and Lourie, 1981; Greenspan, Wieder, Lieberman, Nover, Lourie, and Robinson, 1987). More recently, this understanding has been enhanced by work with infants and young children with interactional difficulties, regulatory problems, and Multisystem Developmental Disorders (including Autistic Spectrum Disorders) (Greenspan, 1992).

This research, plus intensive clinical work with a variety of infants, preschool children, and adults, suggested both the need for and the ingredients of an integrated developmental theory that would reconcile our knowledge of development based on human relationships, cognition, and emerging empirical research on neurophysiological, behavioral, and social development of infants and children.

We observed, for example, that infants progress through a series of emotional tasks, each building on the previous one. Infants without familial or physical challenges often progressed easily through these emotional steps. Infants in challenging familial situations often required assistance to help their caregivers provide the needed experiences that would make it possible for the infant to master the expectable emotional tasks (e.g., the caretakers needed to respond with warmth to the infant's overtures in order to foster relatedness; they needed to read and respond to the infant's signals so that two-way, intentional communication was fostered).

Many infants with marked difficulties in sensory processing and motor planning (e.g., Autistic Spectrum problems) could also achieve emotional health, but only if they progressed through these same emotional stages. Assisting infants and young children with marked constitutional and maturational variations, however, required innovative therapeutic strategies (Greenspan, 1992).

A series of organizational levels of personality, along multiple dimensions, and mediating processes or "structures" was thereby formulated to describe and summarize these observations of core emotional processes. We further observed that these levels which could also be described in terms of "Functional Emotional Milestones" (Greenspan, 1992), organized related motor, language, sensory, and cognitive capacities.

CLINICAL INDICATORS OF THE LEVELS OF DEVELOPMENT IN CHILDHOOD AND ADULTHOOD

These organizational levels, in their partial or full state of early mastery, go through further development and refinement as the child grows. Even though they are continually changing, we have found that these capacities can be observed in the older child or adult. For example, while the infant first learns to engage and relate with intimacy in early infancy, one can observe the child's or adult's evolving capacity to relate to others. Understanding how these capacities develop helps us understand their importance and later forms.

The first level of development involves regulation and shared attention, that is, *self-regulation and emerging interest in the world* through sight, sound, smell, touch, and taste. Children and adults build on this early developing set of capacities when they act to maintain a calm, alert, focused state, and organize behavior, affect, and thoughts. The infant is capable at birth or shortly thereafter of initial states of regulation to organize experience in an adaptive fashion. He or she can respond to pleasure and displeasure (Lipsitt, 1966); change behavior as a function of its consequences (Gewirtz, 1965, 1969); and form intimate bonds and make visual discriminations (Klaus and Kennell, 1976; Meltzoff and Moore, 1977). Cycles and rhythms, such as sleep–wake and alertness states, can be organized (Sander, 1962). The infant's ability for regulation is suggested by a number of basic abilities involving perceiving and processing information and exploring and responding to the world (Berlyne, 1960; Deci, 1977; Harlow, 1953; Hendrick, 1939; Hunt, 1965; White, 1963).

We have been able to observe individual differences in constitutional–maturational characteristics that contribute to one's regulating capacities. They begin in infancy and then can be observed in older children and adults. These maturational patterns may change as one develops, however. The following list may prove helpful in observing regulatory differences:

1. Sensory reactivity, including hypo- and hyperreactivity in each sensory modality (tactile, auditory, visual, vestibular, olfactory);
2. Sensory processing in each sensory modality (e.g., the capacity to decode sequences, configurations, or abstract patterns);
3. Sensory affective reactivity and processing in each modality (e.g., the ability to process and react to degrees of affective intensity in a stable manner);
4. Motor tone;
5. Motor planning.

An instrument to clinically assess aspects of sensory functions in young children in a reliable manner has been developed and is available (DeGangi and Greenspan, 1988, 1989a,b).

Sensory reactivity (hypo or hyper) and sensory processing can be observed clinically. Is the child or adult hyper- or hyposensitive to touch or sound? Do sounds of motors or of a noisy party overwhelm the individual? Is a gentle touch on the hand or face reacted to by a startled withdrawal? The same question must be asked in terms of vision and movement in space. In addition, in each sensory modality processing of sensations occurs. Does the 4-month-old "process" a complicated pattern of information input or only a simple one? Does the $4^1/_2$-year-old have a receptive language problem and is therefore unable to sequence words he hears together or follow complex directions? Is the young adult prone to get lost in his own fantasies because he has to work extra hard to decode the complex verbal productions of others? Is the 3-year-old an early comprehender and talker, but slower in visual–spatial processing? If spatial patterns are poorly comprehended, a child may be facile with words, sensitive to every emotional nuance, but have no context, never see the "forest"; such children get lost in the "trees." In the clinician's office, they may forget where the door is or have a hard time picturing that mother is only a few feet away in the waiting room. Similarly, adults may find it difficult to follow instructions or easily get lost in new settings. They may also have difficulty with seeing the emotional big picture. If the mother is angry, the child may think the earth is opening up and he is falling in, because he cannot comprehend that she was nice before, and she will probably be nice again. Similarly, adults may be overwhelmed with the emotion of the moment, losing sight of the past or future.

It is also necessary to look at the motor system, including motor tone, motor planning (fine and gross), and postural control. A picture of the motor system will be provided by observing how a person sits or runs; maintains posture; holds a crayon or pen; hops, scribbles, or draws; and makes rapid alternating movements. Security in regulating and controlling one's body plays an important role in how one uses gestures to communicate. The ability to regulate dependency (being close or far away); the confidence in regulating aggression ("Can I control my hand that wants to hit?"); and the ability to comprehend social sequences and follow through on tasks or work activities.

The constitutional and maturational variables may be thought of as "regulatory factors." When they contribute to difficulties with attending, remaining calm and organized or modulating affect or behavior and therefore are a prominent feature of a disorder of behavior, affect, or thought, such a disorder may be considered a "regulatory disorder" (Greenspan, 1992). Regulatory differences sometimes are attributed to "lack of motivation" or emotional conflicts. Observing carefully and obtaining a history of regulatory patterns will make it possible to separate maturational variations from other factors and also observe how many factors often operate together.

Another early level concerns *engagement,* or a sense of relatedness, a lifelong capacity. Once the infant has achieved some capacity for regulation in the context of engaging in the world, and the central nervous system (CNS) maturation is increasing between 2 and 4 months of age, the infant becomes more attuned to social and impersonal interaction. There is greater ability to respond to the external environment and to form a special relationship with significant primary caregivers. The stage of forming a human relationship or attachment becomes more prominent. As part of a growing relationship, the infant evidences a variety of affects or affect proclivities (Thomkins, 1963; Ekman, 1972; Izard, 1978), and demonstrates organized social responses in conjunction with increasing neurophysiologic organization (Emde, Gaensbauer, and Harmon, 1976). It is interesting to note that this empirically documented view of the infant is, in a general sense, consistent with Freud's early hypotheses (1900, 1905, 1911) and Hartmann's postulation (1939) of an early undifferentiated organizational matrix. The organization of experience broadens during the early months of life to reflect increases in the capacity to experience and tolerate a range of stimuli, including responding in social interactions in stable and personal configurations (Sander, 1962; Escalona, 1968; Brazelton, Koslowski, and Main, 1974; Sroufe, Waters, and Matas, 1974; Stern, 1974a,b; Emde et al., 1976; Murphy and Moriarty, 1976). The infant's capacity for engagement is supported by early maturational abilities for selectively focusing on the human face and voice and for processing and organizing information from his senses (Meltzoff, 1985; Papousek, 1981; Papousek & Papousek, 1979; Stern, 1985). The sense of shared humanity, a type of rhythmic connectedness, is evident in both the way the infant and parent use their senses, motor systems, and affects to resonate with one another (Butterworth & Jarrett, 1980; Scaife & Bruner, 1975). The early quality of engagement has implications for later attachment patterns and behavior (Ainsworth, et al., 1974; Bates, et al., 1985; Belsky, et al., 1984; Egeland & Farber, 1984; Grossmann, et al., 1985; Lewis & Feiring, 1987; Miyake, et al., 1985; Pederson, et al., 1990).

Relationship patterns, once formed, continue and further develop throughout the course of life. Most clinicians have a great deal of experience in monitoring the quality of relatedness. But sometimes the clinician ignores the quality of engagement while working on specific ideas or thoughts, so that indifference, negative feelings, or impersonal or aloof patterns continue longer than necessary.

For example, the child who walks in and goes right for the toys, ignoring the clinician, is different from the child who looks at the clinician with a twinkle in his eye and points to the toys, waiting for a warm accepting smile. The adult who strides in the office and makes a beeline for the new painting on the wall with nary a wave or a nod in the therapist's direction may be eschewing any initial sense of engagement to cement a relationship. One observes if there is a range of affects used for trying to establish a sense of connectedness and relatedness—warmth, pleasure, a sense of intimacy and trust.

The next two stages involve *purposeful communication and the emergence of an organized, complex sense of self.* They both involve organized patterns of behavior and intentional, nonverbal communications or gestures. These gestures include facial expressions, arm and leg movements, vocalizations, and spinal posture. From the middle of the first year of life onward, individuals rely on gestures to communicate. Initially during the stage of purposeful communication, simple reciprocal gestures such as head nods, smiles, and movement patterns serve a boundary-defining role. The "me" communicates a wish or intention and the "other" or "you" communicates back some confirmation, acknowledgment, or elaboration on that wish or intention.

These capacities are first seen as the infant develops complex patterns of communication in the context of his or her primary human relationship. Parallel with development of the infant's relationship to the inanimate world where basic schemes of causality (Piaget, 1962) are being developed, the infant becomes capable of complicated human emotional communication (Charlesworth, 1969; Tennes, Emde, Kisley, and Metcalf, 1972; Brazelton et al., 1974; Stern, 1974a). There is both a historic and newly emerging consensus among clinicians, developmental observers, and researchers that affects are used for intentional communication (Bowlby, 1973; Brazelton & Cramer, 1990; Mahler & Bergman, 1975; Osofsky & Eberhart-Wright, 1988; Spitz, 1965; Stern, 1985; Winnicott, 1965) and that these affective patterns, for example, for happiness, anger, fear, surprise, and disgust are similar in different cultures and in both children and adults (Campos, et al., 1983; Darwin, 1872; Ekeman, et al., 1972; Izard, 1971). Intentional communication, which involves both intuiting and responding to the caregiver's emotional cues, gradually takes on qualities that are particular to relationships, family, and culture (Brazelton & Als, 1979; Bruner, 1982; Feinman & Lewis, 1983; Kaye, 1982; Kimmert, et al., 1983; Kleinman, 1986; Markus & Kitayama, 1990; Schweder, et al., 1987; Stern, 1977; Trevarthen, 1979; Tronick, 1980).

When there have been distortions in the emotional communication process, as occurs when a mother responds in a mechanical, remote manner or projects some of her own dependent feelings onto her infant, the infant may not learn to appreciate causal relationships between people at the level of compassionate and intimate feelings. This situation can occur, even though causality seems to be developing in terms of the inanimate world and the impersonal human world.

The stage of two-way, causal, intentional communication (or somatopsychologic differentiation) indicates processes occurring at the somatic (sensorimotor) and emerging psychological levels. It is evidenced in the infant's growing ability to discriminate primary caregivers from others and differentiate his or her own actions from their consequences—affectively, somatically, behaviorally, and interpersonally.

With appropriate reading of cues and differential responses, the infant's or toddler's behavioral repertoire becomes complicated, and communications take on more organized, meaningful configurations. By 12 months of age, the infant is connecting behavioral units into larger organizations as he or she exhibits complex emotional responses such as affiliation, wariness, and fear (Bowlby, 1969; Ainsworth, Bell, and Stayton, 1974; Sroufe and Waters, 1977). As the toddler approaches the second year of life, in the context of the practicing subphase of the development of individuation (Mahler, Pine, and Bergman, 1975), there is an increased capacity for forming original behavioral schemes (Piaget, 1962), imitative activity and intentionality, and behavior suggesting functional understanding of objects (Werner and Kaplan, 1963).

There is now in evidence a stage of behavioral organization or a complex sense of self. As interactions become more complex and social patterns involving many circles of intentional communication are observed, toddlers evidence more sophisticated emotional patterns, such as dealing with challenges to their sense of intimacy with a caregiver (Ainsworth, et al., 1978; Bowlby, 1969), trying to help others connect something that is not expected or using emotional signals to figure out if a behavior is acceptable or not (Dunn, 1988; Emde, et al., 1988; Kagan, 1981; Radke-Yarrow, et al., 1983; Zahn-Waxler, et al., 1982).

This stage involves the many preverbal, behavioral interactions that begin in the second half of the first and beginning of the second year of life. Patterns that began with these early capacities can be seen in many behaviors in older children and adults, including simple gestural cues, involving eye contact, finger pointing, interjections or vocalizations, facial expressions, motor gestures, and different subtle affect expressions. The therapist should note whether the patient initiates such gestures and if she in turn responds to the clinician's countergesturing with a further gesture of her own.

The different emotions the patient reveals suggest the range and type of affect gestures they can communicate. The range and degrees of specific affects can be very broad. In the aggressive domain, for instance, there are gradations that run from assertive, competitive, and mildly aggressive behavior to explosive and uncontrolled rage. The same is true for the affectionate and caring domain, which ranges from promiscuous emotional hunger, to mild affection, a sincere sense of warmth, compassion, and to the developmentally advanced emotion of empathy. Affects can be combined with verbal themes showing a pattern during a session.

How does the person begin the session? What happens as he or she moves through the first third to the middle of the session, and then from the last third to saying good-bye? Follow the change in affect. For example, an individual may come in showing apprehension and tentativeness, become warm, and then competitive; show concern with issues of sibling or spousal jealousy and rivalry; and then express concern about separating from the therapist toward the end of the interview. Although several specific feelings have been elaborated in the above example, another patient may show only one or two affects during the entire interview.

The basic emotional messages of life—safety and security versus danger, acceptance versus rejection, approval versus disapproval—can all be communicated through facial expressions, body posture, movement patterns, and vocal tones and rhythm. Words enhance these more basic communications, but most of us form quick, split-second judgments regarding a new person's dangerousness or approachability from his or her gestures before the conversation even gets started. In fact, if a person looks threatening and says, "You know, I'm your friend," we tend to believe the gestures and discount the words.

At a more subtle level, gestural communication also relays to us what aspects of our own emotions are being accepted, ignored, or rejected. The raised eyebrows and head nods we perceive quickly tell us whether the person hearing our message is reacting with excitement, anger, curiosity, or detachment. More importantly, our ever-emerging definition of the uniqueness of our very self is dependent on how others react to our own special tendencies with preverbal gestures. Differential responses stir different affects and are part of the process that refines and defines our maturing behavior and sense of self. How is our mischievous behavior and devilish grin responded to, with an accepting smile or a head-shaking frown? Our natural inclinations toward mischievousness, laziness, and a whole host of other personality traits are in part either accepted and supported, or refined or squelched, as a result of the impact of this nonverbal communication system. The nonverbal, gestural communication system is therefore a part of every dialogue contributing to our sense of who we are and what we perceive.

The clinician who only focuses on a person's words may miss an underlying, critical lack of organized gestural communication ability. For example, the "spacey" child who floats in and out of the room, or misreads the implied social rules of the playroom and hides toys, ignoring the therapist's facial expressions and sounds, and the adult who misreads the intentions of others, seeing, for example, assertiveness as anger or dependence as rejection, both betray an inability to fully process organized gestural communications. Complex, self-defining gestures involving opening and closing many circles in a row (30 or 40) emerges in the second year of life and is seen thereafter in complex, nonverbal interactions, where patterns are communicated and comprehended.

As one observes gestures expressing a complex sense of self, one should take note not only of the range of affects but the richness and depth of affects observed. Are they superficial, as if the person is simply play-acting or imitating someone? Or do they convey a sense of personal depth? In other words, is one able to empathize with the way the patient is feeling?

The next level involves *the elaboration and sharing of meanings.* The individual's ability to represent or symbolize experience is illustrated in the pretend play of a child or the verbal expression of the adult's worries and anxieties.

This level begins as the toddler approaches the end of the second year. Internal sensations and unstable images become organized in a mental representational form that can be evoked and is somewhat stable (Gouin-Decarie, 1965; Bell, 1970; Piaget, 1962; Fenson and Ramsay, 1980). While this capacity is fragile between 16 and 24 months, it soon becomes a dominant mode in organizing the child's behavior.

This stage involves the formation of mental representations or ideas. Related to the ability to create representations is the capacity for "object permanence." This capacity is relative and goes through a series of stages (Gouin-Decarie, 1965); it refers to the toddler's ability to search for hidden inanimate objects. Representational capacity refers to the ability to organize and evoke internal organized multisensory experiences of the animate object. The capacities to represent animate and inanimate experiences are connected and depend both on CNS myelination and appropriate experiences.

At a representational level, the child develops capacities for elaboration, integration, and differentiation. The elaboration of ideas gradually becomes more complex and the sense of self now involves symbols, not just behaviors (e.g., use of words for intent and descriptions, use of personal pronouns, improved recognition of self in mirror) (Fein & Apfel, 1979; Fenson, et al., 1976; Inhelder, et al., 1972; Pipp, et al., 1987; Rubin, et al., 1983). Pretend play and intentional interpersonal use of language illustrate these new capacities (Waelder, 1933; Erikson, 1940; Peller, 1954; Kraus and Glucksberg, 1969; Nelson, 1973; Fein, 1975; Lowe, 1975). Causal schemes are developed at a representational level (Sinclair, 1970; McCune-Nicholich, 1977). As ideas and behaviors are being elaborated, they reflect not only ongoing relationships, but prior negotiations as well. A large number of studies on early attachment patterns and later behavior illustrate the importance of early patterns as well as later relationships (Aber & Baker, 1990; Arend, et al., 1979; Cassidy, 1990; Cassidy & Marvin, 1988; Easterbrooks & Goldberg, 1990; Egeland & Farber, 1984; Goldberg & Easterbrooks, 1984; Main, et al., 1985; Marvin & Stewart, 1991; Maslin-Cole & Spieker, 1990; Matas, et al., 1978; Pastor, 1981; Sroufe, 1983; Sroufe, et al., 1983; Waters, et al., 1979). As children are elaborating their ideas, they are using them to make more sense of their experiences and themselves (Bretherton & Beeghly, 1982; Dore, 1989; Dunn, et al., 1987; Dunn, 1988; Nelson, 1989; Nelson & Gruendal, 1981; Schank & Abelson, 1977).

Building on the capacities of this level, the child or adult uses ideas to indicate their wishes, intentions, or expectations. For example, a child may indicate a certain degree of trust or cautiousness about trying to define what is going to happen in the clinical interview. The child may stage pretend play sequences, featuring hurricanes and disasters or with children getting injections. He may be indicating his expectations of this new relationship. The child whose play focuses on dolls being fed and everyone being happy may be indicating a different set of expectations about the emerging relationship with the clinician. The adult who talks about relationships in the past that have led to disappointment will be giving different messages than the patient who talks of satisfying relationships.

This level in relating not only involves using representations or symbols in both play and verbal communication, but sometimes is evidenced by the use of subtle spatial communications, such as building complicated towers or houses with passages in them. Older children and adults can sometimes use a picture to convey a feeling or complex meaning. Adults often use descriptions of visual imagery from dreams or free associations. One can obscure the depth and range of themes developed at the representational level. Are there only shallow, repetitive dramas or rich deep ones with a range of emotions?

The next level involves *creating logical bridges between ideas.* Shared meanings are used both to elaborate wishes and feelings and to categorize meanings and solve problems. As logical bridges between ideas are established, various types of reasoning and appreciation of reality emerge, including dealing with conflicts and finding prosocial outcomes, and distinguishing what's pretend from what's believed to be real (Dunn & Kendrick, 1982; Flavell, et al., 1986; Harris, et al., 1991; Harris & Kavanaugh, 1993; Wolf, et al., 1984; Wooley & Wellman, 1990). As children become capable of emotional thinking, they begin to understand relationships between their own and others experiences and feelings. They also illustrate these relationships in their narratives. Emotional thinking also enables children to begin to reason about right and wrong (Buchsbaum & Emde, 1990; Emde & Buchsbaum, 1990;

Harris, 1989; Nelson, 1986; Smetana, 1985; Stewart & Marvin, 1984; Wolf, 1990). As children move into latency and become more concerned with peers, they begin to appreciate emotional complexity such as mixed feelings (Donaldson & Westerman, 1986; Harter & Whitesell, 1989). The child begins to elaborate and eventually differentiate those feelings, thoughts, and events that emanate from within and those that emanate from others. The child begins to differentiate the actions of others from his or her own. This process gradually forms the basis for the differentiation of self representations from the external world, animate and inanimate. It also provides the basis for such crucial personality functions as knowing what is real from unreal, impulse and mood regulation, and the capacity to focus attention and concentrate in order to learn and interact.

The capacity for differentiating internal representations becomes consolidated as object constancy is established (Mahler et al., 1975). As the child moves into the oedipal stage, both reality and fantasy become more complex (Bruner, 1986, 1990; Fivush, 1991; Greenspan & Salmon, 1993; Nelson, K., 1989; Singer & Singer, 1990; Wolf, in press.) In middle childhood, representational capacity becomes reinforced with the child's ability to develop derivative representational systems tied to the original representation and to transform them in accordance with adaptive and defensive goals. This permits greater flexibility in dealing with perceptions, feelings, thoughts, and emerging ideals. Substages for these capacities include representational differentiation, the consolidation of representational capacity, and the capacity for forming limited derivative representational systems and multiple derivative representational systems (structural learning [Greenspan, 1979]). Throughout these stages, but especially in the formation of complex behavior patterns and rituals (Reiss, D., 1989) the elaboration of ideas and in creating bridges between ideas, one observes cultural influences, for example, in the way girls and boys construct aspects of their inner worlds. The now-well-known-findings that in Western cultures men tend to be more assertive and competitive and women more caring and relationship-oriented (Gilligan, 1982) is evident during development in greater early signs of empathy in girls and parents inclinations to talk more to boys about anger and girls about sadness (Zahn-Waxler, et al., 1992).

At this level, the child can make connections between different ideas and feelings ("I am mad because you took my toy") and balance fantasy and reality. An adult can similarly hold logical conversations about wishes and feelings and make connections. ("I feel lonely and needy, and I get helpless when I feel that way. Sometimes I get mad because I can't stand being so vulnerable.")

Shared differentiated meanings involve the communication of ideas to another person and building on the other person's responses, not just having ideas. Some people only communicate their own ideas, never building on the responses of the other person. In both childhood dramas and adult conversations they talk, but do not easily absorb or reply to someone else's ideas and comments. For example, whenever a 4-year-old little girl came home from preschool, she played out scene after scene of being a princess, letting her mother hold her imaginary ermine robe, while her mother's casual questions, such as "What does the princess want me to do next?" and "Who did you play with today?" were ignored. Similarly, a 40-year-old businessman seen in therapy could elaborate at great length about how "No one satisfies me." He was unable to wrench his thoughts away from this theme and would obsessively return to it, regardless of the therapist's comments or questions. Without the ability to form bridges between various feelings states, including his own and someone else's, that patient was incapable of exploring a fuller range of feelings. Other individuals are just the opposite; diligently following instructions, listening to every word, but rarely elaborating their own feelings about events or their understanding of them.

Children operating at the level of creating logical bridges between different islands of symbolic or representational communication do not just negotiate via pretend dramas. They also begin to negotiate the terms of their relationship with the clinician in a more reality-based way. "Can I do this?" or "Can I do that?" the child may say. "What will you do if I kick the ball into the wall?" the child may further inquire. The child may also want to know if he and the clinician can play after the session is over because he enjoys the playroom so much (and seems to yearn for a little extra contact with other people). A child's negotiations about bringing parents into the playroom, wanting either to continue or end the session early, or curiosity about where the clinician lives and what his family is like, clearly indicate a use of symbols or words in a logical interactive way. These logical bridges between one thought and another suggest that this more advanced level of negotiating relationships has been mastered. The adult who shifts between free associations and logical reflection, or who wonders about how two feelings are connected, or who makes such connections, also reveals this level.

The stages of representational elaboration and differentiation can be observed and further assessed as one looks at the way in which individuals organize the content of their communications and deal with anxiety. Thematic development (i.e., the content of the communication) helps one assess the individual's representational level. Look first at the overall organization in terms of the presence or absence of logical links connecting the thematic elements. A certain minimum capacity to organize thinking can be expected with adults. With a child, however, the standards vary according to age, and the organization of themes must be weighed against the age-appropriate standard.

For instance, if an adult reveals tangentiality in thinking and mild loosening of associations, we begin to get a picture of the degree of representational differentiation present. With a child the meaning of such signs depends on age. In a 4-year-old, we might not be surprised by the partial absence of logical links; in a $2^1/_2$- to 3-year-old, we would be even less surprised. In children of 6, 7, and 8, however, we expect a greater capacity to form logical bridges between thematic productions.

Making age-appropriate judgments is not always a straightforward process when assessing children. The following cases will assist not only in understanding children, but also in seeing the level attained in an adult. Many adults can only organize contents at certain childhood levels.

A 9-year-old boy comes into the interview room, makes good eye contact with the therapist, smiles, and asks if there are any games or toys to play with. The clinician asks what he has in mind, and the boy says, "Do you have a basketball? I like to play basketball." The therapist responds empathetically, "Oh," and the child is off and running, telling her that he played basketball and made three baskets last week.

As he talks about playing basketball, his facial expression suddenly begins to look morose. When the therapist wonders aloud about his change from glee and elation to a look of sadness, the child says, "Well, I don't have enough friends to play with." He continues, "You've got a fancy-looking office here," and wonders if the therapist has children with whom she plays basketball. The child next reflects on how often he has to play basketball by himself. Although he has a court near his house, neither his father, brother, nor any other kids will play with him. Upon inquiry about his lack of friends, the boy describes a pattern of superficial relationships with schoolmates. Here we see demonstration of an organized communication in the context of playing basketball. The underlying theme is a desire for greater emotional closeness that is accompanied by difficulty in achieving the intimacy comfortably. The theme is organized in the sense that the elements emerge in a logical manner.

As we continue to follow this scenario we may have some questions about the integrity of this child's organization of thinking. The child next wants to know if the therapist will play basketball with him. When she asks how the child envisions this happening, he gleefully says that they could go out to the schoolyard and play one-on-one.

Immediately following this remark, he asks the therapist, "Can people die of heart attacks?" The therapist wonders aloud why that thought occurred to him, and the child responds, "There was a car accident and people had their arms and legs cut off. Can robbers get into a building and steal?" When the clinician asks for further elaboration, the child focuses on robbers entering a building and stealing things. As the child talks about this, the therapist is left with the impression that the boy is talking about his concern over having something stolen from him.

Here we see an abrupt shift from the interwoven themes of basketball, the wish for closeness, and feelings of loneliness and isolation, to themes of heart attack, physical injury, and things being stolen. A breakdown in thematic organization is signified by the absence of the connecting links that one would expect from a 9-year-old. Whereas the child initially displayed a relatively good capacity for thematic organization, he later showed a breakdown in this capacity. If the child had not experienced this breakdown, transitions concerning other sports, people getting hurt playing sports, and the general issue of physical injury, vulnerability and the issue of being robbed could have been expected. Such an alternative sequence would represent an appropriate series for a 9-year-old. Through an explicit, logical process, he would reach the same endpoint. The fantasy material concerning heart attacks, car accidents, and severed limbs wouldn't suddenly come out of left field, but would instead be linked thematically by logical bridges of thought.

The richness and depth of thematic development also deserve attention. Thematic organization reveals the degree to which a person has an age-appropriate capacity for reality testing and organized thinking or communicating. The elaborateness of thematic productions, on the other hand, should reveal the constrictions (characterological or neurotic) in the range of thought and affect available to the individual. The person who is capable of developing rich, broad, age-appropriate themes is telling the therapist that he or she has access to a rich, broad affective and thematic intrapersonal life. The person whose elaborations are constricted and intermittently become fragmented, superficial, or stereotyped, however, is telling the therapist that his or her intrapersonal life must be kept limited.

Soap operas and melodramas, with their shallow plots and cardboard characters, fail to convey a sense of real-life complexity. By contrast, major works of world literature attain that sense, at least to some extent. Similarly, as an individual's thematic development unfolds in the clinical interview, it may range from being complex and meaningful to being constricted, superficial, and fragmented.

In addition to the complexity of the drama, another aspect of the representational level of the patient relates to how he describes his feelings. To the degree that the patient is able to describe feelings at all, he or she is showing an ability to abstract feeling states. This is a sign of true representational ability, and should be compared to the patient's ability to simply describe such behaviors as, "I went to the store and bought a banana. Then I bought an apple and a pear and ate them all." In this last sentence, the patient is using words, to be sure, but is describing a series of behaviors. This is qualitatively different from the patient's ability to say, "I ate the apple and I felt thrilled. I was happy and delighted with the taste of the apple. It reminded me of the spicy applesauce my mother used to make for me."

The ability to abstract feelings is a true indication of the patient's ability to represent experience. The patient's ability to describe his or her feelings may occur at various levels. Patients who are less developmentally advanced, but who can represent experience, tend to talk in undifferentiated feeling states which have a somatic or physical ring to them: "My body feels tight and tense"; "I'm empty or hollow inside." Global descriptors are also often evident at an early level of representation. "I don't like that"; "My feelings feel bad (or good)." More advanced descriptors are used when the person abstracts into a feeling tone, such as sadness, happiness, anger, rage, despair, or excitement.

In general, prerepresentationally, patients use acting out of behaviors rather than representing them. Or they use descriptions of behaviors or actions rather than their feelings. At the representational level three levels in the adult and older child can be elucidated. One has to do with undifferentiated, somatic-based affect descriptions ("my body feels explosive"; "my belly feels full, to the bursting point"). The second level is characterized by fewer somatically based affects, but the affect statements are usually still global and general and not highly specific or differentiated. For example, the patient says, "That makes me feel good" or "That makes me feel bad (or not so good)." At the third and more advanced level, the patient is using the terms we more frequently associate with affect descriptions and is able to abstract feeling tones such as sadness, happiness, excitement, or pleasure. Here the patient says, "When so-and-so said that, it made me feel happy and excited," or "When what's-his-name didn't return my call, I felt very sad and disappointed." Or "When whoosy-whatsis confronted me in front of the other people, I felt embarrassed and enraged."

If the patient hasn't been coached to use certain words (sometimes as a result of the therapist using those words), the patient's spontaneous choice of affect descriptors may reveal where he is in terms of representational level. Therefore, the clinician readily observes whether the patient can represent experience and where he or she is in terms of the representational continuum of experience. The patient who only uses behavioral descriptions (e.g., "I hit my wife and she hit me and I hit her back") or the patient who only describes body aches and pains, is not showing the capacity for representational elaborations. Nor is the patient who only acts out feelings by breaking things or having temper tantrums and hitting people capable of true representational communication. To be sure, the ability to describe behaviors is at a higher level than the ability to simply put the behaviors into actions.

For the child, we look to see if, for example, she is able to elevate a feeling like anger to the representational mode where she can create scenes of soldiers or animals fighting. Or, if she can use words and say things like, "I'm mad." There is a difference between the prerepresentational organization of anger and the representational organization of anger. Similarly, with dependency, do the dolls hug? Does the child say, "I like you," or "I love you," or "Can I come back?" Or does he deal with dependency only with actual hugs or clinging or even grabbing possessions and wanting to take them home? Again, is the behavioral mode used or has the child advanced to the representational mode in dealing with these basic themes of life? Similarly, does the adult hit or reflect on his feeling of anger? Does he grab or reflect on his feelings of love or neediness? If the representational mode has been reached, what themes can it accommodate and at what level of abstraction—somatic, global, or differentiated? Furthermore, does it accommodate all the themes that the individual is likely to be interested in, or only some of these themes? Is it broad and rich, or narrow and constricted?

Along with more differentiated affect descriptions, one often sees the patient putting together the different representations into meaningful patterns. There are logical bridges between the representations. The patient can form categories and see the connections between them. Consider adults who can observe themselves well enough to reason about their anger and wonder, "Why did I get so angry with my wife? Maybe her comments about my not making enough money really got to me. I do get mad when she tends to undermine or humiliate me." This kind of reasoning between feelings reflects a clear ability for representational differentiation. The ability to self-observe and reflect on one's own inner feelings is an indication of a high level of representational differentiation.

With children, one looks to see if the child's dolls are fighting because they are mad at each other, because one doll took the favorite food of another doll. The adult recognizes that his mother-in-law left in a huff because she was angry at him, because he called her a meddlesome old woman. Here we see two "becauses" linking up the different elements. Does the patient argue with the therapist? "Last week you promised to play checkers with me/make up that extra time you owe me/fill out my insurance forms. You forgot, didn't you?" As the therapist explains that he never made the promise, the patient says, "Remember, halfway through the session, right after you took your telephone call, which made me mad by the way, you made a promise to make it up to me. I felt pleased and anticipated liking you again." The clinician, feeling guilty, says, "Oh yes. I think I remember." Here we see a logical, reality-based individual using words in a highly intentional and organized manner, showing differentiated thinking in a disagreement with the clinician about the activity of the day. Whether it is the interlocking of complex themes or legalistic conversation about the rules governing the therapeutic session,

the representationally differentiated individual will have logical
links connecting his feelings and themes.

Besides looking for logical links, the therapist also looks at
how the patient applies these logical links to a broad range of
themes. Is the person's range broad or narrow? Does she bring
in dependency, but not aggression, or only aggression but not
dependency; curiosity but not dependency and pleasure? Which
particular themes have exposure or access to this highly differentiated representational mode?

One also looks at the person's ability to go even beyond basic
representationally differentiated modes of communication and
mobilize extended representational systems. Can he or she construct a complex logical matrix for fantasy elaborations or reality-
based concerns and see the shadings and gray areas between different themes? For example, the person with extended representational systems will derive from his or her basic concerns themes
that are connected to each other in a logical way. Such individuals
are able to reflect that one can compete with someone and still
be friends with that individual, or that alliances forged out of
necessity can shift when a perceived common danger has passed.
This is a highly complex drama, with shades of gray (competition
and aggression in a framework of collaboration).

Anxiety is often not directly observed, but it can be inferred
from signs of distress or disruption in thematic elaboration. Noting and following the signposts of anxiety can further help reveal
the representational level. It also reveals how the patient may shift
from representational to prerepresentational levels. Most importantly, it tells the therapist about a person's concerns. One of
the best clues to points of anxiety is a sudden disruption in a
developing theme, an ongoing style of relating, or a mannerism
or gesture.

With a child during most play sessions, if the clinician stays
out of the child's way by not overstructuring the situation, some
disruption in activity will be seen when the child comes to an area
that is troubling. You will also observe what the disruption pathway is like for the child in terms of personality structure. Did the

child show disorganized thinking and looseness in communication or lose impulse control, throwing or spilling things, or become clinging and want to be held?

Take, for example, the little girl who plays with mother and father dolls and develops an aggressive theme having the dolls fighting. She then darts to the other side of the room and begins behaving in a disorganized way, throwing things or spilling paint on the floor. You say to the child, "That is not permitted, because one rule of the playroom is that you cannot destroy things." She continues doing it, obviously disorganized and out of control. When she finally is about to splatter paint on your new suit, you have to restrain her. Here you have witnessed a profound disorganization occur.

Some children handle their distress by switching activities but carrying on the same theme in a less frightening mode. The same child who first develops the fighting theme with the mother and father dolls, shifts to drawing after trying other intermediate activities. She creates a sketch with mother and father bears fighting. Here one sees that the child has not given up entirely or become disorganized, and has instead shown an ability to persevere and work in a less frightening mode.

At first the therapist will not know the nature of the anxiety, which may be fear of bodily damage, or of separation, or of some even earlier global anxiety. But the therapist will know when there has been a disruption. When the therapist goes back over his notes and sees the sequence of themes and affects, he will get some hints as to what caused the disruption.

The therapist can learn a great deal by noting the sequence of themes that arise during a child's playroom session or in an adult's therapeutic conversation. These may tell one what the patient's fear centers on (bodily damage, world destruction, losing a sense of self, losing the love of another person, abandonment, for example). A sequence might run as follows: the child plays with the father doll, darts over to the other side of the room and gets a toy gun, frantically shoots it at the dartboard, and then goes back to the doll and pretends to shoot its arm off. Thus the child works a new theme—using the gun for violence—into the old drama. He presents a picture of apprehension and anxiety; the theme is temporarily disrupted, but the child later returns to it. He has armed himself but still comes back into the doll "family." The sequence may suggest that he was concerned with some danger for which he felt a gun would be protective. A likely hypothesis would be that the child is more concerned with bodily harm than with separation or a more global loss. An adult may become less logical, harder to follow, going off at a tangent when talking about aggression or perhaps becoming repetitive when talking about dependency, or evidencing a labile mood when discussing sexuality. These shifts suggest anxiety.

By looking at disruptions in a child's play patterns and in an adult's communication skills from a developmental perspective, the clinician may determine if an individual is anxious. He looks for either a shift from a higher level to a lower one, a shift from a more adaptive pattern to a more maladaptive pattern at a given level, or a sudden narrowing of the thematic or emotional range. A shift from a higher level to a lower level does not always indicate anxiety. Sometimes, for example, in the excitement of play or simply in the relaxation of free expression, people may shift developmental levels in their mode of communication. This shift, however, coupled with such other signs of anxiety as a change in facial expression, a sense of tension, an increase in motor discharge patterns, or an abrupt shift in content, will often indicate that anxiety is disrupting the child's play or the adult's ability to communicate.

We may see a person shifting from a representational differentiated mode to a prerepresentational behavior discharge mode, that is, behaving rather than representing experience (e.g., the child goes from talking about anger to throwing toys around; the adult goes from talking about anger to demanding you let her call you at home). Furthermore, in the prerepresentational behavioral mode (the stage of intentional prerepresentational communication), the individual is disorganized and acting in a somewhat chaotic and even a random manner. We therefore see a shift to an earlier developmental level and to a more maladaptive pattern in that earlier developmental level.

In a more subtle manner, the patient may simply shift from a more differentiated representational mode to a less differentiated representational mode. When this kind of change occurs, we see a shift within a representational mode from a more differentiated, logical expression of meanings, even highly fantasized or pretend meanings, to one where the meanings, while still pretend, take on a more fragmented or less differentiated quality. In other words, the primary process aspects of communication can be viewed in terms of the content, as well as in terms of the structure or organization of the communication. Often, patients who develop fantasy themes will do so with secondary process elaboration. There is an evident organization to their drama. When a shift toward fragmentation occurs, however, that organized quality may be lost and primary process, in both the content and the structure, may become more evident. This is a shift from the differentiated to the less differentiated representational level.

The individual who has a broad range of themes at a gestural or representational level, but then shifts to a narrow range of themes, may also be indicating some signs of anxiety. For example, the person who in his gestures is interacting in a warm and assertive, even empathic way, who then shifts to an impersonal mode or an aggressive or clinging mode, may be showing signs of anxiety, even though he stays within the behavioral mode. He is clearly shifting from a broad-ranging flexible pattern to a more narrow and rigid pattern. The same implication would be drawn if this occurred at the representational level or the representational differentiated level.

Therefore, to discern anxiety, one can systematically examine the patient's communication—via play, verbalizations, gestures, or quality of engagement—and watch for shifts from a higher level to a lower level, shifts from an adaptive mode to a maladaptive mode at that level, or a narrowing of thematic range within a level.

When the patient becomes anxious, it is often the interviewer's tendency to comfort him or her right away. The comforting is usually more subtle than putting an arm around the person and saying, "Now, now, things will get better." For example, after witnessing some acute anxiety with a child, the interviewer may quickly begin structuring the activity by saying, "Why don't we try this." Another common tack is to ask the patient a question that diverts attention from the source of the anxiety to another area. We may say, "You know, you haven't told me about your friends recently. Tell me, how are you getting along with them?"

If patients become disorganized and cannot reorganize without help, the therapist may need to move in a supportive way to help them reorganize their thinking and impulses. One can do this without shifting the focus. In fact one can maintain a focus, not only on what is disorganizing but on the ego's coping capacity. For example, the therapist can say something empathetic, indicating that he understands a patient's experience, but the remark should not focus on what stirred him or her up (e.g., "I can see that you don't like remembering your parents"). The child who has played out or the adult who has recalled such a fight scene, and is already disorganized, may not be able to deal with such a comment at that time. But if one says, "I know kids sometimes want to throw things and pull things," one is focusing on the child's tendency to get out of control rather than on what is frightening him or her. Similarly, commenting on the adult's urge to metaphorically "kick the dog," conveys the same message. By empathizing with their coping or lack of coping, one is staying with them. One is moving in on a sensitive area; one is engaging and talking to the patient who will feel somewhat reassured. Such a course is far more supportive than changing the topic. The patient may subsequently be able to tell the therapist about other instances when he or she was out of control.

SUMMARY OF DEVELOPMENTAL LEVELS

The organizational levels described and discussed above are not difficult to observe, but are often taken for granted. When a child comes into the playroom ready to play or talk, there is often some rapport or emotional relatedness that soon develops between therapist and child. As soon as the therapist opens the door and the child makes eye contact with him or her, or perhaps follows a few facial or arm gestures, indicating where the toys are kept, we have an intentional, preverbal communication system going. Therapist and child are engaged and intentional with each other.

As the child begins complex play, staging mock battles with appropriate sound effects, or making noises and pointing to indicate "Get me that!" more complex intentional communication is occurring. When the child puts feelings into words and elaborates pretend play themes, the level of shared meanings, or *representational elaboration* is reached. The next level will be reached when the child not only elaborates themes, but constructs bridges between domains of experience: "I'm scared when I'm mad." The ability to categorize experience indicates emotional thinking (i.e., *representational differentiation*). A symbolic "me" and a symbolic "you" are now in evidence: "I always get so scared of everything." Most importantly, the capacity for categorizing experience helps an individual elaborate feelings and build on another's communications. The patient can have a logical two-way dialogue and tell the difference between fantasy and reality.

Individuals may have clear compromises in their attainment of these organizational levels, such as the patient who comes in to therapy and can only partially engage. When anxious or frightened, this person typically disengages and becomes aloof or withdrawn. Not infrequently, he also gets disorganized and cannot even gesture purposefully and intentionally. His gestures and speech both become disjointed. His capacity for representational elaboration is limited to either disorganized emotional communications or organized descriptions of impersonal events. There is little capacity for balancing subjective elaborations and an appreciation of reality. The person then uses words in a fragmented way, tends to be concrete and impersonal in his descriptions of the world, gesturally signals in a disorganized and chaotic way, and, while capable of engaging with others, easily disengages and becomes aloof.

As the clinician looks at the tendency to use verbal descriptions of behavior, and organize these descriptions rather than put them into acting out behaviors,[1] he further looks to see if the person can represent global, somatically based affects, can represent simple, general affects or more differentiated, abstracted affects. He also looks for the ability to make connections between different affective domains and categories of feelings and behaviors, and the ability for self-observation and reasoning about one's emotional inclinations and tendencies. One can further look at this last category in terms of the ability to observe oneself and reason in different dimensions: in the here-and-now, which is the easiest in a historical sense, to anticipate the future, and to do all the above as part of an active exploration, and obviously, finally to integrate them.

Also, as a person is involved in more differentiated self-observing capacities, he or she can apply this to different types of relationship patterns. Therefore, in terms of comprehending relationships, various levels of representational differentiation can also be noticed. An early level has to do with being able to explore feelings that occur in dyadic relationship patterns, a later one has to do with triangular relationship patterns. A still later level involves group patterns that have many different dyads and triads as well as the relationship between all the members of the group and the group as a whole. Finally, signposts of higher levels of organization can be seen in the ability to move into explorations of feelings having to do with stable internal values and principles, and being able to look at an emerging sense of self against these aspirations and principles.

DEVELOPMENTAL DIAGNOSTIC FORMULATIONS

The developmental structuralist model also lends itself to abstracting categories reflecting overall developmental status from these highly detailed observations of a person's organizational

---

[1]The acting out behaviors are usually characteristic of the person who hasn't yet mastered the complex interchange of behavioral intentions and expectations and who is somewhat arrested between the simple gestural and complex gestural stages.

level and experiential orientation. These categories of functioning may be viewed on a spectrum from maladaptive to adaptive organizational patterns. At one extreme, for example, there are defects in organizational integrity. A determination of a personality defect would be made when there is a severe impairment in the expected level of "core" personality or ego functions, such as reality testing, mood regulation, or impulse modulation.

Another level of maladaptive development may be summarized under the category of constrictions in the flexibility of the personality. In this category there are no major defects in organizational capacities, but the range of experience that can be organized is restricted. For example, a 5-year-old child may have the capacity to test reality, but only in the context of a very impersonal, shallow relationship and with affects of low intensity or affects restricted to the aggressive or negativistic domains. An adult may be able to *talk* about "loving" or "lonely" feelings but *acts out* on hostile ones. The stage upon which an individual's ego develops may not have cracks running through it, or be vulnerable to crumbling, but can still be narrow and therefore accommodate only a very restricted drama.

Constrictions may reveal themselves, ranging from severe ones based on compromises made early in life to minor ones stemming from later compromises. For example, there is a difference between persons who can maintain the integrity of their organizational capacities (the capacity for reality testing) only by totally walling off all human intimacy, and those who have minor limitations in experiencing assertive feelings with authority figures but otherwise function in an adaptive, age-appropriate way. The latter individual simply may not be able to compete fully, whereas the former realizes only a shadow of his or her human potential.

A third, very subtle type of constrictive impairment is called an encapsulated disorder, based on the person's inability to maintain experiential continuity over time in narrowly delineated areas of experience, only minimally compromising the overall age-appropriate flexibility of personality. A patient recently seen in therapy aptly illustrates this sort of constrictive impairment. This lawyer, whose feisty courtroom style intimidated many fellow members of the bar, seemed curiously subdued and flat when in the presence of one particular judge. The balding, bespeckled judge reminded the lawyer of his own father, and the lawyer was extremely frustrated by his inability to act more assertively in the other man's presence.

Once the therapist makes a judgment about the person's level and type of organizational defect and/or constriction, the type of drama being played out can then be categorized. Dramas, some of which are quite painful, may unfold in age-appropriate experiential organizations; less painful dramas may play themselves out in very constricted or even defective organizations.

A few comments should be made about the relationship of the developmental approach to the traditional DSM-III-R (APA, 1987) or DSM-IV (APA, 1994) psychiatric approach to diagnosis. As we have seen, the clinical judgments that can be deduced from the interviewing approach advanced here refer to the integrity or developmental level of basic ego functioning and flexibility, and the nature of concerns or conflicts. These judgments parallel the traditional categories of psychiatric disability: psychosis and borderline conditions (age-inappropriate level of basic ego functioning); character disorders (major limitations in flexibility in critical sectors of the personality); neurotic disturbances (encapsulated limitations in flexibility around certain areas of experience); and developmental conflicts (the difficulties experienced by the person with a flexible structure as he or she works through particular developmental tasks). The focus on selected disorders such as depression does not compete with the developmental approach presented here. In fact, the developmental approach helps the clinician determine just what type of depression a person might be evidencing. Is the person having difficulty with regulating mood to such a degree that such basic personality functions as reality-testing are interfered with? Or is the person experiencing depressive thoughts in an age-appropriate personality structure, where the depressive affect simply constricts the range of experience?

In addition, a variety of learning and behavioral disorders based on neurological and/or physiological malfunctions can be understood in the context of our approach to specific ego functions. These types of disorders, however, are also connected with the psychological aspects of ego functioning. For example, less than full attainment of an expected developmental level may show itself in a global impairment in the capacity to focus concentration; a very circumscribed defect in an ego function, however, may result in only a mild impairment in the same capacity.

Considering the current preference for phenomenology, in contrast to what have been termed "inferred" dynamic states, it is also of interest that our diagnostic approach, although based on dynamic concepts, does not require "a belief" in internal states. Even when referring to individuals with encapsulated neurotic disorders—those who cannot process experience in a specified narrow domain—the diagnosis can be documented *phenomenologically* just as one can document phenomenologically that a person has hallucinations and delusions. The former process is simply a subtler observation requiring, as it were, the high-power lens of the clinician's microscope.

For example, observing whether a patient can represent concerns with dependency and assertiveness allows the therapist to compare him to another asymptomatic patient who nonetheless shows no evidence of symbolizing a range of emotional patterns. Instead, either he simply behaves out his concerns, or quietly inhibits them. The second asymptomatic person may appear healthy, but if he is observed developmentally, we would see limitations.

As noted, the clinical judgments that can be derived from our approach are easily translated into the traditional or classical psychiatric concepts. What is being emphasized here, however, is that there may be an advantage to using a developmental framework because its concepts are not limited in explanatory value; they do have implications for pathogenesis and treatment of disorders. In addition, the developmental approach suggested here has implications for both the level of adaptation and the level of psychopathology or limitation. Moreover, it has the unique virtue of enabling the interviewer to intuit the way a patient experiences his own strengths and weaknesses, and thus to plan appropriate psychotherapeutic approaches.

In practice, the developmental approach presented here may be used together with traditional diagnostic classification schemes. A three-column approach may be used; with diagnoses based on symptoms and personality traits in one column, etiologically based diagnoses in another, and the developmental approach to diagnosis in still another. The developmental approach suggests how a person "organizes" his experience and is in a sense the connection or "experiential pathway" between etiological circumstances and various manifest symptoms.

THEORETICAL BACKGROUND AND MODEL FOR ASSESSING DEVELOPMENTAL LEVELS

The following section will describe how this developmental model was initially formulated. The developmental–structuralist approach to assessing developmental levels builds on a historical foundation for identifying disturbances in the early years of life. Constitutional and maturational patterns which influenced the formation of early relationship patterns were already noted in the early 1900s, with descriptions of "babies of nervous inheritance who exhaust their mothers" (Cameron, 1919) and infants with "excessive nerve activity and a functionally immature" nervous system (Rachford, 1905).

Winnicott, who as a pediatrician in the 1930s began describing the environment's role in early relationship problems (1931), was followed in the 1940s by the well-known studies describing the severe developmental disturbances of infants brought up in institutions or in other situations of emotional deprivation (Lowery, 1940; Hunt, 1941; Bakwin, 1942; Spitz, 1945; Bowlby, 1951). Spitz's films resulted in the passage of laws in the United States prohibiting institutional care for infants (they were instead to be placed in foster care).

Both the role of individual differences in the infant based on constitutional–maturational and early interactional patterns, and the "nervous" infants described by Rachford in 1905 and Cameron in 1919, again became a focus of inquiry, as evidenced by the observations of Burlingham and Freud (1942); Bergman and Escalona's descriptions of infants with "unusual sensitivities" (1949); Murphy and Moriarty's description of patterns of vulnerability (1976); Thomas, Chess, and Birch's temperament studies (1968); Cravioto and Delicardie's descriptions of the role of infant individual differences in malnutrition (1973); and the impressive emerging empirical literature on infants (Sander, 1962; Lipsitt, 1966; Gerwirtz, 1961; Reingold, 1966; Brazelton et al., 1974; Stern, 1974a,b; Emde et al., 1976). More integrated approaches to understanding disturbances in infancy have been emphasized in descriptions of selected disorders and in clinical case studies (Fraiberg, 1979; Provence, 1983; Greenspan et al., 1987). Building on the historical foundations, we conducted clinical and observational studies of infants, young children, and their families (Greenspan et al., 1987; Greenspan, 1992).

At each stage of emotional development, we observed that pathologic as well as adaptive formations are possible. These we postulated could be considered as relative compromises in the range, depth, stability, and personal uniqueness of the experiential organization consolidated at each stage.

It should also be pointed out that, through analyses of videotaped infant–caregiver interactions (Greenspan and Lieberman, 1980), these patterns associated with each stage evidence temporal stability and can be reliably rated and new raters trained and kept at high levels of reliability (Hofheimer, Strauss, Poisson, and Greenspan, 1981; Hofheimer, Lieberman, Strauss, and Greenspan, 1983; Poisson, Lieberman, and Greenspan, 1981). Empirical support for this framework and its related infant–caregiver interaction rating scale (GLOS) is emerging through its application in discriminating clinical disorders and clinical and nonclinical groups (Dougherty, 1991).

This framework has also served as a basis for formulating the stages in early ego development (Greenspan, 1989) (see Tables

TABLE A1

Developmental–Structural Delineation of Stage-Specific Capacities[a]

Stage	Illustrative Adaptive Capacities	Illustrative Maladaptive (Pathologic) Capacities	Adaptive Caregiver	Maladaptive Caregiver
Homeostasis (0–3 months)	Internal regulation (harmony) and balanced interest in the world	Unregulated (e.g., hyperexcitable) or withdrawn (apathetic) behavior	Invested, dedicated, protective, comforting, predictable, engaging, and interesting	Unavailable, chaotic, dangerous, abusive; hypo- or hyperstimulating; dull
Attachment (2–7 months)	Rich, deep, multisensory emotional investment in animate world (especially with primary caregivers)	Total lack of or nonaffective, shallow, impersonal involvement (e.g., autistic patterns) in animate world	In love and woos infant to "fall in love"; effective, multimodality, pleasurable involvement	Emotionally distant, aloof, and/or impersonal (highly ambivalent)
Somatopsychological differentiation (3–10 months)	Flexible, wide-ranging, affective, multisystem contingent (reciprocal) interactions (especially with primary caregivers)	Behavior and affects random and/or chaotic or narrow, rigid, and stereotyped	Reads and responds contingently to infant's communications with a range of senses and affects	Ignores or misreads (e.g., projects) infant's communications (e.g., is overly intrusive, preoccupied, or depressed)
Behavioral organization, initiative, and internalization (9–24 months)	Complex, organized, assertive, innovative, integrated behavioral and emotional patterns	Fragmented, stereotyped, and polarized behavior and emotions (e.g., withdrawn, compliant, hyperaggressive, or disorganized behavior)	Admiring of toddler's initiative and autonomy, yet available, tolerant, and firm; follows toddler's lead and helps him organize diverse behavioral and affective elements	Overly intrusive, controlling; fragmented, fearful (especially of toddler's autonomy); abruptly and prematurely "separates"

TABLE A1 (continued)

Stage	Illustrative Adaptive Capacities	Illustrative Maladaptive (Pathologic) Capacities	Adaptive Caregiver	Maladaptive Caregiver
Representational capacity, differentiation, and consolidation ($1\frac{1}{2}$–4 years)	Formation and elaboration of internal representations (imagery); organization and differentiation of imagery pertaining to self and nonself, emergence of cognitive insight; stabilization of mood and gradual emergence of basic personality functions	No representational (symbolic) elaboration; behavior and affect concrete, shallow, and polarized; sense of self and "other" fragmented, undifferentiated, or narrow and rigid; reality testing, impulse regulation, mood stabilization compromised or vulnerable (e.g., borderline psychotic and severe character problems)	Emotionally available to phase-appropriate regressions and dependency needs; reads, responds to, and encourages symbolic elaboration across emotional and behavioral domains (e.g., love, pleasure, assertion) while fostering gradual reality orientation and internalization of limits	Fears or denies phase-appropriate needs; engages child only in concrete (nonsymbolic) modes generally or in certain realms (e.g., around pleasure) and/or misreads or responds noncontingently or unrealistically to emerging communications (i.e., undermines reality orientation); overly permissive or punitive
Capacity for limited extended representational systems and multiple extended representational systems (middle childhood through adolescence)	Enhanced and eventually optimal flexibility to conserve and transform complex and organized representations of experience in the context of expanded relationship pattens and phase-expected developmental tasks	Derivative representational capacities limited or defective, as are latency and adolescent relationships and coping capacities	Supports more complex, phase- and age-appropriate experiential and interpersonal development (i.e., into triangular and posttriangular patterns)	Conflicted over child's age-appropriate propensities (e.g., competitiveness, pleasure orientation, growing competence, assertiveness, and self-sufficiency); becomes aloof or maintains symbiotic tie; withdraws from or overengages in competitive or pleasurable strivings

"This chart is an illustrative summary and should not imply a level of precision or finality to this conceptualization beyond a relative approximation of important events in early development.
From: Greenspan (1981), Psychopathology and Adaptation in Infancy and Early Childhood: Principles of Clinical Diagnosis and Preventive Intervention. *Clinical Infant Reports*, No. 1. New York: International Universities Press.

TABLE A2

Emotional Milestones, Family and Service System Patterns

Stage-Specific Tasks and Capacities	Infant Maladaptive	Family Maladaptive	Service System Maladaptive	Service System Adaptive
Homeostasis (0–3 months) (regulation and interest in the world)	Unregulated (e.g., hyperexcitable) or withdrawn (apathetic) behavior	Unavailable, chaotic, dangerous, abusive; hypo- or hyperstimulating; dull	Critical and punitive	Supply support structure and extra nurturing
Attachment (2–7 months) (Falling in love)	Total lack of or nonaffective, shallow, impersonal involvement in animate world	Emotionally distant, aloof, and/or impersonal (highly ambivalent)	Angry and inpatient covered by mask of impersonal professionalism	Woo caregiver into a relationship, point out pleasurable aspects of baby
Somatopsychological differentiation (3–10 months) (Purposeful communication)	Behavior and affects random and/or chaotic or narrow, rigid, and stereotyped	Ignores or misreads (e.g., projects) infant's communications (e.g., is overly intrusive, preoccupied, or depressed)	Vacillates between overcontrol and avoidance (of intrusive caregiver) or overprotectiveness (of depressed caregiver)	Combine empathy and limit setting with sensitivity to reading subtle emotional signals, help caregiver read infant's signals
Behavioral organization, initiative, and internalization (9–24 months) (A complex sense of self)	Fragmented, stereotyped and polarized behavior and emotions (e.g., withdrawn, compliant, hyperaggressive, or disorganized behavior)	Overly intrusive, controlling; fragmented, fearful (especially of toddler's autonomy); abruptly and prematurely "separates"	Premature separation from or rejection of family rationalized by notion: "they are okay now"	Support family self-sufficiency, but with admiration and greater rather than less involvement

TABLE A2 (continued)

Stage-Specific Tasks and Capacities	Infant Maladaptive	Family Maladaptive	Service System Maladaptive	Service System Adaptive
Representational capacity, differentiation and consolidation (1¹/₂–4 years) (creating ideas and emotional thinking)	No representational (symbolic) elaboration; behavior and affect concrete, shallow, and polarized; sense of self and "other" fragmented, undifferentiated or narrow and rigid; reality testing, impulse regulation, mood stabilization compromised or vulnerable (e.g., borderline psychotic and severe character problems)	Fears or denies phase-appropriate needs; engages child only in concrete (nonsymbolic) modes generally or in certain realms (e.g., around pleasure) and/or misreads or responds noncontingently or unrealistically to emerging communications (i.e., undermines reality orientation); overly permissive or punitive	Infantalizing and concrete with family providing instructions, but no explanations or real sense of partnership	Create atmosphere for working partnership; learn from caregivers and help them conceptualize their own approaches

TABLE A3
Stages of Ego Development

Self-Object Relationship	Ego Organization, Differentiation & Integration	Ego Functions
Homeostasis—0–3 months		
Somatic preintentional world self-object	Lack of differentiation between physical world, self, and object worlds	Global reactivity, sensory-affective processing and regulation or sensory hyper- or hyporeactivity and disregulation
Attachment—2–7 months		
Intentional part self-object	Relative lack of differentiation of self and object. Differentiation of physical world and human object world	Part-object seeking, drive-affect elaboration or drive-affect dampening or liability, object withdrawal, rejection, or avoidance
Somatopsychological Differentiation—3–10 months		
Differentiated behavioral part self-object	Differentiation of aspects (part) of self and object in terms of drive-affect patterns and behavior	Part self-object differentiated interactions in initiation of, and reciprocal response to, a range of drive-affect domains (e.g., pleasure, dependency, assertiveness, aggression), means-ends relationship between drive-affect patterns and part-object or self-object patterns
		or
		Undifferentiated self-object interactions, selective drive-affect intensification and inhibition, constrictions of range of intrapsychic experience and regression to stages of withdrawal, avoidance, or rejection (with preference for physical world), object concretization

TABLE A3 (continued)

Self-Object Relationship	Ego Organization, Differentiation & Integration	Ego Functions
Behavioral Organization—Emergence of a Complex Self, 10–18 months		
Functional (conceptual) integrated & differentiated self-object	Integration of drive-affect behavioral patterns into relative "whole" functional self-objects	Organized whole (in a functional behavioral sense), self-object interactions characterized by interactive chains, mobility in space (i.e., distal communication modes), functional (conceptual) abstractions of self-object properties, integration of drive-affect polarities (e.g., shift from splitting to greater integration)
		or
		Self-object fragmentation, self-object proximal urgency, preconceptual concretization, polarization (e.g., negative, aggressive, dependent, or avoidant, self-object pattern, regressive state, including withdrawal, avoidance, rejection, somatic dedifferentiation, object concretization)
Representational Capacity and Elaboration—1$^1/_2$–3 years		
Representational self-object Elaboration 1$^1/_2$–3 yr	Elevation of functional behavioral self-object patterns to multisensory drive-affect invested symbols of intrapersonal and interactive experience (mental representations). Interactive experience (mental representations)	Representational self-objects characterized by mobility in time and space; e.g., creation of object representation in absence of object drive-affect elaboration (themes ranging from dependency and pleasure to assertiveness and aggression now elaborated in symbolic form evidenced in pretend play and functional language), gradual drive affect stability (self-object representations slowly survive intensification of drive-affect dispositions)
		or
		Behavioral concretization (lack of representation), representational constriction (only one or another emotional theme, drive-affect liability, regressive states including withdrawal, avoidance, rejection, and behavioral dedifferentiation and object concretization).

TABLE A3 (continued)

Self-Object Relationship	Ego Organization, Differentiation & Integration	Ego Functions
Representational Differentiation—2–4 years		
Differentiated, integrated representational self-object	Abstractions of self-object representations and drive-affect dispositions into higher level representational organization. Differentiated along dimensions of self-other, time, and space	Representational differentiation characterized by genetic (early somatic and behavioral patterns organized by emerging mental representations) and dynamic integration (current drive-affect proclivities organized by emerging mental representations), intermicrostructural integration (i.e., affect, impulse, and thought). Basic structure formation (self-object representations abstracted into *stable* patterns performing ongoing ego functions of reality testing, impulse control, mood stabilization, etc.). Self and object identity formation (i.e., a sense of self and object which begins to integrate past, current and changing aspects of fantasy and reality) or Representational fragmentation (either genetic, dynamic, or both). Lack of, or unstable basic structures (e.g., reality testing, impulse control, etc.), defective, polarized or constricted (global or encapsulated) self-object identity formation

From: Greenspan (1981).

A1, A2, and A3, which summarize the developmental structuralist framework, its relationship to the service system, and the stages in early ego development).

The formulated developmental stages do not exist in a vacuum. During development they are influenced by both constitutional and maturational factors, as well as environmental factors. Each stage, in fact, can be understood as resulting from specific caregiver–child interaction patterns, in which the child's behavior is influenced by his constitutional and maturational patterns and the caregiver is influenced by the family–cultural patterns.

The developmental model can be visualized with the infant's constitutional–maturational patterns on one side and the infant's environment, including caregivers, family, community, and culture, on the other side. Both of these sets of factors operate through the infant–caregiver relationship which can be pictured in the middle. These factors and the infant–caregiver relationship, in turn, contribute to the organization of experience at each of six different developmental levels, which may be pictured just beneath the infant–caregiver relationship.

Each developmental level involves different tasks or goals. The relative effect of the constitutional–maturational, environmental, or interactive variables will, therefore, depend on and can only be understood in the context of the developmental level they relate to. The influencing variables, therefore, are best understood, not as they might be traditionally, as general influences on development or behavior, but as distinct and different influences on the six distinct developmental and experiential levels. For example, as a child is negotiating the formation of a relationship (engaging), his mother's tendency to be very intellectual and prefer talking over holding may make it relatively harder for him to become deeply engaged in emotional terms. If constitutionally he has slightly lower than average motor tone and is hyposensitive with regard to touch and sound, his mother's intellectual and slightly aloof style may be doubly difficult for him, as neither she nor the child is able to take the initiative in engaging the other.

Let us assume, however, that he more or less negotiates this early phase of development (Grandmother, who lives with him as well as his father are very "wooing" caregivers). At age 3, when the developmental phase and task is different, he may have an easier time, even though his mother hasn't changed. His intellectual mother is highly creative and enjoys pretend play as well as give-and-take logical discussions. No longer anxious about her son's dependency needs, she is more relaxed and quite available for play and chit-chat. The task is no longer simply one of forming a relationship but of learning to represent (or symbolize) experience and form categories and connections between these units of experience. Mother's verbal style is now quite helpful to him, especially given his need for lots of verbal interaction. In other words, the same caregiving pattern can have a very different impact, depending on the tasks of the particular developmental level. Each developmental level of experience is, therefore, a reference point for the factors that influence development. There have been very useful intervention models that focus on specific influences such as the caregiver's feelings, fantasies or support system, or on certain phases of early development (Brazelton et al., 1977; Fraiberg, 1980; Provence, 1983; Provence and Naylor, 1983).

What is potentially unique about this particular clinical and research model (Greenspan et al., 1987; Greenspan, 1989, 1992) is the ability it gives us to look at the back-and-forth influence of highly specific and verifiable, constitutional–maturational factors on interactive and family patterns and vice versa, in relationship to specific developmental processes (and to relate these processes to later developmental and psychopathologic disorders). The goal of this model is to look at all the major influences throughout the different stages of development. Genetic, biological, or environmental influences do not influence behavior directly, but influence either the child's or the caregiver's behavior, which, in turn, influences their interaction, which eventually leads to adaptive or maladaptive organizations at each developmental level. This model, therefore, provides flexibility in the ways in which influences can be exerted on the organization of the personality.

References

Aber, J. L., & Baker, A. J. (1990), Security of attachment in toddlerhood: Modifying assessment procedures for joint clinical and research purposes. In: *Attachment in the Preschool Years,* ed. M. T. Greenberg, D. Cicchetti, & E. M. Cummings. Chicago: University of Chicago Press, pp. 427–463.

Ainsworth, M. D. S., Bell, S. M., & Stayton, D. J. (1974), Infant–mother attachment and social development: "Socialisation" as a product of reciprocal responsiveness to signals. In: *The Integration of a Child into a Social World,* ed. M. P. M. Richards. Cambridge, U.K.: Cambridge University Press, pp. 99–135.

———— Blehar, M. C., Waters, E., & Wall, S. (1978), *Patterns of Attachment: A Psychological Study of the Strange Situation.* Hillsdale, NJ: Erlbaum.

Allison, G. H. (1994), On the homogenization of psychoanalysis and psychoanalytic psychotherapy: A review of some issues. *J. Amer. Psychoanal. Assn.,* 42:341–363.

American Psychiatric Association (1987), *Diagnostic and Statistical Manual of Mental Disorders,* 3rd ed. rev. (DSM-III-R). Washington, DC: American Psychiatric Press.

—— (1994), *Diagnostic and Statistical Manual of Mental Disorders* 4th ed. (DSM-IV). Washington, DC: American Psychiatric Press.

Arend, R., Gove, F., & Sroufe, L. A. (1979), Continuity of individual adaptation from infancy to kindergarten: A predictive study of ego-resiliency and curiosity in pre-schoolers. *Child Develop.*, 50:950–959.

Ayers, A. J. (1964), Tactile functions: Their relation to hyperactive and perceptual motor behavior. *Amer. J. Occupat. Ther.*, 18:6–11.

Bakwin, H. (1942), Loneliness in infants. *Amer. J. Dis. Child.*, 63:30–42.

Bates, J. E., Maslin, L. A., & Frankel, K. A. (1985), Attachment, security, mother-child interaction, and temperament as predictors of problem behavior ratings at age three years. *Monographs of the Society for Research in Child Development*, 50(1-2, Serial No. 209).

Bell, S. (1970), The development of the concept of object as related to infant–mother attachment. *Child Develop.*, 41:219–311.

Belsky, J., Rovine, M., & Taylor, D. G. (1984), The Pennsylvania infant and family development project, III: The origins of individual differences in infant–mother attachment: Maternal and infant contributions. *Child Develop.*, 55:718–728.

Bergman, P., & Escalona, S. (1949), Unusual sensitivities in very young children. *The Psychoanalytic Study of the Child*, 3 & 4:333–352. New York: International Universities Press.

Berlyne, D. E. (1960), *Conflict, Arousal and Curiosity*. New York: McGraw-Hill.

Bowlby, J. (1951), *Maternal Care and Mental Health*, Monogr. Series No. 2. Geneva: World Health Organization (WHO).

—— (1969), *Attachment and Loss*, Vol. 1. New York: Basic Books.

—— (1973), *Attachment and Loss*, Vol. 2. New York: Basic Books.

—— (1979), *Attachment and Loss*, Vol. 3. New York: Basic Books.

Brazelton, T. B., Koslowski, B., & Main, N. (1974), The origins of reciprocity: The early mother–infant interaction. In: *The Effect of the Infant on Its Caregiver*, ed. M. Lewis & L. Rosenblum. New York: John Wiley, pp. 49–76.

——— Tronick, E., Lechtig, A., Lasky, R. E., & Klein, R. E. (1977), The behavior of nutritionally deprived Guatemalan infants. *Develop. Med. Child. Neurol.*, 19:364–367.

——— Als, H. (1979), Four early stages in the development of mother–infant interaction. *The Psychoanalytic Study of the Child*, 34:349–369.

——— Cramer, B. G. (1990), *The earliest relationship*. Reading, MA: Addison-Wesley.

Bretherton, I., & Beeghly, M. (1982), Talking about inner states: The acquisition of an explicit theory of mind. *Develop. Psychol.*, 18:906–921.

Bruner, J. (1982), *Child's Talk: Learning to Use Language*. New York: Norton.

——— (1986), *Actual Minds, Possible Worlds*. Cambridge, MA: Harvard University Press.

——— (1990), *Acts of Meaning*. Cambridge, MA: Harvard University Press.

Buchsbaum, H. K., & Emde, R. N. (1990), Play narratives in 36-month-old children. *The Psychoanalytic Study of the Child*, 45:129–155.

Burlingham, D., & Freud, A. (1942), *Young Children in Wartime*. London: Allen & Unwin.

Butterworth, G., & Jarrett, N. (1980), *The Geometry of Preverbal Communication*. Paper presented to the Annual Conference of the Developmental Psychology section of the British Psychological Society. September. *Language, Communication, and Understanding*. Edinburgh.

Cameron, H. S. (1919), *The Nervous Child*. London: Oxford Medical Publications.

Campos, J. J., Barrett, K. C., Lamb, M. E., Goldsmith, H. H., & Stenberg, C. (1983), Socioemotional development. In: *Handbook of Child Psychology*, Vol. II, ed. M. M. Haith & J. J. Campos. New York: Wiley, pp. 783–915.

Caron, A. J., & Caron, R. F. (1982), Cognitive development in early infancy. In: *Review of Human Development*, ed. T. Fields, A. Huston, H. Quay, L. Troll, & G. Finley. New York: John Wiley, pp. 107–147.

Cassidy, J. (1990), Theoretical and methodological considerations in the study of attachment and self in young children. In: *Attachment in the Preschool Years*, ed. M. T. Greenberg, D. Cicchetti, & E. M. Cummings. Chicago: Chicago University Press, pp. 87–120.

——— & Marvin, R. (1988), with the Attachment Working Group of the John D. and Catherine T. MacArthur Network on the Transition from Infancy to Early Childhood. A system for coding the organization of attachment behavior in 3 or 4 year old children. Paper presented at the International Conference on Infant Studies. Washington, DC.

Charlesworth, W. R. (1969), The role of surprise in cognitive development. In: *Studies in Cognitive Development: Essays in Honor of Jean Piaget*, ed. E. Elkind & J. H. Flavell. London: Oxford University Press, pp. 257–314.

Clyman, R. B. (1991), The procedural organization of emotions: A contribution from cognitive science to the psychoanalytic theory of therapeutic action. *J. Amer. Psychoanal. Assn.*, 39(Suppl.):349–382.

Cravioto, J., & Delicardie, E. (1973), Environmental correlates of severe clinical malnutrition and language development survivors from kwashiorkor or marasmus. In: *Nutrition, the Nervous System and Behavior*. Washington, DC: PAHO Scientific Publication No. 251.

Darwin, C. (1872), *The Expression of Emotions in Man and Animals*. London: Murray (Republished by University of Chicago Press, 1965).

Deci, E. (1977), *Intrinsic Motivation*. New York: Plenum.

DeGangi, G., DiPietro, J. A., Greenspan, S. I., & Porges, S. W. (1991), Psychophysiological characteristics of the regulatory disordered infant. *Infant Behav. Develop.*, 14:37–50.

——— Greenspan, S. I. (1988), The development of sensory functioning in infants. *J. Phys. & Occupat. Ther. in Ped.*, 3.

——— ——— (1989a), The assessment of sensory functioning in infants. *J. Phys. & Occupat. Ther. in Ped.*, 9:21–33.

——— ——— (1989b), *Test of Sensory Functions in Infants*. Los Angeles: Western Psychology Services.

—— Porges, S. W., Sickel, R., & Greenspan, S. I. (1993), Four-year follow-up of a sample of regulatory disordered infants. *Infant Mental Health J.*, 14:330–343.

De Jonghe, F., Rijnierse, P., & Janssen, R. (1994), Psychoanalytic supportive psychotherapy. *J. Amer. Psychoanal. Assn.*, 42:421–446.

Donaldson, S., & Westerman, M. (1986), Development of children's understanding of ambivalence and causal theories of emotions. *Develop. Psychol.*, 22:655–662.

Dore, J. (1989), Monologue as reenvoicement of dialogue. In: *Narratives from the Crib*, ed. K. Nelson. Cambridge, MA: Harvard University Press, pp. 27–73.

Dougherty, S. C. (1991), *An Investigation of Depression in Infancy and Early Childhood from a Transactional, Developmental Structuralist Perspective*. Doctoral dissertation. Saybrook Institute, San Francisco, CA.

Doussard-Roosevelt, J. A., Walker, P. S., Portales, A. L., Greenspan, S. I., & Porges, S. W. (1990), Vagal tone and the fussy infant: Atypical vagal reactivity in the difficult infant. *Infant Behav. & Develop.*, 13:352 (abstract).

Dunn, J. (1988), *The Beginnings of Social Understanding*. Cambridge, MA: Harvard University Press.

—— Bretherton, I., & Munn, P. (1987), Conversations about feelings states between mothers and their young children. In: *Symbolic Play: The Development of Social Understanding*, ed. I. Bretherton. New York: Academic Press.

—— Kendrick, C. (1982), *Siblings*. Cambridge, MA: Harvard University Press.

Easterbrooks, M. A., & Goldberg, W. A. (1990), Security of toddler-parent attachment: Relation to children's sociopersonality functioning during kindergarten. In: *Attachment in the Preschool Years*, ed. M. T. Greenberg, D. Cicchetti, & E. M. Cummings. Chicago: University of Chicago Press, pp. 221–245.

Egeland, B. & Farber, E. A. (1984), Infant–mother attachment: Factors related to its development and change over time. *Child Develop.*, 52:857–865.

Ekman, P. (1972), Universals and cultural differences in facial expressions of emotion. In: *Nebraska Symposium on Motivation*. Lincoln: University of Nebraska Press.

—— Freisen, W., & Ellsworth, P. (1972), *Emotion in the Human Face*. New York: Pergamon Press (Guidelines for Research and an Integration of Findings).

Emde, R. N. (1983), The prerepresentational self and its affective core. *The Psychoanalytic Study of the Child*, 38:165–192. New Haven, CT: Yale University Press.

—— Biringen, Z., Clyman, R. B., & Oppenheim, D. (1991), The moral self of infancy: Affective core and procedural knowledge. *Develop. Rev.*, 11:251–270.

—— & Buchsbaum, H. (1990), "Didn't you hear my mommy?": Autonomy with connectedness in moral self-emergence. In: *The Self in Transition: Infancy to Childhood*, ed. D. Cicchetti & M. Beeghly, Chicago: University of Chicago Press, pp. 35–60.

—— Gaensbauer, T. J., & Harmon, R. J. (1976), Emotional Expression in Infancy: A Biobehavioral Study. *Psychological Issues*, Monogr. No. 37. New York: International Universities Press.

—— Johnson, W. F., & Easterbrooks, M. A. (1988), The do's and don'ts of early moral development. Psychoanalytic tradition and current research. In: *The Emergence of Morality*, ed. J. Kagan & S. Lamb. Chicago: University of Chicago Press, pp. 245–277.

Erdelyi, M. H. (1985), *Psychoanalysis: Freud's Cognitive Psychology*. New York: W. H. Freeman.

Erikson, E. H. (1937), Configurations in play: Clinical notes. *Psychoanal. Quart.*, 6:139–214.

—— (1950), *Childhood and Society*, rev. ed. New York: W. W. Norton, 1963.

—— (1959), Identity and the Life Cycle. *Psychological Issues*, Monogr. No. 1. New York: International Universities Press.

Escalona, S. (1968), *The Roots of Individuality*. Chicago: Aldine.

Fein, G. G. (1975), A transformational analysis of pretending. *Develop. Psychol.*, 11:291–296.

———— & Apfel, N. (1979), Some preliminary observations on knowing and pretending. In: *Symbolic Functioning in Childhood*, ed. N. Smith & M. Franklin. Hillsdale, NJ: Erlbaum.

Feinman, S., & Lewis, M. (1983), Social referencing at ten months: A second-order effect on infant's responses to strangers. *Child Develop.*, 54(4):878–887.

Fenson, L., Kagan, J., Kearsely, R. B., & Zelazo, P. R. (1976), The developmental progression of manipulative play in the first two years. *Child Develop.*, 47:232–35.

———— & Ramsay, D. (1980), Decentration and integration of play in the second year of life. *Child Develop.*, 51:171–178.

Fish, B., & Hagin, R. (1973), Visual-motor disorders in infants at risk for schizophrenia. *Arch. Gen. Psychiat.*, 28:900–904.

———— Shapiro, T., Halpern, F., & Wile, R. (1965), The prediction of schizophrenia in infancy: III. A ten-year follow-up report of neurological and psychological development. *Amer. J. Psychiat.*, 121:768–775.

Fivush, R. (1991), Gender and emotion in mother–child conversations about the past. *Journal of Narrative and Life History*, 1. No. 4, 325–41.

Flavell, J. H., Green, F. L., & Flavell, E. R. (1986), Development of knowledge about the appearance-reality distinction. With commentaries by M. W. Watson and J. C. Campione. *Monographs of the Society for Research in Child Development*, 51(1, Serial No. 212).

Fraiberg, S. (1979), Treatment modalities in an infant mental health program. Presentation at the training institute on "Clinical Approaches to Infants and Their Families" sponsored by the National Center for Clinical Infant Programs, Washington, DC.

———— (1980), *Clinical Studies in Infant Mental Health: The First Year of Life*. New York: Basic Books.

Freud, A. (1965), Normality and pathology in childhood. In: *The Writings*, Vol. 6. New York: International Universities Press.

Freud, S. (1900), The Interpretation of Dreams. *Standard Edition*, 4 & 5. London: Hogarth Press, 1953.

—— (1905), Three essays on the theory of sexuality. *Standard Edition*, 7:135–242. London: Hogarth Press, 1953.

—— (1911), Formulations on the two principles of mental functioning. *Standard Edition*, 12:218–226. London: Hogarth Press, 1958.

Gewirtz, J. L. (1961), A learning analysis of the effects of normal stimulation, privation and deprivation on the acquisition of social motivation and attachment. In: *Determinants of Infant Behavior*, Vol. 1, ed. B. M. Foss. London: Methuen, pp. 28–35.

—— (1965), The course of infant smiling in four child rearing environments in Israel. In: *Determinants of Infant Behavior*, Vol. 1, ed. B. M. Foss. London: Methuen, pp. 205–220.

—— (1969), Levels of conceptual analysis in environment-infant interaction research. *Merrill-Palmer Quart.*, 15:9–47.

Gill, M. M. (1984), Psychoanalysis and psychotherapy: A revision. *Internat. Rev. Psycho-Anal.*, 11:161–179.

Gilligan, C. (1982), *In a Different Voice: Psychological Theory and Women's Development*. Cambridge, MA: Harvard University Press.

Goldberg, W. A., & Easterbrooks, M. A. (1984), Toddler development in the family. Impact of father involvement and parenting characteristics. *Develop. Psychol.*, 55:740–752.

Gouin-Decarie, T. (1965), *Intelligence and Affectivity in Early Childhood: An Experimental Study of Jean Piaget's Object Concept and Object Relations*. New York: International Universities Press.

Greenspan, S. I. (1975), A Consideration of Some Learning Variables in the Context of Psychoanalytic Theory: Toward a Psychoanalytic Learning Perspective. *Psychological Issues*, Monogr. No. 33. New York: International Universities Press.

—— (1979), Intelligence and Adaptation: An Integration of Psychoanalytic and Piagetian Developmental Psychology. *Psychological Issues*, Monogr. 47/48. New York: International Universities Press.

—— (1981), Psychopathology and Adaptation in Infancy and Early Childhood: Principles of Clinical Diagnosis and Preventive Intervention. *Clinical Infant Reports*, No. 1. New York: International Universities Press.

—— (1985), Comprehensive clinical approaches to developmental and emotional disorders in infants and young children: Emerging perspectives. In: *Maternal and Child Health Technical Information Series*. Rockville, MD: U.S. Department of Health and Human Services.

—— (1989), *The Development of the Ego: Implications for Personality Theory, Psychopathology, and the Psychotherapeutic Process*. Madison, CT: International Universities Press.

—— (1992), *Infancy and Early Childhood: The Practice of Clinical Assessment and Intervention with Emotional and Developmental Challenges*. Madison, CT: International Universities Press.

—— Lieberman, A. F. (1980), Infants, mothers, and their interaction: A qualitative clinical approach to developmental assessment. In: *The Course of Life: Psychoanalytic Contributions Toward Understanding Personality Development*, Vol. I, *Infancy and Early Childhood*, ed. S. I. Greenspan & G. H. Pollock. DHHS Pub. (ADM) 80-786. Washington, DC: U.S. Government Printing Office.

—— Lourie, R. S. (1981), Developmental structuralist approach to the classification of adaptive and pathologic personality organizations: Application to infancy and early childhood. *Amer. J. Psychiat.*, 138:6–12.

—— & Salmon, J. (1993), *Playground Politics: Understanding the Emotional Life of Your School-Age Child*. Reading, MA: Addison-Wesley.

—— Scharfstein, S. (1981), The efficacy of psychotherapy: Asking the right questions. *Arch. Gen. Psychiatry*, 38:1213–1219.

—— Wieder, S. (1987), Dimensions and levels of the therapeutic process. In: Infants in Multirisk Families: Case Studies in Preventive Intervention. *Clinical Infant Reports*, No. 3. Madison, CT: International Universities Press.

—— —— Lieberman, A., Nover, R., Lourie, R., & Robinson, M. (1987), Infants in Multirisk Families: Case Studies in Preventive Intervention. *Clinical Infant Reports*, No. 3. Madison, CT: International Universities Press.

Grossmann, K., Grossmann, K. E., Spangler, G., Suess, G., & Unzner, L. (1985), Maternal sensitivity and newborns' orientation responses as related to quality of attachment in Northern Germany. *Monographs of the Society for Research in Child Development*, 50(1-2, Serial No. 209).

Harlow, H. F. (1953), Motivation as a factor in the acquisition of new responses. *Nebraska Symposium on Motivation*, I, 24–29.

Harris, P. L. (1989), *Children and Emotion*. Oxford: Basil Blackwell.

────── Brown, E., Marriott, C., Whittall, S., & Harmer, S. (1991), Monsters, ghosts, and witches: Testing the limits of the fantasy-reality distinction in young children. *British Journal of Develop. Psychol.*, 9:105–123.

────── & Kavanaugh, R. (1993), Young Children's Understanding of Pretense. *Monographs of the Society for Research in Child Development*. 58(1, Serial No. 231).

Harter, S., & Whitesell, N. (1989), Developmental changes in children's emotion concepts. In: *Children's Understanding of Emotion*, ed. C. Saarni & P. L. Harris. New York: Cambridge University Press.

Hartley, D. (1993), Assessing psychological levels. In: *Psychodynamic Treatment Research: A Handbook for Clinical Practice*, ed. N. Miller, L. Luborsky, J. Barber, & J. Docherty. New York: Basic Books, pp. 152–176.

Hartmann, H. (1939), *Ego Psychology and the Problem of Adaptation*. New York: International Universities Press.

────── Kris, E., & Loewenstein, R. (1946), Comments on the formation of psychic structure. *The Psychoanalytic Study of the Child*, 2:11–38. New York: International Universities Press.

Hendrick, I. (1939), *Facts and Theories of Psychoanalysis* (2nd edition, original work published in 1934). New York: Knopf.

Hofheimer, J. A., Straus, M. E., Poisson, S. S., & Greenspan, S. I. (1981), The reliability, validity and generalizability of assessments of transactions between infants and their caregivers: A multi-center design. Working Paper, Clinical Infant Development Program, National Institute of Mental Health.

────── Lieberman, A. F., Strauss, M. E., & Greenspan, S. I. (1983), Short-term temporal stability of mother–infant interactions in the first year of life. Paper presented at the 93rd Meeting of the American Psychological Association, Los Angeles, CA.

Horowitz, M. J., Ed. (1991), *Person Schemas and Maladaptive Interpersonal Patterns.* Chicago: University of Chicago Press.

Hunt, J. McV. (1941), Infants in an orphanage. *J. Abnorm. & Soc. Psychol.*, 36:338.

———— (1965), Intrinsic motivation and its role in psychological development. In: *Nebraska Symposium on Motivation,* ed. D. Levine. Lincoln: University of Nebraska Press.

Inhelder, B., Lezine, I., Sinclair, H., & Stambak, M. (1972), Le debut de la function symbolique. *Archives de Psychologie* (as cited in Rubin, K. H., Fein, G. G., & Vandenberg, B., 1983). In: *Handbook of Child Psychology,* 4th ed., Vol. 4, ed. E. M. Hetherington & P. H. Mussen. New York: Wiley, pp. 187–243.

Izard, C. E., (1971), *The Face of Emotion.* New York: Meredith & Appleton-Century-Crofts.

———— (1978), On the development of emotions and emotion-cognition relationships in infancy. In: *The Development of Affect,* ed. M. Lewis & L. Rosenblum. New York: Plenum Press.

Jackson, D. D. (1960), *Etiology of Schizophrenia.* New York: Basic Books.

Kagan, J. (1981), *The Second Year: The Emergence of Self-Awareness.* Cambridge, MA: Harvard University Press.

Kaye, K. (1982), *The Mental and Social Life of Babies: How Parents Create Persons.* Chicago: University of Chicago Press.

Kernberg, O. F. (1975), *Borderline Conditions and Pathological Narcissism.* New York: Jason Aronson.

Kihlstrom, J. F. (1987), The cognitive unconscious. *Science,* 237:1445–1452.

Kimmert, M. D., Campos, J. J., Sorce, F. J., Emde, R. N., & Svejda, M. J. (1983), Social referencing: Emotional expressions as behavior regulators. In: *Emotion: Theory, Research and Experience:* Vol. 2. *Emotions in Early Development,* ed. R. Plutchik & H. Kellerman. Orlando: Academic Press, pp. 57–86.

Klaus, M., & Kennell, J. (1976), *Maternal-Infant Bonding: The Impact of Early Separation or Loss on Family Development.* St. Louis, MO: C. V. Mosby.

Kleinman, A. (1986), *Social Origins of Distress and Disease.* New Haven: Yale University Press.

Kohut, H. (1971), *The Analysis of Self: A Systematic Approach to the Psychoanalytic Treatment of Narcissistic Personality Disorders.* New York: International Universities Press.

Kraus, R., & Glucksberg, S. (1969), The development of communication: Competence as a function of age. *Child Develop.*, 40:255–266.

Lewis, M., & Feiring, M. (1987), Infant, maternal and mother–infant interaction behavior and subsequent attachment. *Child Develop.*, 60:831–837.

Lichtenberg, J., Lachmann, F., & Fosshage, J. (1992), *Self and Motivational Systems: Toward a Theory of Technique.* Hillsdale, NJ: Analytic Press.

Lidz, T. (1973), *Origin and Treatment of Schizophrenic Disorders.* New York: Basic Books.

Lipsitt, L. (1966), Learning processes of newborns. *Merrill-Palmer Quart.*, 12:45–71.

Lowe, M. (1975), Trends in the development of representational play: An observational study. *J. Child Psychol. & Psychiatry*, 16:33–47.

Lowery, L. G. (1940), Personality disorders and early institutional care. *Amer. J. Orthopsychiatry*, 10:546–555.

Luborsky, L., & Crits-Christoph, P. (1990), *Understanding Transference—The CCRT Method.* New York: Basic Books.

Mahler, M. S., Pine, F., & Bergman, A. (1975), *The Psychological Birth of the Human Infant.* New York: Basic Books.

Main, M., Kaplan, N., & Cassidy, J. (1985), Security in infancy, childhood, & adulthood: A move to the level of representation. *Monographs of the Society for Research in Child Development.* 50(1-2, Serial No. 209).

Markus, H., & Kitayama, S. (1990), Culture and the self: Implications for cognition, emotion, and motivation. Unpublished paper.

Marvin, R., & Stewart, R. B. (1991), A family systems framework for the study of attachment. In: *Attachment in the Preschool*

Years, ed. M. T. Greenberg, D. Cicchetti, & E. M. Cummings. Chicago: Chicago University Press, pp. 51–87.

Maslin-Cole, C., & Spieker, S. J. (1990), Attachment as a basis of independent motivation: A view from risk and nonrisk samples. In: *Attachment in the Preschool Years*, ed. M. T. Greenberg, D. Cicchetti, & E. M. Cummings. Chicago: Chicago University Press, pp. 245–272.

Matas, L., Arend, R. A., & Sroufe, L. A. (1978), Continuity of adaptation in the second year: The relationship between quality of attachment and later competence. *Child Develop.*, 49:547–556.

McCune-Nicholich, L. (1977), Beyond sensorimotor intelligence: Measurement of symbolic sensitivity through analysis of pretend play. *Merrill-Palmer Quart.*, 23:89–99.

Meltzoff, A. N. (1985), The roots of social and cognitive development: Models of man's original nature. In: *Social Perception in Infants*, ed. T. M. Field & N. A. Fox. Norwood: Ablex.

———— & Moore, K. (1977), Imitation of facial and manual gestures by human neonates. *Science*, 198:75–78.

Miller, N. (1993), Diagnosis of personality disorders. In: *Psychodynamic Treatment Research: A Handbook for Clinical Practice*, ed. N. Miller, L. Luborsky, J. Barber, & J. Docherty. New York: Basic Books, pp. 127–151.

Miyake, K., Chen, S., & Campos, J. J. (1985), Infant temperament, mother's mode of interaction, and attachment in Japan: An interim report. In: Growing points in attachment theory and research. *Monographs of the Society for Research in Child Development*, 50(1-2, Serial No. 209).

Murphy, L., & Moriarty, A. (1976), *Vulnerability Coping and Growth*. New Haven, CT: Yale University Press.

Nelson, K. (1973), Structure and strategy in learning to talk. *Monographs of the Society for Research in Child Development*, 38(1-2, Serial No. 149).

———— (1986), *Even Knowledge: Structure and Function in Development*. Hillsdale, NJ: Erlbaum.

———— & Gruendel, J. M. (1981), Generalized even representations: Basic building blocks of cognitive development. In:

Advances in Developmental Psychology, Vol. 1, ed. A. Brown & M. Lamb. Hillsdale, NJ: Erlbaum.

Nemiah, J. C. (1977), *Alexithymia: Theories and Models.* Proceedings of the Eleventh European Conference on Psychosomatic Research. Basel, Switzerland: Karger.

Osofsky, J. D., & Eberhart-Wright, A. (1988), Affective exchanges between high risk mothers and infants. *Int. J. Psychoanal.*, 69:221–232.

Papousek, H. (1981), The common in the uncommon child. In: *The Uncommon Child*, ed. M. Lewis & L. Rosenblum. New York: Plenum, pp. 317–328.

——— Papousek, M. (1979), Early ontogeny of human social interaction: Its biological roots and social dimensions. In: *Human Ethology: Claims and Limits of a New Discipline*, ed. K. Foppa, W. Lepenies, & D. Ploog. New York: Cambridge University Press, pp. 456–489.

Pastor, D. (1981), The quality of mother–infant attachment and its relationship to toddlers' initial sociability with peers. *Develop. Psychol.*, 23:326–335.

Pederson, D. R., Moran, G., Sitko, C., Campbell, K., Ghesquire, K., & Acton, H. (1990), Maternal sensitivity and the security of infant–mother attachment: A Q-sort study. *Child Develop.*, 61:1974–1983.

Peller, L. (1954), Libidinal phases, ego development, and play. *The Psychoanalytic Study of the Child*, 9:178–198. New York: International Universities Press.

Perry, J. C. (1993), Defenses. In: *Psychodynamic Treatment Research: A Handbook for Clinical Practice*, ed. N. Miller, L. Luborsky, J. Barber, & J. Docherty. New York: Basic Books, pp. 274–327.

Piaget, J. (1962), The stages of the intellectual development of the child. In: *Childhood Psychopathology*, ed. S. Harrison & J. McDermott. New York: International Universities Press.

Pipp, S., Fischer, K. W., & Jennings, S. (1987), Acquisition of self- and-mother knowledge in infancy. *Develop. Psychol.*, 47:86–96.

Poisson, S., Lieberman, A., & Greenspan, S. I. (1981), *Training Manual for the Greenspan-Lieberman Observation System (GLOS)*.

Typescript. Rockville, MD: The Reginald Lourie Center for Infants and Children.

Portales, A. W., Porges, S. W., & Greenspan, S. I. (1990), Parenthood and the difficult child. *Infant Behav. & Develop.*, 13:573 (abstract).

Provence, S. (1983), *Infants and Parents: Clinical Case Reports*, No. 2. New York: International Universities Press.

———— Naylor, A. (1983), *Working with Disadvantaged Parents and Their Children: Scientific and Practical Issues*. New Haven, CT: Yale University Press.

Rachford, B. K. (1905), *Neurotic Disorders of Childhood*. New York: E. B. Treat.

Radke-Yarrow, M., Zahn-Waxler, C., & Chapman, M. (1983), Children's prosocial dispositions and behavior. In: *Handbook of Child Psychology*, 4th ed., Vol. 4, ed. E. M. Hetherington & P. H. Mussen. New York: Wiley, pp. 469–545.

Rapaport, D. (1959), The structure of psychoanalytic theory: A systematizing attempt. *Psychological Issues*, Monogr. 6. New York: International Universities Press, 1960.

Reber, Arthur S. (1993), *Implicit Learning and Tacit Knowledge*. New York: Oxford University Press.

Reiss, D. (1989), The represented and practicing family: Contrasting visions of family continuity. In: *Relationship Disturbances in Early Childhood—A Developmental Approach*, ed. A. J. Sameroff & R. N. Emde. New York: Basic Books, pp. 191–220.

Rheingold, H. (1966), The development of social behavior in the human infant. *Monographs of the Society for Research in Child Development*, 31:1–28. Chicago: Society for Research in Child Development.

Rubin, K. H., Fein, G. G., & Vandenberg, B. (1983), In: *Handbook of Child Psychology*, 4th ed., Vol. 4, ed. E. M. Hetherington & P. H. Mussen. New York: Wiley, pp. 136–148.

Sander, L. (1962), Issues in early mother–child interaction. *J. Amer. Acad. Child Psychiatry*, 1:141–166.

Scaife, M., & Bruner, J. S. (1975), The capacity for joint visual attention in the infant. *Nature*, 253:265–266.

Schank, R. C., & Abelson, R. P. (1977), *Scripts, Plans, Goals and Understanding*. Hillsdale, NJ: Erlbaum.

Schweder, R., Mahapatra, M., & Miller, J. (1987), Cultural and moral development. In: *The Emergence of Morality in Young Children,* ed. J. Kagan & S. Lamb. Chicago: University of Chicago Press, pp. 1–90.

Shore, M., & Massimo, J. (1991), Contributions of an innovative psychoanalytic therapeutic program with adolescent delinquents to developmental psychology. *The Course of Life,* Vol. IV: *Adolescence,* ed. S. Greenspan & G. Pollock. Madison, CT: International Universities Press, pp. 333–356.

Sinclair, H. (1970), The transition from sensorimotor to symbolic activity. *Interchange,* 1:119–126.

Singer, D. G., & Singer, J. L. (1990), *The House of Make-Believe: Children's Play and Developing Imagination.* Cambridge, MA: Harvard University Press.

Smetana, J. (1985), Preschool children's conceptions of transgressions: Effects of varying moral and conventional domain-related attributes. *Develop. Psychol.,* 21:18–29.

Spitz, R. A. (1945), Hospitalism: An inquiry into the genesis of psychiatric conditions in early childhood. *The Psychoanalytic Study of the Child,* 1:53–74. New York: International Universities Press.

—— (1965), *The First Year of Life: A Psychoanalytic Study of Normal and Deviant Development of Object Relations.* New York: International Universities Press.

—— (1965), The evolution of dialogue. In: *Drive, Affects, Behavior,* Vol. 2, ed. M. Schur. New York: International Universities Press, pp. 171–190.

Sroufe, L. A. (1983), Infant–caregiver attachment and patterns of adaptation in preschool: The roots of maladaptation and competence. In: *Minnesota Symposium in Child Psychology,* Vol. 16, ed. M. Perlmutter. Hillsdale, NJ: Erlbaum, pp. 41–83.

—— Fox, N. E., & Pancake, V. (1983), Attachment and dependency in developmental perspective. *Child Develop.,* 54:1615–1627.

—— & Waters, E. (1977), Attachment as an organizational construct. *Child Develop.,* 48:1184–1199.

———— ———— Matas, L. (1974), Contextual determinants of infant affective response. In: *The Origins of Fear*, ed. M. Lewis & L. Rosenblum. New York: John Wiley.

Stern, D. N. (1974a), Mother and infant at play: The dyadic interaction involving facial, vocal and gaze behaviors. In: *The Effect of the Infant on Its Caregiver*, ed. M. Lewis & L. Rosenblum. New York: John Wiley.

———— (1974b), The goal and structure of mother–infant play. *J. Amer. Acad. Child Psychiatry*, 13:402–421.

———— (1977), *The First Relationship: Mother and Infant.* Cambridge, MA: Harvard University Press.

———— (1985), *The Interpersonal World of the Infant: A View from Psychoanalysis and Developmental Psychology.* New York: Basic Books.

Stewart, R. B., & Marvin, R. S. (1984), Sibling relations: The role of conceptual perspective-taking in the ontogeny of sibling caregiving. *Child Develop.*, 55:1322–1332.

Tennes, K., Emde, R., Kisley, A., & Metcalf, D. (1972), The stimulus barrier in early infancy: An exploration of some formulations of John Benjamin. In: *Psychoanalysis and Contemporary Science*, Vol. 1, ed. R. Hold & E. Peterfreund. New York: Macmillan, pp. 206–234.

Thomas, A., Chess, S., & Birch, H. (1968), *Temperament and Behavior Disorders in Children.* New York: New York University Press.

Thomkins, S. (1963), *Affect, Imagery, Consciousness*, Vol. 1. New York: Springer.

Trevarthen, C. (1979), Communication and cooperation in early infancy: A description of primary intersubjectivity. In: *Before Speech: The Beginning of Interpersonal Communication*, ed. M. Bullowa. Cambridge, England: Cambridge University Press, pp. 321–347.

Tronick, E. (1980), The primacy of social skills in infancy. In: *Exceptional Infant*, Vol. 4, ed. D. B. Sawin, R. C. Hawkins, L. O. Walker, & J. H. Penticuff. New York: Brunner/Mazel, pp. 144–158.

Vitiello, B., Alexander, J. R., Stoff, D. M., Behar, D., & Denckla, M. B. (1989), Reliability of subtle (soft) neurological signs in children. *J. Amer. Acad. Child & Adol. Psychiatry*, 28:749–753.

Waelder, R. (1933), The psychoanalytic theory of play. *Psychoanal. Quart.*, 2:208–224.

Waters, E., Wippman, J., & Sroufe, L. A. (1979), Attachment, positive affect, and competence in the peer group: Two studies in construct validation. *Child Develop.*, 50:821–829.

Weil, A. (1970), The basic core. *The Psychoanalytic Study of the Child*, 25:442–460. New York: International Universities Press.

Weiss, J., Sampson, H., & Mt. Zion Psychotherapy Research Group (1986), *The Psychoanalytic Process: Theory, Clinical Observations and Empirical Research*. New York: Guilford Press.

Werner, H., & Kaplan, B. (1963), *Symbol Formation*. New York: John Wiley.

White, R. W. (1963), Ego and reality on psychoanalytic theory. In: *Psychological Issues*, Monogr. 11. New York: International Universities Press.

Winnicott, D. W. (1931), *Clinical Notes on Disorders of Childhood*. London: Heinemann.

——— (1965), Ego distortion in terms of true and false self. *The Maturational Processes and the Facilitating Environment*. New York: International Universities Press; London: Hogarth Press.

Wooley, J. D., & Wellman, H. M. (1990), Young children's understanding of realities, nonrealities, and appearances. *Child Develop.*, 61(4):946–961.

Wolf, D. (1990), Being of several minds. In: *The Self in Transition: Infancy to Childhood*, ed. D. Cicchetti & M. Beeghly. Chicago: University of Chicago Press, pp. 183–213.

——— (In Press), Narrative worlds: The acts of forming and attending to meaning. In *Affective Processes*, ed. D. Brown. Psychoanalytic Press.

——— Rygh, J., & Altshuler, J. (1984), Agency and experience: Actions and states in play narratives. In: *Symbolic Play*, ed. I. Bretherton. Orlando, FL: Academic Press, pp. 195–217.

Wynne, L., Matthysse, S., & Cromwell, R. (1978), *The Nature of Schizophrenia: New Approaches to Research and Treatment*. New York: John Wiley.

Zahn-Waxler, C., & Radke-Yarrow, M. (1982). The development of altruism: Alternative research strategies. In: *The Development of Prosocial Behavior,* ed. N. Eisenberg. New York: Academic Press.

——— Robinson, J. D., & Emde, R. N. (1992), The development of empathy in twins. *Develop. Psychol.,* 28:1038–47.

Name Index

Abelson, R. P., 396
Aber, J. L., 396
Acton, H., 391
Ainsworth, M. D. S., 391, 393
Alexander, J. R., 116
Allison, G. H., 38
Als, H., 392
Altshuler, J., 397
Apfel, N., 396
Arend, R., 396
Ayers, A. J., 72, 106

Baker, A. J., 396
Bakwin, H., 416
Barrett, K. C., 392
Bates, J. E., 391
Beeghly, M., 396
Behar, D., 116
Bell, S. M., 391, 393, 395
Belsky, J., 391
Bergman, A., 46, 47, 137, 319, 385, 392, 393, 398

Bergman, P., 417
Berlyne, D. E., 388
Birch, H., 417
Biringen, Z., 36
Blehar, M. C., 393
Bowlby, J., 272, 278, 392, 393, 416
Brazelton, T. B., 139–140, 390, 392, 417, 426
Bretherton, I., 396
Brown, E., 397
Bruner, J. S., 391, 392, 398
Buchsbaum, H. K., 397
Burlingham, D., 417
Butterworth, G., 391

Cameron, H. S., 416
Campbell, K., 391
Campos, J. J., 391, 392
Caron, A. J., 124
Caron, R. F., 124
Cassidy, J., 396
Chapman, M., 393

Charlesworth, W. R., 392
Chen, S., 391
Chess, S., 417
Clyman, R. B., 36
Cramer, B. G., 392
Cravioto, J., 417
Crits-Christoph, P., 51
Cromwell, R., 119

Darwin, C., 392
Deci, E., 388
DeGangi, G., 73, 88, 117, 388
deJonghe, F., 38
Delicardie, E., 417
Denckla, M. B., 116
DiGangi, G., 33n
DiPietro, J. A., 88, 117
Donaldson, S., 398
Dore, J., 396
Dougherty, S. C., 417
Doussard-Roosevelt, J. A., 88
Dunn, J., 393, 396, 397

Easterbrooks, M. A., 393, 396
Eberhart-Wright, A., 392
Egeland, B., 391, 396
Ekman, P., 390, 392
Ellsworth, P., 392
Emde, R. N., 36, 47, 390, 392, 393, 399, 417
Erdelyi, M. H., 36
Erikson, E., 4, 46, 385, 396
Escalona, S., 72, 390, 417

Farber, E. A., 391, 396
Fein, G. G., 396
Feinman, S., 392
Feiring, M., 391
Fenson, L., 395, 396
Fischer, K. W., 396
Fish, B., 72
Fivush, R., 398
Flavell, E. R., 397

Flavell, J. H., 397
Fosshage, J., 47
Fox, N. E., 396
Fraiberg, S., 47, 417, 426
Frankel, K. A., 391
Freisen, W., 392
Freud, A., 4, 46, 385
Freud, S., 4, 24, 27, 45–46, 169–170, 319, 371, 390, 417

Gaensbauer, T. J., 390, 417
Gewirtz, J. L., 388, 417
Ghesquire, K., 391
Gill, M. M., 51, 356
Gilligan, C., 398–399
Glucksberg, S., 396
Goldberg, W. A., 396
Goldsmith, H. H., 392
Gouin-Decarie, T., 395, 396
Gove, F., 396
Green, F. L., 397
Greenspan, S. I., 4, 14, 18, 19, 27, 33, 36, 37, 40, 48, 69, 72, 73, 88, 105, 117, 118, 157, 332, 374, 385–386, 387, 388, 390, 398, 417, 418–419t, 420–424t, 426
Grossmann, K., 391
Grossmann, K. E., 391
Gruendal, J. M., 396

Hagin, R., 72
Halpern, F., 72
Harlow, H. F., 388
Harmer, S., 397
Harmon, R. J., 390, 417
Harris, P. L., 397, 398
Harter, S., 398
Hartley, D., 51
Hartmann, H., 27, 47, 141, 314, 390
Hendrick, I., 388
Hofheimer, J. A., 417
Horowitz, M. J., 36, 51
Hunt, J. McV., 388, 416

Inhelder, B., 396
Izard, C. E., 390, 392

Jackson, D. D., 119
Janssen, R., 38
Jarrett, N., 391
Jennings, S., 396
Johnson, W. F., 393

Kagan, J., 393, 396
Kaplan, B., 393
Kaplan, N., 396
Kavanaugh, R., 397
Kaye, K., 392
Kearsely, R. B., 396
Kendrick, C., 397
Kennell, J., 388
Kernberg, O., 46, 47, 337
Kihlstrom, J. F., 36
Kimmert, M. D., 392
Kisley, A., 392
Kitayama, S., 392
Klaus, M., 388
Klein, R. E., 139–140, 426
Kleinman, A., 392
Kohut, H., 4, 46–47, 337, 356
Koslowski, B., 390, 392, 417
Kraus, R., 396
Kris, E., 47, 141, 314

Lachmann, F., 47
Lamb, M. E., 392
Lasky, R. E., 139–140, 426
Lechtig, A., 139–140, 426
Lewis, M., 391, 392
Lezine, I., 396
Lichtenberg, J., 47
Lidz, T., 119
Lieberman, A., 72, 386, 417, 426
Lipsitt, L., 388, 417
Loewenstein, R., 47, 141, 314
Lourie, R. S., 72, 385–386, 417, 426
Lowe, M., 396

Lowery, L. G., 416
Luborsky, L., 51

Mahapatra, M., 392
Mahler, M. S., 4, 46, 47, 59, 137, 319, 385, 392, 393, 398
Main, M., 396
Main, N., 390, 392, 417
Markus, H., 392
Marriott, C., 397
Marvin, R. S., 396, 398
Maslin, L. A., 391
Maslin-Cole, C., 396
Massimo, J., 156
Matas, L., 390, 396
Matthysse, S., 119
McCune-Nicholich, L., 396
Meltzoff, A. N., 388, 390
Metcalf, D., 392
Miller, J., 392
Miller, N., 51
Miyake, K., 391
Moore, K., 388
Moran, G., 391
Moriarty, A., 390, 417
Munn, P., 396
Murphy, L., 390, 417

Naylor, A., 426
Nelson, K., 396, 398
Nemiah, J. C., 59
Nover, R., 72, 386, 417, 426

Oppenheim, D., 36
Osofsky, J. D., 392

Pancake, V., 396
Papousek, H., 36, 390
Papousek, M., 36, 390
Pastor, D., 396
Pederson, D. R., 391
Peller, L., 396
Perry, J. C., 51

Piaget, J., 4, 320–321, 385, 392, 393, 395
Pine, F., 46, 47, 137, 319, 385, 393, 398
Pipp, S., 396
Poisson, S. S., 417
Porges, S. W., 73, 88, 117
Portales, A. L., 88
Provence, S., 417, 426

Rachford, B. K., 416, 417
Radke-Yarrow, M., 393
Ramsay, D., 395
Rapaport, D., 169–170
Reber, A., 36, 37
Reingold, H., 417
Reiss, D., 398
Rijnierse, P., 38
Robine, M., 391
Robinson, J. D., 399
Robinson, M., 72, 386, 417, 426
Rubin, K. H., 396
Rygh, J., 397

Salmon, J., 398
Sampson, H., 51
Sander, L., 388, 390, 417
Scaife, M., 391
Schank, R. C., 396
Scharfstein, S., 14
Schweder, R., 392
Shapiro, T., 72
Shore, M., 156
Sickel, R., 73, 117
Sinclair, H., 396
Singer, D. G., 398
Singer, J. L., 398
Sitko, C., 391
Smetana, J., 398
Sorce, F. J., 392
Spangler, G., 391
Spieker, S. J., 396
Spitz, R. A., 47, 280, 392, 416
Sroufe, L. A., 390, 393, 396
Stambak, M., 396

Stayton, D. J., 391, 393
Stern, D. N., 47, 390, 392, 417
Sternberg, C., 392
Stewart, R. B., 396, 398
Stoff, D. M., 116
Strauss, M. E., 417
Suess, G., 391
Svejda, M. J., 392

Taylor, D. G., 391
Tennes, K., 392
Thomas, A., 417
Thomkins, S., 390
Trevarthen, C., 392
Tronick, E., 139–140, 392, 426

Unzner, L., 391

Vandenberg, B., 396
Vitiello, B., 116

Waelder, R., 396
Walker, P. S., 88
Wall, S., 393
Waters, E., 390, 393, 396
Weil, A., 72
Weiss, J., 51
Wellman, H. M., 397
Werner, H., 393
Westerman, M., 398
White, R. W., 388
Whitesell, N., 398
Whittall, S., 397
Wieder, S., 72, 157, 386
Wile, R., 72
Winnicott, D. W., 392, 416
Wippman, J., 396
Wolf, D., 397–398
Wooley, J. D., 397
Wynne, L., 119

Zahn-Waxler, C., 393, 399
Zelazo, P. R., 396

Subject Index

Abandonment, feelings of, 149
Abstracting capacity
    affective experience in, 21–22
    difficulty with, 124–128
Abusive environment, 280
Acting out, 218–219, 403–404
    avoiding, 223
    unsuccessful gestural communication, 221–222
Adaptation, interference with, 7
Adolescents, representational differentiation in, 332–333
Affective descriptors, 256
Affective disorders, 123–128
    clinical example of, 128–133
    hypothesis on, 118–123
Affective experience
    developmental growth and, 42–43
    in ego capacities, 23–28
Affective-thematic area, avoidance of, 323
Affects. *See also* Emotions; Feelings
    ability to communication, 393–394

absence of, 302–304
abstracted, 229–232, 233, 259–261, 403–404
advanced expressions of, 229–231
boundary-defining, 161–187
capacity for representational elaboration of, 225–251
concrete, 379
constrictions in, 232–233
describing, 403–405
difficulty modulating, 347–348
in ego development and intelligence, 19–23
flat, 198
forming connections with representations, 314
global use of, 227
here-and-now, 356
hierarchy of, 230*t*
inability to appreciate, 338
inability to represent, 303–306
intensity of, 215–216, 291–293, 325

451

isolation of, 286
overload of, 166–168
representation of, 245–246
representational capacity and, 290, 291–293
self and other-defining, 189–224
somatic based, 228
somatically based, 258–259
steps to representing, 233
Aggression, 94–95
   conflicts over, 304–306
   engagement problems and, 150–153
Ambivalence, 304
   at representational level, 324
Analytically oriented psychotherapy, 39
Anger, expression of, 192
Antisocial individual, 338–339
   engagement of, 155–159
Anxiety
   communication of, 403–410
   ego in dealing with, 324–326
   at representational level, 324
Assertiveness, 17–19
Athletic activities, 108
At-risk infants, regulatory disturbances in, 72–73
Attachment stage, 418t
Attention deficit disorder (ADD), 95–96
   therapeutic strategies for, 96–104
Attentional capacity, 86
Attentional problems, 95–104
Attitudes, fixed, 216–224, 301–312
Auditory processing
   differences in sensitivity to, 81–84
   difficulties with, 341, 350–351
   ego differentiation deficits and, 350–351
   of infant, 72–73
Auditory-verbal processing, 118–120, 124–125
   capacity for, 86
   decreased, 94
   difficulties in, 282–283, 285–288

Autism, 282
Autistic Spectrum problems, 387
Autonomous ego functions, 27
Avoidant type, 91–92

Behavioral discharge mode, 225
   activities of, 241
   conflicts over aggression at, 305–306
   determining, 226–227
   hierarchy of, 228–229
Behavioral enactment, 225–226
Behavioral interaction, 162
Behavioral level, 418t
   fixed attitudes and character constrictions in, 301–312
   forming representations at, 239–245
Behavioral negotiations, 212–216
Behavioral patterns, 60–61
   boundary-defining, 161–187
   changing from, 296–301
   description of, 411–412
   exploring, 239–242, 245–246, 368
   helping patient describe, 254
   self and other-defining, 189–224
Behavioral therapy, developmental principles in, 39–40
Big picture perspective, 275–276, 283
Biological variables, 115–117
Borderline personality, 414
   intensity of therapeutic relationship for, 43–44
Boundary defining, 391
   clinical illustrations of problems of, 176–187
   distortion of, 172
   early stage of, 162–163
   gestures, behaviors, and affects in, 161–187
Boundary-defining cues/gestures, 162–164
   absence of, 164–165
   disruption of, 166–167
   establishing of, 168–170

Boundary-defining interactions, 24
  establishing patterns of, 169–171
Bridge building, 314–315
  development of, 397–410
  differentiated, 334
  experiences and, 337–338
  between fantasy and reality, 342–343
  in oedipal triangle, 327
  psychotherapeutic techniques for, 357
  between values and desires, 331–332

Causality, 392
Central nervous system variations, 116–117
Chaotic environment, 280
Character
  constrictions in transition from behavioral to representational levels, 301–312
  disorder of, 414
  problems in forming, 7
Character pathology
  affective experience and, 43
  complex gestures in, 216–224
  developmental approach with, 63–64
  seeds of, 322
Character structure problems, 5
  developmental diagnosis of, 11–12
Children, engaging and working with, 150–155
Clarification, 316
  of age-appropriate patterns, 374
  in building bridges, 262–263
  with complex gestural pattern problems, 208
  failure of, 171–172
  in fostering representational differentiation, 358
  overloading with, 256–257
Clinical practice challenges, 5–6
Clinical techniques, 253–312
Cognitive behavioral therapy, 39–40
Cognitive function, 20–23

Cognitive representation, 245–246
Collaborative constructor of experience, 15–17, 19
Communication
  across space, 277–278
  complex gestural patterns of, 189–224
  developing boundary-defining patterns of, 181–186
  direct behavioral, 195
  fostering sense of shared, 237–239
  gestural and affective, 25
  intentional, 25, 391–395
  learning rules of, 199
  motor system in, 198
  on multiple levels, 200
  within oneself, 262
  opening and closing circles of, 191, 194, 198–199, 288–291, 351, 366–367
  shared, 240–241. See also Meaning, shared
  symbolic circles of, 362
  tools of, 15
Complex gestural patterns
  character pathology and, 216–224
  clinical examples of, 193–196
  determining level of, 197–198
  determining range of, 198–199
  technical considerations of, 196–216
  transference-countertransference reenactments affecting, 201–208
Compliance pattern, 202
Compulsive ritual, 276–277, 279–280
Concrete fixed attitudes, 218–219
Confidence, development of, 25
Conflict
  ego development level and, 54–57
  ego in dealing with, 324–326
  at representational level, 324
  resolving, 372–374
  structure building and, 374–380
  theory of, 336–337

Connectedness
  inability to experience, 137
  lack of, 219
Constitution
  in ego differentiation deficits, 349–355
  focus on variations in, 105–109
  types of, 5
Constitutional-maturational patterns
  deficits in, 119–120
  developmental stages and, 425–426
  variations in, 388, 417
Constitutional-maturational vulnerability
  in affective disorders, 123–128
  high-risk environment for, 126
  optimal environment for, 130–131
Constrictions
  in affects, 232–233
  around dependency and closeness,
      208–212
  at complex gestures level, 200–201
  compulsive ritual in, 276–277
  definition of, 9
  in developmental profile, 29
  diagnosis of, 413–414
  at gestural level, 291–220
  in representational capacities, 246–
      251, 322–323
  in representational differentiation, 321
  in transition from behavioral to repre-
      sentational levels, 301–312
Coping strategies, 279
  concrete, 307
  primitive, 304–305
Core developmental processes, 8–10
  difficulties with, 64–69
  first, 71
Corrective emotional experience, 15
Counterbehavioral intervention, 209–
      210, 212–216
Countertransference, 146
  tendencies, 368

Defenses, selection of, 27–28
Deficits

at complex gestures level, 200–201
constitutional, interactive, and fantasy
      components of, 349–355
constructing lives to support, 371
definition of, 9
determining degree of, 12
in developmental profile, 29
in ego differentiation, 348–349
in paranoid, depressive ideation, 217–
      219
in representational capacities, 322–323
reworking of, 141–142
understanding of, 365–366
visual-spatial processing, 274–275
Dependency constriction, 208–212
Depression
  biological aspects of, 274–275
  as breakdown in representational sys-
      tem, 273–274
  difficulty modulating affects and, 347–
      348
Depressive states, complex gestures in,
      216–224
Development
  affect and interaction in, 19–23
  of complex gestural patterns, 189–190
  mobilizing processes of, 7, 8–10
  need for systematic understanding of,
      4
The Development of the Ego (Greenspan), 40
Developmental diagnosis, initial, 11–12
Developmental diagnostic formulations,
      412–416
Developmental experience, recreating,
      17–18
Developmental framework
  pioneers in, 4
  psychopathology and, 63–69
  unified theory for, 1
Developmental levels
  case illustration working with, 57–63
  clinical assessment of, 385–426
  clinical indicators of, 387–410

ego development in, 422–424*t*
helping patient negotiate, 14–17
meeting patient at, 10–14
presymbolic, 353–354
stages of, 161–162
theoretical background and model for assessing, 416–426
therapeutic techniques and, 243–245
Developmental principles, 37–40
Developmental profile
construction of, 28–37
importance of, 29–31
schematic outline of, 33, 34–36
Developmentally based therapy
in fostering representational differentiation, 373–374
need for, 1–6
principles of, 7–69
representational differentiation in, 357–358
strategies of, 381–383
Developmental-structural approach, 416–426
overview of, 386–387
stage-specific capacities in, 418–419*t*
Diagnostic formulations, developmental, 412–416
Differentiation, primary, 163
Directive questions, 235–236
Disorganized person, 175–176
Distorted perceptions, 243–244
Distractibility, 86
Drama, amplifying of, 263–270
DSM-III-R diagnosis, 414
Dyadic relationship, 363–365
Dynamic integration, 317
Dynamic perspective, 51–54

Ego
arrested differentiation of, 365
characterization of, 317–318
in dealing with anxiety and conflict, 324–326

deficit in differentiation of, 348–355
developmental levels of, 50–51
foundation of, 382–383
in representational elaboration, 242–243
six levels of organization, 23–28
Ego development
affect and interaction in, 19–23
dynamic conflicts and, 54–57
early stages of, 18
stages in, 50–51, 326–349, 386–387, 422–424*t*
Ego function
developmental stages of, 422–424*t*
mental content and, 46
representational differentiation and, 317–326
severe impairment of, 412–413
Embarrassment, 248–250
Emotional deprivation, 278–279, 416
Emotional expressiveness
capacity for, 30
distortions of, 392
Emotional milestones, 420–421*t*
Emotional needs, defining, 25–26
Emotional themes, 11–12, 270
Emotional thinking, 26–27, 313–359. See also Representational differentiation
capacity to create and elaborate, 35
development of, 397–410
levels of, 36
Emotions. See also Affects; Feelings
avoidance of, 263
intelligence and growth in, 19–23
restriction of, 302–304
Empathic support, 212–213
Empathizer-clarifier role, 19
Empathy, 146–147, 229, 258–259
in behavioral pattern, 238–239
with constricted representational capacity, 247–248
developmental level and, 243, 244–245

helping individual experience, 112–113

in identifying behavioral pattern, 307–308

incapacity for, 338–339

with patient's needs and wishes, 154–155

therapeutic, 237–238

Encapsulated disorder, 413–414

Encapsulated distortions, 325

Engagement

antisocial individual and, 155–159

capacity for, 390–391

difficulty with, 92–94, 150–155

family patterns of, 136–137

fostering of, 12–13

of individual with regulatory problems, 109–110

levels of, 34

of patient with complex gestural pattern problems, 208–216

problems with, 135–142

processes of, 25

rules of, 142–150

style of, 29

Environment, in relationship difficulties, 416

Experience

ability to categorize, 313–314, 333–335, 337–338. *See also* Representational differentiation

collaborating in constructing, 263–270

differentiation of, 361–362, 369–370

Facial expression, 175

difficulty reading, 216–217

Family

behavioral patterns in, 308–312

emotional milestones and, 420–421*t*

engagement patterns in, 136–137

"multiproblem," 157

Fantasy

ability to create, 24

capacity to form, 26

content of, 353

dynamic meaning of, 355

in ego differentiation deficits, 352–355

escape into, 289, 314, 342–345, 375–378

Fantasy-reality balance, 399

Feedback

cause-and-effect, 320

lack of, 163

loops of, 162

Feelings. *See also* Affects; Emotions

inability to represent, 49–50

pushing patient to look at, 13

Fine motor skills, 86

Fixed attitudes

complex gestures in, 216–224

in transition from behavioral to representational levels, 301–312

Games, 108

Genetic integration, 317

Gestural challenges, 174–175

Gestural communication, 394–395

difficulty reading, 216–224

Gestural elaboration, interactive, 224

Gestural patterns

boundary-defining, 161–187

complex, 189–224

compulsive ritual in, 276–277

flexibility in, 277–278

ritualistic, 278–280

self and other-defining, 189–224

therapeutic strategies for variations in, 281–291

of toddler, 191–192

undeveloped, 197

Groups, intolerance of, 81–84

Growth producing experience, 17, 42–43

Here-and-now, living in, 255

Homeostasis stage, 418*t*

Humiliation, 248–250

Hypersensitive type, 90–92

Imagination, 111
Impulsiveness, 94–95
Individual differences, 24
    in sensory reactivity, 72–74
Individuation, 393
Information processing
    difficulties with, 282–283, 285–288
    disorders related to limitations of, 341–347
    reactivity and, 72–73
    therapists communication and, 289–290
Insight, 316
    in fostering representational differentiation, 358
    structural change and, 378
Insight-oriented therapy, 141–142
Intelligence, development of, 19–23
Intentional communication, 391–395
    gestural, 25
    in presymbolic learning, 36
Intentional gestures stage, 161–162
Intentionality, 161
    expression of, 162–163
    levels of, 34
Intentions, difficulty perceiving, 67
Interaction
    in ego development and intelligence, 19–23
    in ego differentiation deficits, 349–355
Interactive regulation, 224
Intermicrostructural integration, 317
Internal reality, 330–331
Internal representations, differentiation of, 398–399
Interpretation
    of age-appropriate pattern avoidance, 374
    in building bridges, 262–263
    with complex gestural pattern problems, 208

overloading with, 256–257
    patient's developmental level and, 10–11
Intimacy
    constrictions around, 208–212
    problems with, 135–159
Intuitive approaches, 62–63

Large-muscle activity, 107
Latency phase, 328–330, 398
Learning
    attentional problems and, 102–104
    disorders of, 415
    presymbolic, 33–36
Light, over- or underreactivity to, 85
Limit setting, 113–114
    in representational capacities, 250–251, 253
    in therapeutic relationships, 293
Longing feelings, inability to represent, 59–60
Loss, feelings of, 149
Love
    loss of, 271–273
    mature form of, 229

Maladaptive development, 412–416
Mastery, helping individual experience, 113
Maternal vocalization
    ability to orient to, 72–73
    unresponsiveness to, 121
Maturational variations, 105–109
Meaning
    developmental levels and, 57–63
    elaboration of, 395–397
    shared, 240–242, 247–248, 253, 395–410
Me/not-me differentiation, 326–327
Mental anticipation, 111
Mental content, 44–51
Mental images, 225–251

Mental representations
  deficits in, 5
  inability to create, 59–60
  patient's capacity to express, 8–9
Microtechniques, 253–255, 262–270
Mind
  content of, 44–51
  six levels of, 23–28
Mother, emotional disappearance of, 143–144
Motor activity modulation, 86
Motor discharge type, 94–95
Motor planning, 388
  impaired, 87–88
  problems with, 102, 107–108, 198
  regulation of, 389
  skills in, 86
Motor tone, 388
  poor, 86
  problems with, 107–108
  regulation of, 389
Motor underreactivity, 93
Movement, reactivity to, 86, 93

Narcissistic character disorder, 338
  representational differentiation in, 356
Needs, softening of, 249
Negativism, 91
Nervous system maturation, 382
Neurotic disturbance, 414
Neutrality, therapeutic, 207–208, 374
Noise, reactivity to, 81–84, 85
Nonverbal cues, 165–166
Numbing feeling, focusing on, 299–300

Object, multisensory image of, 283–285
Object identity formation, 317
Object loss, 271–273
Object permanence, 396
Obsessive-compulsive patterns
  origins of, 279–280
  representational capacities in, 275–276
Odors, reactivity to, 86
Oedipal triangle, 327–328

Operant learning theory, 102–103
Order, concerns with, 26–27
Organizational constrictions, 413
Organizational matrix, undifferentiated, 390
Other, presymbolic complex sense of, 24
Other-defining patterns, 189–224
Overloaded feeling, 81–84
Overreactivity, 90–91
Overwhelmed, sense of being, 248–249

Paranoid schizophrenic, judgments of, 172–173
Paranoid states, 216–224
Parent-child relationship, reenactment of, 201–208
Parents
  concrete behavioral patterns of, 308–311
  gestural communication of, 192–193
  inability to engage representationally, 323
  overloading or withdrawal from children, 139–141
  physical separation from, 272–273
  power struggles with, 375
Pecking orders, 328–329
Peer group, 328–330
Personality developmental, 4
Phallic stage, 321–322
Phenomenology, 415
Physical sensations
  capacity for, 258–259
  helping patient describe, 254–255, 256
Play
  activities of, 108
  complex, 411
  disruptions in, 407–408
  parallel, 151
  representational themes of, 319–320
  symbolic, 397
  themes arising in, 403–408
Playtime, therapeutic, 138–139

Power struggle, 175
Prerepresentational level, 145
   issues of, 31–32
   role of conflict in, 55
Presymbolic learning, 33–36
Presymbolic stages, 36–37
Presymbolic structures, 44–51
Principles, 7–69
   application of, 37–40
Problem-solving orientation, 110–111
Psychiatric disorders, biological and con-
   stitutional variables in, 115–118
Psychoanalysis, 38
Psychodynamic approach, 315–316, 335–
   336
Psychological boundary, 65
Psychopathology
   assumptions of, 336–337
   developmental approach with, 63–69
   lack of ego differentiation in, 337
Psychosexual trends, 321–322
Psychotherapeutic techniques, 1–4. *See
   also* Therapeutic techniques
Psychotherapy
   developmental principles in, 37–40
   frequency and intensity of, 40–44
   problems for, 1–2

Rage, 248–250
Reactivity, 72–73
Reality testing, 172–173
   behavioral, 321
Reality-based bridges, 5–6
Reenactment, avoiding, 212–213
Reflective negotiations, 240–241
Regulation, need for, 248–249
Regulatory capacities
   description of, 29
   difficulties with, 64–69
   overreactivity in, 31
   patterns of, 71–73
Regulatory differences, 388–389
   value of focusing on, 78–80

Regulatory disorder, 390
Regulatory environment
   creating, 75–76
   respect for, 174–175
Regulatory patterns, 90–95
   individual differences in, 72–74
Regulatory process difficulties, 53, 71–133
   affective, 123–133
   attentional, 95–104
   clinical illustration of, 74–85
   hypothesis on causes of, 118–123
   range of, 85–90
   research on, 115–118
   severe, 104–105
   therapeutic strategies for, 105–115
Regulatory profiles, 115–116
Relatedness
   features of, 138
   fostering of, 12–13
Relating
   concrete, 145–149
   difficulty with, 135–159
Relationship
   developing patterns of, 390–391
   difficulty maintaining, 65
   enhancing ability to form, 135–136
   environment in, 416
   family patterns and, 136–137
   formation and maintenance of, 24
   fostering sense of, 146–147
   limits, engagement, and empathy in,
      114–115
   prerepresentational, 164
   problems in, 5
Representation
   affective and cognitive, 245–246
   formation of, 239–245
   themes of, 319–320
Representational approach, 296–301
Representational capacities, 418*t*
   case illustration of promoting, 293–296
   clinical techniques to facilitate, 253–
      312

constrictions in, 246–251, 322–323
defects in, 322–323
intensity of affect and, 291–293
maintaining integrity of, 283–284
Representational differentiation, 24, 26–27, 313–359, 396–397, 411
basic ego functions and, 317–326
development of, 397–410
distortions in, 325
global lack of, 325
levels of, 326–327
limitations in, 322–324
missing areas of, 338–341
tactics to foster, 361–380
therapeutic strategies with, 315–316, 355–359
Representational elaboration, 24, 26, 225–251, 411
clinical conditions related to, 271–280
development of, 395–397
Representational fragmentation, 317
Representational integration, compromised, 325–326
Representational level, 61
fixed attitudes and character constrictions in transition to, 301–312
helping patient shift to, 233–237
therapeutic strategies for variations in, 281–291
Representational-symbolic capacities, 200
Research, regulatory processes, 115–118
Rhythmic activity, 106–107
Ritualistic behavior, 220–222, 278–280

Schizoid personality, 275–276
Selective dedifferentiation, 325
Self
complex sense of, 391–395
defined by social reality, 330–332
formation of, 4, 317
fragmented, 128, 344–346
presymbolic complex sense of, 24
preverbal sense of, 35

Self image, 353–355
Self therapy, 46–47
Self-absorption, 93, 346–347
Self-calming behavior, 220–221
Self-cuing ability, 163–164
Self-defining patterns, 189–224
Self-esteem, loss of, 273–274
Self-hate, 271
Self-nonself boundary, 164
Self-object relationship, 422–424t
Self-observing capacity, 24, 242–243
lack of, 173–174
Self-other differentiation, 318–319
limitations in, 320–321
Self-reflective capacities, 46–47
limited, 53
Self-regulation, 24, 25, 387–390
failure to achieve, 222
levels of, 34
Self-stimulatory behavior, 220–221, 281–282
obsessive-compulsive patterns and, 279–280
Self-sufficiency, promotion of, 17–19
Sensations
defenses and, 27–28
describing, 258–259
helping patient describe, 254–255, 256, 292
overreactivity to, 67–68, 275
reactivity to, 27–28, 281–282
Sensory processing, 388
Sensory reactivity
affective, 388
clinical case of difficulties with, 74–85
individual differences in, 72–74
patterns of, 90–95
variations in, 388–389
Sequencing capacities, 318–319
Shared meaning, 240–242, 395–410
with constricted representational capacity, 247–248
security of, 253

Social reality, 330–332
  adolescents in, 332–333
Social skills, 156–157
Socialization, birth of, 250
Somatic affect states, 222–223, 228
Somatic descriptors, 256
Somatic states, undifferentiated, 262
Somatopsychological differentiation, 418t
Stimulus nutriment, balanced, 169–170
Stimulus-seeking, 94–95
Structural capacities
  focus on, 377–380
  frequency and intensity of therapy
    and, 41–42
  lack of, 48
  mental content and, 44–51
Structural deficits
  reworking of, 141–142
  understanding of, 365–366
Structural perspective, 51–54
Structure building, 113–114, 317
  conflict resolution and, 374–380
Stubbornness, 91
Subtle sensitivity, lack of, 286–288
Superego, 331–332
  in representational elaboration, 242–
    243
Supportive psychotherapy, 38–39
Symbolic capacities, 26, 201
Symbolic communication, 397
Symbols, 225

Tactile defensiveness, 85–86
Tactile sensitivity, 88, 107
  clinical illustration of, 74–85
  differences in, 73, 78–81
Temperature, reactivity to, 86
Thematic organization, 401–402
Therapeutic goals
  based on developmental diagnosis, 12–
    13
  of recreating developmental experi-
    ences, 17–18

Therapeutic process
  boundary-defining aspects of, 167–172
  steps in, 158t
Therapeutic relationship, 9
  affect state in, 23, 363
  aspects of, 52
  comfort in, 239–240
  creating interactive experience in, 361
  dimensions of, 158t
  intensity of, 40–44
  limiting setting and structure of, 293
Therapeutic strategies
  for attentional problems, 96–104
  for constitutional and maturational
    variations in gestural/repre-
    sentational levels, 281–291
  of developmentally based psychother-
    apy, 381–383
  for patients lacking representational
    differentiation capacity, 315–
    316, 355–359
  for regulatory problems, 105–115
Therapeutic techniques. See also Psycho-
    therapeutic techniques
  changing from behavioral to represen-
    tational mode, 296–301
  to facilitate representational capaci-
    ties, 253–312
  to foster representational differentia-
    tion, 361–380
  promoting representational capacities,
    293–296
Therapeutic tools, 52–53
Therapist
  abstracting (nonconcrete) posture of,
    234–235, 236–237
  as collaborator in construction of expe-
    rience, 15–17
  as constructor of drama, 263–270
  counterbehavioral view of, 205–208
  directive questions of, 235–236
  dual role of, 19
  empathic range of, 137–138

fostering sense of shared communication with patient, 237–239
as interactive differentiating object, 366–368
misempathizing, 362
neutrality of, 374
as savior, 370–371
silent, self-absorbed, 174
Therapy
frequency and intensity of, 40–44
verbal content in, 44–51
Thought disorders, 118–123
Thought-behavior dedifferentiation, 325
Thought-drive-affect dedifferentiation, 325
Transference
immediacy of, 356
intensity of, 368
prerepresentational, 141–142
undifferentiated, 373
Transference neurosis, 186–187
Transference relationships, 358
Transference-countertransference reenactments
awareness of, 201–208
preverbal, 200
Transforming differentiational linkage, 325
Triadic relationship deficit, 363–365

Triadic thinking, 327–328
Trust, inability to feel, 137

Unconscious cognitive learning, 36
Unconscious fantasy, content of, 46
Underreactive type, 92–94
Unpleasant affect
tolerance of, 141
withdrawal from, 138–141

Values, internal, 330–331
Verbal cues, insensitivity to, 286–288
Verbal insight, 44–51
Visual images, reactivity to, 85
Visual information processing, 72–73
Visual-spatial processing, 86, 124–125, 285
abstract, 124–128
in depression, 274–275
difficulties with, 87, 282–283
ego differentiation deficits and, 351–352
helping with, 131–132
Vocal rhythms, 106
Vulnerability patterns, 417

"What Must Have Been" sense, 141
Withdrawal, 92–94
collaborating with, 15–17
therapeutic strategies with, 138–141